AF361530

IMAGINING THE JEW IN ANGLO-SAXON
LITERATURE AND CULTURE

Imagining the Jew in Anglo-Saxon Literature and Culture

EDITED BY SAMANTHA ZACHER

UNIVERSITY OF TORONTO PRESS
Toronto Buffalo London

ISBN 978-1-4426-4667-4

Printed on acid-free, 100% post-consumer recycled paper with vegetable-based inks.

Library and Archives Canada Cataloguing in Publication

Imagining the Jew in Anglo-Saxon literature and culture / edited by Samantha Zacher.

(Toronto Anglo-Saxon series ; 21)
Includes bibliographical references and index.
ISBN 978-1-4426-4667-4 (cloth)

1. English literature – Old English, ca. 450–1100 – History and criticism.   2. Christian
literature, English (Old) – History and criticism.   3. Jews in literature.   4. Antisemitism
in literature.   5. Civilization, Anglo-Saxon, in literature.   6. Antisemitism – England –
History – Medieval, 500–1500.   7. England – Ethnic relations – History – Medieval,
500–1500.   8. England – Church history – 449–1066.   9. Great Britain – History –
Anglo Saxon period, 449–1066.   I. Zacher, Samantha, 1973–, editor   II. Series: Toronto
Anglo-Saxon series ; 21

PR179.J49I43 2016   829'.093529924   C2016-900727-8

University of Toronto Press gratefully acknowledges the financial assistance of the Centre
for Medieval Studies, University of Toronto in the publication of this book.

University of Toronto Press acknowledges the financial assistance to its publishing
program of the Canada Council for the Arts and the Ontario Arts Council, an agency
of the Government of Ontario.

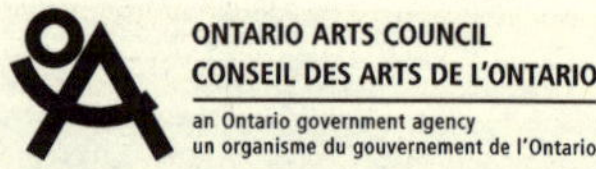

Funded by the   Financé par le
Government   gouvernement
of Canada   du Canada

Canadä

Contents

Literary Types and Anglo-Saxon Audiences

Visual Media: Representations of Jews and Jewish Spaces

Epilogue: Pre- and Post-Conquest Identifications: Continuity and Difference

Illustrations

Acknowledgments

I am immensely indebted to all the folks at University of Toronto Press who helped to bring this project to fruition, in particular the incomparable Suzanne Rancourt, together with Barb Porter, and Evelyn Mackie. I am also grateful to the contributors who patiently and graciously waited for the final pieces of this volume to come together. The idea for this project grew out of a mini-conference that I hosted many years ago at Cornell University (2008), entitled *New Views on Jews in Anglo-Saxon England*. Some of the essays in the present volume were presented in one form or another at that conference, while others are entirely new. That initial event was sponsored by the Society for the Humanities at Cornell (for which I received a Research Grant), and also by the Medieval, English, and Near-Eastern studies departments and programs. I also received unexpected and incredibly generous contributions from my colleagues Ken McClane, W.E.B. Du Bois Professor of Literature (in the English Department and Creative Writing Program at Cornell) and Dominick LaCapra, Bryce and Edith M. Bowmar Professor in Humanistic Studies (The Department of History at Cornell). I cannot thank these colleagues enough for giving me the means and confidence to pursue this project. I interpret their lavish support as an attestation of the interdisciplinary nature of this project and its appeal within wider cultural, religious, and political domains. I am also enormously grateful to all my brilliant contributors for their astonishing work. Their essays genuinely broaden and advance our understanding about the perceptions and attitudes towards Jews in early English, literature, theology, art history, and, for lack of a more precise term, the imagination. Finally, I want to take this opportunity to commemorate Deborah Marcum, a graduate student in the Medieval Studies at Cornell program who participated in the 2008 conference, and who sadly passed away not long after the event. Her co-participants at Cornell, Tom Hill, Sarah Harlan Haughey, and Matt Spears remember her fondly.

Contributors

Daniel Anlezark is Associate Professor at the University of Sydney, Australia, where he teaches medieval English language and literature. He has edited and translated the Old English Dialogues of Solomon and Saturn, and biblical poems from manuscript Junius 11. He has published widely on Old English literature, on topics ranging from Anglo-Saxon biblical verse, to the influence of early Irish literature on Old English texts and role of the pre-Christian religion of the north in Old English poetry. In 2014 he was awarded an Australian Research Council Future Fellowship to work on Anglo-Saxon literature and science.

Adam S. Cohen is an Associate Professor in the Department of the History of Art at the University of Toronto. His research focuses on medieval illuminated manuscripts and monastic art; publications include *The Uta Codex: Art, Philosophy, and Reform in Eleventh-Century Germany* (2000); *Eye and Mind: Essays in Anglo-Saxon and Early Medieval Art by Robert Deshman* (2010); "Monastic Art and Architecture: 700–1050," in *The Cambridge History of Medieval Western Monasticism* (forthcoming). With Linda Safran, he is the current editor of *Gesta*, the biannual journal of the International Center of Medieval Art.

Heide Estes is Professor of English at Monmouth University. She has published articles on Old English language and literature, gender studies, disability studies, and Hebrew and Judaic Studies. She is editor with Haruko Momma of *Old English Across the Curriculum: Contexts and Pedagogies*, a special issue of *Studies in Medieval and Renaissance Teaching* forthcoming in 2016. Her book *Ecotheory and the Environmental Imagination* is under contract with Amsterdam University Press. She is the founder of the scholarly group Medieval Ecocriticisms and a member of the advisory board for the series Environmental Humanities in Pre-modern Cultures from Amsterdam University Press.

Damian Fleming is an Associate Professor of English and Linguistics at Indiana University-Purdue University, Fort Wayne, where he directs the minor in Medieval Studies and teaches Old and Middle English, History of the English Language, and Latin. His research especially focuses on Anglo-Saxon perceptions of the Hebrew language and has appeared in *Anglia, JEGP, Old English Literature and the Old Testament* (2012) and *Latinity and Identity in Anglo-Saxon England* (forthcoming).

Thomas N. Hall taught Old English at the University of Illinois at Chicago and the University of Notre Dame. He has written on Old English poetry and homilies, biblical and apocryphal literature, Anglo-Saxon manuscripts, and medieval Latin sermons.

Stephen J. Harris is a Professor at the University of Massachusetts in Amherst. He is author of *Race and Ethnicity in Anglo-Saxon Literature* (2004) and *Bede and Aethelthryth* (2015), and co-editor of *Misconceptions about the Middle Ages* (2007) and *Vox Germanica* (2013).

Thomas D. Hill, Professor of English and Medieval Studies at Cornell University, received his BA from Harvard University in 1961 and studied with R.E. Kaske at the University of Illinois and Cornell University where he received his PhD in 1967. Since then he has taught at Cornell, chiefly Old and Middle English and occasionally also Old Norse–Icelandic. He has published a number of papers and edited volumes and an edition of the Old English *Solomon and Saturn and Adrian and Ritheus* in collaboration with the late Professor J.E. Cross of the University of Liverpool.

Catherine E. Karkov is Chair of Art History at the University of Leeds and has published widely on Insular and Anglo-Saxon art and archaeology. She is the author of *Text and Picture in Anglo-Saxon England: Narrative Strategies in the Junius 11 Manuscript* (2001), *The Ruler Portraits of Anglo-Saxon England* (2004), and *The Art of Anglo-Saxon England* (2011). She has also published articles on Anglo-Saxon art and archaeology, and has edited numerous collections pertaining to these subjects.

Kathy Lavezzo teaches English literature at the University of Iowa. She is the author of *Angels on the Edge of the World: Geography, Literature and English Community, 1000–1534* (2006) and the editor of *Imagining a Medieval English Nation* (2004) and *Jews in Britain – Medieval to Modern* (PQ 92.1). She is completing a book, *The Accommodated Jew: English Antisemitism from Bede to Milton* (forthcoming).

Asa Simon Mittman (Professor, Art History, California State University, Chico) wrote *Maps and Monsters in Medieval England* (2006), co-wrote with Susan Kim *Inconceivable Beasts: The Wonders of the East in the Beowulf Manuscript* (2013), and many articles on monstrosity and marginality (*Gesta, postmedieval, Peregrinations*, and elsewhere). He coedited the *Research Companion to Monsters and the Monstrous* (2012), co-directs *Virtual Mappa*, is president of MEARCSTAPA and a member of the Material Collective. His research has been supported by CAA, ICMA, Kress, Mellon, and NEH. He edits book series with Boydell and Brill, and is researching the Franks Casket, and images of Jews on maps.

Andrew Scheil is the Donald V. Hawkins Associate Professor of English at the University of Minnesota. He is the author of *The Footsteps of Israel: Understanding Jews in Anglo-Saxon England* (2004), which won both the International Society of Anglo-Saxonists Best First Book Prize and The Medieval Academy of America's John Nicholas Brown Prize. He is also the author of *Babylon Under Western Eyes: A Study of Allusion and Myth* (forthcoming).

Charles D. Wright received his PhD from Cornell University in 1984, and has taught at the University of Illinois at Urbana-Champaign since 1986. He is author of *The Irish Tradition in Old English Literature* (1993) and of more than forty essays on Old English poetry and prose, medieval Irish and Hiberno-Latin literature, and biblical apocrypha. He has co-edited collections honoring J.E. Cross and Thomas D. Hill, and since 1995 he has been co-editor of *JEGP*. In 2014 he received the CARA Award for Excellence in Teaching from the Medieval Academy of America.

Samantha Zacher is Professor of English and Medieval Studies at Cornell University. She is the author of *Preaching the Converted: The Style and Rhetoric of the Vercelli Book Homilies* (2009), and *Rewriting the Old Testament in Anglo-Saxon Verse: Becoming the Chosen People* (2013). She has also published two collections of essays: *New Readings in the Vercelli Book*, co-edited with Andy Orchard (2009), and *A Companion to British Literature*, 4 volumes, co-edited with Robert DeMaria, Jr and Heesok Chang (2014). Recently, she has written articles on the treatment of Jews, and the role of animals in medieval literature, law, and culture.

Abbreviations

ASE	*Anglo-Saxon England*
ASPR	*The Anglo-Saxon Poetic Records*. Edited by G.P. Krapp and E.V.K. Dobbie, 6 vols. New York: Columbia University Press, 1931–53.
CCCM	Corpus Christianorum, Continuatio Mediaevalis
CCSL	Corpus Christianorum, Series Latina
CH 1	*Ælfric's Catholic Homilies: The First Series*. Edited by P. Clemoes. London: Oxford University Press, 1997.
CH 2	*Ælfric's Catholic Homilies: The Second Series*. Edited by M. Godden, EETS, s.s., 5. London: Oxford University Press, 1979.
CSASE	Cambridge Studies in Anglo-Saxon England
CSEL	Corpus Scriptorum Ecclesiasticorum Latinorum
DOE	*Dictionary of Old English*
EETS	Early English Text Society
e.s.	Extra Series
o.s.	Original Series
s.s.	Supplementary Series
ES	*English Studies*
HE	Bede, *Historia Ecclesiastica*
JEGP	(formerly) *Journal of English and Germanic Philology*
JMEMS	*Journal of Medieval and Early Modern Studies*
MGH	Monumenta Germaniae Historica
MIP	Medieval Institute Publications
MRTS	Medieval and Renaissance Texts and Studies
NM	*Neuphilologische Mitteilungen*
PIMS	Pontifical Institute of Medieval Studies

PG   *Patrologia Graeca*, ed. J.-P. Migne, 162 vols. (Paris, 1857–66)
PL   *Patrologia Latina*, ed. J.-P. Migne, 221 vols. (Paris, 1844–64)
PQ   *Philological Quarterly*
SN   *Studia Neophilologica*
TU   Texte und Untersuchungen zur Geschichte der altchristlichen
         Literatur: Archiv für die griechisch-christlichen Schriftsteller
         der ersten [drei] Jahrhunderte (Leipzig and Berlin, 1882–)

IMAGINING THE JEW IN ANGLO-SAXON
LITERATURE AND CULTURE

Introduction: The Jew in the Anglo-Saxon Imagination

SAMANTHA ZACHER

Studies of Jews in medieval English history, culture, and literature typical-ly begin with the year 1066 or later.[1] The reasons for establishing this date as a terminus *a quo* are perhaps self-explanatory: Anglo-Saxon England was, by all accounts, a land without Jews.[2] There are no records of Jewish inhabitants or visitors to England during the Anglo-Saxon period; and it was not until after the Conquest that Jews were brought as merchants and traders to the island by the Norman invaders.[3] Moreover, despite frequent

---

1 Virtually all studies of Jews in Medieval English literature and culture begin after the Norman Conquest, and even more commonly after 1290, when the Jews were expelled from England. Recent book-length examples include Bale, *The Jew in the Medieval Book* and *Feeling Persecuted*; Delaney, ed., *Chaucer and the Jews*; chapters in Kruger's *The Spectral Jew*; Julius, *Trials of the Diaspora*; and Krummel, *Crafting Jewishness in Medieval England*.

2 There have been relatively few studies of the representation of Jews in Anglo-Saxon literature and culture. The most comprehensive is Scheil, *The Footsteps of Israel*. There have also been several book-length treatments of Jews in Anglo-Saxon biblical texts, including Old Testament poetry, translations of the Hexateuch, and illuminated bibles. Important in this context is Remley, *Old English Biblical Verse*, which treats Jewish identities as part of its larger investigation of these biblical poems; Karkov, *Text and Picture in Anglo-Saxon England*, which presents a systematic study of the illumina-tions that accompany the Old Testament poem *Genesis* in MS Junius 11; Withers, *The Illustrated Old English Hexateuch, Cotton Claudius B.iv*, which analyzes the program of biblical illuminations in this manuscript; Anlezark, *Water and Fire*, which traces allusions to the Genesis flood in Anglo-Saxon texts; and Zacher, *Rewriting the Old Testament*, which investigates the adaptation of Old Testament narratives for theologico-political reasons.

3 The scholarly consensus has been that the Jews came to England only after the Norman Conquest. See Michaelson, *The Jew in Early Medieval Literature*, 12–21; Roth,

travels to the continent, there are no reports of Anglo-Saxon encounters with Jews. If we are to believe the surviving early textual sources, it may be that no Anglo-Saxon ever met a Jew in the flesh.[4]

By sharp contrast, the history of the Jews in England between 1066 and 1290 (the year of their expulsion) is extremely well documented.[5] Although there were periods of relative peace and productive intellectual exchanges between Jews and their Christian neighbours,[6] the late twelfth and thirteenth centuries were marked by turbulent conflict and discord. At different times, and with different legislative intensity, Jews were banned from practising their religion openly, from building synagogues, from entering public office, from owning property, and from earning independent incomes.[7] Without access to free enterprise, many Jews were forced into

---

A History of the Jews in England, 2; Hyams, "The Jews in Medieval England: 1066–1290," 174; and Golb, *The Jews in Medieval Normandy*, 112–14. Stacey provides a lucid and compelling account of the possible economic reasons for the importation of Jews in the first place, in his "Jewish Lending and the Medieval English Economy," 78–101, at 82. On the possible presence of Jews in Roman Britain, see Applebaum, "Were there Jews in Roman Briton?" Wasserstein ("The First Jew in England"), by contrast, argued the presence of a single Jew at the court of King Athelstan in England, on the basis of a questionable reference to an "Israel" (also identified to as a *Iudeus Romanus*, or a "Roman Jew"), in a text known as the *Alea euangelii* ("Gospel Dice"), which survives only in a twelfth-century manuscript in Oxford, Corpus Christi College 122 (written ca. 1140). Lapidge ("Israel the Grammarian," 87–110 at 89), however, summarily dismissed this interpretation by arguing that the "Israel" in question reflects a botched reference to the famed Breton scholar Israel the Grammarian.

4 See further Estes, chapter 12 below.

5 The scholarship on medieval English Jewry is vast. The classic study remains Roth, *A History of the Jews in England*, although scholars have since corrected many details (see, for example, Langmuir's chapter on "Historiographic Crucifixion" in *Toward a Definition of Antisemitism*, 282–98). For recent overviews of the subject, including essays by some of the foremost scholars in the field (including essays by Joe Hillaby, Robert C. Stacey, and Robin R. Mundill), see the collected essays in Skinner, ed., *Jews in Medieval Britain*; and Dobson and Birkett, eds. *The Jewish Communities of Medieval England.*

6 See, for example, Roth, *The Intellectual Activities of Medieval English Jewry.*

7 Although the language in the laws regulating Jewish life tended to repeat inter-generationally and even across borders, the actual implementation of these laws differed radically from regime to regime. Bachrach presents a still very useful comparative analysis in *Early Medieval Jewish Policy* (although some of his conclusions about royal interests in Jewish-Christian relations have been challenged by recent scholars; see, for example, Langmuir, *Toward a Definition of Antisemitism*, 63–99 at 78–80); Blumenkranz, "The Roman Church and the Jews"; Rokéaḥ, *Medieval English Jews and Royal Officials*; Stacey, *Politics, Policy, and Finance.*

money lending – an occupation reviled by the church, and at the same time controlled, protected, and heavily taxed by the crown. There were also anti-Jewish libels and countless acts of anti-Jewish violence. The very first accusation of ritual murder levied against Jews occurred in England in 1144,[8] and the 1190 massacre and mass suicide at York is remembered as the most bloody of many assaults against Jews on English soil.[9] As Jewish communities grew, measures were taken to contain and segregate them: in addition to the ghettoization (however fluid the physical borders were), from 1253 forward (following an institute established during Lateran IV in 1215), Jews were forced to wear identifying badges that visually marked them as different. The final exile of Jews in 1290 – the first and only mass expulsion of a people in this region, and the first systematic exile of Jews in Western Europe – marked the boiling point of intolerance towards Jews in this period.[10]

Given this all-too-brief sketch of Jewish life in medieval England, one might reasonably conclude that Anglo-Saxon conceptions of Jews had little in common with the derisive and far more damaging stereotypes that emerged in the centuries after Jewish settlement in England. To a large extent this would seem a correct assessment. Scholars of medieval anti-Semitism locate a decisive change in attitudes towards Jews in England (and western Europe in general) in the twelfth century, as violence against Jews escalated and new irrational fictions about Jewish belief, practice, and bodies began to take root in the form of accusations of Jewish ritual murder (including charges of ritual crucifixion and cannibalism) and Host

---

8 It seems that Jews were accused of murdering Christian children whenever a child went missing or a corpse was found (see further Langmuir, *Toward a Definition of Antisemitism*, 141). Later accusations of ritual murder on English soil include the following cases: Bury St Edmunds (1181); Lincoln (1202); Stanford (1222); Winchester (1225); London (1244).

9 Crusader fervor abroad often led to violence against Jews at home. See, for example, Liebeschütz, "The Crusading Movement"; Cohen, "A 1096 Complex?"; and Nirenberg, "The Rhineland Massacres of Jews in the First Crusade." On the York Massacre, see the collected essays in Jones and Watson, eds., *Christians and Jews in Angevin England*.

10 There were however, many previous attempts at smaller and more localized Jewish expulsions. For example, Simon de Montfort attempted to exile Jews from parts of Leicester in 1232 (see further Maddicott, *Simon de Montfort*, 15–16. Many accounts have been given of the political, economic, and in particular royal pressures that led to Jewish exile. Two important accounts can be found in Stacey, "Parliamentary Negotiation and the Expulsion of the Jews," and Mundill, *England's Jewish Solution*.

desecration.[11] However, it is also clear that these new "anti-Semitisms" did not *replace*, but rather *supplemented*, older forms of "anti-Judaic" rhetoric, which targeted Jewish misbelief, and highlighted the Jews' rejection of Christ and his message.[12] These older views implicated Jews as the killers of Christ; as willful dissenters from the true faith; as blind servants of the flesh; and as conspirators who sought to destroy Christendom.

Imagining the Jew in Anglo-Saxon Literature and Culture makes a case for the importance of studying representations of Jews *before* 1066. Despite the complete absence of evidence for the presence of Jews in pre-Conquest England, early English authors nevertheless wrote copiously, and at times, even obsessively about them. They culled their ideas about Jews from a host of sources – from the writings of the Church Fathers, from contemporary continental materials, from widespread cultural stereotypes, and of course from their own imaginations. Although Anglo-Saxon authors looked to patristic and continental paradigms when writing about Jews and Jewish history, their writings were never simply imitative or derivative; on the contrary, poets, homilists, and historiographers wrote about Jews and Jewishness in original ways that constructed and reflected their own unique politico-theological experience. Anglo-Saxon depictions of Jews reveal more than simply the mechanisms by which authors constructed ideas about "others"; they also elucidate the self-understanding of early English religious and political communities. This volume, therefore, in order to explore these issues, poses and seeks to answer the following questions: how might the study of pre-Conquest – and therefore pre-settlement – English writings about Jews alter, complicate, and more

---

11 On the differences between these types of libels, see Langmuir, *Toward a Definition of Antisemitism*, chapters 9–12.

12 In his seminal book *Toward a Definition of Antisemitism*, Langmuir argued that there is a fundamental difference between earlier forms of anti-Judaism and later anti-Semitism. While "anti-Judaism" is characterized by xenophobic hostility grounded in differences between systems of belief, "anti-Semitism" can be characterized by irrational prejudices against Jews, which cannot be corroborated by empirical fact. For the social, political, institutional, and commercial factors impacting upon this change see Langmuir, *Toward a Definition of Antisemitism*, chapters 3 and 4. Langmuir cites many contributing factors, including the extreme decentralization of Europe, the Investiture Controversies, and the Gregorian Reform. The two most important factors, however, were the rapid growth of heterodoxies, which forced the Church to define, contain, and punish heretics and apostates, and the connected growth of lay "spirituality," which empowered lay people to claim the zeal of reform, crusade, and persecution. Some have challenged Langmuir's definitions. See Chazan, *Medieval Stereotypes and Modern Antisemitism*, 127–34, and Maccoby, *Antisemitism and Modernity*.

generally add to our understanding of the dynamics of medieval anti-Judaism and anti-Semitism? How might these writings about Jews force us to renegotiate or reassess identity politics in early medieval England? And how might absence itself function as a theoretical force in exposing the insidious nature of anti-Jewish stereotypes and hatred? What, in short, might an "imaginary Jew" look like in this period?

In order to contextualize this project, it is important to acknowledge the substantial work already in place on the subject of the "imaginary Jew" in earlier and later periods of Jewish scholarship. Looking back to the patristic period, Jeremy Cohen has persuasively argued that the "imaginary Jew" has always played a critical role in the construction of Christian identities. Cohen has argued that "the Christian idea of Jewish identity crystallized around the theological purpose the Jews served in Christendom; Christians perceived Jews to be who they were *supposed* to be, not who they actually *were*."[13] This "hermeneutically and doctrinally crafted Jew" could be shaped to fit different theological and doctrinal purposes. Thus, according to Cohen, even Augustine – arguably the most influential theologian to articulate a theory of Jewish survival in Christendom and the role of Jews in salvation history – was not particularly concerned with the legal or social status of actual Jews; rather his writings about Jews echoed themes of long-established Pauline doctrine and earlier patristic traditions that were to remain largely unchanged for centuries to come.[14] The fact that all major theologians after Augustine (even those who held far less tolerant attitudes towards Jews) continued to employ the same basic repertoire of anti-Judaic rhetoric highlights precisely the constructedness of such formulations.

Following Cohen, medievalists working in different disciplines have devised similar terms to explain the rhetorical and virtual position of Jews in medieval theology, literature, and the visual arts: hence the terms "spectral Jew" (Kruger); "paper Jew" (Biddick); "virtual Jew" (Tomasch and Krummel).[15] What these formulations have in common is the recognition

---

13 Cohen, *Living Letters of the Law*, 2. Cohen traces the utility of "the hermeneutically- and rhetorically-crafted Jew" from Augustine to Aquinas.

14 Cohen, *Living Letters*, 20. Augustine thought about Jews differently at different stages in his life. On his important "doctrine of witness," see Cohen, *Living Letters* and "Augustine's Doctrine of Jewish Witness Revisited," 564–78; and Fredriksen, *Augustine and the Jews*.

15 See Kruger, *The Spectral Jew*; Biddick, "Paper Jews"; Tomasch, "Postcolonial Chaucer and the Virtual Jew"; and Krummel, *Crafting Jewishness in Medieval England*. For a review and summary of these terms, see Bale, *The Jew in the Medieval Book*, 20.

that, as Kruger writes, "the Jew" was first and foremost "a fantasy construction that had as much or more to do with Christian identity as it did with actual Jews and Jewish communities."[16] As an ideological construct grounded in the collective imaginary, the rhetorical Jew took on a life of its own; this construct had the effect of suppressing or evacuating all traces of Jews in the flesh. Although traditional Christian hermeneutics insisted upon the stubborn carnality of the Jew, who was shackled to the Letter of the Law and therefore blind to New Testament revelation, there was a paradoxical tension that denied Jews actual, physical presence. This ideological "de-materialization" of "the Jew" had real-world consequences. Focusing on twelfth- and thirteenth-century England, Sylvia Tomasch has argued that the consistent and frequent use of anti-Jewish stereotypes enabled the permanent abjection of the Jew in Christian thinking – the consequence of which was to render Jews less than human.[17] Thus, Jewish bodies become at once "imaginary constructions and actual people" who "exist only in a fabricated past or phantasmic future."[18] Tomasch uses the analogy of post-colonialism to explain this condition of virtuality: although "Jews were not strictly speaking a separate "geo-political entity" within England, they were a distinct religious entity, with separate political responsibilities, privileges, and liabilities."[19] By the thirteenth century, the ghettoization of Jews, together with laws that restricted Jewish dress, worship, practice, and sources of livelihood, rendered them comparable to what post-colonial discourse might label an "internally colonized" people.[20] If Jews were not "serfs" in the historical sense of the word, they were nevertheless forced to labour "in the service" of the king in ways that denied them civic freedoms.[21]

---

16   Kruger, *Spectral Jew*, xvii.

17   Tomasch, "Postcolonial Chaucer and the Virtual Jew."

18   Ibid., 252.

19   Ibid., 250.

20   Ibid. Tomasch utilizes a distinction made by Anne McClintock between "colonization" and "internal colonization." According to McClintock, "*Colonization* involves direct territorial appropriation of another geo-political entity, combined with forthright exploitation of its resources and labor, and systematic interference in the capacity of the appropriated culture (itself not necessarily a homogenous entity) to organize its dispensations of power. *Internal colonization* occurs where the dominant part of a country treats a group as it might a foreign colony" (McClintock, "The Angel of Progress," 88; quoted by Tomasch, "Postcolonial Chaucer," 250).

21   The question as to what "Jewish service" meant in late England is a matter of some debate. Were Jews considered to be "*servi*" as they were called in Capetian France around

The same tactics of erasure also arguably applied to the Jew in the historical and biblical past, with obvious differences in terms of consequence and effect. Miriamne Ara Krummel has therefore argued that "typological figurations" that used "supersessionist thinking" were dangerous precisely because "they erase[d] the efficacy of the Jewish past." Thus, "in the rewriting of Jewish scriptural myths, the Jewish bodies that lived before the Christian bodies [were] made to disappear."[22] Krummel locates this particular vanishing point somewhere along the horizon of Christian typology, which in its most extreme application denied autonomous meaning to the Old Testament, its figures, and events, except when they were read as a "shadow" or revelation of the New Testament. As the essays in the present volume collectively demonstrate, this balance between presence and erasure is evident everywhere in Anglo-Saxon sermons, biblical commentaries, poetry, and the liturgy.

By focusing on the imaginary conception of Jews, it might be objected that we are sidestepping a recent trend in the academy, which favours "materialisms" in all of its applied theoretical domains (with its emphasis upon the historical person, the archive, and more generally the "thing"). However, in addition to exposing new and different imaginings of Jews, the present volume maintains that the study of "immaterial Jews" in Anglo-Saxon England sheds important light on the popular, institutional, and cultural frameworks that produced these imaginings. This is because at the very heart of anti-Jewish fictions we can locate doubts and uncertainties about Christian doctrine and belief. As Gavin I. Langmuir, Anthony Bale, and others have argued, the very fact that Judaism managed to survive its long history of attack, rejection, and abnegation means that the various narratives surrounding Christian messianism and supersessionism were subject to scepticism – if Christianity did indeed supersede Judaism,

---

1230 and in Germany by 1236? See further Abulafia, "Notions of Jewish Service"; Langmuir, "*Tanquam servi*" in *Toward a Definition of Antisemitism*; and Mundill, *The King's Jews.*

22 Krummel, *Crafting Jewishness*, 5. Steven Kruger has further complicated this dynamic by calling attention to the phenomenological status of the "absentee Jew." He argues that the same logic that produced the construct of the virtual or hermeneutic Jew resulted in a double-bind for its Christian practitioners. Citing Derrida's *Specters of Marx*, Kruger demonstrates that "the specter is a paradoxical incorporation, the becoming-body, a certain phenomenal and carnal form of the spirit." Hovering between spirit and body, the spectral Jew haunted Christian doctrine and practice with its stubborn antecedence (Kruger, *Spectral Jew*, xxi, citing Derrida, *Specters of Marx*, 6).

why were Jews still practicing their false religion?[23] In the twelfth and thirteenth centuries, doubts about aspects of Eucharistic doctrine contributed to the invention of blood libels against Jews, first in England, and then elsewhere in Europe. As Miri Rubin and Langmuir have argued, these "blood fictions" can be linked directly to rising doubts in the church and in the popular realm about the doctrine of Transubstantiation – that is, to the question of the physical presence of Christ in the Eucharist.[24] The associated allegations that Jews maliciously profaned and destroyed the host (the symbol of Christian community and God's presence) and that they murdered Christian children and cannibalistically drank their blood betrayed "psychic distress or rather the resurfacing of anxiety (about, for instance, the act of eating God)."[25] In such cases, Jews were not only depicted as being excluded from the Christian *communitas*, but also as willful destroyers of it.

It is our contention that the religious and cultural frameworks that produced the "imaginary Jew" in earlier texts demand similar scrutiny. Although it may well be the case that the most harmful and aggressive fictions about Jews developed in the twelfth century, it is also true that many of these "anti-Semitisms" developed from earlier, widespread misconceptions about Jews. For instance, late medieval accounts of Jewish Host desecration had their roots in earlier miracle stories about the Bleeding Host, which date at least as far back as the sixth century; in these texts, Jews typically appeared as reluctant witnesses to the truth and efficacy of the Eucharist.[26] One example of such an account is recorded in Ælfric's tenth-century *Life of St. Basil*, in which a Jew sees a Host "turn into a bloody child on the altar" before being doled out to the congregants. In Ælfric's version of the story, the doubting Jew takes part in the miracle by eating "a morsel of flesh" and sipping "blood from the chalice."[27] Compacted in this legend are a series of anxieties about Jews: the fear that Jews might actually eat the sacred Host and thereby profane it (an apprehension that recalls

---

23 Langmuir, *Toward a Definition of Antisemitism*, 100–34; Bale, *The Jew in the Medieval Book*.

24 Rubin, *Gentile Tales*, 25–8; Langmuir, *Toward a Definition of Antisemitism*, 100–34.

25 Krummel, *Crafting Jewishness*, 7.

26 On the role of Jews in stories conveying miracles of the host, see Rubin, *Gentile Tales*, 27–39. Rubin mentions the tale of Evagrius Scholasticus of Antioch (ca. 536–600), which was popularized by Gregory of Tours (d. 595).

27 *Ælfric's Life of St. Basil the Great*, ed. and trans., Corona, 160.

the numerous penitential bans against consumption of the host by non-Christians, animals, and other agents); and the sublimated fear that Jews might have valid doubts about its phenomenal transformation.[28] In such cases, the figure of the doubting Jew can be read as an expression and projection of uncertainties that corrosively lingered in the minds of Christian readers.[29] In fact, many of the essays in the present volume demonstrate the use of imaginary Jews as a means of channelling and allaying similar fears and doubts about Christian faith.

If the rhetorical construction of the imaginary Jew played an instrumental role in the creation and maintenance of religious ideologies both in the early and late medieval periods, it did so as well in the political sphere. The concretization of the idea of the Jewish "other" became central to the idea of the developing English nation. Most of the scholarship on this topic has focused on the thirteenth-century expulsion of the Jews from England. As James Shapiro has argued, "the desire on the part of the English to define themselves as different from, and indeed free of, that which was Jewish, operated not only on an individual level but on a national level as well: that is, between 1290 and 1656 the English came to see their country defined in part by the fact that Jews had been banished from it."[30] In the process of refining and honing what it meant to be "English," different textual ideologies began to take prominence surrounding the depiction of the Jew. Augustine (in a distinctly Pauline vein) had articulated many centuries before the presence of two Israels – namely, the Israel of the Flesh (Judaism) and the Israel of the Spirit (Christianity).[31] According to the hermeneutics of supersession, the latter was to replace the former. At the time of the Jewish expulsion, English authors adopted this trope of the two Israels and applied it to their own situation, establishing the Jews in England as representative of the Israel of the Flesh, and the Christian

---

28 Rubin, *Gentile Tales*, 27–39.

29 These doubts, had, after all, been given official voice in monastic circles since the ninth-century Eucharistic controversies, when Ratramnus and Radbertus (at Corbie) debated whether the Host received in communion contained the actual blood and flesh of Christ. See Chazelle, *The Crucified God in the Carolingian Era*.

30 Shapiro, *Shakespeare and the Jews*, 42.

31 The scholarship on the topic of the two Israels as figured through depictions of *Synagoga* and *Ecclesia* is vast. See especially Seiferth, *Synagogue and Church in the Middle Ages*; and Schlauch, "The Allegory of Church and Synagogue." For examples before the eleventh century, see Bishop, "An Iconographical Study of the Appearance of *Synagoga*."

community in England as the New Israel of the Spirit. As Sophia Menache explains, "the expulsion … serve[d] the interests of the monarchy in the long run, by providing a unifying element of national consciousness, the idea of a 'chosen people.'"[32] Moreover, "the removal of 'Israel of the [F]lesh' made it easier for the English to identify with 'Israel of the [S]pirit,' a concept deeply rooted in Christian society."[33] After the expulsion, the fantasy of a *judenrein* England became associated with the idea of a homogeneous nation and empire.[34]

It is clear that this configuration of England as the New Israel had idiosyncratic rhetorical force in the late thirteenth century. Numerous examples of this same trope had appeared much earlier, however, in Anglo-Saxon texts and culture as authors began to imagine their own *communitas* (defined in different ways in different historical periods) as the New Israel.[35] Thus, in his eighth-century *Historia Ecclesiastica*, the Venerable Bede used the trope of chosenness to establish his own *gens Anglorum* as the New Israel, united under one church. Bede's application of the concept both adopted and broke with Paul's understanding of Christian universalism: although Bede's imagined community was ecclesiastical (not political), his concept of unity pertained to Britain, not a pan-Germanic or pan-Christian ideal. This application changed and became increasingly political and "Anglo-centric" (in both senses of the word) in subsequent periods as the nascent concept of "nation" began to take shape.[36] Although it remains a contested issue as to whether Anglo-Saxon England might be considered a nation-state, the conditions for such an imagined community were nevertheless established

---

32 Menache, "Faith, Myth, and Politics," 360.

33 Ibid.

34 See Shapiro, *Shakespeare and the Jews*, for evidence against an England completely without Jews in the post-exile period.

35 See Zacher, *Rewriting the Old Testament*. For discussions of Bede's use of this theme of chosenness, see especially Wormald, "*Engla Lond*," 12–16 and "Bede, The *Bretwaldas* and the Origins of the *Gens Anglorum*," 121–5; Scheil, *The Footsteps of Israel*, 111–42; and Harris, *Race and Ethnicity*, 45–82.

36 Such claims for special election were hardly original to Anglo-Saxon authors: similar assertions had been made by virtually every conquering people that followed in the footsteps of Rome, and also in the Holy Roman Empire. The closest cultural and textual analogues for Anglo-Saxon England were Frankish, and these can be traced at least as far back as the reign of Pippin, whose anointing in 751 asserted his status as a divinely sanctioned ruler, and the status of the Frankish people, collectively, as the New Israel. See further Wallace-Hadrill, *Early Germanic Kingship*, 48–50; Wormald, "*Engla Lond*," 11–15; Zacher, *Rewriting the Old Testament*, 28–30.

by the consolidation of tribal power under a single West-Saxon dynasty at
the very end of the ninth and early tenth centuries, and were bolstered by
developing West-Saxon claims to rulership over "all the English people,"
and subsequently "over all of Britain."[37] Thus, from the age of Alfred the
Great onward, West-Saxon kings forged specious genealogies that claimed
ancestral descent directly from Adam and Noah, and used Old Testament
iconography in order to assert divinely mandated rule.[38] These "propagan-
dist" moves were calculated to give credence to an emerging conception of
a united English people.[39] Moreover, as I have argued in my recent book,
*Rewriting the Old Testament in Anglo-Saxon Verse: Becoming the Chosen
People*, the same general claims to identification with the New Israel were
reiterated and applied more widely in tenth-century Old English versifi-
cation of the Old Testament, since poets obsessively cited the scriptural
theme of "chosenness" in order to characterize the ongoing and exclusive
covenant between the English people and God.[40]

By offering this brief analogy between the ideologies of "two Israels" in
Anglo-Saxon England and in the thirteenth century, we can see that the
process of "othering" Jews in Anglo-Saxon texts and visual arts did not

---

37 It is not until the ninth century that we begin to witness the emergence of a recog-
nizable "English" polity, when Alfred the Great (king of Wessex 871–99) cultivated
the title "king of all of the English." For more details, see Wormald, "The Making of
England"; Foot, "The Making of *Angelcynn*"; Zacher, "Multilingualism at the Court
of King Æthelstan."

38 On the West-Saxon genealogies going back to Noah and Adam, see Anlezark, "Sceaf,
Japheth and the Origins of the Anglo-Saxons." On the West-Saxon dynastic use of
Biblical iconography, see Wormald, *The Making of English Law*, 416–30, and Pratt,
Political Thought of King Alfred, 170. On portraits affiliating rulers with biblical kings,
see Chaney, *Cult of Kingship*, and Karkov, *Ruler Portraits*.

39 Turville-Petre argued in *England the Nation* that the development of a national
consciousness occurred in Chaucer's England, while Lavezzo made a case for the era
just after the Norman Conquest (*Imagining a Medieval English Nation*, vii–xxviii).
Still others have reconstructed a developing ideology of nationhood beginning as early
as the eighth and ninth centuries in England. See Campbell, "The United Kingdom
of England" and *The Anglo-Saxon State*; Wormald, "*Engla Lond*" and "Bede, The
Bretwaldas and the Origins of the *Gens Anglorum*"; Foot, "The Making of *Angelcynn*";
Pratt, *Political Thought of King Alfred the Great*; Zacher, "Multilingualism at the
Court of King Æthelstan." From early on such claims were expressed through the
self-identification of Anglo-Saxon England as the New Israel and as the chosen nation
of God (Scheil, *The Footsteps of Israel*; Zacher, *Rewriting the Old Testament*).

40 Zacher, *Rewriting the Old Testament*.

merely assert theological and religious difference, but rather forged a state of mind fundamental to the construction of communal and individual identity in Anglo-Saxon England.[41] That the Jewish "other" resided entirely outside Anglo-Saxon time and space did not neutralize its importance and impact upon Anglo-Saxon thought. Rather, as many of the essays in this volume demonstrate, such a strict emphasis on the physical encounter with the Jewish other may indeed prove to be too limiting and simplistic. Jews were not simply abstract concepts that had been imported wholesale through the adoption of Christian thought and typology in Anglo-Saxon England; rather they represented continuing sites of abhorred opposition and admired familiarity.

Several key points emerge from this brief discussion. The first is that Anglo-Saxon representations of Jews exemplified some of the same pressure points of opposition and intimacy reflected in writings and depictions of Jews in later medieval periods in England and elsewhere. The second is that many of the scholarly tools used to evaluate the role of the rhetorical Jew in the literature and visual arts of late antiquity and the late medieval period prove useful for the evaluation of Anglo-Saxon imaginings. And the third is that the condition of Jewish absence in Anglo-Saxon England only brings further into relief the essential idea – vital to the study of Jewish representation by external sources in *any* period of history – that the rhetorical figure of "the Jew" is fundamentally disconnected from actual Jews. These concepts underpin the essays in this volume, dedicated to the study of "the imagined Jew" in Anglo-Saxon England.

Contributions: Past and Present

In contrast to the impressive amount of scholarship devoted to the study of Jews in late medieval English texts and culture, few comparable studies exist which examine Anglo-Saxon texts and culture. The contributors to this volume have all significantly advanced this work in the fields of literature, manuscript studies, and art history, as the collective bibliography at the end of this volume indicates. The most comprehensive study of the subject to date remains Andrew P. Scheil's *The Footsteps of Israel: Understanding*

---

41   As Scheil has eloquently argued, "pointing the finger at the embodiment of alterity in the cultural landscape is one strategy by which a culture regulates its boundaries, its cohesiveness and integrity" (*The Footsteps of Israel*, 5).

Jews in Anglo-Saxon England (2003), which surveys writings about Jews and ancient Hebrews in contexts as varied as Anglo-Saxon sermons, histories, poetry, saints' lives, and theological tracts. Scheil's book demonstrates the diversity of attitudes towards Jews, ranging from hate, revulsion, and repudiation, to love, admiration, and the desire for imitation. The texts also reflected multiple and conflicting discourses about Jews:

> Jews were a meditative vehicle for exegesis; an exemplum of the direction of God's shaping hand throughout history; a record of the divine patterns of the historical imagination; a subject for epic and elegy; an outlet for anger and rage; a dark, fearful image of the body; a useful political tool – in all, a variform way of fashioning a Christian *populus* in England and continually refining its nature. In Anglo-Saxon England, Jews and Judaism signify not image but process; not stable concept, but complex negotiation.[42]

Jews and Judaism in Anglo-Saxon texts were not merely "static motifs," nor were they "simply an unchanging, universally despised, unproblematic 'Other'."[43] Rather, Jews were seen to inhabit the borderline between "otherness" and "sameness" in a fashion that made them flexible to different rhetorical needs and demands. For this very reason, authors could – without seeming in the least inconsistent or unreliable – combine oppositional depictions of Jews as sick, blind, and corrupted on the one hand, and as a righteous and cherished *populus Dei* on the other.

Scheil's book concentrates heavily on the works of the Venerable Bede, and on the historiographical models that influenced his view of history (including chronicles, histories, and commentaries by such authors as Eusebius, Orosius, Salvian, and Paulinus of Nola), revealed especially in his *Ecclesiastical History of the English People*. Scheil is surely correct to suggest that Bede is a nodal figure, whose writings were read and admired throughout the Anglo-Saxon period and beyond, and whose attitudes towards Jews clearly shaped and guided those who followed, especially theologians and homilists such as Alcuin, Ælfric, and Wulfstan.[44] However, there are other historical and textual models that require analysis.

---

42 Scheil, *The Footsteps of Israel*, 3.
43 Ibid., 6.
44 For an account of authors who read Bede, see Gransden, *Legends, Traditions and History in Medieval England*.

Following in the footsteps of Scheil, the essays in this volume (including a new essay by Scheil himself) explore different discursive treatments of Jews in the Anglo-Saxon world. In the process, they treat a wide cross-section of perspectives addressing Anglo-Saxon treatments of race, religion, and ethnicity, textual and visual representations of Jews, the translation and interpretation of Scripture, theology, uses of Hebrew words and etymologies, and the treatment of Jewish spaces and landmarks. Collectively, the essays engage numerous topics that have not hitherto been adequately theorized or explored in scholarship. This work comes at an auspicious moment in medieval scholarship, as scholars have begun to think more critically about medieval categories of race and ethnicity, and to explore possible connections with and dissociations from contemporary classifications.[45] Since the publication of Scheil's book in 2003, there have been pioneering explorations of the connections between Jews and other minorities – Muslims, heretics, witches, lepers, etc.[46] – in addition to numerous studies of proto-Orientalism in the medieval period, a field which has examined representations of Jews, both on their own terms, and in relation to Muslims, their Semitic counterparts.[47] In *Imagining the Jew in Anglo-Saxon Literature and Culture*, these new directions in the study of early medieval conceptions of Jews can be seen at work.

Part 1: Defining the Jew: A Question of Race, Ethnicity, or Religion?

The task of defining Jewish identity has never been an easy one. Even today, Orthodox, Conservative, and Reform Jews cannot agree on the essential question as to whether Jewishness is determined by birth, by normative religious statutes, by distant ancestry, or by self-identification. These disagreements converge not simply around aspects of Jewish practice and

---

45 On the category of race in the Middle Ages, see, for example Bartlett, "Medieval and Modern Concepts of Race and Ethnicity"; Hahn, "The Difference the Middle Ages Makes" (both essays appear in a special volume of *JMEMS* devoted to the concept of race in the Middle Ages). See also Yeager, "Racial Imagination and the Theater of War."

46 See, for example, Moore, *The Formation of a Persecuting Society*; Nirenberg, *Communities of Violence*; Heng, "Jews, Saracens, 'Black Men,' Tartars."

47 See especially Akbari, *Idols in the East* and "Placing the Jews in Late Medieval English Literature." For Anglo-Saxon writings on Muslims, see Scarfe Beckett, *Anglo-Saxon Perceptions of the Islamic World*.

observance, but also in some instances around secular policy making, such as Israel's "Law of Return," which grants Jews living in the diaspora the right to live in Israel and to gain citizenship. Christians in the Middle Ages, looking from the outside in, faced other concerns regarding categories of Jewish identity. A recurring point of contention was the problem of conversion in both directions: were Jews able to "relinquish" their Jewish identity if they chose to do so? What about Jews who were forced to convert by non-Jews against their will – were they "false Christians"? Was Jewishness a racial, ethnic, or religious category? The first two essays in the volume take up some of these questions with regard to Anglo-Saxon texts. Stephen J. Harris begins by providing a rigorous examination of the terms designating Jews and Jewish identity in Anglo-Saxon texts as well as their biblical, rabbinic, and patristic cognates and sources. As Harris points out, from the patristic period forward, there was a hierarchy of valuation in which the term "Jew" was seen to be pejorative, "Israelite" relatively neutral, and "Hebrew" laudatory. According to this schema, "the Jew" became a type of the faithless Christian, while faithful Christians began to identify themselves as the *New Israel*. In the Anglo-Saxon period, these designations gained special significance when writers such as Bede (and later Alcuin) actually envisioned the Church as well as the *gens Anglorum* as the New Israel. As we have seen in the discussion above, this identification with the biblical Israel – itself understood as a nation – became a major topic of discussion in a range of Anglo-Saxon texts.

Thomas N. Hall continues this discussion in his study of the Anglo-Saxon version of the apocryphal *Vindicta Salvatoris*, a story that was ultimately based upon the account Josephus gives in his *Jewish Wars* of the sacking of Jerusalem by the Roman emperors Titus and Vespasian. A branch of the *Vindicta* also served as one source for the thirteenth century *Siege of Jerusalem* – a text that has been at the centre of Jewish-Muslim studies in medieval scholarship.[48] Hall traces the evolution of this story to a fourth-century Latin adaptation by Hegesippus, who Christianized Josephus's account by reframing Vespasian and his son Titus as unwitting instruments of God's vengeance in the plot to overthrow the Jewish race. It was, however, the medieval apocryphon known as the *Vindicta Salvatoris* or *Avenging of the Saviour*, which introduced the character of

---

48 For related scholarship on the *Siege of Jerusalem*, see Akbari, "Placing the Jews"; Yeager, "The Crusade of the Soul in *The Siege of Jerusalem*"; Millar, *The Siege of Jerusalem;* Van Court, *"The Siege of Jerusalem and Recuperative Readings."*

Nathan, who set in motion a campaign to avenge Christ's death. While the earliest surviving text of the Latin *Vindicta Salvatoris* identified Nathan as an Ishmaelite, the first vernacular translation in Old English identified him as a Jew. Hall asks, "what does it mean in this story that Nathan is an Ishmaelite or a Jew, and what is the point of having an Ishmaelite or a Jew serve as the single-handed inspiration for the crusade to destroy the Jewish race?" Hall's analysis reveals the extent to which this Anglo-Saxon text blurs racial and religious identities in its confused effort to label and thus segregate Jewish identity. In ways that are often unintentionally comical, the Old English text reflects widespread ontological uncertainty surrounding the identity of Jews in this period.

Part 2: The Jew in Anglo-Saxon Theology and Liturgy: Aspects of Language, Place, and Time

It has often been implied, and sometimes asserted outright, that with the possible exception of Bede, Anglo-Saxon authors were not the real "movers and shakers" of Christian theology, doctrine, and belief.[49] The three chapters by Damian Fleming, Kathy Lavezzo, and Andrew P. Scheil explore the figure of "the Jew" in Anglo-Saxon theology and liturgy, and seek to map points of continuity and difference with the various Latin patristic sources that inform Anglo-Saxon texts. Collectively, the essays consider what fundamental concerns were expressed, lauded, and repudiated in Anglo-Saxon theological conceptions of Jewishness and Jewish practice. More specifically, the essays question whether Anglo-Saxon authors generally followed the lead of patristic authorities, or whether, and in what contexts, they developed *sui generis* theological traditions.

The essay by Fleming investigates Anglo-Saxon attitudes towards the Hebrew language in patristic and Anglo-Saxon writings, especially those of the Venerable Bede. While the majority of work on the subject of Jews in Anglo-Saxon England has focused on corporeal and representational depictions of Jews, Fleming's focus is on language as an alternative, and important point of access for thinking about philo- and anti-Judaic attitudes in early medieval England. His detailed analysis of embedded

---

49   For Bede's influence on later writers, see Gransden, *Legends, Traditions and History in Medieval England*.

Hebrew words in Anglo-Saxon grammars and biblical commentaries poses a series of hitherto unexplored questions: did Anglo-Saxon writers revere Hebrew as one of the *tres linguae sacrae* or did they approach the language from the viewpoint of conventional "supersessionist" rhetoric, which assumed a felicitous move from the Jewish Letter to the Christian Spirit? What did it mean for an author to claim textual authority by citing Hebrew language? In the course of his study, Fleming demonstrates that Bede played an instrumental part in promoting Jerome's Vulgate Bible in the West as the most authoritative and truthful translation of the Bible.

Lavezzo investigates a more sinister side of Bede's writings on Jews, focusing on those passages in Bede's *oeuvre* that are critical of the Jewish past. Lavezzo provides a close reading of Bede's theological writings on the Temple in his *De Templo* (and in various other allegorical commentaries on Old Testament books). Claiming to seek the "spiritual mansion of God" within the "material structure" of the temple, Bede implies that the literal temple is superseded by the new, spiritual church, whose figurative cornerstone is Christ. In this way, Bede reframes the typical Pauline rhetoric of temporal supersession so that it fits the spatial and imaginative coordinates of the temple itself. This typological redefinition of building materials would seem to carry with it a straightforward anti-Judaic message: by ascribing to the Jews a "tectonic mentality," Bede repeats and perpetuates the stereotype that the tomb-like Jews are closed to the spiritual Christian message. However, Lavezzo complicates this paradigm by citing moments in the *De Templo* and in the *Historica Ecclesiastica* where Bede stresses the religious and spiritual value of earthly dwellings, thereby establishing the temple as a holy place of worship to the Anglo-Saxon church.

Scheil's essay also refers back to the paradigm of supersession by exploring the ways Jews and Judaism are appropriated by the textual culture of Anglo-Saxon England in order to signal moments of temporal and historical transition. Anglo-Saxon England inherited many methods used to measure, demarcate, and understand the progress of Christian time and salvation history; one powerful tradition uses the rhetorical or hermeneutic Jew as a signature or attendant marker of transition, particularly when that moment of transition is in the service of a discourse of renewal and rebirth. Using a variety of homilies and other texts mostly by Bede and Ælfric, Scheil explores the spectral presence of the Jews in the liturgical calendar. Jews are located at these moments of Christian transition and renewal in the calendar, and come to embody the notion of transition itself. The *transitus* of the Jews – that is, the Christian apprehension of Jews and Judaism as belated, superseded, passed over, spiritually dead and lost – comes to be seen as a logical adjunct to understanding the structure of time in the Christian textual tradition of Anglo-Saxon England.

Part 3: Literary Types and Anglo-Saxon Audiences

The cluster of essays by Daniel Anlezark, Thomas D. Hill, and Charles D. Wright explore depictions of Jews in Old English literature. These essays focus on individual texts and themes with the aim of addressing the following general questions: In what literary contexts do discussions of Jews appear? What kinds of audience responses did authors anticipate in constructing complementary or negative portrayals of Jews? Were there discrepancies between the representations of Jews in Anglo-Latin and Old English texts? Did treatments of Jewish topics differ when addressed to lay as opposed to clerical audiences?

The essay by Anlezark focuses on references to and discussions of Abraham and the Abrahamic covenant in Anglo-Saxon poetry and prose, particularly in the verse *Exodus* and the sermons of Ælfric. In these works, Abraham is depicted as the father of Christian gentile nations, rather than of the Jewish people. In the hands of Anglo-Saxon writers, biblical narratives were stripped of their specific Jewish significance, so that they could be adapted to a typological reading that treated the larger Christian community as heirs to the promises made to Abraham. Old English texts thus absorbed and reflected the Pauline view that the promises made by God to Abraham and the Israelites were fulfilled in Jesus, who was interpreted literally and uniquely as the promised seed of Abraham. Anlezark demonstrates that while Anglo-Saxon authors drew readily upon patristic interpretations of the covenant, they nevertheless adapted these materials allegorically to reflect their own contemporary circumstances.

Hill's essay focuses on the precarious treatment of Jews in the poem *Elene*, which presents a version of the well-known legend of the finding of the true cross by the eponymous mother of Constantine the Great. Elene finds the true cross by interrogating the Jewish community and imprisoning and torturing Judas, a Jew who eventually converts to Christianity. Traditionally, scholars (Hill included) have looked to the Latin *Inventio crucis* legend as the main source for themes such as the contrast between the Letter and the Spirit and the role of Jews as unwitting witnesses to the truth of Christ. However, in this essay, Hill turns to a new body of texts – namely, the liturgical materials associated with the feast of the *Inventio crucis* on 3 May and the feast of the exaltation of the Cross on 15 September. Hill suggests that if these feasts were in fact celebrated in England in the ninth century, then the poet and his auditors would have been intimately familiar with the associated prayers and treated them as part of the larger repertoire concerning the *Inventio crucis*. As such they would have interpreted the *Inventio crucis* legend "not as a straightforward historical event, but as a symbolic event in which the history of the fourth century, the passion of Jesus, and the ongoing tradition of Christian worship and praxis in the medieval world were linked together." Reading *Elene* in light of these paratexts conjoins the traditional association of the Jews with the Crucifixion, and reveals their role as symbolic fixtures in the Anglo-Saxon liturgy and imagination.

In the essay following, Wright turns to the poem *Andreas*, which narrates the journey of the apostle to the land of the Mermedonians in an attempt to rescue Matthew from his impending death at the hands of cannibals. The focus is on one difficult passage in the poem, which lauds the apostle Matthew's resilience and his ability to withstand the *galdorcræftas* of the Jews – a term perhaps best translated as "witchcraft" or "black magic," though usually explained away as "evil machinations," or "blasphemous deceits" to fit conventional anti-Judaic rhetoric. Wright, however, proposes a novel interpretation, reading *galdorcræftas* as a reference to *tefilin* – Jewish "phylacteries" worn on the forehead and arm, which were often interpreted by Christian exegetes as superstitious or magical forms of protection. While the association of magic with Jews may at first seem to isolate the Jews as uniquely pernicious and misguided others, Wright demonstrates that similar concerns pervaded patristic and medieval writings on Christian worship, in the form of warnings against the use of amulets and trinkets made from the gospels or the wood of the Cross. Building upon these associations, Wright examines Anglo-Saxon attitudes towards Jewish practice and ritual, and also towards the use of apotropaic devices in both Judaism and Christianity. Wright's reinterpretation of the term reveals a latent fear that the excessive or misguided worship of religious objects might result in Judaizing behaviour.

Part 4: Visual Media: Representations of Jews and Jewish Spaces

Most contemporary stereotypes about Jews and Jewish physiognomy have their ultimate roots in medieval depictions. Jews in medieval manuscripts from the eleventh century onwards were depicted as having hooked noses, shaggy beards, horns, and tails.[50] They also sometimes wore identifying clothing, which included hats of different varieties, such as the *pileum cornutum*, also called *Judenhut*, or Phrygian cap. From the thirteenth century, Jews were depicted as wearing badges of the type enforced by Lateran IV (such insignia poignantly prefigure the *Judenstern* Jews were forced to wear during the Nazi regime). It is therefore all the more striking that similar grotesque images of Jews did *not* generally appear in Anglo-Saxon manuscripts. One reason is surely that most Anglo-Saxon illuminations depicted either biblical figures or else established Christian types, such as *Synagoga and Ecclesia* (which in the later periods would likewise absorb the negative depictions of Jews). Two exceptions in which Jews are made to look visually different appear in a manuscript containing the Old English Hexateuch (MS Cotton Claudius B.iv). The first image depicts Jews with pointed hats, a detail that would seem to reveal familiarity either with actual Jews, or more likely, how Jews were commonly represented in continental manuscripts.[51] The second appears in a series of images depicting Moses with horns. This image of the "horned Moses" represents the first attested appearance of this figure in art history, preceding Michelangelo's sculpture (housed in Rome, in San Pietro in Vincoli) by over 500 years. While the Anglo-Saxon "horned Moses" is clearly the ancestor of the damaging anti-Judaic stereotype of the "horned Jew," which comes to represent carnal difference and willful otherness associated with the devil, in Anglo-Saxon England and indeed throughout much of the Middle Ages, this figure represented victory, power, and even divine election.[52]

Turning to the corpus of graphic media in illuminated bibles and other manuscripts, Catherine Karkov, Adam S. Cohen, and Asa Mittman focus on the variety of visual markers Anglo-Saxon artists used to depict Jews. These essays collectively examine whether artistic visual representations of Jews conformed to their textual counterparts. Moreover, they ask whether the emphasis in visual media on physical difference intensifies

---

50 For negative physical depictions of Jews in medieval manuscripts and visual art, see Trachtenberg, *The Devil and the Jews*, esp. 44–52; Lipton, *Images of intolerance*; Strickland, *Saracens, Demons & Jews*; Camille, *Gothic Idol*, ch. 4; and Mellinkoff, *Outcasts*.

51 See Mellinkoff, "The Round, Cap-shaped Hats Depicted on Jews."

52 On the figure of the horned Moses, see Mellinkoff, *Horned Moses*. On the Anglo-Saxon illuminations in particular, see Withers, *The Illustrated Old English Hexateuch*; and now the chapter by Asa Mittman, below. I am grateful to Peter Gilgen for reading a draft of this essay, and for offering his expert editorial comments.

the patristic conviction that Jews were a "carnal" people set apart from "spiritual" Christians. Karkov focuses on images of women in the Anglo-Saxon Hexateuch, concentrating in particular on the figures of Sarah, the *progenitrex* of the line of the Jews, and Hagar, the illegitimate mother of Ishmael and forbear of the Muslim people. While patristic commentary has generally stressed the ethnic and even moral differences between these women, the Anglo-Saxon artist joins them through an uncanny doubling, which at times depicts them as mirror opposites, and at times as virtually indistinguishable figures. This doubling performs a powerful commentary on the status of women in the bible as marginalized figures, exiled from the dominant world of men. Moreover, these visual connections force a comparison between Jews and Muslims, who are depicted (respectively) as the chosen and outcast people of God, and by extension between Jews and Christians, the latter of which come to represent the new elect through the advent of Christ.

Cohen turns to other Old Testament *exempla*, focusing on the positive use of Pentateuchal figures as models for English kingship in Anglo-Saxon manuscripts. His essay focuses in particular upon a rare and awkward depiction of King Edgar, which appears at the beginning of the manuscript containing the New Minster Charter – a document that charts the King's central involvement in the re-foundation of the New Minster as a monastery, and his agency in the Benedictine Reform. This beautifully executed, rather strange illumination depicts Edgar standing on tiptoe, with his body contorted and arms raised to Christ – a posture that has defied explanation. Through a series of comparisons with other Carolingian and Byzantine manuscripts, Cohen is able to suggest that New Minster Edgar is modelled on the story of King David dancing in humility before the Lord, in 2 Samuel 6. With this cultural, political, and religious focus firmly in mind, Cohen interrogates the ways in which Old Testament exempla were used to communicate positive notions of humility, kingship, and revelation. Such positive connections reinforced the persistent Anglo-Saxon self-identification as the newly proclaimed chosen people.

Mittman explores one of the earliest surviving depictions of the horned Moses in an eleventh-century Old English Illustrated Hexateuch. Building on previous studies of this figure, Mittman focuses in particular on Moses's unusual size, which links him visually to a host of giants in the Hexateuch. The connection is troubling, since – as one prolific twelfth-century commentator notes in the margins of the manuscript – the monstrosity of the giants' bodies betrays the monstrosity of their minds. Mittman further demonstrates that the Anglo-Saxon artist strategically misplaces some of these images of giants in relation to the biblical text in order to emphasize links between their monstrosity and God's wrath. Although in the case of Moses, it is clear that his size is intended positively to emphasize his tremendous power and strong leadership, the visual analogy with enemy giants nevertheless calls attention to the marginal, and ultimately foreign status of the biblical Jew. As Mittman concludes, "images of Moses, the great Jewish prophet, as not only horned but also gigantic complicate what might otherwise have been a simplistic dichotomy of 'us' and 'them', thereby creating a more fertile basis for contemplative viewing."

Epilogue: Pre- and Post-Conquest Identifications: Continuity and Difference

The final essay by Heide Estes ventures beyond the purview of the Anglo-Saxon period to explore points of continuity and difference between pre- and post-Conquest identifications of Jews. The article offers a speculative analysis of how Ælfric's late tenth-century homilies that comment on Jewish difference might have been read and experienced in the twelfth century, when many of Ælfric's homilies were recopied, reproduced, and reinterpreted. Using this group of texts as a platform for discussion, the essay seeks an understanding of what kinds of Jewish stereotypes and depictions were original to Anglo-Saxon productions by tracing lines of intellectual transmission from the works of specific Anglo-Saxon authors to post-conquest representations of Jews. Estes reads Ælfric's sermons specifically in the context of the anti-Jewish riots in London (during the coronation of Richard I in 1189), the York massacre (1190), and also the rise of blood-libels against Jews. She postulates that twelfth-century readers who experienced political and social antipathy towards actual Jews would have had very different views of Ælfric's Jews and his anti-Jewish rhetoric.

Defining the Jew: A Question of Race, Ethnicity, or Religion?

1 Anglo-Saxons, Israelites, Hebrews, and Jews

STEPHEN J. HARRIS

God has spoken once. Two things have we heard.

Ps 62:12

The term *Jew* as used in Christian exegesis conceals a complicated relationship between Christians and the historical Jews of Scripture, on one hand, and on the other, living Jewish people of the early Middle Ages. From the perspective of authoritative Catholic writers, as Kenneth Stow explains, the relationship between Jews and the Church is governed by the theory that "originated in St. Paul's view, expounded in the Epistle to the Romans, that the true Israel is a spiritual body, composed of believers in Christ, and not the Israel of the flesh, the Jews."[1] Spiritually, *Israel* is a term that can refer both to Jews and to Christians. But more terrestrially, *Israel* is the nation that emerges out of the Egyptian captivity of the *Hebrews*. *Israel* is also the name of the Northern Kingdom, set next to the southern Kingdom of Judah, comprised of the tribes of Judah and Benjamin, whose capital was Jerusalem. *Judah* is the source of the name *Iudaeos*, from which English speakers derive *Jew*. As Christians develop the theory of the spiritual body of Israel, the three terms *Hebrew*, *Israelite*, and *Jew* come to take on theological significance. As Bernhard Blumenkranz explains, among medieval Christian writers there is a hierarchy of valuation

---

1 Stow, "Jews and the Catholic Church," 7:75–9, at 75. My thanks to Andrew Scheil, Andrew Rabin, and Scott DeGregorio for their generous advice and direction, and to Samantha Zacher for her invitation to participate in this volume.

in the terms, *Iudaei* being pejorative, *Israelitae* being relatively neutral, and *Hebrew* being laudatory.[2] Particular Christian writers, such as Isidore of Seville, were very careful with their terminology, but others, such as Leo the Great, were not. The clarity of the distinctions in the terms is compromised by their use in two narratives: a narrative of physical kinship to Abraham and a narrative of spiritual kinship to Abraham. These two narratives were known as the *Ecclesia ex circumcisione* and the *Ecclesia ex gentibus* (as in Amalarius of Metz), or the *Israel of the flesh* and the *Israel of the spirit* (as in Bede).[3] When searching for "the Jew" in Anglo-Saxon England, then, we ought to be aware of both narratives and how they contextualize the three terms.

Some Anglo-Saxon authors keep to patristic tradition, some do not. Perhaps as a consequence, in searching the vast expanse of Anglo-Saxon textual evidence, we find discrepancies in portraits of "the Jew." And perhaps not unsurprisingly, Andrew Scheil concludes that the image of "the Jew" in Anglo-Saxon England is not singular, but multiple, the result of a discursive practice reshaped by shifting contexts.[4] Is this conclusion influenced to some degree by the manner in which evidence is collected? In other words, in trying to be capacious, is the researcher overlooking lines of influence and hierarchies of theological competence? (One worries, for example, whether in the eyes of a researcher a clearly anti-Semitic remark from a marginal author has the same value as a laudatory remark from a major author.) But even when focusing on the writing of a particular Anglo-Saxon, is the terminology clear enough across the millennia to allow us to understand what he thinks of *Jews*? The question is complicated by the obvious fact that there were no Jews in Anglo-Saxon England, so Jews were imagined, spectral, phantasmic. Or perhaps such a question cannot be answered generally, if only because there was no uniform manner of speaking about *Jews* across the many languages of Anglo-Saxon

---

2 Blumenkranz, *Les Auteurs chrétiens latins*, 59, on Cassiodorus. I am deeply indebted to Blumenkranz's work. Bauer, *Adversus Judaeos*, offers a fuller explanation in a quote from Blumenkranz (her 28), but I cannot locate it in Blumenkranz. Bauer's work is extremely useful, and she points out quite correctly that the term "Juden" is bound up in context (30).

3 Amalarius of Metz, quoted in Blumenkranz, *Les Auteurs chrétiens latins*, 172n1; Bede, at 134.

4 Scheil, *The Footsteps of Israel*. Heide Estes calls the image of the Jew in Anglo-Saxon England "multifarious, not simply dualistic"; see her "Lives in Translation: Jews in the Anglo-Saxon Literary Imagination" (PhD diss.), 6.

England. Moreover, Anglo-Saxons, like their Continental neighbours, held many different views. The contemporaries Agobard of Lyons and Amalarius of Metz held drastically different views about the connection between followers of Christ and those faithful to Torah. Even if one draws distinctions along national lines in the evidence, no such distinctions can be drawn in any conclusion – the extant sample of Anglo-Saxon authors is statistically insufficient. Given these challenges, a reasonable if inconclusive result might be a catalogue of images and ideas that were available for adoption in textual culture. We can't say what Anglo-Saxons thought about Jews, but we might be able to say what they *could have thought*.

Scheil limits his own study to particularly important Anglo-Saxon authors, and then to a selection of their works, cataloguing some of the images of Jews. In a review of Scheil's *Footsteps*, Scott DeGregorio lamented the fact that Scheil had not been able to go further into the Latin tradition of Anglo-Saxon England.[5] This concern was shared by other reviewers, as well, Andrew Rabin notable among them. The number of Anglo-Latin authors is daunting enough and the topic so capacious as to moderate the ambitions of any researcher. But Scheil's focus allows for further contributions to his larger discussion about available images of Jews. As those images are collated, it is important to prepare categories by which to sort them. My more limited aim is therefore to describe in slightly more detail a categorical distinction already observed by scholars of Anglo-Saxon England between the Jewish *gens* and the people of Israel.[6] The distinction is observed by early Latin authors, but it is difficult to say to what degree it was maintained. Some Christian authors sometimes refer to Jews as the *gens Iudaeorum*, or the *Iudeos*. *Iudeos* derives from *Judah*: Hraban Maur, for example, a student of Alcuin, writes, "Christians are named from Christ, just as the Jews are named from Judah."[7] The same authors also refer to Jews with the phrase *populus Israhel*. When Hraban writes of the *gens Iudaeorum* or the *populus Israhel*, the respective plural and singular qualifiers (*Iudaeorum* and *Israhel*) are freighted with theological

---

5 DeGregorio, review of Scheil, *The Footsteps of Israel*; see also the review by Rabin, 227–30.

6 Although not otherwise acknowledged, Arno Borst's unparalleled historiographical research on the relation of the Hebrew language to the Jewish people has been invaluable; *Der Turmbau von Babel*.

7 Hraban Maur, *De Universo*, IV, vii, trans. Throop, 90. Scheil, *The Footsteps of Israel*, 41, translates *Iudaea* as Judaea.

connotations. We might note, for example, that the Anglo-Saxon Church saw itself as a part of the New Israel, not the New Judea. And as Scheil points out, the Latin poet Salvian thought "Israel" a designation of chosenness that could be lost – while tribal identity, connoted by Judah, is presumably a more permanent quality.[8]

We find a philological distinction between Judah and Israel in Hebrew: *iehudah* and *yisrael*. The name *iehudah* is the Tetragrammaton, the name of God, with the addition of a Deled. The name is given to Judah by his mother Leah in Genesis 29:35. Leah combines the name of God with the word *odeh*, to make supplication to or to acknowledge (the Lord). Thus, in the name Judah, Leah and all Jews humbly acknowledge the Lord. In his study of the use of these terms in Antiquity, S.J.D. Cohen points out that using "Jew" to designate pre-medieval communities more often than not fails to respect historical distinctions:

> The predecessors of the English word, *Jew*, Greek *Ioudaios* and Latin *Iudaeus*, were originally ethnic-geographic terms, like "Egyptian," "Syrian," "Cappadocian," "Thracian," and so forth. Thus instead of "Jews" we should, in many cases, speak rather of "Judaeans," the residents of Judaea (geography), who constitute the ethnos, "nation" or "people," of the Judaeans (ethnicity).[9]

Cohen reports that his lucid distinction is unfortunately incapable of making sense of wide variations in historical and Scriptural data. Historically, as Cohen points out, "Augustine knows Christians who still call themselves *Iudaei*, and the Bishop of Hippo explains to them that Christians can and should be called Israel, but not *Iudaei*, even though in theory this name belongs to them as well."[10] Although *Iudaei* designates people from Judah (Jews), by the end of the first century CE, *Iudaei* comes to designate the religious faith of Judeans (i.e., the Jewish faith), as well. In fact,

---

8 Scheil, *The Footsteps of Israel*, 129; and Estes, "Lives," 14. Thomas D. Hill also notes the influence of Salvian in medieval distinctions between Israel and Judah; see his "Hebrews, Israelites, and Wicked Jews," 358–61. Blumenkranz reports that Salvian observes the twelve tribes of *Hebrews*, after leaving Egypt, taking on two names, the *People of God* and *Israel*; *Jews* are both, he says, but neither the one nor the other. See Blumenkranz, *Les Auteurs chrétiens latins*, 42.

9 Cohen, *The Beginnings of Jewishness*, 14.

10 Epistle 196, cited by Cohen, *The Beginnings of Jewishness*, 26n3.

Haymo of Auxerre suggested in the ninth century that the term *Iudaei* designates all the faithful, Jews and Gentiles.[11] But as we have already seen, the name (New) *Israel* is also used to designate the faithful. J.S. Bergsma notes that in Hebrew Scriptures, the term "Israel" tends to refer to the patriarch Jacob, the nation of Israel (which comprises all twelve tribes) and "the Northern Kingdom, composed of the ten northern tribes, *to the exclusion of Judah*."[12] So, *Judah* sometimes refers to all twelve tribes (and to ten northern ones), and *Judah* sometimes refers to the patriarch Judah, the single tribe descended from him, and the whole of the Southern Kingdom ("which also includes Levites and Benjamites").[13] And sometimes not *Judah*, but *Israel* is used to refer to the entirety of the Jewish people.[14] No consistency can be discovered from examining the evidence indiscriminately. If a consistent distinction exists between *Judah* and *Israel*, it apparently exists only for specific writers within specific contexts.

Who are the people of Israel? And who precisely are the *gens Iudaeorum*? The *locus classicus* of a distinction between these two phrases or tropes is the historical narrative of Torah. Employing the phrases eschatologically, Jeremiah prophesizes, "In those days the House of Judah will unite with the House of Israel; together they will come from the land of the North to the land I gave your ancestors for a heritage" (Jer 3:18; 32:32). Jeremiah's prophetic distinction is cited by Byrhtferth of Ramsey in describing the battle at Maldon in Essex in the year 991. Having described the battle, Byrhtferth writes:

Talis enim olim comminatio Iudeis promissa est, quam nostrates tunc et nunc sustinebant et sustinent. Dicet enim comminans propheta: "Pro eo quod non audistis verba mea, ecce ego mittam et assumam uniuersas cognationes aquilonis (ait Dominus) et adducam eas super terram istam, et super habitatores eius, et super omnes nationes que in circuitu eius sunt, et interficiam illos."

---

11 Blumenkranz, *Les Auteurs chrétiens latins*, 202n5: "notandum autem nomine Iudaei, omnes Iudaeos credentes debere intelligi." He may have been following Cassiodorus; Blumenkranz, *Les Auteurs chrétiens latins*, 59.

12 Bergsma, "Qumran Self-Identity: 'Israel' or 'Judah'?", 172–89, at 173; italics original.

13 Bergsma, "Qumran Self-Identity," 174.

14 Weinfeld, "Jeremiah and the Spiritual Metamorphosis of Israel," 17–56, at 17: Jeremiah heralds "not only a physical but also a spiritual rebirth of Israel – and the reference is to Israel in the broad and original sense as including the northern tribes."

(A threat was once issued to the Jews (*Iudeis*), similar to what our people, then and now, were and are enduring. For the prophet Jeremiah said, reproachfully, "Because (said the Lord) you have not heard my words, behold I will send and take all the kindreds (*cognationes*) of the north, and I will bring them against this land, and against the inhabitants thereof, and against all the nations (*nationes*) that are round about it, and I will destroy them.")[15]

With *cognationes*, Byrhtferth is referring to nations that share a common (*co-*), familial (*gnatus*) relation, an Israel of the flesh. The connection by blood (*cognationes*) also relates to a narrative of faith (*pro eo quod non audistis verba mea*), an Israel of the spirit. But the Israel of Byrhtferth's allusion is divided against itself. Byrhtferth alludes here to an interpretation of two royal branches of the Jewish people as symbols of religious conviction – Israel of the flesh is a type of Israel of the spirit. The spiritual interpretation was based in part on the historical exclusion in Nehemiah 13 of the Moabites and Ammonites from the Jewish community in Jerusalem.[16] That historical exclusion created two groups of Jews, each distinguished by its relative faithfulness to the Law. As Samantha Zacher has pointed out, an historical interpretation that isolates a distinctive, faithful portion of Israel gave Christian interpreters "sufficient grounds for further reinterpretation of the concept of chosenness."[17] Put another way, the claim could be made that Christians do not inherit the mantle of Israel by blood, but by faith; and that seems plausible to Christians because Nehemiah and Jeremiah suggest that blood is insufficient. Like Jeremiah, Isaiah in chapter 11 contemplates the eventual return of both royal branches, branches that Jeremiah calls "Israel" and "her faithless sister Judah" (Jer 3:8). Jeremiah says: "In those days the House of Judah will unite with the House of Israel; together they will come from the land of the North to the land I gave your ancestors for a heritage" (Jer 3:18). Allen Godbey explains this image: "People of Judah and Benjamin were all restored [to Israel] following the triumph of Cyrus. Descendants of other tribes were not included in the recorded return. They were to be restored at some time in the far future."[18] *Israel* and *Judah* seem to distinguish the faithful (Israel) from

---

15 Lapidge, "The *Life of St Oswald*," 51–8, at 55.
16 Godbey, *The Lost Tribes a Myth*, 675.
17 See Zacher, "The Chosen People," 457–77, esp. 460–2.
18 Godbey, *Lost Tribes*, 666.

the faithless (Judah). But *Israel* sometimes refers to both. God promises, "Now I will bring on you all a nation from afar, House of Israel" (Jer 5:15) to kill most, but not all, disloyal people.[19]

Amid a great deal of anti-Jewish polemic, some writers recalled that the first Christian churches were comprised of Jews – Amalarius of Metz, for example.[20] But did a Jew continue to be a Jew once he confessed Christ? Is a Jew ethnically defined? In some patristic exegesis, *Israel of the flesh* provides an image of Jews as a family, as brethren. Isidore of Seville describes four means of speaking of brothers in Scripture: by nature, by *gens*, by maternal relation, and by affect. He gives some examples. Brothers by nature are Esau and Jacob, Andrew and Peter, and so forth. He describes brothers by *gens*, "as all Jews are called in Deuteronomy (15:12)."[21] Any Jewish man or woman is a brother in this sense, as members of the same ethnicity. Although Romans 9:3 declares all Christians to be brethren, all Christians are not members of the same ethnicity. Christians are brothers by affect, by spiritual communion. In the famous passage that Isidore cites, Paul goes further in helping to explain the relationship between Christian brethren and the Jews:

[3] For I could wish that myself were accursed from Christ for my brethren, my kinsmen according to the flesh: [4] Who are Israelites; to whom pertaineth the adoption, and the glory, and the covenants, and the giving of the law, and the service of God, and the promises; [5] Whose are the fathers, and of whom as concerning the flesh Christ came, who is over all, God blessed for ever. Amen. [6] Not as though the word of God hath taken none effect. For they are not all Israel, which are of Israel: [7] Neither, because they are the seed of Abraham, are they all children: but, In Isaac shall thy seed be called. [8] That is, They which are the children of the flesh, these are not the children of God: but the children of the promise are counted for the seed.

---

19 I discuss this tradition in relation to *Maldon* in my *Race and Ethnicity in Anglo-Saxon Literature*, chapter 6. My views there are now substantially changed; see "Oaths in the Battle of Maldon."

20 Blumenkranz, *Les Auteurs chrétiens latins*, 172.

21 Isidore of Seville, *Etymologiarum sive originum*, ed. Lindsay, 1:379; IX, vi. The same terminology is used by Sidonius Apollonarius; see Blumenkranz, *Les Auteurs chrétiens latins*, 43–4.

Spirit, not flesh brings salvation. In verse 6, Paul is recollecting the distinction between Israel and Judah: "For they are not all Israel, which are of Israel." With his first "Israel" Paul describes the select who follow the Law; with his second "Israel," Paul describes the land and people of Israel, Judaea and the *Iudaeos*, the *eretz Yisrael* (the homeland of Israel). So, in verse 8, Paul reminds his readers that biological descent is insufficient to attain the name of Israel. Only those who are called spiritually to Torah – specifically the Pentateuch, and generally commentaries on it, and the laws and traditions that derive from it – are *Israel* in the first sense. Here we see a justification for the adopted Christian concept of "chosenness" that Zacher identifies. We also see that faith, not ethnicity, is the Scripturally-based, patristic measure of Christian religious identity.[22]

The distinction between *Israel of the spirit* and *Israel of the flesh* is not only a Christian one, but is also observed in Torah's portrait of Jews struggling with faithfulness both to Torah and to one another. An important theme in rabbinic commentary is the tension between (and within) Israel and Judah. Jacob wrestles with an angel and gains his name *Israel* from that struggle with God. Judah struggles alongside Benjamin with the other tribes. These tensions and differences point to larger, symbolic lessons. The names *Judah* and *Israel* are occasionally used in the Mishna – a record of the oral tradition of rabbinical teaching – to distinguish all Jews from gentiles. For example, Jews are the circumcised and the clean (Neusner, 1–2).[23] But, the nomenclature also allows an interpreter to make a distinction between faithful Jews and unfaithful Jews. So, those who leave the land in peacetime are rejecting the gift of God, and therefore accepting idolatry (3). These faithless Jews are sometimes called *Judah*. But Judah is also the faithful tribe – faithful to the House of David. Is Judah faithful or faithless? The moral ambiguity in the name's symbolism indicates that "God is always ready to accept the penitent" (4), and that the covenant of circumcision is eternal (6). Following Jeremiah, the Mishna confirms the coming of a new covenant. We read, "This will not be like the original covenant, which was broken" (14); and in Sifra CCLXII:I, "a new covenant, which will never be broken from now on" (D). Again, "as it is said, 'Behold

---

22   Another complication is the relation of a people to its language. Consider Jerome's view that as Hebrew was the first language, so will it be the last language when the entire world serves the Lord. See Borst, *Der Turmbau von Babel*, v. 2.1, 389.

23   Neusner, *Jeremiah in Talmud and Midrash*. Page references in this paragraph and the next are to Neusner.

the days are coming, says the Lord, when I will make a new covenant with the house of Israel and the house of Judah'" (E). Again, "Jeremiah speaks of bringing the exiles back from the north country" (138). In Leviticus, Rabbah 9:6, R. Eleazer and R. Yosé ben Haninah converse about the Scripture, "Awake, O north wind, [and come, O south wind]." They say, "When the exiles who are located in the north will awake, they will come and make camp in the south." Similarly, Jeremiah writes, "Lo, I shall bring them from the north country" (Jer 31:8). One meaning of this passage from Leviticus is that "[w]hen Gog, who is located in the north, will awake, he will come and fall in the south" (137). The salient distinction in these discussions lies in faithfulness to Torah.

We see this distinction again in rabbinical commentary on Numbers. Speaking of Israel, one commentator writes that "when he calls them 'my people,' he means not my people in general but only the suitable ones among them" (17, Sifré to Numbers 85:2), i.e., "the suitable Israelites among the larger community." One is reminded here of the separation and fall of Korah and his followers at Sinai in Numbers 16. Nevertheless, separation is not separation from the Jewish people; a Jew can never become a gentile. "God does not raise up prophets for the gentiles, but Jeremiah was explicitly called a prophet for the gentiles. This is understood to refer to Israelites who behave like gentiles; the gentiles get no prophet at all" (26). In other words, Jeremiah was a prophet for Judah. Again, acting like a gentile is not the same as being one.[24] The gentiles are wicked. R. Eleazer ben Azariah says, "Detestable is uncircumcision, for the wicked are reproached with it: 'For the nations are uncircumcised' (Jer 9:25)" (55). Furthermore, there is a supernatural bond between all Jews, which testifies to the unity of the people regardless of internal divisions. The familial and spiritual bond between Jews is proved because "[e]ach Israelite is punished for the sin of any other" (57). Those who obey the Law are Israelites; thus, R. Ishmael says that "it is upon Israel that he has conferred his name in particular" (79:2, p. 59). And in Leviticus Rabbah 2:4, Moses asks Ha-Shem, "Among the seventy distinct nations that you have in your world, [why] do you give instructions to me only concerning Israel?" Ha-Shem replied, "[It is because] they accepted my dominion on them at Mount

---

24 Sedulius Scotus makes a similar point following Romans 2:17, when he distinguishes "entre le fait d'«être» Juif et de «s'appeler» Juif. Pour être vraiment Juif, il faut l'être d'une façon cachée, dans la circoncision du coeur"; Blumenkranz, *Les Auteurs chrétiens latins*, 201.

Sinai, saying, 'Whatever the Lord has spoken we shall do and we shall hear'" (134). And in Jer 13:11, we read, "As the girl cleaves to the loins of a man, so I have made all the house of Israel cleave to me" (r.149).

Israel as a token of fidelity to God is adopted into Christian eschatology, as well. Faith in Christ will distinguish the saved from the damned. And faith informs Bede's understanding of why Jews in the sixth age refuse to recognize Christ as Messiah; this refusal is "a veil before their heart." Among the Jews, says Bede, there are some "from whom the fog of error will be removed."[25] In Bede's larger view,

> After the Jews have been enlightened by faith and have received the grace of the Holy Spirit, the Church will arrive for them in order that there may be "one sheepfold and one shepherd" [Jn 10:16], and one house of Christ established on one cornerstone.

This conversion, or *returning*, brings Judah (the Jews) and Israel (the Church) together. In his commentary on Ezra, Bede notes that "those who had formerly been known because of the diversity of their religion by the different names Israel and Judah were now because of the unity of their devotion all called by the ancient name Israel."[26] Again, in his commentary on the Temple, Bede says, in accordance with Patristic tradition, that both Jews and Gentiles *who are faithful* to the Word will be saved.[27] We see this same claim in *Christ III*: at the Day of Judgment, those "meotude getrywe" ("faithful to the Lord," line 876) will come from the four corners of the earth to Mount Sion.[28] Whatever role ethnicity was thought to play in corporate salvation (and that role is complicated), faith is salvation's *sine qua non*.[29] Thus, in the scene depicting the conversion of the Jews in

---

25 Bede, "On Tobias," in *Bede: A Biblical Miscellany*, trans. Foley and Holder, 75.

26 *Bede: On Ezra and Nehemiah*, trans. DeGregorio, 36. See also *Bede: On the Temple*, trans. Connolly, xxxviii.

27 *De Templo* 2; I owe this reference to the remarkable dissertation by Peter Darby, "Bede's Eschatological Thought" (PhD diss).

28 *Christ III*, ASPR 3, 27; I owe this reference to Thomas N. Hall, "Medieval Traditions about the Site of Judgment," 79–97, at 85.

29 Hall discusses an Irish story in which the Irish people are brought to Sion by St Patrick for judgment. Patrick and Christ negotiate over whether or not sinful Irishmen, on account of their race, should be permitted into Heaven. Likely whimsical, according to Hall, the story nevertheless indicates the complexity of early medieval eschatological traditions. See Hall, "Traditions," 87–9.

Cynewulf's *Elene*, Jews profess faith in Christ. Cynewulf's likely source, the *Acta Sanctorum*, says that those Jews who did not profess faith were persecuted.[30] (One might remark on a possible distinction here between a profession of faith and submission to baptism, something that plays out in typological readings of the Exodus.) From out of the Jewish people, *Judah*, comes a faithful portion, *Israel*.

In short, the history of Judah and Israel in Torah read typologically offers Christians a means of distinguishing between faithful and unfaithful Christians. Bede saw moments of correspondence between Anglo-Saxon history and the Jewish history of Torah. The complexities of those correspondences caution readers of Bede and of relevant Anglo-Saxon texts to be alert to a distinction between *Judah* and *Israel*. The terms offer shorthand for two distinct roles in Christian history and eschatology. These two roles, as Byrhtferth demonstrates, were means of elucidating the spiritual dimension of early English history. Careful writers such as Bede were more likely than not to understand those terms, their typological relation to historical processes, and their eschatological implications. Calvin Kendall points out that in his commentary on Genesis, Bede distinguishes "between 'Israelites' on the one hand and 'Jews' on the other." Bede's moral distinction between *Judah* and *Israel* stretches back even to the sons of Noah. Kendall reports that in Bede's view, "Christians descend biologically from Japheth, the third son of Noah, but typologically from Shem, the first son."[31] Here, descent crosses the boundary of body and soul. And the metaphor of fleshly inheritance is extended to ideas in the mind. *Israel* and *Judah* are inflected biologically and typologically, and also eschatologically. In time, divisions of the flesh will be overcome by a unity of the faithful. And it is faith, *Israel*, not flesh, *Judah* that will stand surety for the soul.

Eschatological symbols that distinguish between Christian faithful and Christian faithless are found throughout Bede's exegesis of the temple and the tabernacle – the first full exegesis on the tabernacle, and probably the most influential.[32] The tabernacle signifies God's presence with Israel during her wandering in the desert. Arthur Holder explains that the tabernacle and the temple were "figures of the Old and New Testament

---

30 Anderson, "Cynewulf's *Elene* 1115b24, the Conversion of the Jews," 1–3, at 2.
31 *Bede: On Genesis*, trans. Kendall, 27.
32 Noted by Scheil, *The Footsteps of Israel*, 64–5. *Bede: On the Tabernacle*, trans. Holder, xv.

communities," and also of "the Church militant and the Church triumphant."[33] Bede, in his discussion of the cups, bowls, and lilies that sit on the lamp-stand in the tabernacle, writes that there are three periods of time "in which the elect lived devotedly for God." Before Christ, there were righteous Jews under the law (called *Israel*); "after the Lord's ascension the primitive Church was gathered from Israel, now it is gathered from the gentiles, and at the end of the world it will be gathered from the remnants of Israel."[34] Bede reminds his readers in the words of Matthew, Christ came not to abolish the law, but to fulfil it. Thus Bede writes,

> For in all humility, we too belong among those descendants of whom it was said that "it shall be an everlasting law for him, and for his descendants throughout their generations" [Ex 30:31]. We are not born of the lineage of Aaron, but we have believed in him in whom Aaron also, with the saints of that age, believed. Concerning him, it was promised to Abraham that "in your descendants all the families of the earth shall be blessed" [Acts 3:25]. Isaiah makes mention of these families when he says, "All who see them shall acknowledge them, that these are the descendants whom the Lord has blessed" [Isa 61:9].[35]

Bede likely means that blessedness extends by faith to Christians, an Israel of the spirit.[36] Again, Israel is the historical body as well as the type of that faithful, blessed family. Bede held not that all Christians would be saved, but only that an elect would be saved, the Christian faithful.[37] The two *Jewish* tribes separated from *Israel* in the time of Ezra, the Moabites and Ammonites, Bede notes in his commentary on Ezra and Nehemiah, "figuratively represent heretics."[38] Only faithful Jews belong to *Israel*, and only faithful Christians belong to the new *Israel*.

---

33 *Bede: On the Tabernacle*, trans. Holder, xix.

34 Ibid., 36.

35 Ibid., 162–3.

36 The terms are from Blumenkranz, *Les Auteurs chrétiens latins*, 134.

37 On the elect, see Bede's *Thirty Questions on the Book of Kings*, 100–1. In *Bede: A Biblical Miscellany*, trans. Foley and Holder, 81–143. On Israel as the city of Christ, see 137.

38 *Bede: On Ezra and Nehemiah*, trans. DeGregorio, 219. DeGregorio rightly notes that this commentary is an important but unremarked witness to patristic claims about Jews.

In the mental world of tropes and images, *Judah/Jew/Jude* becomes a type of the faithless[39], and typology sadly shades into lived experience. One antagonism fuels another on a pathological continuum, and the tropes that govern one's reading begin to govern one's life. One must remember the long, terrible history of relations between Christians and Jews, and also observe that from Paul to Auerleius Autpertus to Alcuin to Hraban Maur, the *populus Israhel* is a trope that refers to those who have received the favour of God, whether they be Jews or Christians. In searching for "the Jew," the people of Israel should not be lost in translation.

---

39 It was common among caustic Christian writers to equate *Judah* to *Judas*.

2 Nathan the Jew in the Old English *Vindicta Salvatoris*

THOMAS N. HALL

When medieval Christians thought of Jews, a story that likely shaped their thinking was the well-known legend of the destruction of Jerusalem by the Roman emperors Titus and Vespasian. First told in Greek by Josephus in his *Jewish War*, then retold in countless Latin and vernacular sermons, histories, saints' lives, poems, plays, romances, and *chansons de geste*, this is a story that played a major role in popularizing the idea that the Romans under Titus and Vespasian sought to annihilate the Jews in order to punish them for plotting Christ's execution and for refusing to be converted to Christianity.[1] Christ was murdered by the Jews, the story goes, and to avenge that murder God compelled the Romans to retaliate by launching a crusade to massacre the Jews in Jerusalem. The idea that the siege of Jerusalem was an act of divine vengeance is not part of the story as originally told by Josephus, but was introduced in the fourth-century Latin adaptation of Josephus attributed to one Hegesippus, who Christianized Josephus's account of the Jewish war and explained the Roman victory as a "miracle of divine destiny."[2] In Hegesippus, Nero appoints Vespasian supreme commander of the Roman army, and God sends Vespasian into Syria and Palestine on a mission to overthrow the Jewish race. Even in Hegesippus, however, Vespasian and his son Titus are still Roman pagans who are unaware of the fact that they are instruments of God's vengeance; the Christian moralizing operates entirely at the level of the narrative

---

1 The growth of the legend is discussed by Dobschütz, *Christusbilder*, 197–262, 273*–335*; Ohly, *Sage und Legende in der Kaiserchronik*, 53–66; Wright, *The Vengeance of Our Lord*, 18–32; and Millar, *The Siege of Jerusalem*, esp. 42–75, 105–40, and 150–5.

2 *Hegesippi qui dicitur Historiae libri V*, ed. Ussani, 3: "de sanctae constitutonis miraculo."

voice, not at the level of the plot. But the legend underwent a crucial transformation when it turned Titus and Vespasian into Christian converts seeking to avenge the death of their own saviour, and that transformation took place in the early medieval apocryphon known as the *Vindicta Salvatoris* or *Avenging of the Saviour*. After Hegesippus, the *Vindicta Salvatoris* is the real starting point for the medieval legend of the destruction of Jerusalem, and one of its innovations that was to have a lasting impact on later versions of the story was its introduction of a character named Nathan who was singularly responsible for converting Titus and Vespasian and setting in motion the campaign to avenge Christ's death. Nathan is arguably the most important person in the story since without him there would be no siege of Jerusalem and no avenging of the saviour. He is, however, a complicated character who is especially difficult to understand given that the earliest surviving text of the Latin *Vindicta Salvatoris* calls him an Ishmaelite, whereas the earliest vernacular translation (into Old English) calls him a Jew. What does it mean in this story that Nathan is an Ishmaelite or a Jew, and what is the point of having an Ishmaelite or a Jew serve as the single-handed inspiration for the crusade to destroy the Jewish race?[3]

A first step in addressing these questions is to consider Nathan's role in the story, which weaves together a series of loosely related adventures concerning the destruction of Jerusalem by Titus and Vespasian, the trial and death of Pontius Pilate, and the miraculous cloth owned by Veronica impressed with a likeness of Christ, which is used to cure the emperor Tiberius of leprosy.[4] Parts of this story grow directly out of the *Gospel of Nicodemus* and the medieval continuations of the *Gospel of Nicodemus*, and it is no coincidence that in many medieval manuscripts the *Vindicta Salvatoris* occurs side by side with the *Gospel of Nicodemus* as if these were thought to be companion texts.[5] There is no critical edition of the *Vindicta Salvatoris* that takes into account more than even a couple of its manuscripts, and there is no authoritative study of its textual transmission,

---

3 On the perceptions of Ishmael and his progeny in Anglo-Saxon England, see further chapter 9 by Karkov below.

4 On the textual and literary history of the *Vindicta Salvatoris*, see Hall, "The *Evangelium Nichodemi* and *Vindicta Salvatoris* in Anglo-Saxon England," 58–81.

5 Twenty-eight manuscripts containing both the *Gospel of Nicodemus* and the *Vindicta Salvatoris* are identified by Izydorczyk, *Manuscripts of the Evangelium Nicodemi*, Index 3, s.v. *Vindicta salvatoris*. Several such pairings are also noted by Millar, *The Siege of Jerusalem*, 138.

42   Thomas N. Hall

so it is difficult to answer even the most basic questions about when and where this work was composed or how widely it was known, but the earliest surviving copy is in a manuscript (Saint-Omer, Bibliothèque municipale 202) which was written at the abbey of Saint-Bertin in Flanders in the late ninth century. This manuscript is of particular interest to students of Old English literature because it left Flanders and migrated to England by the eleventh century, when two of its contents, the *Gospel of Nicodemus* and *Vindicta Salvatoris*, were both translated into Old English, probably at Exeter, and it is consequently one of the very few manuscripts we know about that can be identified as the actual source-manuscript consulted by an Old English translator.[6] The ninth-century Saint-Omer 202 Latin text of the *Vindicta Salvatoris* and its eleventh-century Old English translation were edited together by J.E. Cross in 1996 and form the basis for the following discussion, although I will also make reference to the only other published edition of the *Vindicta Salvatoris*, the one issued by Constantin von Tischendorf in 1876 based on two fourteenth-century Italian manuscripts.[7] The texts edited by Cross and Tischendorf vary in a number of details, but the story they tell is consistent enough to permit some observations about the basic structure of the narrative and the role Nathan plays within it.

The part of the story that concerns us here is the opening episode of the *Vindicta Salvatoris*, which introduces us right away to Nathan, whose travels have taken him from his homeland in Judea to the distant shores of Aquitaine, where he meets an ailing *regulus* named Tyrus. The Saint-Omer 202 version of the story begins as follows:

In diebus illis Tyberii caesaris teth<r>archa sub Puntio Pilato traditus fuit a Iudeis, celatus a Tyberio. In diebus illis erat quidam homo nomine Tyrus, regulus Tyberii in regnum Aquitaniẹ in ciuitatem Libiae, que dicitur Burdigala, et

---

6   See Cross and Crick, "The Manuscript: Saint-Omer, Bibliothèque Municipale, 202," and Cross, "Saint-Omer 202 as the Manuscript Source for the Old English Texts." The Saint-Omer 202 Latin text and the Old English translation are both edited and translated by Cross with assistance from Brearley and Orchard in *Two Old English Apocrypha*, ed. Cross, 248–92. In the following notes, I refer to the Latin text as the *Vindicta Salvatoris* and the Old English translation as the *OEVSal* (a slight modification of its *DOE* short title), with citations from both taken from Cross's edition in *Two Old English Apocrypha*.

7   Tischendorf, ed., *Evangelia apocrypha*, 471–86.

erat insanus in narem dextram habens cancrum faciem delaceratam usque ad oculum. Exiuit quidam homo de Iudaea cui nomen Nathan, filius Naum, erat enim de Ismahelitis, pergens de terra in terram, de mare in mare, de terminis terre usque ad orbem terrarum. Missus est a Tyberio imperatore ad portandam sibi pactam in urbem Rome. Erat ipse Tyberius cęsar insanus ulceribus sanus plenus de fimbrię, id est, ramus de lepra nonus. Voluitque Nathan pergere in Roma. Insufflauit uentus septentrion, que dicitur hauster, et imperauit nauigium illius et deduxit ad portas Libię ciuitatis. Viditque eum Tyrus nauigium uenientem et cognouit que de Iudęa erat, admirans, omnes dicentes: "Numquam talia uidimus aliquando." Iussit eum Tyrus ad se uenire et interrogauit quidnam esset et ille dixit: "Ego sum Nathan, filium Nau, de regno Grecorum, subditus in Iudaea, sub Puntio Pilato. Missus fui ut uenirem ad Tyberium in urbe Roma ad portandam pactam eius de Iudaeam. Inruit uentus ualidus in mare et deduxit me in loco isto, et nescio ubi sum."

(In the days of the emperor Tiberius, (while Herod was) tetrarch under Pontius Pilate, He (Christ) was betrayed by the Jews, and (it) was kept secret from Tiberius. In those days there was a certain man, Tyrus by name, an underking of Tiberius in the kingdom of Aquitania in a city of Libia, which is called Burdigala, and he was ill, having a cancer on the right nostril, his face being destroyed up to the eye. A certain man whose name was Nathan, son of Naum, went from Judea, for hc was an Ishmaelite, going from land to land, from sea to sea, from the ends of the earth to the edge of the world. He was sent by the emperor Tiberius to bring him a treaty to the city of Rome. The emperor Tiberius himself was ill with ulcers, very full of fever, which is the ninth kind of leprosy. And Nathan wanted to go to Rome. The north wind, which is called Auster, blew and directed his ship and brought it to the gates of the city of Libia. Tyrus saw him (and) the ship coming, and he knew that it was from Judea, (and) everyone was amazed, saying: "We have never seen such things, ever." Tyrus ordered him to come to him and asked him who he was and he said: "I am Nathan, son of Naum, from the kingdom of the Greeks, subject under Pontius Pilate in Judea. I have been sent to come to Tiberius in the city of Rome to take his treaty from Judea. A strong wind raged on the sea and brought me to this place, and I do not know where I am.")[8]

---

8 *Vindicta Salvatoris* §§1–4, ed. Cross, 248–52.

Once Nathan and Tyrus are introduced to one another, Tyrus apparently judges Nathan to be knowledgeable and well travelled, and he asks Nathan whether he knows of any herbs or medicines that might cure the disfiguring cancer on his face. Tyrus even promises Nathan that if he will help him find a cure, he will see to it that Nathan completes his journey to Rome. Nathan confesses that he has no such medical knowledge himself, but that not very long ago there was a great prophet in Judea named Jesus Christ who became famous for performing countless miracles – raising the dead, curing the infirm, and giving sight to the blind – and if there was ever anyone who could cure Tyrus of his illness, it would have been Jesus, except that Jesus was unfortunately murdered by the Jews. Nathan goes on to relate with great enthusiasm the whole of Christ's earthly ministry and his passion and resurrection, recalling several beneficiaries of Christ's miraculous cures, including the woman named Veronica who suffered from an issue of blood for twelve years and who was healed when she touched the hem of Christ's garment. Nathan ends his dramatic account of Christ's career by quoting the promise of Christ's second coming in the traditional Ascension Day antiphon, "Men of Galilee, why are you amazed, looking at heaven? So shall he come just as you have seen me going into heaven."[9] Tyrus listens intently to Nathan's message, then at once professes belief in Christ as his saviour, curses Tiberius for allowing Christ to be executed in Nathan's homeland, and pledges to travel to Jerusalem to avenge Christ's death by murdering his enemies, the Jews. As Tyrus utters this pronouncement, the cancer falls from his face, and his flesh is "restored like the flesh of a small boy."[10] Tyrus rejoices, praises God, and asks to be baptized in Christ's name. Nathan the Ishmaelite then baptizes Tyrus in the name of the Father, Son, and Holy Ghost, and changes Tyrus's name to Titus, which is said to mean "holy" (*pius*). The newly converted, healed, and renamed Titus then enlists the help of Vespasian (who is otherwise unidentified at this point), and together they round up seven thousand armed men and set off for the Holy Land to avenge the death of

---

9 *Vindicta Salvatoris* §7, ed. Cross, 256: "Viri Galilei quid admiramini aspicientes in caelum? Sic ueniet quemadmodum uidisti me euntem in caelum." This antiphon, a standard text for the Introit of Ascension Day in the earliest surviving Mass-texts, is indexed by Chevalier, *Repertorium Hymnologicum*, II:764 (no. 21921); Hesbert, ed., *Antiphonale Missarum Sextuplex*, 120–1; and Hesbert, *Corpus Antiphonalium Officii*, III:544 (no. 5458).

10 *Vindicta Salvatoris* §9, ed. Cross, 258: "restituta est caro eius sicut caro pueri paruuli."

Christ and slaughter the Jews. In both the Saint-Omer 202 Latin text and
the Old English translation, Nathan then disappears from the story, but
in Tischendorf's fourteenth-century version he reappears at the very end
after several intervening episodes and is summoned to baptize the emperor
Tiberius after Tiberius has been cured of his fevers, ulcers, and leprosy
through the aid of Veronica's miraculous cloth. Tischendorf's late version
of the story thus ends with an encore performance by Nathan, who stages
yet another conversion and baptism scene, reenacting his role as Christian
apologist and missionary, preaching the Gospel in foreign lands and converting the heathen.

This story is full of problems. To begin with, how Nathan manages to
sail to the coast of Aquitaine in southwestern Gaul while travelling from
Judea to Rome is a geographical conundrum, and the location of the city
of Libia is equally mysterious. Tyrus is said to live "in the kingdom of
Aquitania in a city of Libia which is called Burdigala," and when Nathan
reaches the end of his journey he arrives at "the gates of the city of Libia,"
so that Libia seems to be understood as a city in Aquitaine, but exactly
how it relates to Burdigala (the present-day city of Bordeaux in the north
of Aquitaine) is not clear, particularly since the only commonly used place
name in ancient and medieval geographies that resembles the name *Libia* is
Libya, the name of the north African country.[11] Is it possible that Libia is
not a city after all but a region of Aquitaine in which the city of Burdigala
is located? Or is *Libia* supposed to be another name for *Burdigala*, and do
these names both refer to the same place? Maybe so, since when Titus and
Vespasian set out for Jerusalem, "they went out of the city of Libia, which
is called Burdigala."[12] The Old English translator was apparently troubled
by this geographical muddle and sought to rectify it by eliminating all
references to Burdigala, claiming only that Tyrus lived "on þære ceastre,
þe wæs genemned Lybie ... on Equitania rice" ("in the city called Libya ...

---

11 L'abbé Chevin, *Dictionnaire latin-français des noms propres de lieux ayant une certaine
notoriété principalement au point de vue ecclésiastique et monastique*, 168, s.v. Libya;
Graesse, Orbis Latinus, II:387 s.v. Libya; Egger, *Lexicon nominum locorum*, 179. The
only other place name I have come across that resembles this one is the Latinized place
name Libia, once used for the present-day town of Leyva in Asturias, northern Spain:
see Deschamps, *Dictionnaire de géographie ancienne et moderne*, 732 s.v. Libia. That
the country of Libya is located in North Africa, west of Egypt, is affirmed in The Old
English Orosius I.1, ed. Bately, 11 line 2. In the *OEVSal*, the place name in question is
variously spelled Lybie, Libie, and Libia.

12 *Vindicta Salvatoris* §12, ed. Cross, 262: "exierunt de ciuitate Libia, que dicitur Burdigala."

within the kingdom of Aquitania").[13] The nineteenth-century apocrypha scholars R.A. Lipsius and Ernst von Dobschütz both took the references to Aquitania and Burdigala in Tischendorf's edition to imply that the *Vindicta Salvatoris* was written in Aquitaine, but that was just a guess, and neither Lipsius nor von Dobschütz had an explanation for the location or identity of Libia.[14] Some of this confusion over place names and geography may conceivably be due to faulty transmission of the text, but it is probably more realistic to think that it simply reflects a lack of actual familiarity with these places, so that the site of Nathan's encounter with Tyrus is nothing more than a fictional place outfitted with place names the author has only heard or read about. The important point seems to be that in journeying from the Holy Land to Rome, Nathan is thrown off course, and he finds himself unexpectedly diverted to a foreign land inhabited by pagans ripe for conversion. From this perspective it doesn't really matter what foreign land Nathan ends up in – Libia could just as well be Ethiopia or India or Mermedonia – but it is remarkable nonetheless that the author of the earliest surviving version of the *Vindicta Salvatoris* seems to have had difficulties with real-world geography.

Much the same can be said about the story's historical setting, which is vaguely placed sometime in the first century AD not long after Christ's death, but which hardly aims for any kind of historical accuracy. Nathan's adventure takes place during the reign of the emperor Tiberius, while Herod is tetrarch under Pontius Pilate in Judea within "the kingdom of the Greeks," and it culminates in the siege of Jerusalem by Titus and Vespasian. Some of these details would have been known from the New Testament gospels, which tell us that Christ was born in the reign of Tiberius Caesar, when Pontius Pilate was governor of Judea and Herod was tetrarch of Galilee (Luke 3:1 etc.), but we run into trouble when we try to fit all these figures and events into a single historical time frame that bears any relationship to reality. Even the Bible tells us that Herod died when Jesus was still a child (Matt. 2:14, 19), and the imperial reign of Tiberius (AD 14–37) doesn't come close to overlapping with the reigns of Vespasian

---

13 *OEVSal* §1, ed. Cross, 249.

14 Lipsius, *Die Pilatus-Acten kritisch untersucht*, 37; Dobschütz, *Christusbilder*, 216, 276, 277*. Without explanation, both Lipsius and von Dobschütz date the text to the early eighth century. It has recently been dated to the second half of the fourth century by Yuval, *Two Nations in Your Womb*, 48, although Yuval does not locate the text geographically.

(AD 69–79) and Titus (AD 79–81). Most curious of all, the identification of Tyrus as a petty ruler in Aquitaine who evolves into the Christian convert Titus of the anti-Jewish crusading duo Titus and Vespasian is a strong indication that the author of this text had no clue that the historical Titus and Vespasian were Roman emperors, and he must have been oblivious of the quite substantial literary tradition, originating with Josephus, that chronicles the siege of Jerusalem by Titus and Vespasian during the Jewish-Roman war of AD 66–70.[15] The Saint-Omer 202 text says nothing about the identity of Vespasian, but the Old English translation at least makes an effort to explain who he is by referring to him as Titus's "fyrdgemacan, þe wæs genemned Vespasianus, þe wæs eac hæðen" ("fellow-soldier, who was called Vespasian, who was a heathen too").[16] As with the story's vexed geography and confused place names, the historical backdrop of Nathan's exploits is essentially a crude fiction that betrays a sweeping ignorance of Roman history of the first Christian century.

Other details in the story are similarly problematic. The wind that blows Nathan off course and drives him to Libia is said to be "the north wind, which is called Auster," whereas in fact *Auster* is the standard name for the *south* wind in Roman and medieval cosmologies, as anyone would know who was familiar with the traditional names of the winds.[17] The *Vindicta Salvatoris* has also evidently invented a new name-etymology by

---

15 The transmission and reception of Josephus's *Jewish War*, and its influence on well over a hundred authors from the second century to the sixteenth, is carefully documented by Schreckenberg, *Die Flavius-Josephus-Tradition in Antike und Mittelalter*.

16 *OEVSal* §10, ed. Cross, 261.

17 Interestingly, the Old English translation drops the name *Auster* and properly credits "se suðerna wynd" ("the southern wind") with directing Nathan's course: *OEVSal* §3, ed. Cross, 251. *Auster* is the name routinely given for the south wind in the most influential classical and medieval treatises on natural science, including Pliny the Elder, *Naturalis historia* II.47 (46), ed. Mayhoff and von Jan, *C. Plini Secundi Naturalis historiae libri XXXVII*, I: 170; Isidore, *De natura rerum* XXXVII.3, ed. and trans. Fontaine, *Isidore de Séville: Traité de la nature*, 297; Bede, *De natura rerum* XXVII, ed. Jones, CCSL 123A, 218; and *Ælfric's De temporibus anni*, ed. and trans. Blake, 94 line 406. The same identification appears in several Old English glosses and notes: see Wright, *Anglo-Saxon and Old English Vocabularies*, I: cols. 8, 143, 350; Logeman, "Anglo-Saxonica Minora," 104–5; Hessels, *An Eighth-Century Latin-Anglo-Saxon Glossary*, 23 (A 951); Kindschi, "The Latin–Old English Glossaries in Plantin-Moretus MS 32 and British Museum MS Additional 32, 246," 134; and Pulsiano, "Old English Nomina ventorum." The same tradition is also recorded in *Byrhtferth's Enchiridion* IV.i.53–4, ed. and trans. Baker and Lapidge, 200. On the common use of the name *Auster* for the south wind in classical meteorology, see Böker, "Windnamen," esp. cols. 2290–1.

claiming that the name *Titus* means "holy,"[18] and the story makes a number of other perplexing claims that depart from common knowledge or defy simple explanation. How is it, for example, that the Jewish betrayal of Christ was kept secret from Tiberius? What exactly is meant by the "kingdom of the Greeks" in Judea? Why would a Roman emperor at the time of Christ commission an Ishmaelite to convey a treaty from Judea to Rome? How is Tyrus able to tell that Nathan's ship originates from Judea? What are the nine kinds of leprosy? And how does cancer fall from a person's face anyway?[19] Most intriguing of all, who is Nathan the Ishmaelite, and what is it that empowers him to baptize heathens and convert them to Christianity? Nathan is easily the most interesting and complex character in the story, and his complexity derives in large measure from the odd mixture of details that are used to sketch the shadowy outlines of his religious, national, and ethnic identity. In the Saint-Omer 202 Latin text, Nathan is introduced as an Ishmaelite (*de Ismahelitis*), but in the context of the *Vindicta Salvatoris* it isn't clear what that means.[20] Today the term *Ishmaelite* is normally used to refer to Arabs who claim descent

18   No etymology of *Titus* is proposed by Jerome in his handbook of biblical name-etymologies, the *Liber interpretationis Hebraicorum nominum*, nor by Isidore in his *Etymologiae*, which are the two likeliest places where one might expect to find one. However, it may conceivably be of some significance, given King Tyrus's unfortunate nasal condition, that the biblical place-name *Tyrus* is understood by both Augustine and Jerome to mean *angustia sive tribulatio*: see Augustine, *Enarrationes in Psalmos* LXXXII.7, ed. Dekkers and Fraipont, CCSL 39, 1143; and Jerome, *Liber interpretationis Hebraicorum nominum*, ed. Lagarde, CCSL 72, 97; as well as the discussion by Wutz, *Onomastica Sacra*, I:425.

19   To be fair, instantaneous miraculous cures, including cures of facial diseases such as cancer or leprosy, are not uncommon in medieval saints' lives, which plausibly exerted some influence on this scene in the *Vindicta Salvatoris*. When St Martin kisses the face of a leper at the city gates of Paris, for instance, the leper is instantly healed and his skin made clean, as we learn from Sulpicius Severus, *Vita S. Martini* XVIII.3–4, ed. and trans. Fontaine, Sources Chrétiennes 133, 292–3. Likewise, Gregory the Great, *Dialogi* II.26, ed. and trans. de Vogüé and Antin, Sources Chrétiennes 260, 214–15. Other miraculous cures of leprosy are noted by Brewer, *A Dictionary of Miracles*, 151, 239–41.

20   Nathan is also identified as an Ishmaelite in the fourteenth-century Latin *Vindicta Salvatoris* edited by Tischendorf, *Evangelia apocrypha*, 471 ("Nathan filius Naum: erat enim Ismaelita"), and in the undated Latin *Vindicta Salvatoris* edited from London, British Library, Harley 495 by Kölbing and Day as an appendix to their edition of the Middle English prose *The Siege of Jerusalem*, 83–5 (83: "Nathan filius Nahim; erat enimYsmaelita").

from Ishmael, the son of Abraham by his Egyptian slave woman Hagar.[21] These are the Arabs who long occupied the desert to the east of Palestine and from the Persian Gulf to the northeast edge of Egypt, including the whole of northern Arabia, where according to Genesis, the twelve sons of Ishmael established their residence. The biblical Ishmaelites were nomads who were shunned by the Hebrews and are best remembered for the episode in Genesis 37 where Joseph's brothers sell him to a band of roving Ishmaelite merchants, who then sell him into slavery in Egypt. The Old Testament Ishmaelites are associated with Midianites and Hagarenes, tribes hostile to Israel, and hostility is one of their defining characteristics. As descendants of Ishmael, the Ishmaelites inherited the prophetic curse directed at their forefather by the angel of the Lord in Genesis 16:12: "He shall be a wild man: his hand will be against all men, and all men's hands against him, and he shall pitch his tents over against all his brethren." The Ishmaelites of biblical tradition are thus violent, uncivilized outcasts who wander the desert and pose a threat to the Israelites, with whom they share a common ancestry through their descent from Abraham, though they remain culturally distinct.

The Ishmaelites were not well understood in the medieval West, however, since neither the Bible nor its commentaries do much to clarify the relationship between the Ishmaelites and their Arab descendants, or between the Ishmaelites and the later inhabitants of the Arabian desert who came to be known as Saracens. Jerome speaks of the Saracens, Midianites, Hagarenes, Ishmaelites, and sometimes even the Arabs as if these were a single people known by different names,[22] and Isidore of Seville likewise associates the Ishmaelites with the Saracens because the Saracens lived in the desert and were thought to descend from Sarah, the wife of Abraham and mother of Isaac.[23] The seventh-century biblical commentaries produced under Archbishop Theodore and Abbot Hadrian at Canterbury similarly explain that "Midianites and Ishmaelites and Madiani and Agarreni are the

---

21 The difficult history of the term *Ishmaelite* is discussed in detail by Scarfe Beckett, *Anglo-Saxon Perceptions of the Islamic World*, 90–189.

22 Scarfe Beckett, *Anglo-Saxon Perceptions of the Islamic World*, 90–1, citing examples from Jerome's *Epistulae*, *Interpretatio chronicae Eusebii Pamphili*, *In Isaiam*, and *Commentarii in Ezechielem*.

23 Isidore, *Etymologiae* IX.ii.57, ed. Lindsay, *Isidori Hispalensis episcopi Etymologiarum sive originum libri XX*; English translation by Barney, Lewis, Beach, Berghof, with the collaboration of Hall, *The Etymologies of Isidore of Seville*, 195.

same peoples as those who are now appropriately called Saracens."[24] To serious readers of the Bible it was important to know who these tribes were and how they were related to one another, but no such attempt at careful ethnographic discrimination is attempted in the *Vindicta Salvatoris*, where the only significance of Nathan's designation as an Ishmaelite seems to be that like the biblical Ishmaelites, he traces his origins to the Holy Land and is in a perpetual state of wandering. This appears to be the thrust of the story's claim that Nathan is "an Ishmaelite, going from land to land, from sea to sea, from the ends of the earth to the edge of the world." The biblical and patristic understanding of the Ishmaelites as desert bandits who were enemies of Israel plays no part in Nathan's story. He is certainly not a Saracen or an Arab, and as a native citizen of Judea subject to Pontius Pilate who is engaged in what sounds like an ambassadorial peace mission between Rome and Judea, he is hardly inimical to Jews. Although its intended meaning may not be crystal clear, the label *Ishmaelite* is not a slight on Nathan's character.

The identification of Nathan as an Ishmaelite in the earliest Latin version of the *Vindicta Salvatoris* is not paralleled in the Old English translation, however, which omits reference to Nathan's Ishmaelite heritage and simply says that he had travelled widely: "Ac se ylca Nathan wæs swa gelyðen, þæt he hæfde gefaren fram ælcum lande to oðrum and fram sæ to sæ and swa þæt he hæfde ealle eorðan ymbfaren" (And this same Nathan was so well travelled that he had journeyed from land to land, from sea to sea, so that he had gone around the whole earth).[25] In fact, when Nathan's ship appears at the gates of Libia, Tyrus immediately recognizes him as a Jew, declaring in amazement: "Næfre ic ær on þyssum lande swylc wundor ne geseah, þæt æfre Iudeisce men hyder on land myd scype sceoldon cuman" (Never before have I seen such a wonder in this land, that Jewish folk should come ashore here by ship).[26] Later versions of the siege of

---

24 *Biblical Commentaries from the Canterbury School of Theodore and Hadrian*, ed. and trans. Bischoff and Lapidge, 338–9: "Madianitae et Hismahelitae et Madianei et Agarreni ipsi sunt qui nunc abusiue Sarraceni nominantur" (PentI.195), with commentary at 466–7. Cited and discussed by Scarfe Beckett, *Anglo-Saxon Perceptions of the Islamic World*, 118–19. The *Madianei* are probably the Medes.

25 *OEVSal* §2, ed. Cross, 249–51.

26 *OEVSal* §3, ed. Cross, 251.

Jerusalem legend commonly report that Nathan hails from Judea,[27] or that he is on "an eraunde fram the Jewes,"[28] but to the best of my knowledge, only the Old English *Vindicta Salvatoris* explicitly calls Nathan a Jew, apparently in an effort to revise or correct his identification as an Ishmaelite in the Latin text. But why would the Old English translator reinterpret Nathan as a Jew? This last detail is surely one of the most remarkable features of the Old English translation, not least because it sets up two antithetical and polarized representations of Jewish morality, one thoroughly positive and one thoroughly negative, and it makes a Jew indirectly responsible for the destruction of the Jews in Jerusalem.

One thing that does make sense in both the Latin and Old English versions of the story is that Nathan is in a position to preach the Gospel because he lived in Judea during the time of Christ and was a first-hand witness to the miracles Christ performed. In the Latin *Vindicta Salvatoris* in Saint-Omer 202, Nathan recalls Christ's resurrection by saying, "*we have seen and witnessed him*, just as he foretold himself beforehand, in that very flesh in which he was born, in which he suffered, in which he was buried, in which he lay two days in the tomb, in which he rose from the dead on the third day as true God and true man, in which he appeared to his disciples for forty days and ascended to the heavens with strength and great power *in our sight*."[29] The Old English translation enhances this up-close perspective by giving Nathan the additional comment: "And I tell you truly, that in the same body in which he was buried he arose again within two days, just as *I truly know* that he is the true God."[30] Nathan is

---

27 For instance, *Titus & Vespasian or The Destruction of Jerusalem in Rhymed Couplets*, ed. Herbert, 60; *The Siege of Jerusalem in Prose*, ed. Kurvinen, 74; and *La Vengeance de Nostre-Seigneur: The Old and Middle French Prose Versions*, ed. Ford, 197. This may be why one of the leading authorities on the apocrypha associated with the Gospel of Nicodemus refers to Nathan as "a Jewish emissary to Rome": Izydorczyk, "The Evangelium Nicodemi in the Latin Middle Ages," 60.

28 *Siege of Jerusalem*, ed. Livingston, 43 line 50.

29 *Vindicta Salvatoris* §7, ed. Cross, 256: "*quem nos uidimus et testificati sumus*, sicut ipse antea predixerat, ipsa carne in que natus, in ipsa passus, in ipsa sepultus, in ipsa per dies duos in sepulchro iacuit, in ipsa die tertia sicut uerus Deus et uerus homo a mortuis resurrexit, in ipsa per dies .XL. apparuit discipulis suis, et ad cęlos, *nobis uidentibus*, cum uirtute et potestate magna ascendit" (emphasis mine).

30 *OEVSal* §7, ed. Cross, 257: "Ac ic secge to soðon, þæt on þam ylcan lychaman þe he myd bebyrged wæs, on þam ylcan he eft aras bynnan twam dagum, eall swa *ic to soðon wat* þæt he ys se soða God" (emphasis mine).

an informed witness and a believer in Christ, and his immediate personal experience is what enables him to become the instrument of Tyrus's conversion to Christianity and the narrative trigger for the avenging of the saviour and the destruction of Jerusalem. That he is a native of Judea, and in the Old English translation explicitly a Jew, is not really surprising since it is crucial for the story that he be closely associated with Christ. He is of Christ's own people, he lived where Christ lived, he experienced the political and social realities that Christ experienced, and he saw the events from Christ's life which he relates to Tyrus, so that he is a trustworthy and reliable Christian apologist. But he is also, in the earliest version of the story, an Ishmaelite, which makes him an outcast and a wanderer alienated from and opposed to the Jewish community, so that he can claim cultural kinship with Christ but he can also disassociate himself from the Jews of Jerusalem who were responsible for Christ's death. He can speak with authority about Christ's life among Jews, but he is immune from charges against Jewish crimes. The Old English translation retains this multifaceted dimension of Nathan's character – a pro-Jesus anti-Jew from Judea – but abandons the Ishmaelite connection and modifies the anti-Jew element to produce an archetypal "Jew for Jesus" who is unlike any other Jew. This leaves us with two very different ideas about the nature of Jews in the Old English *Vindicta Salvatoris*. On the one hand, it was the Jews who were responsible for crucifying Christ, an act so evil that it sparks a crusade that results in the deaths of thousands of Jews in Jerusalem. As a race, Jews are categorically wicked and have been judged worthy of extinction. But on the other hand, there is one Jew in particular who bears witness to Christ's ministry, preaches the Gospel, converts the heathen to Christianity, heals the sick just as Christ did, and is an agent for universal justice who inspires the campaign to avenge the crimes of the Jews. How are we to explain this fractured and seemingly contradictory depiction of Jewishness in the Old English *Vindicta Salvatoris*?

If we search for literary ancestors for the character of Nathan, an obvious place to look is the Bible, and sure enough this is where we find a promising figure who helps explain a fundamental aspect of Nathan's role in the *Vindicta Salvatoris*. There are two Nathans in the Old Testament who are relevant here, the first a prophet under Kings David and Solomon who reproves David for his adulterous affair with Bathsheba, and the second the son of David and Bathsheba (apparently named after Nathan the prophet) who later appears within the genealogy of the Virgin Mary in the third chapter of Luke (3:31).[31] Nothing else is known about this second Nathan, the son of David and Bathsheba, but his precursor and namesake, Nathan the prophet, is an important figure in early Christian exegesis because his prophecy that a successor to David will someday come to build a temple in Jerusalem and perpetuate David's line was understood to have messianic implications. In the book of the Vulgate Bible known as 2 Kings (the book which Protestant Bibles, including the King James Version, designate as 2 Samuel), God, speaking through Nathan, announces to David that he will crown David's success by establishing an everlasting kingdom for the Israelites and erect a house of cedar for God to dwell in. This will not happen during David's lifetime, however, but one of David's descendants will inherit his throne and build God's temple. In the words of God delivered to David by Nathan, "And when thy days shall be fulfilled, and thou shalt sleep with thy fathers, I will raise up thy seed after thee, which shall proceed out of thy bowels, and I will establish his kingdom. He shall build a house to my name, and I will establish the throne of his kingdom forever" (2 Kings 7:12–13).[32] Nathan's prophecy is again related in the book of 1 Paralipomenon or 1 Chronicles, where the oracle to David is presented in very similar language: "And when thou shalt have ended thy days to go to thy fathers, I will raise up thy seed after thee, which shall be of thy sons, and I will establish his kingdom. He shall build me a house, and I will establish his throne forever" (1 Par. 17:11–12). From the Dead Sea scrolls onward, Nathan's prophecy was understood to look forward to the Messiah,[33] and Christian interpreters naturally saw its fulfilment in Christ, who was indeed a direct descendant of David through David's son Nathan and a self-proclaimed symbol for the new temple.[34]

---

31 The several Nathans named in the Hebrew Scriptures (as many as seven depending on how many are counted as the same person) are distinguished in the *Dictionnaire de la Bible*, ed. Vigouroux, IV.2: cols. 1481–3.

32 Here and elsewhere, English translations of the Vulgate are taken from the Douay-Rheims version, *The Holy Bible Translated from the Latin Vulgate*, with minor adjustment to the punctuation.

33 The Qumran text known as the *Florilegium or Midrash on the Last Days* (4Q174), dating probably to the first century BCE, interprets the prophecy of 2 Kings 7:11–14 as referring to "the Branch of David who shall arise … at the end of time": Vermes, *The Complete Dead Sea Scrolls in English*, 494.

34 Key witnesses to this Christological interpretation of Nathan's prophecy include Tertullian, *Adversus Marcionem* III.xx.8–10, ed. Braun, Sources Chrétiennes 399, 178–81; Lactantius, *Divinae Institutiones* IV.xiii.18–27, ed. Monat, Sources Chrétiennes

Isidore of Seville represents this interpretive tradition well when he explains that Nathan's prophecy was not fulfilled in David's son Solomon but in "our Lord Christ, who was begotten from the line of David,"[35] and Hrabanus Maurus affirms that Nathan's prophecy of a house of God to be erected by David's seed refers not to the physical earthly temple built by Solomon but to the eternal house of God established by Christ.[36] This Christological reading of Nathan's prophecy became standard throughout the Middle Ages, and one of its consequences was that it promoted the understanding of Nathan as a Jewish prophet who proclaimed the Christian message by foretelling Christ's advent to found the everlasting temple of God's kingdom. The very name by which Nathan is known in the *Vindicta Salvatoris* thus marks him as a symbolic heir of Nathan the court prophet of King David and, more to the point, as a Jewish prophet who preaches the Christian Gospel.

That Nathan is to be understood as a Jewish *prophet* is reinforced, moreover, by his identification in the Latin *Vindicta Salvatoris* as "Nathan, filius Naum" (Nathan, son of Naum),[37] or as the Old English translation puts it, "anes burhmannes sunu on Ysrahela lande, þæs nama wæs Nau" (the son of a city-dweller in Israel whose name was Nau).[38] In the Old English, the omission of the final *-m* in *Naum* is likely due to a misreading of the exemplar, where the name was probably written as *Naū*, with a nasal suspension mark over the *u*.[39] In any case, the name that is clearly intended in

---

377, 118–23; Augustine, *De civitate Dei* XVII.8, ed. Dombart and Kalb, CCSL 48, 570–2; Angelome of Luxeuil, *Enarrationes in Libros Regum* II.7 (*PL* 115:353–7); and Peter Damian, *Sermo* 49, ed. Lucchesi, CCCM 57, 308–9.71–88. This interpretation continues to play a part in present-day commentary: e.g., *The New Interpreter's Bible*, ed. Keck, II:1259–60; and *The Expositor's Bible Commentary*, ed. Longman III and Garland, III:391.

35 Isidore, *De fide catholica contra Iudaeos* I.ix.5 (*PL* 83:466): "Non est ergo ille Salomon, sed nec iste David dilatus est Christus. Ecce apparuerunt promissiones praedictae, non in Salomone, sed in Christo Domino nostro, qui ex David genere ortus est, fuisse completae."

36 Hrabanus, *Commentarius in Paralipomena* II.xvii (*PL* 109:365).

37 *Vindicta Salvatoris* §2, ed. Cross, 248.

38 *OEVSal* §2, ed. Cross, 249–51.

39 This is a common form of scribal error that hardly needs to be documented, but note by way of comparison the several words in manuscripts of the Latin *Evangelium Nicodemi*, as reflected in the apparatus to Cross's edition, which omit a final *-m*

both versions is *Naum*, a name so rare and distinctive in Judeo-Christian literature that it inevitably calls to mind the Old Testament minor prophet Nahum, whose name is spelled *Naum* in the Vulgate, and who foretold in rather stark, apocalyptic terms the destruction of the city of Nineveh, the capitol of the Assyrian Empire, by the Medes and Babylonians during the reign of King Josiah in the seventh century BCE. The fine details of Nahum's prophecy aren't important to the *Vindicta Salvatoris*, but the general message which he delivers concerning the impending destruction of a wicked city by a wrathful God to take just vengeance against the enemies of his people does provide an interesting biblical parallel for the destruction of Jerusalem resulting from Nathan's preaching of the Gospel to Tyrus. The opening verses of Nahum's prophecy, in the Old Testament book that bears his name, characterize God as a jealous, wrathful God who "taketh vengeance on his adversaries" and is "angry with his enemies" (Nahum 1:2), a characterization that is fully consonant with the depiction of God in the *Vindicta Salvatoris* as a militant, vengeful God who orders Titus and Vespasian "to go down into Judea to avenge His [Christ's] death"[40] and to carry out a merciless and exacting form of retributive justice for the crimes perpetrated by the Jews. When Titus and Vespasian reach Jerusalem, God sends an angel to instruct the two generals to inflict a series of punishments on the Jews which are chosen to correspond to the nature of their deeds:

Just as they [the Jews] did with Christ, so also let us do to them. They hung our Lord on a green tree and let us hang them on a dry tree; they killed Him without fault and let us kill them with the foulest death; they took his tunic and divided it into four parts and let us rend them into four parts and give their bodies to the beasts of the earth and birds of the air; they sold Christ for

---

for the same reason: e.g., *principatu* for *principatum* (140), *acta* for *actam* (140), *principe* for *principem* (140), *terra* for *terram* (142 [2x], 158), *uindicta* for *uindictam* (168), *monte* for *montem* (178, 192, 194), *die* for *diem* (188), *oratione* for *orationem* (188), *dormitione* for *dormitionem* (196), *nemine* for *neminem* (196), *specie* for *speciem* (204), *forma* for *formam* (218, 220), *fulgore* for *fulgorem* (224), *obsecratione* for *obsecrationem* (228), and *multitudine* for *multitudinem* (232). Likewise, in the various texts of the Old English *Gospel of Nicodemus* reflected in Cross's apparatus, note *helda* for *hældan* (155), *nama* for *naman* (179), *bydda* for *byddan* (179), and *lychama* for *lychaman* (191).

40 *Vindicta Salvatoris* §§30–1, ed. Cross, 290: "descendere in Judęa ut uindicarent mortem eius."

thirty pieces and we gave thirty of them for one piece of silver and let their names be obliterated from the earth.[41]

The threat of God's wrathful vengeance against his iniquitous enemies is of course a familiar theme in the Old Testament and is voiced by a number of prophets other than Nahum, but Nahum is an especially apt figure to identify as Nathan's father in the *Vindicta Salvatoris* not only because of the nature of Nahum's prophecy but also because he is named, along with David's son Nathan, as a direct ancestor of Christ in the genealogical roll-call in the third chapter of Luke (3:25, 31). Just as Nathan the prophet under King David foretells events that can be seen as coming to fruition in Christ, so the prophet Nahum is a direct forebear of Christ who literally and historically prepares the way for Christ's coming. Taken together, the biblical and exegetical associations conjured up by the names *Nathan* and *Naum* predispose us to imagine that a character known as "Nathan, son of Naum" will in some way enact the role of a Jewish prophet who proclaims the Christian Gospel, who warns of God's wrathful vengeance against the enemies of his people, and who is himself intimately associated with Christ. When that character turns out to originate from Judea, draws on his own experience to tell the story of Christ's ministry and earthly career, quotes an Ascension Day antiphon to prophesy Christ's second coming, incites a bloodthirsty crusade to the Holy Land to punish God's enemies, and heals the sick and baptizes heathens in Christ's name, the name begins to ring true.

The biblical roots of the names *Nathan* and *Naum* explain a great deal about the personal history and motivation of Nathan and his function in the story, but they don't account for what is perhaps the most perplexing aspect of Nathan's character, namely his role as the solitary good Jew in a story that categorically denounces Jews as evil. Even if we can see that Nathan's biblical heritage provides clear models for his ability to preach the Gospel, precipitate the crusade to avenge Christ's death, and convert

---

41 *Vindicta Salvatoris* §§30–1, ed. Cross, 290: "Quomodo fecerunt de Christo, ita et nos faciamus illos. Suspenderunt dominum nostrum in lignum uiride, et nos suspendemus eos in arido; occiderunt illum sine culpa, et nos occidamus illos morte turpissima; acceperunt tonicam eius et fecerunt de ea partes .IIII.ᵒʳ, et nos scindamus eos in quattuor partes et damus carnes illorum bestiis terre et uolatilibus caeli; uendiderunt Christum .XXX. argenteos, et nos damus pro uno argenteo .XXX. ex illis et deleantur nomina illorum de terra." The literary and iconographic topos of Christ's crucifixion on a green tree is discussed by Hall, "The Cross as Green Tree in the *Vindicta Salvatoris*."

the heathen, it is still difficult to reconcile the notion of an exemplary Christ-like Jew with the story's overarching condemnation of the Jewish race as unredeemable and worthy of destruction for their unforgivable crimes against Christianity. This is the central crux of Nathan's character, and if we want to find an influential model for an exemplary Jew in a world filled with wicked Jews, the best place to look is in the apocryphon that ultimately gave rise to the *Vindicta Salvatoris* and that frequently accompanies it in manuscripts, namely the *Gospel of Nicodemus*.[42] There is of course no character in the *Gospel of Nicodemus* named Nathan, but there are characters who stand out in sharp relief as atypical Jews who advocate for Christ and are instrumental in carrying the passion narrative forward. To recognize this pattern, one has to be aware that the fundamental dynamic of Jewish identity in the *Gospel of Nicodemus* is that as a collective the Jewish people are universally wicked and deceitful, motivated by guile and envy and a stubborn allegiance to the old law, whereas individually they include Jews who stand out as uncommonly good men.[43] As a race, in other words, the Jews are Christ's worst enemies, but there are a select few among them who are Christ's strongest supporters. In the first half of the *Gospel of Nicodemus* (the part known as the *Acts of Pilate*), a crowd of Jews demands that Christ be brought to trial before Pilate, and they plot to bring about Christ's death and attempt to conceal their role in doing so. This Jewish mob invokes the Jewish sabbatical laws to accuse Christ of healing and performing miracles on the sabbath, and they accuse him of committing blasphemy, of casting out demons through sorcery, of being born through fornication, and of causing the deaths of all the children in Bethlehem. When Pilate confesses that he can find no fault in Jesus, the Jews declare in a single collective voice: "His blood be upon us and upon our children."[44] Then after the Jews demand that Christ be crucified,

---

42 For basic orientation on the *Gospel of Nicodemus*, see Hall, "The *Euangelium Nichodemi* and *Vindicta Saluatoris* in Anglo-Saxon England," 36–58; and Izydorczyk, "The *Evangelium Nicodemi* in the Latin Middle Ages." The rather idiosyncratic spelling of the name *Nicodemus* as *Nichodemus* throughout Cross's volume, contrary to standard practice elsewhere, simply reflects the spelling of the name in the Saint-Omer 202 Latin text (e.g., 140 lines 2 and 4).

43 The anti-Jewish rhetoric of the *Gospel of Nicodemus* is briefly discussed by Scheil, *The Footsteps of Israel*, 215–16, 218.

44 I cite from the Latin text of the *Evangelium Nichodemi* in Saint-Omer 202 (from Cross's edition) since it was clearly a version known in Anglo-Saxon England: here, *Evangelium Nichodemi* IV.1: "Sanguis eius super nos et super filios nostros," 160.

Pilate surveys the crowd, sees several of the Jews crying, and says: "Not all of the crowd wants him to die."[45] But the Jewish elders retort: "For this end we have come *as the entire multitude* that He might die."[46] Later on, when "the Jews" learn of Christ's resurrection from the tomb, they gather a large sum of money to bribe the soldiers who had been assigned to guard Christ's tomb to spread the word that Christ's body had been stolen by his disciples. Throughout the *Gospel of Nicodemus*, the Jews behave as a single character in the drama. They suppress their own individuality, they accuse Christ in a single voice, and they are blamed collectively for hanging Christ on the Cross. They have no identity apart from their designation as "the Jews," and they are guided by a single consciousness and a single will.[47]

This monolithic Jewish plot to murder Christ is opposed, however, by two Jews in particular who come to Christ's defence and who are characterized as good and just individuals, namely Nicodemus and Joseph of Arimathea. Nicodemus first comes forward at the trial after the Jews have stated their accusations against Christ, and he reminds them that Christ has performed many miracles that have never been witnessed before. He asks the Jews what they want with Jesus, and he implies that they have no legitimate complaint against him. Immediately after this, Joseph of Arimathea is introduced as "a good and just man" who awaits the kingdom of God and who likewise disagrees with the accusations of the Jews.[48] As Christ is dying on the Cross, Joseph asks Pilate for Christ's body, which he wraps in a clean linen cloth and places in his own tomb, and he has a stone rolled in front of it. Then when Joseph reproaches the Jews for crucifying Christ and piercing his side with a lance (and it's the Jews who are accused of these acts, not the Romans), the Jews are said to be "exceedingly bitter in their souls,"[49] and they shut Joseph up in a windowless chamber and plot to kill him. At this point Joseph becomes a type of Christ when the Jewish mob comes to drag him out of the sealed chamber to kill him, but they

---

45 *Evangelium Nichodemi* IV.5, 164: "Non omnis multitudo uult eum mori."

46 *Evangelium Nichodemi* IV.5, 164: "Ideoque uenimus *uniuersa multitudo* ut moriatur" (emphasis mine).

47 Readers of Old English poetry will recognize a similar pattern in Cynewulf's *Elene*, where the council of Jewish wise men summoned by Elene speak in one voice as *we Ebreisce* ("we Hebrews") and reply to her interrogations *anmode* ("unanimously"): *The Vercelli Book*, ed. Krapp, 77 (lines 397a, 396a).

48 *Evangelium Nichodemi* XI.3, 166: "uir bonus et iustus."

49 *Evangelium Nichodemi* XII.1, 170: "exacerbati sunt animo eius."

open the chamber only to find it empty. This scene is immediately followed by the report of the soldier who had been set to guard Christ's tomb that the stone had just been rolled away from the entrance to the tomb, only to reveal that Christ had mysteriously disappeared. Nicodemus and Joseph of Arimathea both stand out in this story as exemplary Jewish men of authority who are opposed to the Jewish mob and who come to Christ's defence, exhibiting compassion and generosity.

Anyone familiar with the *Gospel of Nicodemus* would have been able to recognize this basic pattern of good and just Jewish individuals who distinguish themselves from the wicked Jewish mob and who associate themselves with Christ. In the *Gospel of Nicodemus* this pattern is an important one from a narrative perspective because it promotes Nicodemus as a rational and trustworthy insider, and we want Nicodemus to be a rational and trustworthy insider because the *Gospel* is said to have been written down by Nicodemus in Hebrew, so his integrity as a narrator and the credibility of the entire story are at stake. The *Vindicta Salvatoris* is a very different story from the *Gospel of Nicodemus*, but it enacts precisely this same opposition between a wicked Jewish mob and an exemplary Jewish individual who is sympathetic with Christ. Nathan simply takes this opposition to an extreme by assuming the role not just of a Christ sympathizer but of a Christian apostle who baptizes and converts in Christ's name. The *Gospel of Nicodemus* is not by any means the only text known to early medieval audiences that involved an opposition between an exemplary individual and a wicked mob. Readers of Old English poetry and early saints' lives will recognize this broader hagiographic trope as present in *Andreas* and *Elene* and a score of virgin martyr legends. But the opposition as developed in the *Gospel of Nicodemus* is a refinement of this standard hagiographic trope that particularizes the exemplary individual and the wicked mob as Jewish, and there can be no question that the *Gospel of Nicodemus* had considerable influence in broadcasting this particularized version of the trope.

Nathan the Jew in the Old English *Vindicta Salvatoris* has a complex literary pedigree. Originally declared an Ishmaelite in the Latin *Vindicta Salvatoris* to underscore his alienation and independence from the Jewish community at large and thus indemnify him against any allegation of Jewish crime, he nevertheless has emphatic Jewish credentials as a namesake of both Nathan the prophet and Naum the prophet, a pair of connections that authorizes him to preach the Gospel to Tyrus. The fact that he is a subject of Pontius Pilate in Judea further betrays Nathan's essential underlying Jewishness, which is a dominant feature of his character in spite of his alleged Ishmaelite origins. The Old English translator evidently recognized Nathan's Jewish ties and simply outed him as a Jew to make explicit what the Latin text merely hints at through geographical, historical, exegetical, and onomastic clues. The Latin text is so full of problems that it may not be possible to reason out its author's intentions fully, but one consequence of his decision to call Nathan an Ishmaelite is that he makes the crusade to eliminate the Jews originate with a traditional enemy of the Jews, an arrangement that has a certain logic to it. The Old English text abandons this scheme and instead makes a Jew ultimately responsible for the destruction of the Jews, replicating the dramatic opposition between a solitary good Jew and the evil Jewish mob popularized by the *Gospel of Nicodemus*. One possible motivation for this shift is that the Old English translator didn't quite understand what an Ishmaelite was, and he knew he needed to create a character who could function as a Jewish prophet, a Christian apologist, and an agent for divine justice. A Jew could perform these roles better than an Ishmaelite, and the result was Nathan, son of Naum, a Jew from Judea who had served under Pontius Pilate and who knew Christ. He is a unique literary creation and one of the most extraordinary representations of a Jew in early English literature.

The Jew in Anglo-Saxon Theology and Liturgy: Aspects of Language, Place, and Time

3 *Hebraeam scire linguam*: Bede's Rhetoric of the Hebrew Truth

DAMIAN FLEMING

The traditional perception that Bede's biblical commentaries are largely derivative can be traced to a face-value reading of his own frequent claim that he is merely *patrum uestigia sequens* (following in the footsteps of the fathers).[1] Despite this apparent humility, however, he advanced to his readers his conception of the Hebraic source of scripture and the implications of this idea, even going so far as to determine a new age for the world. Of course, he quotes extensively from the writings of his patristic predecessors; a superficial reading of Bede's texts might view them as a scholastic catena, a mere string of others' words. Bede nevertheless often uses patristic quotations to articulate unprecedented arguments. An examination of two of Bede's works demonstrates his strikingly modern and philologically responsible understanding of Hebrew: he advances Jerome's idiosyncratic insistence on the primacy of the Hebrew Bible but does not hesitate to disagree with Jerome when he feels it is necessary. Bede's *Commentary on Genesis* reveals his controversial innovations and deft rhetorical posturing as he establishes himself as a scholar of Hebrew comparable to Jerome, and his *Letter to Plegwine* defends his original argument for the age of the world by distinguishing himself and other scholars who appreciate the importance of Hebrew from the sadly misguided Christians and even Jews who fail to do so.

---

1 See Ray, "Who Did Bede Think He Was?"; the work of Ray and other current Bede scholars (see, for example, the essays in the same collection) has done much to fight this image. See in particular DeGregorio, "Introduction: The New Bede," 6–9.

Bede could not read Hebrew – in any modern sense – nor would he have any opportunity to do so.[2] There were no Jewish populations in the British Isles before the Norman Conquest and there is no evidence of the study of Hebrew during this time period.[3] Nevertheless, Bede knew a lot about Hebrew, and his linguistic abilities place him among the most exceptional Latinists of the Middle Ages, evidenced by his prodigious output of Latin poetry and prose, as well as writings on the Latin language. He additionally taught himself a substantial amount of Greek with the help of a bilingual manuscript of the Acts of the Apostles.[4] Had the appropriate resources been available, there can be no doubt that Bede could have learned Hebrew. In place of Hebrew manuscripts or Jewish teachers, Bede had to rely on the collected works of Jerome, which offer the literal meanings of hundreds of Hebrew proper names and dozens of comments about the structure, orthography, and even paleography of Hebrew texts.[5] Most importantly, Bede takes from Jerome the idea that Hebrew deserves primacy as the language that contains the oldest record of salvation history, and thus, the language from which translations are made.[6]

Before the time of Bede, the importance of Hebrew in the Christian world was primarily advanced by Jerome, who devoted his life to translating the Old Testament from Hebrew to Latin and to crafting a body of commentaries and letters that justified his project. Bede follows Jerome, accepting his philological argument for a return to the Hebrew text of the Old Testament – the "Hebrew Truth" – as the ultimate source of the biblical text. We perhaps take it for granted that Jerome's translation according to the Hebrew – what we call the Vulgate – was then the foremost medieval Latin text of the Bible, but that was not a given in Bede's day. Jerome's translation competed for centuries with the Old Latin translations based on the Greek Septuagint, which were well established and

---

2 Sutcliffe, "The Venerable Bede's Knowledge of Hebrew."

3 Scheil, *The Footsteps of Israel*, 7.

4 Dionisotti, "On Bede, Grammars, and Greek"; Lynch, "The Venerable Bede's Knowledge of Greek."

5 In addition to the examples below, see Sutcliffe, "The Venerable Bede's Knowledge of Hebrew," 304; he notes "the care with which Bede collected scraps of information about Hebrew ... and enables us to judge how eagerly he would have embraced the study of the language had he had any opportunity of doing so."

6 The importance of Hebrew rests then on its historical role in the transmission of scripture, not on any mystical or "sacred" nature that set it apart from other languages. See Dekker, "Pentecost and Linguistic Self-Consciousness," 352.

continued to be known as the texts cited by Latin patristic authors before Jerome.[7] Jerome's Latin translation was not officially declared the Bible of the Roman Church until the sixteenth century.[8] Bede, however, was part of a cultural milieu in seventh- and eighth-century Northumbria that strongly supported the Vulgate. Christopher de Hamel notes the special attention paid to textual considerations of the Bible in Bede's world, which ultimately "played a remarkable part in the dissemination of Jerome's translation. It is tempting to see the Venerable Bede, Doctor of the Church, like Saint Jerome, as having a role too in completing the publication of the Vulgate."[9]

Bede's frequent and vocal advocacy of the importance of the Hebrew basis of biblical translation had led nineteenth- and early twentieth-century scholars to believe that he possessed some independent knowledge of Hebrew.[10] Bede often follows closely the footsteps of Jerome, not only borrowing from him many facts about the Hebrew language but also a pointed rhetorical stance that was originally born out of the hostility Jerome faced during his own lifetime because of his translation. Jerome's biblical prefaces, commentaries, and letters bear witness to his lifelong struggle – most famously with his contemporary Augustine – to replace the Greek Septuagint with the Hebrew Bible as the starting point for biblical translation. Jerome dubs his source text the *hebraica ueritas*, "the Hebrew Truth," a loaded term which weds his access to Hebrew with truth itself and conversely casts suspicion on any other source text.[11]

---

7 De Hamel, *The Book: A History of the Bible*, 25–30; Marsden, *The Text of the Old Testament in Anglo-Saxon England*, 8–11.

8 Sutcliffe, "The Name 'Vulgate'"; Marsden, *The Text of the Old Testament in Anglo-Saxon England*, 8.

9 De Hamel, *The Book: A History of the Bible*, 34.

10 Sutcliffe, "The Venerable Bede's Knowledge of Hebrew," 302, who cites scholars such as J.A. Giles, S.A. Hirsch, and Charles Singer attributing genuine knowledge of Hebrew to Bede; see also Stinson, "'Northernmost Israel': England, the Old Testament, and the Hebraic 'Veritas' as Seen by Bede and Roger Bacon." Perhaps owing to the easy availability of nineteenth-century texts on-line, the notion that Bede knew Hebrew has re-emerged in popular online references; see for example: http://www.britannia.com/ bios/bede.html and http://www.stbedeepiscopalchurch.org/st-bede-episcopal-church- st-pete-fl-33704-st-bede-the-venerable.html.

11 Kamesar, *Jerome, Greek Scholarship, and the Hebrew Bible*, 42–9; Cain, *The Letters of Jerome*, 54.

Bede supports Jerome's logic and refers to him as *noster interpres* (our translator – in contrast to the *LXX interpretes* of the Septuagint) and his translation as the *hebraica ueritas*. In transferring Jerome's term for the Hebrew source to the resultant translation, Bede bestows the authority of the Hebrew text on Jerome's translation. Bede is able then to act with the authority of Jerome himself, effortlessly discussing a given reading from the Hebrew Truth compared with the Septuagint or the "old translation."[12] These are the types of comments that originally fuelled the speculation that Bede himself could read Hebrew. Our modern *index fontium* may defuse the force of these statements by pointing directly to Bede's immediate source, usually Jerome; and many editors print such verbatim quotations entirely in italics as if to remind us that this is not really Bede.[13] We ought to beware, however, of dismissing comments made by Bede as irrelevant simply because we can source them; Bede's commentaries give the impression of direct engagement with, and wholehearted support of, the Hebrew language. Given his complete mastery of classical Latin, his continually improving knowledge of Greek, and his concern with language generally, it would not be surprising if many medieval authors, like some modern ones, believed that Bede could actually read Hebrew. Although late in his career Bede himself developed a novel system of indicating his sources; these were regularly misunderstood and miscopied by scribes and do not appear in his works under consideration here.[14] And though most of his information is lifted directly from Jerome, Bede also makes original deductions about the Hebrew language and uses his own understanding of Hebrew to disagree with Jerome.

A large number of comments concerning the Hebrew language are found in Bede's *Commentary on Genesis*, which draws heavily on Jerome's

---

12 Kendall, trans., *Bede: On Genesis*, 56, gives a number of examples.

13 See, Jenkins, "Bede as Exegete and Theologian," 163, who challenges "anyone who desires to establish the contention that Bede was a student of Hebrew to produce any evidence for it which cannot be explained as being taken from the writings of other authors."

14 Laistner, "Source-marks in Bede Manuscripts," 350–4; Gorman, "Source Marks and Chapter Division in Bede's Commentary on Luke," 246–90. Gorman points out the problematic nature of many of the twentieth-century editions of Bede's works, especially regarding the *index fontium* and use of italics.

Hebrew Questions on Genesis.[15] The casualness with which Bede makes references to the spelling of words in the Hebrew alphabet vividly suggests a personal knowledge of the material. Commenting on an element in a genealogical list at Genesis 10:7, "Filii Regma: Saba et Dadan," Bede first notes that two occurrences of a seemingly identical word actually represent two different words when written in Hebrew and thus have different meanings, "Hic Saba per SIN litteram scribitur, supra uero per SAMECH … Interpretatur ergo nunc Saba Arabia" (This Saba is written with the letter SIN, but above with the letter SAMECH … therefore now Saba is interpreted Arabia). Then he makes reference to a separate verse in the psalms which – again, when read in Hebrew – demonstrates the distinction between the two words:

> Nam in septuagesimo [primo] psalmo, ubi nos habemus *Reges Arabum et Saba munera offerent*, in Hebraeo scriptum est *Reges Saba et Saba*, primum nomen per SIN, secundum per SAMECH, quae nostrae litterae similis est.[16]

> (For, in the seventy-first psalm, where we have *the kings of Arabia and Saba offered gifts*, in Hebrew it is written *kings of Saba and Saba*: the first name with SIN, the second with SAMECH, which is similar to our letter.)[17]

Although almost all of this is borrowed verbatim from Jerome's comments on the same verse in his *Hebrew Questions in Genesis*, Bede presents this information as part of his own running prose without attribution, giving the impression that he knows about the spelling of these words in the

---

15 Bede's *Commentary on Genesis* was written during two separate periods in his career; the second half was completed some years after the first. A consideration of the development of this biblical commentary is outside the scope of this article, though it is worth noting that almost all of Bede's citations from Jerome's *Hebrew Questions* appear in the latter half of the commentary. Further study of Bede's entire corpus might reveal the diachronic development of Bede's appreciation of Jerome's work and his attendant insistence on the importance of the Hebrew Truth. See Kendall, trans. *Bede: On Genesis*, 40–53.

16 Jones, ed., *Libri quatuor in principium Genesis usque ad natiuitatem Isaac et eiectionem Ismahelis adnotationum* (hereafter Bede, *In Gen.*); 144.

17 All translations are my own unless otherwise noted.

Hebrew alphabet.[18] Bede also leaves his own mark in the comment on the letter SAMECH: "quae nostrae litterae similis est" (which letter is similar to *ours*), adding a level of personal immediacy which is not found in the passage from Jerome's *Hebrew Questions.* This additional comment is ultimately derived from Jerome's commentary on Ezekiel.[19] Bede pulls together disparate information about the Hebrew language and redeploys it in his own works, thus bestowing upon himself the authority of the Hebrew language.

Bede's confidence in his control of the Hebrew language is even more impressive when he uses it to disagree with or even correct Jerome. As noted above, Bede is an avid supporter of Jerome's translation project and agrees with his decision to prioritize the Hebrew text over the Septuagint. But in at least one occurrence, Bede uses his own understanding of Hebrew paleography to prefer a reading from the Septuagint over the reading chosen by Jerome. In explicating the descendants of Noah at Genesis 10, Bede notes the following:

Dodanim Rhodii: melius enim legitur Rhodanim siue Rhodim, ut septuaginta interpretes transtulerunt, et in libro Hebreorum nominum etiam noster interpres posuit; similitudo enim litterarum DALETH et RES hunc apud Hebreos saepe facit errorem, ut alia legitur pro alia.[20]

---

18 Jerome writes: "Hic Saba per SIN literam scribitur, supra uero per SAMECH ... interpretatur ergo nunc Saba Arabia. Nam in septuagesima primo psalmo, ubi nos habemus *reges Arabum et Saba munera offerent*, in hebraeo scriptum est *reges Saba et Saba*: primum nomen per SIN, secundum per SAMECH," De Lagarde, ed., *S. Hieronymi presbyteri hebraicae quaestiones in libro Geneseos* (hereafter *Hebrew Questions*), 12: "Here [in Hebrew] Saba is written with the letter SIN, but above [where Saba is written, it is spelled] with the letter SAMECH ... therefore this occurrence of Saba is interpreted Arabia. For, in the seventy-first psalm, where we have *the kings of Arabia and Saba offered gifts*, in Hebrew it is written *kings of Saba and Saba*: the first name with SIN, the second with SAMECH." See Sutcliffe, "St. Jerome's Pronunciation of Hebrew"; Barr, "St. Jerome and the Sounds of Hebrew."

19 "In Psalmis, ubi scriptum est: *Reges Arabum et Saba munera offerent tibi*, in hebraeo habet: *Reges Saba et Saba munera offerent tibi*, quorum una 'Saba' per 'sen' litteram scribitur, alterum per 'samech' quae nostrae litterae similis est," Glorie, ed., *S. Hieronymi presbyteri commentariorum in Hiezechielem libri xiv*, 376; "In the Psalms, where it is written, *the kings of Arabia and Saba offered gifts*, in Hebrew it is written, *the kings of Saba and Saba offered gifts*, where one 'Saba' is written with the letter SEN and the other with SAMECH, which is similar to our letter."

20 Bede, *In Gen.*, 142–3.

(*The Dodanim are the people of Rhodes*: it is better to read Rhodanim or Rhodim, as the Septuagint translated, and our translator put in the *Book of Hebrew Names*; for the similarity of the letters DALETH and RES often creates this mistake among Hebrews, as the one is read for the other.)

The core of his commentary – that the Dodanim are the people of Rhodes and this is what the Septuagint says – comes from Jerome's *Hebrew Questions*; the rest of the passage is unsourced.[21] Bede does not merely note that these two words refer to the same people but suggests a possible emendation to the Vulgate text: that we should read *Rhodanim* in place of *Dodanim*. Naturally, in suggesting a change to the text of Jerome's translation, Bede has to look elsewhere for his justification, hence the unusual appeal to the authority of the Septuagint. He also uses another text of Jerome's as evidence ("as our translator puts in the *Book of Hebrew Names* …"), but fails to mention that, although *Rhodim* is included in Jerome's *Book of Hebrew Names*, *Dodanim* is as well.[22] Strikingly, Bede gives the impression of knowing the Hebrew language at the level of spelling – paleography even – noting the common confusion of the letters *dalet*: ד and *resh*: ר in the present tense ("facit errorem"), as if this were a mistake he himself has witnessed Hebrews making. Bede's awareness of this potential letter confusion also derives from Jerome but not in reference to this text; in fact, to make this connection, Bede synthesized information from two separate references in Jerome's commentary on Ezekiel.[23]

---

21 "Dodanim Rhodii: ita enim LXX interpretes transtulerunt," Jerome, *Hebrew Questions*, 12.

22 Lagarde, ed. *Liber interpretationis hebraicorum nominum*, 64, 70.

23 "*Filii Dadan negotiatores tui*: Pro quo, nescio quid uolentes, Septuaginta filios Rhodiorum interpretati sunt, nisi forte primae litterae falsi similitudine, ut pro Dadan legerunt Radan … sed melius est Dadan alterius loci nomen accipere, et ut in hebraico et apud ceteros interpretes habetur," Glorie, ed., 368, "*The sons of Dadan were thy merchants*: For this, I don't know what they were wishing, the Septuagint translates 'sons of Rhodians,' unless by chance they were deceived by the similarity of the first letter, so that they read Radan for Dadan … but it is better to accept Dadan as the name of the other place, as is found in the Hebrew and among the other translators." "*Syrus negotiator tuus*: Syrus quoque fuit negotiator Tyri, pro quo in hebraeo positum est *aram* in cuius loco Septuagesima homines interpretati sunt, pro *aram* legentes *adam*, et RES et DALETH litterarum, sicut supra, decepti similtudine," Glorie, ed., 369–70, "*Syrus was thy merchant*: Syrus was also the merchant for Tyrus, for whom in the Hebrew it has 'aram' in place of which the Septuagint has translated 'men,' reading 'adam' for 'aram,' having been deceived by the similarity of the letters RES and DALETH, as above."

Bede shows himself here to be comfortable drawing upon diverse, and even conflicting texts, and ultimately deciding issues for himself. He uses his own knowledge of Hebrew – though derived from Jerome – to go so far as to make an argument that corrects Jerome's translation of the Bible. The overall impression of the passage leaves one with the feeling that Bede is sympathetic, or perhaps even patronizing, towards what he characterizes as a mistake by Jerome: "It's okay Jerome, sometimes even the Jews get this wrong."

There are other passages within Bede's *Commentary on Genesis* that lack an immediate source, yet present the appearance of direct knowledge of Hebrew, as in the following example, in which Bede comments on God's seemingly unusual syntax. In reference to Genesis 4:7, God's rebuke to Cain following the rejection of his offering, "Sed sub te erit appetitus eius, et tu dominaberis illius" (but the lust thereof shall be under thee, and thou shalt have dominion over it), Bede explains:

> Iuxta idioma linguae hebreae indicatiuum modum pro imperatiuo posuit, qualia habes innumera: *Diliges Dominum Deum tuum, Diliges proximum tuum, Non fornicaberis, Non furtum facies, Non falsum testimonium dices,* pro eo, ut diceretur, "Dilige," "Et ne occidas," "Ne forniceris," "Ne furtum facias," "Ne falsum testimonium dicas."[24]

> (Following Hebrew usage [God] uses the indicative mood in place of the imperative; you have many examples, *Thou shalt love the Lord your God, Thou shalt love thy neighbour, Thou shalt not fornicate, Thou shalt not steal, Thou shalt not speak false testimony,* as if it should say, "Love!," "And do not kill," "Do not fornicate," "Do not steal," "Do not speak false testimony.")

No source has been identified for this comment, though Jones[25] suggests comparing a line from Jerome's translation of Origen's homily on the Song of Songs, which reads, "Moris est scripturarum, imperatiuum modum pro optatiuo ponere" (It is the custom of scripture to put the imperative mood in place of the optative).[26] This comment locates the unusual syntax in

---

24 Bede, *In Gen.*, 75.
25 Ibid.
26 Vallarsi, ed. *Sancti Eusebii Hieronymi Stridonensis presbyteri operum, tomus tertius,* col. 506.

the context of scripture, in general, rather than the Hebrew language, and addresses the use of the imperative and the optative as opposed to the imperative and indicative. Expressions of the type "mos scripturarum" are common in Jerome and Bede to explain unusual grammatical constructions, but that is not what is at issue here. Bede is not talking about *scriptural* usage but *Hebrew* usage. The phrase "iuxta idioma hebreae linguae" is also not uncommon in Jerome, but he never suggests that in Hebrew the indicative is used for the imperative. The statement as a whole represents an original induction on the part of Bede, who has drawn his own conclusion about the Hebrew language by combining his knowledge of Latin grammar and the text of the Vulgate, which he knows is very often derived from Hebrew usage.[27] We can only imagine the impact such a statement could have had on Bede's readers: because he presents seemingly new information about Hebrew usage as compared with Latin usage, one might conclude that Bede himself had knowledge of Hebrew. The fact that Bede makes such a statement based on personal observation demonstrates his comfort discussing Hebrew on his own authority; he likely believed he had some knowledge of Hebrew as he did in the case of Greek. This brief overview shows why Bede's readers – from the eighth to the nineteenth century – could easily suppose that Bede had a real knowledge of Hebrew. Bede felt comfortable enough in his knowledge of Hebrew to refer to it throughout his commentaries, drawing together often disparate comments from Jerome, making original observations, and even dissenting from Jerome. The full force of his confidence in his understanding is seen when someone dared to challenge his conclusions derived from his understanding of Hebrew.

Perhaps the most significant and pointed rhetorical use of Hebrew in the writings of Bede concerns the age of the world. Bede's claim to merely follow in the footsteps of the fathers is most suspect in the case of chronology, as few of his patristic predecessors wrote anything on the subject.[28] Lacking a direct model to follow, Bede's original deductions and calculations in his works on time and the calendar led him to suggest a new figure for the age of the world; he was thus perceived as undermining established

---

27 As Kendall points out, some of Bede's examples are in fact from the Greek New Testament, "But, of course, the phrasing in Greek or Aramaic is influenced by the idiom of the Old, which is Bede's point" (trans. *Bede: On Genesis*, 143).
28 Wallis, "Bede and Science" and "Introduction" to *Bede: The Reckoning of Time*.

eschatology. Although he draws upon the work of a number of fathers, he follows none of them directly and ultimately rests his authority on the Hebrew Truth itself in direct opposition to the Septuagint, which in this context he debases as an inaccurate, Jewish text. Bede is so confident in the foundation of the Hebrew Truth that he departs from the work of Jerome, Augustine, and others, only to turn around and line those same authorities up behind his own view.

In addition to Bede's role as biblical commentator, he was also the foremost authority on the calendar in the Middle Ages. His decision to employ Dionysus Exiguus's dating scheme starting at the birth of Christ established the use of *anno domini* as the norm for dating years in Western Europe, and his comprehensive *Reckoning of Time* served as the foundational work on the Latin calendar until the Renaissance.[29] Early in his career, Bede sought to fill a gap in the corpus of Christian learning by writing a concise introduction to the calendar, *On Times*.[30] This short computistical manual would allow clerics to understand the reasoning behind the dating of Easter.[31] At the end of this highly influential text, Bede appended a short *Chronicle*, which traces the highlights of world history from creation to his own time.[32] This *Chronicle* begins with an overview of the six ages of the world, the sixth and current age having begun at the Incarnation, a concept not original to Bede. Like so many of Bede's works, this *Chronicle* represents a synthesis, modelled in great part on the fourth-century *Chronicon* of Eusebius of Caesarea as translated into Latin by Jerome, combined with the chronicle found in Isidore of Seville's *Etymologies* – which itself combined Eusebius's dates with Augustine's scheme of six ages of the world.[33] The numerical figures in both Eusebius-Jerome and Isidore are based on the Septuagint; Augustine does not particularly care about literal dates. Bede's innovation in his *Chronicle* was recalculating the individual years that made up the dates leading to the Incarnation based solely on the information found in Jerome's translation

---

29   Wallis, "Bede and Science"; Declercq, *Anno Domini*, 169.
30   Both of Bede's treatises on time are published in Jones, ed., *Bedae opera de temporibus*; reprinted in CCSL 123B.
31   Wallis, trans., *Bede: The Reckoning of Time*, lxiv.
32   Mommsen, ed., in MGH AA 13 (Berlin, 1898), 223–354; this is reprinted in Jones' CCSL edition of Bede's works on time.
33   Wallis, lxiii–lxxi; Darby, *Bede and the End of Time*, 17–34.

of the Bible – the Hebrew Truth.[34] As a result of recalculating these figures, Bede offered a new age for the world. Where the Eusebius-Jerome *Chronicon* placed the Incarnation at *anno mundi* 5199, Bede's calculation placed it at 3952; he removed 1247 years from the traditionally accepted age of the world.

Bede's radical reconfiguration, produced out of strict reverence for the Hebrew text of the Old Testament, was apparently not well received by some. The popular opinion had developed that each of the ages of the world was roughly a millennium long, based on the fact that Augustine outlined six ages of the world and that in the established chronicles Christ was born in the sixth millennium. Bede's new figure of Christ's birth in 3952 seemed to suggest that the Incarnation did not occur in the sixth age of the world, and therefore, might seem to undermine the six-age scheme altogether. As a result of his recalculations, Bede was apparently accused of heresy in England; all that remains of the controversy is Bede's heated letter to one Plegwine responding to the charge, in which he concisely outlines his logic and reckoning for his figures.[35]

This letter represents one of the clearest moments showing Bede coming into his own as an authority and church father in his own right, vehemently defending his original work where he has clearly departed from the footsteps of the fathers.[36] He opens the letter by questioning how on earth he could be charged with heresy or be said to deny that the Incarnation occurred in the sixth age. He channels the spirit of Jerome here, asserting his own authority because of its base in the Hebrew Truth, deriding those whose linguistic abilities are inferior to his, and equating the Septuagint with its dubious Jewish translators in contrast to Jerome, "our Christian translator."

---

34 Daniel McCarthy has recently argued that Bede in fact borrowed these figures from Adomnan's copy of the Iona Annals. McCarthy's article came to my attention too late to be given full consideration here; nevertheless, if McCarthy's thesis is correct, Bede's rhetorical posturing which I outline below becomes even more impressive; "Bede's Primary Source for the Vulgate Chronology."

35 Wallis, "Bede and Science," 120–1. Wallis is skeptical as to the seriousness of the charge of heresy; the only evidence we have of it is Bede's own letter. Nevertheless, the vehemence with which Bede attacks the charge shows its importance to Bede. See Darby, *Bede and the End of Time*, 35–64.

36 Ray, *Bede, Rhetoric, and the Creation of Christian Latin Culture*; ibid., "Cicero and Bede."

In quo annorum series iuxta **hebraicam ueritatem**, ubi LXX interpretibus longe breuior habetur, erat annotata, ita ut usque ad Aduentum Saluatoris in carne nec quinque annorum millia sint completa. Suadebamque illi fraternae, fateor, charitatis et ipsius **ueritatis** intuitu ut Scripturae Sacrae post Christianum nobis interpretem translatae potius quam Iudaicis interpretationibus uel chronographorum imperitiae, fidem accommodare disceret, digito ostendens quod Eusebius in descriptione temporum neque **hebraicam ueritatem** neque LXX translatorum per omnia sit editionem secutus.[37]

(In this work [*On Times*], the sequence of years was given according to the **Hebrew Truth**; this is far shorter than the Septuagint, so that up to the Advent of the Savior in the flesh, five thousand years were not completed. And I believe that I advised, in consideration of fraternal charity and **truth** itself, that credence be given to the Holy Scripture as it is translated by our Christian translator [Jerome], rather than to Jewish translators [Septuagint], or the ignorance of chronographers, pointing out how Eusebius in his designation of times followed neither the **Hebrew Truth** nor the Septuagint in every instance.)[38] (my emphasis added)

Taking a clever rhetorical turn, which again he inherits from Jerome, Bede is able to elevate the Hebrew Truth while at the same time distancing himself from the Jews.[39] The Hebrew Bible is not the suspect Jewish text: the Septuagint is.

Bede also learned from Jerome that one cannot completely denigrate the Jews if one is to rely on the authority of the Hebrew text. Bede quotes Jerome's commentary on Isaiah to counter the hypothetical objection that the Jews may have maliciously altered their texts to deceive Christians; picking up Jerome's rhetoric here and below, Bede contrasts the notion of the truth (*ueritas*) and specifically the *hebraica ueritas* with what is falsified or mendacious: "Quod si aliquis dixerit Hebraeos libros postea a Iudaeis esse **falsatos**, eosque dum nostris inuident auctoritatem sibi abstulisse **ueritatem**, audiat Origenem ..." (Should anyone say that the

---

37 Bede, *Epistola ad Pleguinam*, ed. Jones, 617–26.
38 Wallis, trans., *Bede: The Reckoning of Time*, 406.
39 For a study of Bede's ambiguous portrayal of the Jews, see Scheil, *The Footsteps of Israel*, 30–97.

Hebrew books were **falsified** later on by the Jews and that they, when they begrudge authority to us, deprive themselves of the **truth**, let them listen to Origen ...), who demonstrates that this cannot be the case.[40] Bede cites the Jewish historian Josephus, who verifies the shorter chronological figures and the fact that the Jews did not falsify the texts, and Jerome: "Audiat beatum Hieronimum quod non Hebraeos sed Graecos codices dicat esse **falsatos**" (Let him listen to the blessed Jerome who says that the Greek, and not the Hebrew manuscripts are **false**).[41] Finally, Bede directly invokes the trials Jerome suffered as a result of his translation from the Hebrew as a model for himself:

> Quippe qui in tam necessaria diuinae Scripturae translatione paene a Latinis simul et Hebraeis est lapidibus oppressus – ab Hebraeis quidem quod eis inridendi Christianos et calumniandi pro codicibus **mendosis** occasio foret ablata; a Latinis autem quod noua eis et insolita tam etsi meliora pro ueteribus ingererentur et solitis.[42]

> (Indeed, on account of such a necessary translation of Holy Scriptures, [Jerome] was pelted with stones by both the Latins and the Hebrews, almost at the same time – by the Hebrews, because he robbed them of the opportunity to mock and revile the Christians on account of their **fallacious** books, by the Latins because he had introduced new and unfamiliar, albeit better, things in place of old and familiar ones.)[43]

Although forging his own path, Bede envisions himself following in the footsteps of Jerome's persecution, even by fellow Christians, for introducing material that is "new and unfamiliar, albeit better." In his later, much longer *De temporum ratione* Bede more explicitly draws attention to the novelty of his enterprise: "Should anyone be annoyed that I have presumed to try my hand at this subject, since I have labored to confect a new work out of what can be found scattered here and there in the writings of the ancients, then let him listen to what St Augustine says, 'It is necessary

---

40 Bede, *Epistola ad Pleguinam*, 620; Wallis, trans., *Bede: The Reckoning of Time*, 409.
41 Bede, *Epistola ad Pleguinam*, 621; Wallis, trans., *Bede: The Reckoning of Time*, 410.
42 Bede, *Epistola ad Pleguinam*, 623.
43 Wallis, trans., *Bede: The Reckoning of Time*, 412.

that many men make many books ....'"[44] When discussing his conception of world chronology, Bede is forced to acknowledge the newness of the undertaking, which he justifies by citing his adherence to the truth. The tradition – even the well-worn path of the fathers – cannot be followed when it is shown to be erroneous.

In the *Letter to Plegwine*, Bede is further able to muster Augustine in support of his case. Quoting *The City of God,* Bede makes the reasonable, philological claim that when disagreement is found between two texts "ei linguae potius credatur unde est in aliam per interpretes facta translatio" (greater faith should be put in [the version] in the language from which the translation was made into another language by translators).[45] Although in principle Augustine supported the Septuagint over Jerome's new translation, he had to admit that in a case of disagreement, the text in the original language should be preferred.[46] This concession on Augustine's part is significant because the Septuagint carried the weight of tradition and, in some circles, divine inspiration. Over the course of his writings, Augustine generally sides with the Septuagint. Bede, however, is able to cherry-pick evidence to obscure the division on this issue between two of the most important Latin Fathers and use both in support of his own argument.

In the letter, Bede builds a rhetorical tour-de-force in defence of the Hebrew Truth and his reliance on it. He concludes by placing himself among the noble crowd of authorities whom he has cited to support his reliance on the Hebrew and rhetorically brackets this list with the words "Hebrew Truth" and "Hebrew language" (in bold):

Agnoscas etiam ... qua ipse auctoritate assertionem meae computationis astruam: **hebraica** uidelicet, **ueritate**, per Originem prodita, per Hieronymum edita, per Augustinum laudata, et per Iosephum confirmata. Quibus ego in rebus talibus non ullos inuenio doctiores. Neque autem mirandum, laudabilem uirum Eusebium, quamuis miro sapiendi dicendique ingenio testam

---

44   Wallis, trans., *Bede: The Reckoning of Time*, 4; "Si quem sane uel illud offendit cur aliquid de huiusmodi negotio temptare praesumpserim, quare de his quae sparsim in ueterum scriptis inueniri potuerant ipse nouum opus condere studuerim, audiat dicente sancto Augustino quia ideo necesse est plures a pluribus fieri libros..." *De temporum ratione*, ed. Jones, 265.

45   Bede, *Epistola ad Pleguinam*, 622; Wallis, trans., *Bede: The Reckoning of Time*, 410.

46   Goodwin, *Take Hold of the Robe of a Jew*, 78–94.

ferrumque, ut dicitur, conglutinare ualeret, non ualere tamen quod non didicerat, hoc est, **hebraeam** scire **linguam**.[47]

(For you should know … by what authority I build the assertion of my computation: namely by the **Hebrew Truth**, recorded by Origen, published by Jerome, praised by Augustine, confirmed by Josephus. I have found none more learned in such matters than these. Nor is it to be wondered at that that praiseworthy man, Eusebius, although he was able, as they say, to bind iron and brick by his marvelous talent in speaking and thinking, nevertheless could not do what he had not learned to do, that is, to know the **Hebrew language**.)[48]

Bede places himself among this group of "the most learned on these matters" who support the Hebrew Truth, a group of scholars he ranks more highly than Eusebius, excluded for the singular reason that he did not know Hebrew. The rhetorical implication looms large that the other scholars, including Bede, know Hebrew so that their opinions concerning the Old Testament carry much more weight. The charges of heresy brought against Bede, such as they were, are wrong-headed because they are due to ignorance of the Hebrew language. Of course, when we think of eighth-century Northumbria – or all of Western Europe, even – we generally imagine that ignorance of Hebrew was widespread, if not universal. This is not how Bede imagines the situation. Like Jerome, Bede is confident enough in his understanding of Hebrew, and its special claim to truth, to draw a line in the sand: he places himself squarely on one side, backed up by Jerome, Augustine, Origen, and Josephus, in opposition to the praiseworthy – though ultimately misguided – Eusebius, the Jews who translated the Septuagint, and the foolish monk who accused Bede of heresy.

It has long been established that Bede's knowledge of Hebrew is derivative and that all his information can be traced primarily to the Latin texts of Jerome. Sourcing passages, however, should not be an end in itself. The fact that the question of Bede's knowledge of Hebrew was ever raised is suggestive of the historical perception of his acquaintance with Hebrew and how deep and frequent his borrowings from Jerome are. Furthermore, not all of Bede's references to Hebrew can be classified as

---

47 Bede, *Epistola ad Pleguinam*, 625.
48 Wallis, trans., *Bede: The Reckoning of Time*, 414.

simply derivative. Most of Bede's information originates with Jerome, but he uses it to make his own observations about the Bible on the basis of his understanding of the Hebrew language. A modern conception of what constitutes knowledge of a language ought not to obscure the value of the texts examined here as evidence for language contact by medieval readers. Bede, following Jerome, insists on the importance of Hebrew in biblical study; in doing so, he presents Hebrew as accessible even in the farthest corner of the earth. But in addition to following and proclaiming the importance of Jerome's translation, Bede was also a trailblazer himself. As recent scholarship has shown, the old image of Bede – which originates with Bede himself – merely following in the footsteps of the fathers must be taken with a healthy grain of salt. The fact that Bede made a point of engaging with texts and subjects in a way no previous church father had, shows he was not simply a compiler. This is patently clear when considering the role of Hebrew in his exegesis and its importance in his study of the calendar. Standing on Jerome's shoulders and waving the flag of the Hebrew Truth, Bede traced new paths of Christian scholarship, even proposing a new date for the age of the world. And he could dismiss those who disagreed with him because they were ignorant of Hebrew.

4 Building Anti-Semitism in Bede

KATHY LAVEZZO

As Nicholas Howe has observed, despite Bede's fame as a writer deeply invested in questions of time and date, "throughout Bede's writing there runs an abiding concern with ideas of place."[1] The Northumbrian scholar famous for his contributions to calculating the date of Easter, chronicle writing, and the adoption of the *anno domini* method, also emphasized issues of geography and location.[2] For example, Bede's work on dating had a crucial spatial dimension: the *computus* mapped the communal identity of the faithful via its shared observance of Easter throughout Christian territories.[3] And, in Bede's renowned chronicle, the marginal positioning of Britain "on the mental map of Christendom" in the *Ecclesiastical History of the English People* (hereafter *EH*) performs a key structural role in his account of historical action, shifting the vantage point of one surveying Christendom from a Roman gazing upon the distant northern land of the Britons to an Anglo-Saxon "looking from the island south towards Rome and the remains of the old empire."[4]

For Howe, Bede's cultural geography is particularly noteworthy for its emphasis on natural spaces, on landscapes and topographies, as opposed to man-made places. For example, through an extended discussion of English landscape in the *EH*, Howe shows how Bede offers his readers not only "a deep geographical setting for historical exposition" but also

---

1 Howe, *Writing the Map*, 126.
2 Ibid.
3 On the *computus* see also Edson, *Mapping Time and Space*.
4 Howe, *Writing the Map*, 133.

an environmental rationale for historical change.[5] The sheer fertility and plenitude of Britain was what brought Britons, Romans, Saxons and others to the island. Howe's analysis of natural locations in Bede comprises part of a larger argument on how the Anglo-Saxons tended to devalue built environments as spiritually void and ephemeral material entities, turning instead to embrace natural locations. Drawing evidence from architecture as well as poetry, chronicles, wills and charters, Howe shows that the Anglo-Saxons admired "the land itself, the work of God's creation ... far more than ... anything built on the land," such as homes, churches, and halls.[6] That dismissal of built environments responded not simply to the physical unreliability of such structures, which often were constructed from impermanent and flammable wood, but also to the God-centred thrust of Christian thinking. Even the vaunted built environment of the mead-hall falls below the divine standard achieved during God's work of creation.[7] Even the use of "home" or *ham* in the vernacular poetry of the period resonates with a sense of "earthly transience" that "gains pathos from its accompanying faith in heavenly permanence."[8] For the Anglo-Saxons, buildings made of wood or even stone become inconsequential in light of both divine creation and the final, otherworldly destination which members of the faithful piously anticipated.

Interpreted in one way, the Anglo-Saxon rejection of built environments is laudable and even poignant, insofar as it bolstered an early medieval people enduring war, famine, disease, slavery, a harsh climate, and a low life expectancy. At the same time, however, if we turn from the community of Anglo-Saxon Christians to their religious others, we see how that embrace of spirituality had certain disturbing aspects, which emerged from the origins of Christian discourse in Pauline hermeneutics. Because Christians "are not in the realm of the flesh but are in the realm of the Spirit," as Paul claimed in Romans 8:9, they supplant the carnal aspects of Judaism – e.g., the physical inscription of the body via circumcision – with new and superior spiritual counterparts.[9] Paul's interpretive method proved so influential that Christianity emerged as a religion whose very coherence hinged on its supposed supersession of a Jewish carnality, literalism, and materialism.

---

5 Howe, *Writing the Map*, 141.
6 Howe, *Writing the Map*, 50–1.
7 Neville, *Representations of the Natural World*, 37, 62–74.
8 Howe, *Writing the Map*, 47.
9 Biblical citations are from the New International Version.

From an architectural standpoint, this meant that Judaism was associated with physical, built environments that were supplanted in Christianity by "higher" mystical locales such as the living church of Christian souls and the heavenly Jerusalem. Consider, for example, Augustine's *City of God*, which takes as its controlling figure the typological celebration of a new, Christian Jerusalem – the City of God that is "above," "on high," "free," and "mother of us all" – that is foreshadowed by historical Jerusalem.[10] The subordinate status of the terrestrial Jerusalem emerges starkly in *City of God* 18.45, where Augustine interprets Haggai 2:9, "Greater shall be the glory of this latter house than of the former" (Magna erit gloria domus istius novissimae, plus quam primae).[11] Augustine writes that when the Jews rebuilt the temple in Jerusalem after their return from exile in Babylon, they thought that their reconstruction fulfilled Haggai's prophecy. But, Augustine claims, the Jews were wrong to interpret literally Haggai, who looked towards not so much the rebuilding of the historical temple as the building with living stones of a church "far more glorious than that temple was which was built by King Solomon, and restored after the captivity" (longe gloriosior quam templum illud fuit quod a rege Salomone constructum est et post captivitatem instauratum).[12] This is not to say that Augustine fails to admire the Jerusalem temple, which he refers to in XVII.3 as Solomon's "most magnificent temple" and in XVII.8 as "that highly renowned temple" (nobilissimum templum; templum illud ... excellentissime diffamatum).[13] Nevertheless, however excellent and noble the temple may be, far more glorious is the Christian church, composed of living stones.

In their inability to read Haggai correctly, Augustine's Jews join in the debasement of their temple. Like the physical temple, the "populis ... carnalis" or carnal people of the Jews are subordinated to a physical sphere, supplanted by mystical Christian truths.[14] Moreover, Augustine claims, the Jews are punished for their literal-mindedness by losing the capacity to tell the future altogether: because they linked Haggai's "latter house"

---

10 Augustine, *The City of God Against the Pagans*, trans. Levine, Vol. 4, XV.18–19; cf. Gal. 4:21ff and Heb: 8.8–10. Those passages from Augustine are cited and discussed in Meyer, *Medieval Allegory and the Building of the New Jerusalem*, 63.

11 *The City of God*, trans. Greene, vol. 6, 40–1.

12 Ibid.

13 *The City of God*, trans. Sanford and Green, vol. 5, 218–19; 278–9.

14 *The City of God*, trans. Greene, vol. 6, 40–1.

to the reconstructed temple, "that people had no prophets from that time on" (nec prophetas ex illo tempore habuit illa gens).[15] Here, the special, if somewhat fraught, relation to time enjoyed by the Old Testament Jews diminishes alongside their special relation to place. Personages like Haggai impart to biblical Jews a privileged relation to time because of their ability to prophesy (although the messages of these prophets are often misunderstood by the Jews, according to Augustine). Solomon's temple, the dwelling of none other than God, endows the Jews with a privileged relation to space. But when the Jews described by Augustine overinvest in and mistakenly glorify that carnal space, they lose their ability to foretell the future. The temple thus proves pivotal to the history of the Jews' declining relationship with God, who ceases to bestow on them the gift of prophecy.

Bede, in one of his fifty homilies on the gospels, also uses architecture to connote Jewish carnality. The sermon focuses on a pericope or gospel passage from Luke in which the evangelist recounts how, after the crucifixion, Mary Magdalene and other women wishing to anoint Christ's corpse with spices "found the stone rolled away from the tomb, and on entering they did not find the body of the Lord Jesus" (Inuenerunt autem … lapidem reuolutum a monumento et ingressae non inuenerunt corpus domini Iesu).[16] As Bede does throughout his homilies, he teases out several meanings of the passage for his fellow monks. Bede's multi-level exegesis begins with the historical sense, by reminding his readers that Matthew's gospel "tells us that an angel came down from heaven and rolled the stone away from the mouth of the tomb"; the angel, Bede stresses, did not move the stone to "make a way for the Lord to go out, but so that the open and empty space of the tomb might divulge to human beings that he had risen again" (the full quotation reads: Notum iuxta historiam est narrante euangelista Matheo quia descendens de caelo angelus reuoluit lapidem ab ostio monumenti non quidem ut exeunte domino uiam faceret sed ut apertus uacuusque monumenti locus hominibus eum resurrexisse proderet).[17] Jewishness then enters into Bede's hermeneutics as he begins to consider the spiritual meaning of the passage. Employing the pericope to assert the supersession of Judaism by Christianity, Bede writes that, "mystically, the

---

15 Ibid. Augustine focuses on the end of Jewish prophets in this chapter, but he also points to the Jews' oppression "with many plagues by kings of alien race, and by the Romans themselves" as another indicator of their incorrect reading of Haggai's prophecy.

16 Bede, Homily II.10, ed. Hurst, 247; trans. Martin-Hurst, 90.

17 Bede, Homily II.10, ed. Hurst, 247; trans. Martin-Hurst, 90.

rolling away of the stone implies the disclosure of the divine sacraments, which were formerly hidden and closed up by the letter of the law. The law was written on stone."[18] Echoing Paul's contrast of letter and spirit, Bede's interpretation of the rolling away of the stone thus construes Christianity as the revelation of a higher, spiritual order that displaces and supplants a Jewish law that is carnal – written "on tablets of stone" (2 Corinthians 3:3) – and bound to a literal and earthly sensibility.

Bede's denigration of "Jewish" literalism and carnality centers on an architectural feature, the stone over the tomb, whose removal Bede links to the "stripping away of the Old Law." Bede thus ties the built environment of the tomb and the carved-in-stone laws of Judaism to an obsolete physicality. The usual function of a sepulcher – to enclose and protect the body of a dead person – does not pertain to Christ, whose resurrection rendered the built environment unnecessary. Moreover, Christ's triumph over the physical world and mortality is such that he didn't need his tomb opened by an angel to depart from it. The angel turns away the stone not to assist Jesus but to disclose his resurrection. Instead of sheltering Christ, the empty tomb manifests Christ's transcendence of material objects like tombs. The tomb thus morphs from quotidian sepulcher into a vehicle of faith.

Members of the Christian faithful, Bede continues, mystically reenact the work performed by the angel: "[w]hen we acknowledge our faith in the Lord's passion and resurrection, his tomb, which had been closed, is opened up" (Etenim et nobis singulis cum fidem dominicae passionis et resurrectionis agnouimus monumentum profecto illius quod clausum fuerat apertum est).[19] In contrast, Jews and pagans "continue to be like a tomb still closed by a stone."[20] While Bede addresses both pagans and Jews in this passage, the function of the latter group as his primary focus emerges in his reference in the next line to the *duritia* or hardness of their unbelief, which prevents them "from becoming aware that a dead person, who has destroyed death's right of entry and has already passed into

---

18 Ibid.

19 Ibid.

20 See the full quotation in Bede, Homily II.10: ed. Hurst, 247–8; trans. Martin-Hurst, 90–1: "Ac uero Iudaeus ac paganus qui mortem quidem redemptoris nostri quam credunt inrident triumphum uero resurrectionis eius prorsus credere recusant quasi clausum lapide adhuc monumentum permanet nec ualent ingredi ut ablatum resurgendo corpus domini respiciant."

the heights of the heavens, cannot be found on earth."[21] Even by Bede's time, the idea of the ossified or stone-like heart of the Jew was a familiar anti-Semitic trope. As an inanimate and hard entity that, according to classical and medieval authorities, occupied the bottom rung of the Great Chain of Being, and as the material on which the Ten Commandments were written, stone served as a popular means of characterizing Judaism as a lethal and debasing investment in the letter of the law over the spirit. In Jeffrey Cohen's words, "rock seems as inhuman a substance as can be found."[22] This "geological" component of medieval anti-Semitism flourished in Anglo-Saxon writings.[23] Bede characterizes the Jew as hard- or stone-hearted repeatedly in his works.[24] In the case of the Luke homily, he develops the stereotype by adding to the duality of the superseded stone tablets and hard heart a stone structure associated with death, the tomb. In Bede's homily, while Christians mystically open Christ's tomb anew, Jews become like tombs themselves. The provision of shelter – even for a corpse – is normally beneficial; but here, architectural enclosure connotes a hardness of unbelief that renders the Jew akin to the space abandoned by Christ.[25]

Bede's likening of Jews to the closed and lethal space of a tomb is undeniably offensive. But, as Andrew Scheil has shown, there is much more than anti-Semitism to Bede's approach to Jews.[26] At the same time that Bede denigrated contemporary Jews as sepulchers, he evinced an unprecedented appreciation for buildings associated with biblical Jews, i.e., the holy sanctuaries of the Hebrew bible. Epitomizing Bede's interest in biblical spaces are three exegetical works: *On the Tabernacle* (ca. 721–5), an interpretation of the account in Exodus 24:12–30:21 of the erection of

---

21 See further, ibid.: "quia duritia suae infidelitatis repelluntur ne animaduertant quia non potest in terris mortuus inueniri qui destructo mortis aditu iam caelorum alta penetrauit."

22 Cohen, "Stories of Stone," 58. Cohen's recent publication, *Stone*, inverts received thinking on stones through an ecological inquiry that sheds light on lithic liveliness.

23 Scheil, *The Footsteps of Israel*, 46.

24 Cf. Bede, *Commentary on the Acts of the Apostles*, 7:58.158–60, 76; Scheil, *The Footsteps of Israel*, 40–1.

25 Scheil offers a valuable discussion of the aesthetics of Bede's hermeneutics in the passage on the tombstone (ibid., 32–3).

26 Scheil, *The Footsteps of Israel*, 67. Scheil stresses not simply collecting Anglo-Saxon authors like Bede into a grand tale of Jewish oppression, but understanding "the humanity" that informs anti-Judaic writings (5).

the Mosaic tabernacle; *On the Temple* (ca. 729–31), on the description in *3 Kings* 5:1–7:51 of Solomon's erection of the Temple of Jerusalem; and *On Ezra and Nehemiah* (ca. 725–31), on Ezra-Nehemiah's portrayal of the post-exilic construction of the Second Temple.[27] Those texts mark an important achievement in the history of Christian exegesis. Before Bede, no author had undertaken a full-scale interpretation of any biblical built environment. The "first Christian exegete to produce complete verse-by-verse commentaries on these subjects," Bede broke "new ground" in the history of Christian exegesis.[28]

In *On the Tabernacle*, *On the Temple*, and *On Ezra and Nehemiah*, Bede reads Old Testament sanctuaries as figures for a variety of Christian "structures" associated with "the past, present and future states of the Ecclesia" including: Christ as cornerstone, the living church of the faithful on earth, the sanctuaries created in the heart of individual pious persons, and the heavenly Jerusalem. Thus, ironically, at the same time that Bede connotes the useless space of the sepulchral Jew in his Easter homily, he demonstrates in his exegetical works the utility of biblical Jewish spaces in "building up" symbolic Christian locations. Alongside the idea of the lethal and barren Jew-as-tomb, Bede suggests the fecundity of biblical Jewish spaces, from which a plethora of Christian meanings proliferate.

Bede's reference to the sepulchral Jew appears in a single line in a homily, while his works on biblical sanctuaries figure prominently in his vast corpus of writings. The disparity between the amounts of text Bede devoted to contemporary Jews and to biblical Jewish buildings might urge us to jettison the former as irrelevant to the latter. However, putting those two notions alongside each other heightens our understanding of just how fraught and contradictory Bede's stance on Jews and Christians was. Like his use of the closed tomb to connote a stubborn attachment to a lethal and defunct "Jewish" carnality, Bede's stress in his architectural allegories on the supremacy of the spiritual buildings of Christianity attributes to Jews an outmoded materialism. For example, in one of two sermons Bede wrote on the dedication of a church, he contrasts Solomon's Temple with Anglo-Saxon churches and Christian souls. Glossing John 10:23, Bede writes that

---

27 On the dating of *In Ezram et Neemiam*, see DeGregorio, "Introduction," *On Ezra and Nehemiah*, trans. and ed. DeGregorio, xlii. On the dating of *De Tabernaculo*, see Holder, "Introduction," *On the Tabernacle*, trans. and ed. Holder, xvi. On the dating of *De Templo*, see O'Reilly, "Introduction," *On the Temple*, trans. and ed. Connolly, xvii.

28 DeGregorio, "Bede and the Old Testament," 136, 131.

if Christ "chose to walk in the temple, where the flesh and blood of brute animals used to be offered, much more will he rejoice to visit our house of prayer, where the sacrament of his own body and blood is celebrated" (Si ergo ambulare uoluit in templo in quo caro et sanguis brutorum animalium offerebatur, multo magis nostram orationis domum ubi carnis ipsius ac sanguinis sacramenta celebrantur uisitare gaudebit).[29] Bede goes on to write that even as the Christian sacrifice celebrated in an Anglo-Saxon church renders it a greater source of delight than Solomon's temple, most privileged of all are the living stones or *lapides uiui* of Christian souls, who are "more fully" God's temple than any physical house of prayer whether Jewish or Christian.[30] Echoing Peter's idea that Christians are "as living stones built up, a spiritual house" (1 Peter 2:5), Bede elevates the Christian house of God over its Jewish predecessor. While the biblical sanctuaries discussed in Bede's works might seem at first glance to be diametrically opposed to the tomb-like space of the contemporary Jew, they all occupy a continuum of claims regarding the Christian supersession of Judaism.

In what remains of this essay, I consider how, for all their stress on spirituality, Bede's writings on Jewish space expose a host of Christian materialisms. In his recent reading of "the Jew" in *The Merchant of Venice*, David Nirenberg speaks to such materialisms, noting how the very "areas of human life – letter, law, flesh –" stigmatized by supersession are "difficult to transcend in this world." In the case of Bede's exegeses, in tension with his stress on the temple as an interpretive vehicle for grasping Christian spiritualisms which supplant that physical built environment, are aspects of his architectural exegeses that reveal the charged coexistence, confusion, conflation, and interdependence of matter and spirit. Indeed, for Bede, not only do "Jewish" materialisms prove "difficult to transcend," but also they emerge as highly desirable. An unstable and contradictory dynamic, of course, characterizes virtually all Christian rhetorics of supersession as they emerge in typological readings of the Old Testament. As critics such as Jill Robbins and Steven Kruger demonstrate, Christian hermeneutics always register the value of the "old" Jewish perspectives they claim

---

29   Bede, Homily II.24, *Homiliarum evangelii libri II*: ed. Hurst, 358–9; trans. *Homilies on the Gospels. Book Two: Lent to the Dedication of the Church*, Martin-Hurst, 241–2.

30   Cf. ibid., "Necque enim putandum est quia domus solummodo in qua ad orandum uel ad mysteria celebranda conuenimus templum sit domini et non ipsi qui in nomine domini conuenimus multo amplius templum eius et appellemur et simus."

31   Nirenberg, "Shakespeare's Jewish Question," *Renaissance Drama* ns 38 (2010): 77–113, at 78.

to supplant.[32] Christian spirituality never truly trumps its Jewish material counterpart; rather the material dimensions of Jewish historical life persist in the "new," figural interpretation. In his "Figura," Erich Auerbach suggests such an interrelation, writing that "[f]igural prophecy implies the interpretation of one worldly event through another; the first signifies the second, the second fulfills the first. Both remain historical events; yet both, looked at in this way, have something provisional and incomplete about them; they point to one another."[33] Auerbach's words suggest the dialectical and therefore interdependent quality of the Christian-Jewish analogies generated in hermeneutic works like *On the Temple, On the Tabernacle* and *On Ezra and Nehemiah*. In how the material of the temple and its Christian meanings "point to one another," we see how the figural turn is always incomplete.

While this hermeneutic instability always informs Christian readings of the Old Testament, it seems to especially emerge in Bede, whose investment in the temple and tabernacle extends beyond the appropriations of allegory to a noteworthy interest in the those structures as literal edifices. As Charles Jones points out, Bede, throughout his architectural exegesis, "has a master's interest in the literal meaning despite his preacher's aim to surmount it."[34] Haunting Bede's celebration of Christian living stones, temple hearts, and even the heavenly Jerusalem is his undeniable fascination with the materiality of Jewish built environments. Importantly, however, Bede never overtly affirms those materialisms, thanks to his fraught relationship to "the Jew." The writer can't make too explicit his investment in literal space, because such an embrace of matter would risk evacuating Christianity of its unique status and exposing Christian ties to a prior "Jewish" literalism. Yet by attending to the uneasy transmission of "Jewish" materialisms to Anglo-Saxon England, we can, at times, uncover telling moments that both problematize claims about the Anglo-Saxon dismissal of built environments, and dismantle the stereotype of

---

32 Robbins, *Prodigal Son, Elder Brother*; Kruger, *The Spectral Jew*.

33 Auerbach, "Figura," 58. As Howe observes, Auerbach's theory of *figura* insists "that each event must be treated as actual, as within 'the stream of historical life,' and not as a mere idea or concept" ("The Figural Presence of Erich Auerbach," 139); thanks belong to Andrew Scheil for drawing my attention to this piece. We should also note, with Howe, that as a Jewish émigré writing in the late 1930s, Auerbach "had a political and moral responsibility in the late 1930s to assert the continuing presence of the historical events of the Hebrew bible and thus of the Jewish people" (ibid., 139–40).

34 Jones, "Some Introductory Remarks," 157. See also DeGregorio, "Introduction," *On Ezra and Nehemiah*, xxi.

the tomb-like Jew. Ultimately, if we look carefully at Bede's works, we discover an image of the lithic and enclosed Christian that collides with and demolishes the fantasy of the sepulchral Jew.

I: Bede's Virtual Temples

The construction of both the tabernacle and the temple mark, in Scott DeGregorio's words, "a critical phase of development in God's covenantal relationship with Israel."[35] Because Bede lived during a similarly foundational moment in the relationship between God and man in England, the example of the Israelite's literal erection of God's house was apt.[36] Important evidence of this historical motivation emerges in the fact that Bede wrote his three major works on holy sanctuaries while he was composing his most famous work, the *EH*. Taken together, those texts situate the spiritual "building" of the church in England in relation to God's overall providential plan, as figured in the making of the sanctuaries of the Old Testament.[37] Bede's portrayal of Christianity pointed not only to the pivotal historical moment those texts engage, but also to the spatial aspect of the Old Testament passages, with their focus on idealized built environments. The architectural coherence, organic unity, and structural solidity of the tabernacle and temple often serve in his exegetical works as prompts for discussing best practices for the creation of a strong Anglo-Saxon church.[38] Demonstrating Bede's view that God's human agents in England had in many respects failed to help create a strong "living" church, works like *On the Temple* comment on the failings of Anglo-Saxon religious leaders and advocate for reform. The strength and cohesion of Jewish sanctuaries serve for Bede as figures for early Christian evangelizers who, as firm "pillars" of the faith, exemplify how a reformed Anglo-Saxon church should behave.[39]

---

35 DeGregorio, "Bede and the Old Testament," 136.

36 Ibid.

37 DeGregorio, "Bede and the Old Testament," 136–7; Mayr-Harting, *The Venerable Bede*, 13; O'Reilly, "Introduction," *On the Temple*, trans. Connolly, xxxv.

38 Holder, "Allegory," 120.

39 Cf. *De Templo* 18.4, 18.5 18.7, 18.16 (Bede, *De tabernacvlo, De templo, In Ezram et Neemiam*, ed. Hurst CCSL 119A [Turnholt: Brepols, 1969], 198–200, 205–6; *On the Temple*, trans. Connolly, 74–6, 83–4. Further citations of *De Templo* will cite book, chapter, and section numbers followed by page numbers in Hurst and Connolly. On Bede's reformist stress on strong pillars of the church, see O'Reilly, "Introduction," *On the Temple*, trans. Connolly, xxxix–xlvi; and DeGregorio, "Bede and the Old Testament," 137–9.

While Bede's interest in spiritual cohesion, permanence, and strength helps to explain his architectural focus, we would be wrong to play down the material side of the equation when considering what drew him to write about the temple and tabernacle. After all, both the temple and tabernacle were the most exalted buildings-qua-buildings in human history, edifices whose physical components and form were dictated by God, as recorded by scripture. The tabernacle and temple were not only designed by a divine architect, they also served as divine sanctuaries. Composed of stone like the tomb of Christ discussed in Bede's Easter homily, but hardly empty, the temple merits attention due to its status as nothing less than the *domus dei* or "house of God."[40] Similarly, the tabernacle served as the mobile home for God before the building of the first and second temples. The holy sanctuaries thus embody how, during the time of the Old Law, faith was bound up with a certain material, geographic, and communal exclusivity: only in Jewish spaces did God reside, only Jews could enjoy a physical proximity to the divine.

Christians had grounds to view biblical sanctuaries as possessed of an enviable material privilege, because their worship spaces, medieval churches, neither were designed by God nor hosted God in the manner of the temple or tabernacle. But there are other reasons why an Anglo-Saxon such as Bede might have had special cause to admire the materiality of the temple and tabernacle. For while Jews enjoyed an exalted physical *intimacy* with the divine the Anglo-Saxons' relationship with the faith was characterized by geographic *isolation*, thanks to their habitation of the island of Britain. Who better, then, to admire the exalted materiality of the temple – and the divinity of both its design and occupant – than a monk living in the hinterland of God's new Christian kingdom, far from holy centers such as Jerusalem, where God once deigned to dwell, and Rome, the seat of Christianity? Bede's keen awareness of Anglo-Saxon isolation emerges repeatedly in his writings. The *EH* opens with an account of Britain/Albion as *Oceani insula*, i.e., an island located in the oceanic border thought to encircle the known world, and goes on to elaborate English isolation "on a grand scale, both as an exegetical theme and a narrative device, using classical, biblical and patristic concepts of centre and periphery."[41] The *EH* makes clear Bede's interest in understanding Anglo-Saxon insularity and isolation in relation to the centrality of Christendom's Roman centre. But

---

40 *De Templo*, 1.1.1: ed. Hurst, 147; trans. Connolly, 5.
41 Bede, *HE*, 1.1; O'Reilly, "Islands and Idols at the ends of the earth," 119.

Bede also was attuned to the geographic differences between his isolated people and God's chosen people, who possessed built environments shaped by and inhabited by God.

Bede's concern over the radical spatial differences between biblical Jews and Anglo-Saxon Christians appears, not coincidentally, in the same Easter homily in which he likens Jewish unbelievers to sepulchers closed by stones. Near the end of that sermon, citing Isaiah 11:10, Bede writes that Jesus is the root of Jesse whom the "nations will entreat … because by the grace of his visitation he has summoned not the Jews alone, but us too, who are able to cry out to him from the ends of the earth."[42] Here Bede juxtaposes England's location in the world with that of the Jews and their biblical homeland. The homily very much concerns Jerusalem as a religious centre, i.e., as the place where Christ lived, died, and revealed his divinity via resurrection.[43] Immediately after this Bede discusses the holy places of contemporary Jerusalem, drawing on Adomnán; he then turns to Isaiah 11:10 and alludes to the location of his auditors on "the ends of the earth." Sensitive to the privileged status of Jerusalem and the great distance of the English from that holy capital, Bede stresses the "democratization" of space under Christianity. Christ, Bede writes, summons "not the Jews alone, but us too," e.g., Anglo-Saxons who live far from Jerusalem, who "cry out to him from the ends of the earth." Geography, Bede assures his readers and auditors, doesn't undermine Christian spirituality. While God interacted with a single people associated with the circumscribed space of Jerusalem during the time of the Old Law, Christianity radically remaps the faith, allowing for its miraculous spread throughout the earth, even to its outlying regions.

Bede's architectural allegories connote this remapping of the faith by reading the tabernacle and temple as structures that look towards and are superseded by Christian "buildings" whose mystical nature renders them mobile and thus accessible to anyone on earth, even the far-flung Anglo-Saxons.[44] By meticulously linking Christian mystical "buildings" to biblical

---

42 "ipsum gentes deprecabuntur quia non solum Iudaeos sed et nos qui de finibus terrae ad eum clamare nouimus gratia suae uisitationis aduocauit," Bede, Homily II.10: ed. Hurst, 252; trans. Martin-Hurst, 96.

43 Ibid., ed. Hurst, 251–2; trans. Martin-Hurst, 94–6.

44 Paul was one of the first writers to render the temple a figure of incorporation rather than exclusivity. For example, in Ephesians 2:19–22 and 1 Peter 2:6–8, Paul "enlarge[s] 'access to a deity'" so as "to transcend local ethnic boundaries" (Whitehead, *Castles of the Mind*, 10).

sanctuaries, Bede affirms that Christians, even though they have neither a material temple nor access to God in the manner of the biblical Jews, nevertheless enjoy on earth – and can anticipate in the afterlife – a spiritual relationship to the divine, via the mystical sanctuaries of a church composed of the "living stones" of the faithful joined together by Christ, "the uniquely chosen and precious cornerstone" presaged in Isaiah 28:16 (lapidis angularis singulariter electi et pretiosi).[45] Supersession in Bede's writing allows him to bring virtual versions of the temple and tabernacle to Britain, and serves as a means of overcoming Anglo-Saxon marginality even as it raises the problem of a twinned investment in material privilege and geographic centrality. In other words, problematizing the spiritual thrust of Bede's exegesis is its basis in both an appreciation of literal Jewish spaces and an anxiety over the literal place of England in the world.

Bede remaps the faith by transforming the material particulars of the temple and tabernacle into signs of the miraculous expansion of Christianity over space. Developing an idea from Gregory the Great, Bede stresses the transcendence of geographic borders, signified through verbs like *dilatare* (spread out, extend, dilate) and *diffundere* (spread or pour out).[46] Frequently in *On the Tabernacle*, when he comes across sets of four, Bede links the discrete space of the tabernacle to the vast space constituted by the entirety of a four-cornered earth.[47] Writers had long described the tabernacle as a window into the organization and shape of the world.[48] But Bede goes beyond earlier works by embedding in the tabernacle mystical meanings which permit that signifier of Jewish privilege, paradoxically, to signify a Christian incorporation that had special resonance for the Anglo-Saxon border of a Rome-centred Christian imperium. For example, Bede

---

45 *De Templo* 1.1.1: ed. Hurst, 147; trans. Connolly, 5.

46 Cf. *De Tabernaculo* 2: ed. Hurst, 77; trans. Holder, 86; ibid., 2.12: ed. Hurst, 82; trans. Holder, 93; *De Templo* 1.5: ed. Hurst, 158; trans. Connolly, 19. See Bede's citation of Gregory's *Pastoral Care*, 2.11, in *De Tabernaculo*, 1.4 and 1.6: ed. Hurst, 16 and 24; trans. Holder, 14 and 25. See also Bede's invocation of Paul, Rom. 15:19 (on the geographic spread of Christianity) in *De Tabernaculo* 2.5: ed. Hurst, 60; trans. Holder, 67.

47 E.g., Bede's citation of Psalms 19:4 in relation to the four bronze rings of the tabernacle in *De Tabernaculo*, 2.12: ed. Hurst, 82; trans. Holder, 93. See the boards of the tabernacle, in ibid., 2.5: ed. Hurst, 60; trans. Holder, 66; Bede's citation of Rev 5:9 in discussing the curtains of the tabernacle, ibid., 2.2, ed. Hurst, 44; trans. Holder, 48; and Bede's citation of James 1:12 while discussing the wood of the ark, ibid., 1.5, ed. Hurst, 20; trans. Holder, 20.

48 See Carruthers, *Craft of Thought*, 236; Kominko, *The World of Kosmas,* 109–27; Revel-Neher, "Du Codex Amiatinus," 8–10.

writes that "the width of the boards" of the tabernacle mystically signify "the expansion of the faith and the sacraments, which formerly lay hidden among the one Israelite people but through" the ministry of the apostles and their successors "came [to fill] the wideness of the whole world."[49] Here the very materials that indicate the status of a biblical sanctuary as a bounded and delimited built environment accessed only by a singular Jewish people signify their reverse: the spread of Christian faith throughout the earth.

Central to Bede's project of ironically finding in the discrete spaces of the tabernacle and temple the expanse of Christendom is the erection of individual temples within Christian hearts. Paul's idea of the relationship between the temple and believers (e.g., 1 Corinthians 3:16) would have a particular appeal to a remote Anglo-Saxon people, because it replaces the fixed geography of a singular Jerusalem temple with a preponderance of mobile, mystical edifices. In *On the Tabernacle*, Bede identifies the grate in the middle of the tabernacle altar as a figure of the "place for the Lord" prepared by the elect "in the inmost affections of their hearts, where they gather thoughts devoted to him" (in intimo sui cordis affectu ubi deuotas ei cogitationes collecent).[50] And in the aforementioned homily on the dedication of a church, Bede describes how Christ "desire[s] to inspect and enlighten the innermost recesses of our hearts" and "regards them as equivalent to the portico of Solomon," when those hearts wisely fear the lord, are open to the faith, and inspire good deeds.[51] Going beyond Paul in specifying God's presence in the core of a person's being – the heart – and moreover its "innermost recesses," Bede offers a reassuring notion of how believers, regardless of where they live, may recreate the intimacy of tabernacle and/or temple through good deeds and a pious faith.

But as the Eastertide homily on Luke evinces with its notion of the tomb-like Jew, the spread of faith Bede describes is neither as mobile nor as universal as it appears. While under Christianity, God no longer limits

---

49   The full passage in Bede is as follows: "Latitudo etenim tabularum dilatatio est fidei et sacramentorum quae prius in una Israhelitica plebe latebat sed horum ministerio ad totius orbis amplitudinem peruenit," *De Tabernaculo* 2.5: ed. Hurst, 60; trans. Holder, 66. See also *De Templo* 2.20: ed. Hurst, 217–19; trans. Connolly, 97–8.

50   The full passage reads: "Habet ergo altare Dei in medio sui craticulam ad suscipienda holocausta paratam quia praeparant electi locum domino in intimo sui cordis affectu ubi deuotas ei cogitationes collecent," *De Tabernaculo* 2.12: ed. Hurst, 82; trans. Holder, 92.

51   Homily II.24, ed. Hurst, 358–9; trans. Martin-Hurst, 241–2.

himself to one space but instead travels widely abroad; he never resides in a "Jewish" space. Jews who deny the Christian message, instead of enjoying the privileged architectural intimacy with God possessed by their biblical ancestors, suffer the inverse (i.e., exile from God), becoming "like a tomb still closed by a stone." While biblical Jews had special access to a space enlivened by nothing less than God's presence, contemporary Jews shut themselves away from God through their hardened and resolutely carnal hearts. While the faithful Christian opens himself up to spiritual truths, allowing for God's mystical entry into the heart/temple, the closed heart of the literal-minded and thus unbelieving Jew is empty, lifeless, and sepulchral. Bede's exegesis thus wrenches away from contemporary Jews the privileged architecture of biblical Jews to bestow it upon Christians, and utterly debases the "architecture" of contemporary Jewish identity.

As we have seen, however, the material basis of Bede's geography of supersession troubles his elevation of Christian over Jew. Bede's exegetical works don't so much exhibit a transcendent Christian spirituality as suggest an envy over the exalted materiality of biblical buildings and an anxiety over the literal isolation of England. Indeed, Bede's deep investment in bringing the privileged intimacy of the temple and tabernacle to an isolated England extends beyond the appropriations of allegory to an investment in those structures as historical edifices. At the start of *On the Tabernacle*, Bede makes his interest explicit when he stresses that, before discussing the figural meanings of the tabernacle and its contents, it is important to discuss the *circumstantiae* referred to by Paul in 1 Corinthians 10:11, i.e., particulars of time and place and of material objects themselves.[52] A similar practice of interpretation emerges in *On the Temple*, where "[e]very part of the structure … every detail of ornament, every number, measurement or point of the compass described in the biblical accounts, presented Bede with a mystery of Christ or the Church."[53] Bede's interest in getting an accurate grasp of the physical details of the tabernacle and temple is such that, when possible, he supplements his works by citing extra-biblical sources, such as Cassiodorus and Josephus.[54] Bede claims that he is only interested in the materiality of the biblical sanctuaries as

---

52 *De Tabernaculo* preface: ed. Hurst, 5; trans. Holder, 1. See also *De Tabernaculo* 2.1: ed. Hurst, 43; trans. Holder, 47.

53 Holder, "Allegory and History," 121.

54 Cf. *De Tabernaculo* 2.6: ed. Hurst, 65; trans. Holder, 72, and *De Tabernaculo* 2.12: ed. Hurst, 82; trans. Holder, 92. On Bede's use of Josephus and Cassiodorus, see Holder, "New Treasures and Old," 241–2; and Meyvaert, "Bede, Cassiodorus."

a means to uncovering spiritual truths. Near the beginning of *On the Temple*, Bede states that he seeks "the spiritual mansion of God in the material structure [of the temple]" (in structura materiali spiritalem Dei mansionem).[55] And in *On the Tabernacle*, he writes that "we must reflect for a little while upon the text of the material letter itself, *so that* we shall be able to discuss the spiritual sense with greater certainty" (my emphasis).[56] But Bede's figural interpretations are attended by an attention to physical details that is so minute and so scrutinizing that it effectively renders the temple and tabernacle imaginative presences on which the reader continues to train her eye. Even as Bede stresses building up the living Christian church, he brings long-gone Jewish built environments to vivid imaginative life. Indeed, in somewhat the same way that late medieval fantasies about contemporary Jews would lead to the generation of what Sylvia Tomasch and others have termed a "virtual" Jew on the island after the 1290 expulsion, Bede's exegetical works make virtually present the spaces of the temple and tabernacle.[57] If the English lack the Jews' intimate material proximity to God, works like *On the Temple* allow an English reader to experience a kind of mental intimacy with the physical particulars of those biblical sanctuaries.

Loving Stone

An attachment to a supposedly "Jewish" materiality emerges especially in Bede's attention to material hierarchies such as the physical superiority of a certain building or architectural element over another structure or component. Above all, his discussion of building materials – i.e., stone and wood – in *On the Temple* offers an especially telling appreciation of material excellence. In these remarkable moments, Bede's hermeneutic witnesses an instability arising from the fraught nature of supersession as an ideology which embraces the very attachments it claims to trump. Caught between his spiritual thrust and his material investments, Bede demonstrates what we might call an interpretive panic, as he stumbles over just how the stones and timber of the temple figure Christians and Jews.

---

55 Cf. the full passage: "Tractaturi igitur iuuante domino de aedificatione templi et in structura materiali spiritalem Dei mansionem" (*De Templo* 1.2: ed. Hurst, 148; trans. Connolly, 6).

56 *De Tabernaculo*: ed. Hurst, 43; trans. Holder, 47.

57 Tomasch, "Postcolonial Chaucer and the Virtual Jew."

As we have seen, stones were a favoured means by which Anglo-Saxons connoted a debased Jewish carnality. In his Eastertide homily on Luke, Bede represents the stubbornness, imperceptiveness, and even inhumanity of Jews by likening them to hardened, insentient stone. Solomon's Temple, however, offers an entirely different and exalted brand of stoniness. While the stony Jew is closed off and blind to Christian truths, the stones of the temple merit careful scrutiny by Christians seeking figures of the *lapidum uiuorum* or living stones of the church. The attraction of stones-qua-stones appears in a section of *On the Temple* referring to 1 Kings 5:18, which concerns how "the men of Biblos prepared wood and stones to build the house" (Biblii praeparauerunt ligna et lapides ad aedificandam domum).[58] Here Bede's exegesis embraces the unique physical properties of the stone used for the temple. Bede stresses the enduring permanence of stone to evoke not stubborn, senseless Jews but constant, faithful Christians. He describes how the Church metaphorically lays "large precious stones ... in the foundation" of the "temple" of the faithful when it sets before the people exemplary Christians, who "cling in a special way by the virtue of humility to the Lord ... persevering unflinchingly with invincible constancy of spirit like squared stones."[59] Here the durability of stone isn't a matter of Jewish obstinacy but the kind of Christian immutability celebrated at the opening of the Anglo-Saxon poem *Christ I*, which hails Christ as the cornerstone who "binds with firm fastening the wide walls, the flint unbroken" (gesomnige side weallas / fæste gefoge, flint unbræcne).[60] By using the functional aspect of stones to connote the lithic durability of not Judaic refusal but Christian faith, Bede acknowledges the benefits of the hardness of stones. In tension with Bede's elevation of mystical Christian buildings over literal Jewish edifices is his tendency to use the practical aspects of stone as a means of giving heft and permanence to the former.[61] In his commentary on Acts, Bede elevates living

---

58 *De Templo* 1.4: ed. Hurst, 155; trans. Connolly, 15.

59 See the full reference: "specialiter domino adhaerere nouerimus quos inuincibili mentis stabilitate quasi quadratos quodammodo atque ad omnes temptationum incursus immobiles perdurare" (*De templo* 1.4, ed. Hurst, 155–6, trans. Connolly, 156).

60 *Christ I*, lines 6–7, ed. and trans. Muir, *The Exeter Anthology of Old English Poetry*, 46. My translation is adapted from Muir.

61 See also *On Genesis*, 236, and *On Ezra and Nehemia* 1 (*De tabernaculo, De templo, In Ezram et Neemiam*, ed. Hurst, 273–4; *On Ezra and Nehemiah*, ed. DeGregorio, 56–7); subsequent citations of *On Ezra* by book number will cite page numbers from Hurst and DeGregorio.

over literal stones, writing that "the Lord does not place a high value on dressed stone, but rather desires the splendor of heavenly souls"; but here the precise way in which the temple stones figure Christian virtue registers his regard for the latter, physical entity.[62]

Bede's appreciation of the temple's stony permanence especially manifests itself in his discussion of 1 Kings 6:18, which refers to the cedar lining of the temple boards. Bede's exegesis begins by describing how the stones of the temple walls signify the "living stones" of the saints "cemented to each other by the strength of their faith in the one and the same rule."[63] Here again, the supreme durability of stone figures spiritual durability, i.e., the "unconquered faith" of the saints, while other building materials signify different virtues (e.g., "fragrant action" and cedar, "transcending love" and gold).[64] Then, after interpreting stone as a figure of undefeated belief, Bede ponders the place of stone in the Old Law and another building material – wood – in the New Law:

Verum quia lex in lapide scripta doctrina uero euangelii per lignum est dominicae passionis confirmata unde et populus lapide circumcidebatur in praeputio nos signo crucis consecramur in fronte. Possunt non incongrue parietes templi lapidei siue pauimentum pretiosissimo marmore stratum eorum qui in lege fideliter ac perfecte uixerunt typum gerere, tabulae uero cedrinae siue abiegnae noui testamenti iustos indicare qui uolentes post dominum uenire abnegant semet ipsos et sumpta cruce sua cotidie sequuntur illum.

… because the law was written in stone whereas the teaching of the Gospel was confirmed by the wood of the Lord's passion, so too the people were circumcised by a flintstone in the foreskin whereas we are consecrated by the sign of the cross on the forehead. The stone walls of the temple or the floor paved with most precious marble can quite appropriately be taken as a type of those who lived faithfully and perfectly in the law, whereas the planks of cedar or fir can signify the righteous of the New Testament who in their desire to go after the Lord deny themselves and take up their cross daily and follow him.[65]

---

62 *Commentary on the Acts of the Apostles*, 7:58.158–60, 76.
63 *De Templo* 1.11: ed. Hurst, 174; trans. Connolly, 41.
64 "fortitudine fidei in unam eandemque regulam sibimet agglutinati … fidei namque inuictae lapis figuram," ibid.
65 Ibid. On the literal and figural explication of the circumcision in Anglo-Saxon texts, see further Zacher, "Circumscribing the Text," 89–118.

In part, Bede's formulation distinguishes the carnal life of Jews from Christian spirituality; while Jews, under their law written in stone, literally alter their bodies through circumcision by flint, Christians symbolically mark themselves with the sign of the cross. But the Christian event memorialized by the symbolic gesture also has a physical element, namely the wood of the cross on which Christ died. Thus while Bede earlier imputed to the Christian faith the permanence of stone, now he likens the faith to ordinary, impermanent wood. Moreover, Bede attributes to devout, biblical Jews the very stony permanence he had just a few lines earlier associated with the saints. Of course, the humble nature of wood is part of Bede's theological point in the passage. One of the central paradoxes of Christianity is that God deigned to become man and take on mortal flesh.[66] Christians imitate Christ when they humbly deny themselves and take up their spiritual cross. But I would suggest that, because Bede's reference to the wood of the cross comes on the heels of a passage so clearly invested in stone's permanence, the association of Christians with timber is problematic. Bede's realignment of Christians with wood at some level proves disturbing, given its subordination to stone as a building material.

At the start of the subsequent section of *On the Temple*, Bede writes "Nor should there seem to be any conflict between this and what we said above to the effect that the portico which was in front of the temple was a figure of the faithful of old, whereas the temple is a figure of those who came into the world after the time of Lord's incarnation" (Nec contrarium debet uideri quae supra diximus porticum quae erat ante templum antiquorum ipsum fidelium figuram gestare templum uero eorum qui post incarnationis dominicae tempus in mundum uenerunt).[67] Bede refers here to an apparent contradiction in his treatise, insofar as it first associates Jews only with the portico of the temple described in 1 Kings 6:3 and then later associates them with the stone walls and floors of the building. That earlier designation of the entrance as a figure of holy Jews at once grants them priority in Christian history (since one reaches the portico first when entering the temple) and exiles them from the space of the temple itself.[68] But

---

66 The Incarnation epitomizes the materialism at the heart of Christian practice. In his homily on the dedication of a church, Bede registers the materiality of the Incarnation and links it to the building of the temple; *Homily II*.24, ed. Hurst 375; trans. Martin-Hurst, 250.

67 *De Templo* 1.11: ed. Hurst, 175; Connolly, 41–2.

68 Cf. *De Templo* 1.6: ed. Hurst, 161; trans. Connolly, 23.

in his reading of 1 Kings 6:18, as we have seen, Bede associates Jews with the stone used for the whole temple. Bede assures his readers that such seeming inconsistencies are fine, and indeed are central to his exegetical program: "in the different materials there is a manifold repetition of the same figures" (multiplex namque est in diuersis rebus earundem repetitio figurarum).[69] But Bede seems uncomfortable with the turns his analysis has taken, and he goes on to engage in some rapid and rather confusing manoeuvering. First he writes that the stone walls signifying righteous people before Christ pertain to the portico, not the temple itself, and that the cedar of the portico signifies the Jews who "with greater perfection" (*maiori perfectione*) led a Christian life before Christianity.[70] Then, turning to the interior of the temple, Bede links Christians who sacrifice all for God with the stone wall of the temple; people who are content merely to do the minimum necessary to enter heaven signify its wooden board work.[71] Bede shifts rapidly between interpretations, moving between associating first Jews then Christians with stone, with wood, with inner and outer temple, finally resting upon the association of the holiest Christian with the most durable material entity, the stone of the temple proper. The slipperiness and shifting nature of Bede's exegesis partly serves to confirm his own stress on the "manifold" or multiple nature of exegetical interpretation. But his rapid manoeuvering also seems to signify a kind of hermeneutic panic, an interpretive crisis stemming from his discomfort with the turns his analysis has taken. In other words, the fact that those rapid interpretive shifts immediately follow Bede's association of Jews with stone and Christians with wood and culminate in the association of stone with the holiest of Christians may be no accident, but rather the result of his investment in stone-qua-stone.

Stones were in fact crucial to the Anglo-Saxon Christianity promulgated by monks such as Bede. Stones were so important that, as John Blair puts it, "at least on the richest monastic sites, the really revolutionary change" effected by Christians in England "was the revival, for the first time since the Romans left, of technologies for building and carving in stone."[72] The

---

69 *De Templo* 1.11: Hurst, 175; trans. Connolly, 42.

70 Ibid.

71 Bede, *De Templo*, 1.11, *De tabernaculo, De templo, In Ezram et Neemiam*, ed. Hurst, 175–6; trans. Connolly, 42–3.

72 Blair, *The Church in Anglo-Saxon Society*, 137.

Christian missionaries who reintroduced stone architecture in England restricted the practice to buildings associated with the Church. That unique investment in stone buildings made monastic complexes "decidedly different" from lay structures.[73] While royal vills like Yeavering "were used only sporadically and could be deserted in favour of other sites nearby," monasteries "were continuously occupied and were explicitly founded as permanent sites."[74] The permanence of those Christian structures is such that they endured well beyond the Anglo-Saxon period.

Bede's monastic home at Jarrow, and its sister monastery at Monkwearmouth (founded ca. 673), lie at the centre of this ecclesiastical building program. As David Brown puts it, "Jarrow and Monkwearmouth are among the earliest examples of Anglo-Saxon architecture, and it was from buildings like them that the later styles were to develop."[75] In large part due to the archaeological work of Rosemary Cramp, we have a good sense of the eventual layout of the two monasteries, each of which involved a church and a pair of buildings that stood end-to-end. In Jarrow, the structures were parallel to the minster and separated from it by a yard, fifteen to twenty metres in length.[76] All of the buildings and walls of those monastic complexes were constructed of stone. In the case of Monkwearmouth, its fabric consisted of a mixture of Upper Permian Magnesian Limestone (aka Roker Dolomite), glacier erratics, Coal Measure sandstone, as well as ashlar taken from Roman sites.[77] Jarrow's fabric was composed entirely of cut and dressed stones taken from Roman sites, such as "the Roman wall and fort at Wallsend, across the Tyne to the north-west, and the remains of the substantial supply fort at South Shields to the east."[78]

The stones of Monkwearmouth and Jarrow exemplify how Bede, while celebrating the possession of a faith that is firm as stone, himself inhabited built environments that possessed a literally stony permanence. Indeed, at Bede's home monastery of Jarrow, "much of the original seventh-century monastic church" of St Peter's proved so durable that it "survived more

---

73 Turner et al., *Wearmouth and Jarrow*, 107.

74 Ibid.

75 Brown, *Anglo-Saxon England*, 68.

76 Cramp, "Monkwearmouth and Jarrow: The Archaeological Evidence," fig. 5.14.

77 Turner et al., *Wearmouth and Jarrow*, 141.

78 Ibid., 146.

or less intact until 1782."[79] Bede spent the majority of his life within the stone walls of the Jarrow complex. In an oft-cited autobiographical passage in the *EH*, he writes that, having been raised "in the territory of this monastery," at age seven "I was, by the care of my kinsmen, put into the charge of the reverend Abbot Benedict and then of Ceolfrith, to be educated. From then on I have spent all my life in this monastery."[80] In R.W. Southern's words, "Few men can have spent more years or worked more hours on the same spot than Bede did."[81] On the question of what Bede's nearly lifelong habitation of Wearmouth/Jarrow meant to him, Howe writes that "remaining in place allowed a monk to practice the contemplative life, and if he was a scholarly monk, like Bede, it also enabled him to explore the meaning of place in Christian history and belief."[82] From Howe's perspective, place for Bede entailed an appreciation of Jarrow's Roman connections and even its status as "a type of Rome set at the end of the road that led from the papal city to Northumbria."[83] Key factors influencing his perception of this space would be the reuse of stones originally used for Hadrian's wall to build St Peter's, and the fondness of Benedict Biscop for churches built in the Roman style. But it is important to consider the more immediate meaning that Jarrow and its stone edifices held for Bede. A life spent within the monastic precinct – a place whose stone walls, stone sculpture, colourful paintings, and glass windows likely rendered it, in O'Reilly's words, "a wonder of the northern world," – doubtless attuned Bede to the exceptional materiality of monastic existence on the island.[84] The stone components of the buildings were fundamental in defining Jarrow and other monastic communities as distinctly Christian entities, groups who enjoyed an architectural permanence that was absent elsewhere on the island.

---

79   Ibid., 144. Today, a museum called "Bede's World" centers around the remains of St Peter's and other monastic buildings (http://www.bedesworld.co.uk).

80   The full passage is as follows: "Qui natus in territorio eiusdem monasterii, cum essem annorum VII, cura propinquorum datus sum educandus reuerentissimo abbati Benedicto, ac deinde Ceolfrido, cunctumque ex eo tempus uitae in eiusdem monasterii habitatione peragens, omnem meditandis scripturis operam dedi, atque inter obseruantiam disciplinae regularis, et cotidianam cantandi in ecclesia curam, semper aut discere aut docere aut scribere dulce habui" (*HE* V.24: ed. and trans. Colgrave-Mynors, 566–7).

81   Southern, "Bede," 1.

82   Howe, *Writing the Map*, 130.

83   Ibid., 131.

84   O'Reilly, "Introduction," *On the Temple*, trans. and ed. Connolly, xlviii.

Bede's view of architecture as crucial to Christian practice in Britain emerges in the *EH* where, in his account of the dissemination of the faith on the island, preaching goes hand-in-hand with building and restoring physical churches.[85] Still, however much he appreciated the architecture that surrounded him, Bede offers no extensive celebration of it. Even in his homilies on the dedication of a church, he refrains from discussing both the makeup of the church at Jarrow and its possible relationship to the temple. Both Holder and O'Reilly explore the sources of Bede's reluctance to write about contemporary religious buildings, a reluctance that contrasts starkly with the elaborate allegories of monasteries and churches generated by twelfth-century English writers.[86] While Holder stresses Bede's sense that only biblical sanctuaries merit allegorical interpretation, O'Reilly emphasizes how, for Bede, "the churches built by human hands ... are but figures or copies of the true Jerusalem and can themselves become an earthbound preoccupation or idol."[87] Both critics thus return us to Howe's point regarding the Anglo-Saxon denigration of the man-made and concomitant faith in divine creation.

I would add that a full understanding of Bede's resistance to celebrating physical, built environments requires attending to the place of "the Jew" in his exegetical practice. In other words, Bede refrained from writing about contemporary structures, because any overt embrace of Christian buildings would shore up a version of the degraded materialism he attributed to Jews. Behind Bede's refusal to apply his exegetical approach to Christian buildings is a concern that Christians might start exhibiting the "Jewish" carnality they supposedly transcend. And yet, when Bede stumbles in *On the*

---

85 Cf. *HE* I.26 and II.3: ed. and trans. Colgrave-Mynors, 76–7, 142–3. Holder affirms the "great significance for Bede" churches had "as concrete manifestations of missionary advance," "Allegory and History," 121; similarly Mayr-Harting notes how "Bede's explanation in moral terms of the stones used in the building of the Temple may have another side in his interest to say in the *HE* when actual churches were built of stone, e.g., at York (*HE* II, 14), Lincoln (*HE* II, 16), after some time at Lastingham (*HE* III, 23)"; *The Venerable Bede*, 20. Inverting the approaches of critics like O'Reilly and Holder, who stress the spiritualism linking both texts, Mayr-Harting implies a materialism lurking within *De Templo* – i.e., another aspect of Bede's attention to stones – that emerges more clearly in the stone churches of the *HE*.

86 On medieval English allegories of Christian buildings, see Whitehead, *Castles of the Mind*, 49–61.

87 O'Reilly, "Introduction," *On the Temple*, trans. and ed. Connolly, li.

Temple over how the stones and timber of the temple figure Christians and Jews he proves unable to demonize matter completely. Bede's investment in the stones that defined his monastic life doesn't lead to a full-blown allegory, but rather results in a certain interpretive incoherence. While Bede suggests throughout *On the Temple* how Christians supplant Jews in their ascent to a higher, mystical plane, he proves so invested in stone-qua-stone that he can't sustain his association of Jews with that building material (and Christians with the lesser material of wood), and must link Christians anew with stone. Through his efforts to minimize the link between stones and Jews and heighten instead the linking of stones with Christians, Bede exposes the fictional nature of the ostensible opposition of the two religious groups. Bede's materialism undermines the fantasy of "living" Christian stones and their "dead" Jewish counterparts. Stones no longer strictly signify the debased literalism of his image of the Jew as "a tomb still closed by a stone," but also represent a vitally strong material entity.

Give Me Shelter

If Bede's embrace of stone as an exalted building material in *On the Temple* dismantles the idea of the stony Jew, elsewhere he reveals an investment in quotidian buildings that undermines the idea of the sepulchral Jew. In such passages Bede again reveals his attachment to the home where he spent virtually his entire life, but this attachment has roots far more mundane than the political symbolism evidenced by the stones that set Wearmouth-Jarrow apart from other sites on the island. Rather, Bede reveals his awareness of the fact that, for anyone inhabiting the northern border of the world, the exigencies of life in a harsh climate make it hard to dismiss architectural enclosure.

Bede's sensitivity to his northern climate appears early on in one of his two homilies on the dedication of a church. Bede devotes considerable space in the second half of the homily to the history of the temple, from its erection by Solomon, through its demolition by the Chaldeans, its reconstruction under Zerubbabel and Jeshua, its profanation by Antiochus, and eventual restoration by Judas Maccabeus. While that history makes clear the unique relationship of the Jews to the Jerusalem temple, Bede begins the sermon by stressing how Christian piety creates mystical temples in the hearts of every Christian. After introducing the Pauline notion of Christians as "the temple of the living God" (2 Cor 6:16), Bede urges that listeners "take great care and busy ourselves with good deeds, so that [God] may deign to come more often into this temple of his, and to make his dwelling place there. Let us avoid winter's image, lest the Lord, on coming into our hearts, find them numb from [lack of] charity's ardor, and so, since he has been turned away, quickly leave them."[88] While Bede exhibits in *On the Temple* his identification with the stones that rendered Christian buildings exceptional in his insular homeland, here his claim that Christians should ensure that their hearts "avoid winter's image" recalls built environments at their most basic and humble: as havens from the elements.

Bede's stress on the heart as haven recalls two crucial references to buildings as refuges in the *EH*. The first emerges in Bede's narration of the life of St Alban (ca. 3rd century CE), whose initial, catalyzing, good deed is the opening of his home to a fugitive priest fleeing his pagan persecutors.[89] While the priest's prayers and vigils shore up the spiritual emphasis of this episode, it is clear that that prayerful activity and the conversion it enables would not have happened had it not been for the priest's fundamental need for shelter and the time spent by both men in that house. Alban's vita reminds us that for all Christianity's emphasis on mystical mansions, the lived experience of Christian life necessitated the provision of shelter. A similar message obtains in the famous comparison made in the *EH* by King Edwin's pagan counsellor, likening life to a sparrow's flight in and out of a hall during the winter season. "For the few moments," the counsellor tells his king, that the sparrow occupies the hall where "the fire is burning on the hearth … and all inside is warm … and the wintry tempest cannot touch it, but after the briefest moment of calm, it flits" back into the bad weather.[90] Because human existence, the advisor stresses, possesses just such a fleeting nature, the promise of an everlasting, heavenly dwelling urges conversion to Christianity. The advisor's take on things earthly and carnal is undeniably fraught. At the same time that he derides the impermanent nature of earthly existence, he also portrays a man-made built environment at its most inviting: as a cozy shelter from a

---

88 CCSL, 122, II.24, 359; trans. Martin-Hurst, 242.

89 *HE* I.7: ed. and trans. Colgrave-Mynors, 28–9.

90 The full reference is as follows: "'Talis' inquiens 'mihi uidetur, rex, uita hominum praesens in terris, ad conparationem eius quod nobis incertum est temporis, quale cum te residente ad caenam cum ducibus ac ministris tuis tempore brumali, accenso quidem foco in medio et calido effecto cenaculo, furentibus autem foris per omnia turbinibus hiemalium pluuiarum uel niuium, adueniens unus passerum domum citissime peruolauerit; qui cum per unum ostium ingrediens mox per aliud exierit, ipso quidem tempore

raging storm. The hall may allow for the entrance of a bird into it, but it keeps out "wintry storms of rain and snow."[91]

The counsellor's description of the banquet-hall may reflect how the Anglo-Saxons had special cause to value closed built environments, even more so than other more recent inhabitants of England. Neville refers to evidence suggesting that "the weather endured by the Anglo-Saxons was more severe than that experienced now."[92] The fall of the Roman Empire was matched by a fall in climate, so that "in the centuries following the Anglo-Saxons lived through colder, stormier weather, rougher seas and more snow than that experienced previously and worse weather than that experienced now."[93] Living as they did in a cold, northern climate typified by harsh rain and snowstorms, the Anglo-Saxons would have been especially attuned to the appeal of a snug, man-made shelter.[94]

To return to the homily on the dedication of a church, in which Bede encouraged his auditors to make their hearts as spiritually cozy as a home ideally should be during cold weather, our author presented his audience with a concept they could appreciate. However, after the encouragement to Christians to make their hearts cozy for God, Bede's homily takes a distinctly anti-Semitic turn. Linking John's observation regarding the time of Jesus' visit to the temple (the winter season) to Jesus' words in Matthew 24:12 on the decline of *caritas*, Bede interprets winter weather as a sign of Jewish impiety. Bede writes:

> Why did the evangelist trouble to record that it was winter time, except that he wished to indicate by the harshness of the winter winds and storms the hardness of the Jews' unbelief, and that his utterance was appropriate for

---

quo intus est hiemis tempestate non tangitur, sed tamen paruissimo spatio serenitatis ad momentum excurso, mox de hieme in hiemem regrediens tuis oculis elabitur. Ita haec uita hominum ad modicum apparet; quid autem sequatur, quidue praecesserit, prorsus ignoramus. Vnde, si haec noua doctrina certius aliquid attulit, merito esse sequenda uidetur'"; *HE* II.13: ed. and trans. Colgrave-Mynors, 182–5.

91   Ibid.

92   Neville, *Representations of the Natural World*, 4.

93   Ibid.

94   *HE* II.13: ed. and trans. Colgrave-Mynors, 184–5. Neville comments on how the hall-sparrow episode in the *HE* defines human existence "in its physical place, surrounded by the forces of the natural world" in *Representations of the Natural World*, 24–5.

many of those he found then in the temple, whom he told, *"because iniquity will abound, the charity of many grows cold."*[95]

(Quid enim pertinuit ad euangelistam hiemis tempus commemorare nisi quia duritiam perfidiae Iudaeorum per asperitatem aurarum uoluit designare brumalium et quia plurimis eorum quos tunc in templo inuenit congruebat sermo quem dixit: *Et quoniam abundabit iniquitas refrigescit caritas multorum.*)

Surely this passage evinces Bede's anti-Semitism at its most offensive. Later in the same sermon, Bede likens the Jews to ferocious beasts in their failure to follow Christ.[96] As Scheil points out, when Bede implies that to deny Christ is to sink to "the level of the Jews, those beasts who could not apprehend the voice of reason," he engages in a "hortatory use of Jewish rage and frenzy" akin to Hamlet's idea that humanity, devoid of spirituality, devolves into "[b]estial oblivion."[97] Even worse, though, is Bede's use of the weather to exemplify Jewish rage and frenzy, for it likens the Jew not even to a living creature, but to the elements at their world-destroying worst: a bitter winter storm.

Here, as in the famous passage about the sparrow and the hall in the *EH*, Bede uses bad weather to engage matters of faith and disbelief.[98] The metaphor of the sparrow in the hall is voiced by a pagan counsellor who, like the Jew, is a religious Other. Yet the counsellor is imbued nevertheless with human traits. Thanks to his positioning on the verge of conversion to Christianity, this pagan evinces a poetic and philosophical capacity to appreciate both the appeal of a warm home and the need for a more secure, spiritual dwelling. In contrast, the Jews described in Bede's homily are likened to harsh elements that a building is intended to keep out; more precisely, Jews resemble the very climatic phenomenon that especially resonated in the Anglo-Saxon north. Perhaps more than anything else, the frigid harshness of their northern climate represented misery and tribulation for the Anglo-Saxons.[99]

---

95 CCSL, 122, II.24, 359: trans. Martin-Hurst, 242.

96 CCSL, 122, II.24, 360: trans. Martin Hurst, 244.

97 Scheil, *The Footsteps of Israel*, 42–3.

98 *HE* II.13: ed. and trans. Colgrave-Mynors, 182–5.

99 See for example lines 23–4, "ic hean þonan / wod wintercearig ofer waþena gebind" (I, wretched, thence, mad and desolate as winter, over the wave's binding sought) in *The Wanderer*, and lines 29–33 of *The Seafarer*: "hu ic werig oft/ in brimlade bidan

In many respects, the elemental Jew of this homily reiterates the anti-Semitic overtones of Bede's architectural Jew. Like Bede's idea of the Jew as a "tomb still closed by a stone" – and like Shylock's sober house – Bede's simile involving winter weather associates the Jew with the inhuman and the inanimate. Both cold weather and the closed tomb are associated with sterility and death, notions that oppose the vitality of both biblical sanctuaries and their Christian counterparts. And yet there are important differences between the two figures of speech, differences that remind us that while the risen Christ may have relinquished the world, Christians are very much still there. For all Bede's stress on mystical churches composed of "living stones," his writings register how the community of the faithful was composed not of ether but of persons bearing vulnerable bodies that required homes for protection, churches in which to pray, and monasteries where monks could practice a cenobitic life. Even the most otherworldly of Christians – e.g., ascetic Celtic missionaries such as Colman – needed built environments.[100]

When put alongside each other, Bede's anti-Semitic notions of the "elemental" and "architectural" Jew adumbrate the instability, incoherence, and ambiguity associated with later anti-Semitic thinking, such as the multitude subject positions that, as Bryan Cheyette has shown, were attributed to the Jew in "semitic discourse" in British modernist texts.[101] Scheil suggests as much when he stresses "the essential ambiguity of the Jews" in Bede's writings.[102] Generally speaking, however, understanding what Denise Despres has called the "protean Jew" entails viewing philo-Semitism alongside its anti-Semitic inverse, a phenomenon epitomized by the contradictory idea of chosen biblical Jews and unbelieving contemporary Jews.[103] What Bede's "elemental" and "architectural" Jew evinces, however, is that even when we view just the anti-Semitic half of that binary,

---

sceolde./Nap nihtscua, norþan sniwde,/ hrim hrusan bond, hægl feol on eorþan,/ corna caldast" (I, weary, often on sea-path had to abide. Night-shadow darkened; snow fell from the north; rime bound the soil; on earth hail fell, coldest of corns). *Exeter Anthology*, ed. Muir, 215–16; 230; trans. Glenn [http://lightspill.com/poetry/oe/wanderer.html; http://lightspill.com/poetry/oe/seafarer.html].

100 Cf. *HE*, II.3 and III.26, ed. and trans. Colgrave-Mynors, 142–3, 310–11.
101 Cheyette, *Constructions of "The Jew."*
102 Scheil, *The Footsteps of Israel*, 27.
103 Despres, "The Protean Jew," 145–64.

we still witness a radical contradiction. The Jew is at once hard stone *and* the harsh element that attacks that material. While the Jew as closed tomb connotes architectural obsolescence, the Jew as bad weather connotes architectural utility. Such antinomies arise out of the contradictions of supersession in its geographic manifestations, where the fraught status of the mystical church as both an entity that supersedes the historical temple and an ideal made unattainable by the ineluctable materiality of lived experience on earth is revealed.[104]

---

104 Many thanks belong to Andy Scheil, Jon Wilcox, and Stacy Klein for reading an early draft of this essay and providing valuable advice on it.

5 Transition and Renewal: Jews and the Church Year in Anglo-Saxon England

ANDREW P. SCHEIL

In medieval Christian texts, Jews sometimes appear in unexpected places. These moments of abrupt intrusion speak to the integral place of fictive Jews in certain mechanisms of the Christian imagination.[1] I begin with a textual example a bit removed from Anglo-Saxon England, the Old Irish *Aided Chonchobuir*, "The Death-Tale of Conchobar," pagan king of Ulster. This brief tale opens with the creation of the fateful regicidal weapon – the rock-hard trophy-brain of Mess Gegra, former king of Leinster; the text explains that "Ba bēs d'Ultaib ind inbaid sin cach curaid nomarbdais ar galaib ōenfir nogatta a n-inchind assa cendaib ocus commesct[h]a āel airthib co ndēnad līathrōite crūade díb" (At that time it was a custom with the men of Ulster to take the brains out of the head of every warrior whom they slew in single combat, and to mix lime with them, so that they were made into hard balls).[2] Conchobur keeps Mess Gegra's brain in Ulster as a trophy, but it had been foretold that Mess Gegra would avenge

---

1 This study is concerned not with real Jews and Jewish communities in the early Middle Ages, but rather with Jews and Judaism as they function rhetorically in early medieval Christian texts. For an introduction to historical Jews in the early Middle Ages see Toch, "The Jews in Europe 500–1050," 547–70; on the absence of Jewish communities in Anglo-Saxon England see Scheil, *The Footsteps of Israel*, 7n14.

2 Quotations from the *Aided Chonchobuir* are from *The Death-Tales of the Ulster Heroes*, ed. and trans. Meyer, 4. Meyer edits four versions; my citations are drawn from "Version A" edited from the Book of Leinster and Edinburgh MS. xl. I have expanded the Tironian sign to *ocus*; the translation is by Meyer with my own occasional modifications. Embedded within the *Aided Chonchobuir* is Conchobur's *retoiric* or *roscad*, a poem dated possibly to the early eighth century by Corthals, "The *Retoiric* in *Aided Chonchobuir*," 59.

himself after his death. In a battle with the men of Connacht, the warrior Cet mac Mágach slings Mess Gegra's brain at Conchobur, lodging the missile two-thirds of the way into the king's head. But Conchobur is not dead yet; his men return him to Ulster where he is given the bad news: if the stone is taken out, Conchobur will die; but if the stone is left in, the king's perfect body will be marred.[3] His physician warns him not to do several things that will, apparently, eject the stone from his head and kill him: get angry, mount a horse, have sex with women, and so forth. Conchobur lingered "in this doubtful (or uncertain) state" (*isin chunta-bairt*) for seven years, incapable of action (*nírbo engnamaid*, which means literally "he was not an active warrior") and immobile on his throne "until he heard that Christ had been crucified by the Jews" (naco cúala Críst do chrochad do Iudaidib).[4] The earth trembles on the day of the crucifixion and Conchobur asks his druid counsellor, "What great evil is being done this day?" (Cia olc mór dognīther isind lathiu-sa indiū?)[5] The druid tells him of the crucifixion and notes a correlation: "That man [i.e., Christ] now was born in the same night in which you were born, even on the eighth before the calends of January, though the year was not the same" ("In fer sin dano," ar in drúi, "i n-óenaidchi rogein ocus rogenis-[s]iu .i. i n-ocht calde Enair cen cop inund bliadain").[6] This stunning temporal coincidence causes Conchobur to convert to Christianity, and he rouses himself with a desire to fight the Jews and avenge – as some versions put it

---

3 On the tradition of the ideal, unblemished body of the king in Old Irish literature see McCone, *Pagan Past and Christian Present in Early Irish Literature*, 121–4; McCone notes that "A physical defect, debility or niggardliness can cause lack of sovereignty," 123.

4 Full quotation: "Robói dano isin chuntabairt sin céin robo beō .i. secht mbliadna ocus nīrbo engnamaid, acht a airisium inna suidi nammā .i. naco cūala Crīst do chrochad do Iudaidib" (Meyer, *The Death-Tales*, 8). See *Dictionary of the Irish language*, ed. Quinn et al., s.v. *cuntabart*: (a) "doubt, uncertainty, perplexity"; (b) "danger, peril; doubtful state; doubtful nature or result." The noun *engnam* refers to skill or dexterity, particularly with reference to arms and battle or a valorous deed achieved by such skill (*DIL*, s.v. *engnam*). The related nouns *engnamach* and *engnamaid* both denote "one proficient in arms, an active warrior, a champion" (*DIL* s.v. *engnamach, engnamaid*). References to the *DIL* are drawn from the electronic *DIL* (http://edil.qub.ac.uk).

5 Meyer, *The Death-Tales*, 8.

6 Ibid.

– his "foster-brother" Christ (*comalta*, Meyer, *The Death-Tales*, 16); but the exertion, alas, causes Mess Gegra's brain to pop out of Conchobur's head and the king dies. According to the story, Conchobur was therefore the first pagan to go to heaven, because he believed in Christ and the blood that poured out of his own head baptized him.[7]

While it may seem surprising to a modern reader for Jews to appear in an Old Irish legendary tale, this sudden, seemingly random manifestation of what we would call anti-Judaism is not a rare phenomenon.[8] What is significant in this Irish story, and an important analogy for my argument, is the signal presence of the Jews at a moment of key temporal change: in the Irish tale, the passing of Ulster's legendary king marks the end of the pagan world and the advent of Christian Ireland.[9] Jews, those creatures of the Old Law (according to the Christian tradition), existing only to be superseded, are, I will argue, an appropriate presence at such a transitional moment and appear in analogous Anglo-Saxon examples defined by points of onset, inception, and change in the narration of sacred history.

The Christian re-interpretation of history in late antiquity gave time a specific narrative shape: salvation history, *Heilsgeschichte*, from Genesis

---

7 Meyer, *The Death-Tales*, 15 ("Version B").

8 For example, unprovoked anti-Judaic invective suddenly appears at the end of Ælfric's vernacular lives of Saint Edmund and Saint Swithun: Ælfric, *Lives of Saints* I.21.435–42 (Swithun) and *Lives of Saints* 2.32.264–75 (Edmund); see the discussion in *The Footsteps of Israel*, 291–3. For a summary discussion of the distinction between anti-Semitism and anti-Judaism, following the work of Gavin Langmuir, see Scheil, *The Footsteps of Israel*, 7–9 and the references there. Langmuir's distinction between the two forms of prejudice has been challenged: see, e.g., Chazan, *Medieval Stereotypes and Modern Antisemitism*, 127–34, and Maccoby, *Antisemitism and Modernity: Innovation and Continuity*. The secondary literature on Christian anti-Semitism in the Middle Ages is enormous and ever-growing. For introductory references see Scheil, *The Footsteps of Israel*, 7–11; selected, important recent studies of relevance include Bauer, *Adversus Judaeos: Juden und Judentum im Spiegel alt- und mittelenglischer Texte*; Biddick, *The Typological Imaginary: Circumcision, Technology, History*; Lampert, *Gender and Jewish Difference from Paul to Shakespeare*; Cox, *The Judaic Other in Dante, Chaucer, and the Gawain Poet*; Kruger, *The Spectral Jew*; Bale, *The Jew in the Medieval Book*, and his *Feeling Persecuted*; Cohen, *Christ Killers: The Jews and the Passion from the Bible to the Big Screen*; Biale, *Blood and Belief: The Circulation of a Symbol between Jews and Christians*; Nirenberg, "Figures of Thought and Figures of Flesh," 398–426, and his magisterial *Anti-Judaism: The Western Tradition*; and Krummel, *Crafting Jewishness in Medieval England*.

9 See McCone, *Pagan Past and Christian Present*, 197–9.

to Final Judgment, with the moment of Incarnation at the Nativity as the great centre and pivot of the whole story. While we might think of the Jews as being simple characters in this grand Christian narrative, they also carry out hermeneutic functions: in various ways, the Jews serve as structural elements in the Christian pattern of history. Jews help provide the structure for the traditional "Six Ages of the World," the scheme for organizing time and history promulgated by Augustine and Bede, among others. The Six Ages are structured as follows: the First Age (Adam to Noah, ending with the Flood); the Second Age (Noah to Abraham); the Third Age (Abraham to David); the Fourth Age (David up to the Babylonian exile of the Jews); the Fifth Age (from the Babylonian exile until the coming of Christ); and finally the Sixth Age, initiated by the birth of Christ and now in progress, to be concluded at the Second Coming.[10] Jewish patriarchs, Jewish kings, Jewish exile: the Christian understanding of time and history is constructed, in part, through an appropriation of the *populus Israhel.*

Jews have a place at all the key moments in Christian salvation history, from the establishment of the covenant with Abraham, through the long saga of God's chosen people, the patriarchs and kings, to the exile in Babylon, to the Incarnation and the Jews' role in the crucifixion, to the conversion of the Jews at Final Judgment; what Kruger calls the "spectral Jew" inhabits the very structural principles of Christian time and history.[11] The most common way of understanding the Jews in the early Middle Ages – as witnesses to Christian history and "living letters of the Law" (to borrow Jeremy Cohen's phrase) – is therefore an important part of the Christian sense of time: the time before Christ was the Age of the Law; the time after is the Age of the Gospel.[12] In this way, Jews often serve as

---

10 On the Six Ages of the World in Augustine and others see Ladner, *The Idea of Reform,* 222–38; Dean, *The World Grown Old in Later Medieval Literature,* 39–46; Allen, "Universal History 300–1000," 31–5.

11 Kruger elaborates: "Christianity thus claims to recognize a new and universal structure of time instituted by the incarnation, and it claims for itself a similar universality …. It is the truth breaking into a history that until then contained only glimpses of truth – that is, glimpses of the Christian dispensation to come. And that now-finished history is largely identified with Judaism" (*Spectral Jew,* 3; see also generally 1–8). Kruger's concept of the "spectral Jew" is similar to Jeremy Cohen's term "the hermeneutical Jew" (see *Living Letters of the Law,* 2–3).

12 On the doctrine of Jewish witness see Cohen, *Living Letters of the Law,* 23–65.

a proximate signature of a certain Christian sense of temporal change.[13] I suggest that this deeply embedded connection between Jews and temporal change in the Christian imagination renders them particularly apposite for representation when medieval authors have occasion to think about the progress of time, to give a shaping direction to the events of sacred history, and to meditate upon the power of God's will in the world.

An Anglo-Saxon example of this irruption of the rhetorical (or "spectral" or "hermeneutical") Jew at moments of historical transition can be seen in Ælfric's *Libellus de veteri testamento et novo*, also known as the *Letter to Sigeweard*, his so-called "Treatise on the Old and New Testaments," a brief didactic summary of the Bible and of Christian history.[14] There are two primary organizing structures to Ælfric's explication of history in the *Libellus*: the traditional sequence of biblical books and the Six Ages of the World. Ælfric begins with Creation and proceeds chronologically, explicitly noting the beginning and end of each of the six ages: *in þissere ylde* (in this age) or a similar phrase is a narrative organizing marker in the text.[15] But Ælfric's conclusion to his treatise on time and history finds a place for the Jews. He winds up the final age of the world (852–65), briefly discusses the three orders of society (866–88), and then, before closing, introduces the Jews in a sudden short digression, as sudden as their intrusion into Conchobor's death-tale. With no apparent prompting from any source or obvious cue in the text, Ælfric explains that he wishes to say more about the Jews, "that wretched people" (*þam ungesæligum folce*;

---

13   See Kruger, *Spectral Jew*, 1–8, who notes that the "Christian reorganization of history has had remarkable staying power – though of course its deployment in various historical circumstances has functioned in markedly different ways"; he then goes on to cite some of the "devastating" effects of that staying power in nineteenth- and twentieth-century racial theory (6). Similarly, Kathleen Biddick argues that the temporal notion of modernity itself is closely allied to the Christian ideology of supersession: "The purported 'secularization' of modernity … has never overtaken this core Christian conception of supersession. Supersessionary thinking and notions of modernity are closely bound …" (*Typological Imaginary*, 1). She "term[s] this captivating bundle of supersessionary fantasies about temporality the *Christian typological imaginary*" (2; emphasis hers). See also Kathleen Davis's analogous discussion of Bede and the politics of time in *Periodization and Sovereignty: How Ideas of Feudalism and Secularization Govern the Politics of Time*, 103–31.

14   The first title is the one adopted by Richard Marsden in his authoritative new edition: *The Old English Heptateuch and Ælfric's Libellus de veteri testamento et Novo*, ed. Marsden, vol. 1, 201–30; citations are from this text, by line numbers.

15   For the demarcation of each Age in the *Libellus* see lines 134–5, 164–5, 280–1, 343, 846–7.

889) who crucified the Lord. Ælfric informs us that some Jews believed in Christ, but most did not and they perished, dying in sudden violence (*mid færlicum onræsum*; 894); furthermore, they killed Christ's apostles, continued in their evil ways and did not ask for mercy or forgiveness (894–9). Ælfric then relates their destruction by the Romans (899–914): the desperate famine and descent of the besieged Jews into frenzied madness during the sack of Jerusalem, a tale so awful that "the most shameful abomination done there can not be uttered" (Nys us na to secgenne þone sceamlican morð þe þær gedon wæs; 909–10). The remaining Jews are carried off to slavery in distant lands, and, he tells us, "from these young ones comes the race (of Jews) that yet remains everywhere," and "this was the final retribution (*edlean*) for their evil deeds" (And of þam cnapum ys þæt kynn git gehwær ... þis wæs þæt edlean heora yfelan dæda; 916–18). Once again, as in the tale of Conchobur's death, we have a sudden swerve to the subject of the Jews, appended to a discussion of world history and one of its watershed moments.

I wish to illustrate and explore this strange conjunction, this sublimated logic that links Jews and the passage of Christian time at moments of historical and temporal transition; I proceed through a perhaps unexpected angle: the temporal narrative of the church liturgical year.[16] To be more specific, in what follows I wish to take a portion of the traditional church calendar – Advent, through the Christmas season, to Epiphany – and track the role Jews play in the Anglo-Saxon understanding of those seasons.[17] The liturgical year was one of the prime modes for organizing time, particularly at the level of day-to-day life, and theologically served a number

---

16 Introductory discussions of the liturgical year include McArthur, *The Evolution of the Christian Year*; Horn, III, *The Christian Year*; Adolf Adam, *Das Kirchenjahr mitfeiern*, trans. by O'Connell as *The Liturgical Year: Its History and Its Meaning after the Reform of the Liturgy*; Nardone, *The Story of the Christian Year*; Borgehammar, "A Monastic Conception of the Liturgical Year," 13–44; Connell, *Eternity Today: On the Liturgical Year*, 2 vols. For an interesting discussion of the literary influence of the liturgical year, see Hassel, Jr, *Renaissance Drama and the English Church Year*.

17 I leave out Lent and Easter because the anti-Judaic prompts are all too obvious there: the crucifixion, the deicide charge, and so forth. For a survey discussion of the place of Jews in the Christian liturgy see Frizzell and Henderson, "Jews and Judaism in the Medieval Latin Liturgy," 187–214. In the Good Friday liturgy, there were nine prayers (*orationes solemnes*) for Jews, heretics, pagans. The celebrant would use the formulaic petition *Oremus et pro ...* ("Let us pray for ..."); the congregation would kneel and pray silently before moving on to the next response. When it was time to pray for the "faithless Jews" (*Oremus et pro perfidis Judaeis*), however, the command to kneel was omitted,

of purposes, creating a unity of the faithful through an endlessly reiterated memorial structure, and continually re-enacting the past in the present, year after year. As Heffernan and Matter put it, "Sacred time, although it had a teleological trajectory from Creation through the Incarnation to the Apocalypse, was embodied in the ever-repeating patterns of the liturgy."[18] My exploration of the evidence will illuminate several issues. It shows how Jews are associated with temporal supersession in Christian ideology; they could thus be slotted easily into a Christian representation of time (in this case, the circuit of the liturgical seasons) at just those threshold or liminal moments where change or *transitus* beckons. Further, once the Jews are placed in the seasonal narrative in this fashion, the cyclical character of the church year reinforces this temporal association through each new seasonal iteration, creating a powerful normalizing fiction that grinds on, year after year, embedding the connection between Jews and the *transit* of time at a fundamental level of Christian ideology and imagination.[19] I draw my examples mainly from Bede's and Ælfric's homilies for the Advent, Christmas, and post-Christmas seasons; this choice of authors and texts is obviously an artificial and partial selection, meant to be representative rather than comprehensive. My intent here is to use these texts to reconstruct a representative sketch of the particular ideas that would be likely to circulate as a phenomenon during these liturgical seasons in Anglo-Saxon England and then to examine what part the Jews would have played in that phenomenon.[20]

---

a defiant Christian recognition of Jewish culpability. In 1955 Pope John XXIII inserted the command to kneel during the petition for the Jews back into the rite; in 1960 he ordered that the word *perfidis* be omitted. The prayer itself was completely revised after Vatican II; see Frizell 197–9.

18 Heffernan and Matter, "Introduction to the Liturgy of the Medieval Church," 8.

19 On time in the Anglo-Saxon homiletic corpus, see Lees, *Tradition and Belief: Religious Writing in Late Anglo-Saxon England*, 78–105 ("Chapter 3: Conventions of Time in the Old English Homiletic Corpus").

20 Cf. the methodology of Harris in "The Liturgical Context of Ælfric's Homilies for Rogation," 144–5. Yet even as I assemble the images and themes of the season into a composite form through a selection of homilies in Old English and Latin, I am aware that such a picture has its limits as evidence: as Christopher A. Jones notes (speaking of liturgical practices generally), "… in its actuality the liturgy must have resisted a totalizing view, if only by the sheer diversity and variability of its parts, both written … and unwritten" ("The Book of the Liturgy in Anglo-Saxon England," 659).

Advent

We begin with Advent, often the beginning of the liturgical year in the early Middle Ages, the other leading candidate being Christmas.[21] One prominent figure in this season serves as an elusive symbolic figure for change and transition: John the Baptist. John appears in the Advent season, at the beginning of the liturgical cycle, preparing the way of the Lord, and he also returns later in the Epiphany tradition at the baptism of Christ in the river Jordan. Recurring themes throughout this section of the calendar include rebirth, baptism, initiation, renovation, and the passage from darkness to light. Bede composed a pair of advent homilies centering on John the Baptist.[22] The gospel prompt for the first homily (Mark 1:4–8) tells us that the wild man John eats locusts and wild honey in the desert, and Bede provides multiple figural interpretations of this diet, incorporating the Jews into his explication. The important resonant gospel details for Bede are the flighty movement of locusts and the sweetness of wild honey. Bede explains that the sweetness of the wild honey refers to the "sweetness of the natural wisdom by which the wild people of foreign nations [i.e., the Gentiles] were refreshed" and "on account of its short flight, the locust suggests the inconstant mind of the Jewish nation, by which they were borne up and down between the Lord and idols" (Locusta propter breuem uolatum mobilem Iudaicae gentis animum quo inter dominum et idola sursum iusumque ferebatur insinuat. Mel siluestre dulcedinem naturalis ingenii qua inculti exterarum nationum populi reficiebantur significant; *Homeliae* I.1.108–12). Bede follows his source here, an exegetical interpretation of John's diet in Gregory the Great's *Moralia on Job* (31.25.6–24).

---

21 For discussions of Advent see McArthur, *Evolution of the Christian Year*, 70–6; Horn, *Christian Year*, 54–65; Adam, *Liturgical Year*, 130–8; Borgehammar, "Monastic Conception," 24–9; Connell, *Eternity Today*, vol. 1, 53–87. For an analysis of the Anglo-Saxon liturgy of Advent, and associated literature (e.g., vernacular homilies and *Christ I*) see Bedingfield, *The Dramatic Liturgy of Anglo-Saxon England*, 217–22; Bedingfield notes that "Advent serves both as an end and a beginning, and liturgical books giving forms for a year inconsistently begin with Advent rather than Christmas (though Christmas is the usual beginning in Anglo-Saxon witnesses)," 217. Other possibilities for the beginning of the year included 25 March (the Incarnation) and even Easter; see also below, note 52.

22 Bede, *Homeliarum evangelii libri II*, ed. Hurst, CCSL 122 (Turnhout: Brepols, 1955), 1.1 and 1.2.

But is there a deeper logic that links John the Baptist and the Jews for both Gregory and Bede?

An answer perhaps lies in the liminality that characterizes both. Jews occupy their singular place in Christian ideology due to their ambivalent status – they are not Christians, of course, yet they are also not as alien as pagans. The faiths share histories and sacred texts; Christianity includes and excludes the Jews at the same time; Jews are defined by both alterity *and* proximity.[23] John the Baptist likely conjures up the presence of the Jews in the minds of Gregory and Bede due to his analogous liminality. While John is certainly an orthodox figure in Christian theology, there is also a sense that he does not quite fit – he is exceptional.[24] Bede, Ælfric, and others note many times that John was "greater than any other man," yet he is still a man.[25] He is singular, one of only three people (Ælfric tells us) whose birth is celebrated by the church (along with Jesus and Mary).[26] He is Christ's great, belated "fore-runner" (*forrynel*).[27] With a pithy and resonant sentence, Ælfric places John at the centre of a temporal transition, explaining that "John is the end of the Old Law and the beginning of the New" (Iohannes is geendung þære ealdan æ and angin þære niwan; Ælfric, *CH* 1.25.80–1). There is something of a paradox in Ælfric's expression: the simple copula asserts that he is the end of the Old Law and the beginning of the New, yet he cannot *be* both. The binary division between Old Law / Jew and New Law / Christian has no place for ambiguity; so to what great temporal period does John truly belong?[28] Ælfric then elaborates, using a series of similes: "He was sent before the Lord, as the day-star goes before the sun, as a herald before a judge: as the Old Testament before the New, for the Old Law was like a shadow and the New Testament is

---

23 A point many scholars of Christian anti-Semitism make; see, e.g., Kruger, *Spectral Jew*, 8–17.

24 See Godden's headnote to *CH* 1.25 in *Ælfric's Catholic Homilies: Introduction, Commentary and Glossary*, 200.

25 E.g., Bede, *Homeliae* I.12.46–51; Ælfric *CH* 1.25.101–4, I.32.29–30; *Blickling XIV*.161, 162 (*The Blickling Homilies*, ed. Morris).

26 Ælfric, *CH 1*.25.67–8. Cf. also the interesting depiction of John the Baptist, the "foremost of city dwellers" (*burgwarena ord*), in *The Descent into Hell*, lines 56–75 in *The Exeter Book*, ASPR III, 219–23.

27 Ælfric, *CH* 1.25.117, 224; I.32.148.

28 As Biddick notes, a threshold is important in the construction of time "since it suggests the moment in which retroactive construction is suspended, thus allowing for temporalities that are not one" (*Typological Imaginary*, 105 n. 2).

the truth through the grace of the Savior" (He wæs asend toforan drihtne swa swa se dæigsteorra gæð beforan þære sunnan: swa swa bydel ætforan deman: swa swa seo ealde gecyþnys . ætforan þære niwan, for þan ðe seo ealde æ wæs swilce scadu and seo niwe gecy[ð]nys is soðfæstnyss þurh hælendes gife; Ælfric, *CH* 1.25.96–100). In the binary figural structure of Ælfric's comparison, John is to Jesus as the Old Testament is to the New, as the Jews are to Christians; this would make John "Jewish," a creature of the Old Law, yet he is simultaneously the beginning of the New Law, a day-star before the sun. *Blickling XIV* follows a similar line of thought, explaining that John was the "union (*fæstnung*) both of the old and the new law."[29] Bede uses similar language to express John's liminal status as a figure on the exact threshold of a new age: he explains that John is the last of the witnesses and prophets sent to the people of Israel and that he is "a kind of boundary line (*limes*) between law and gospel, figure and truth."[30] We know from anthropologists that boundaries and thresholds are places of power and also places of ontological uncertainty.[31] In the language of these Anglo-Saxon texts we can sense the paradox or potential "category error" that is John, the belated herald of Christ, and thus his potential relationship to the similarly paradoxical, belated Jews, who, like John, are also

---

29 *Blickling XIV* (*Seo Gebyrd S. Johannes þæs Fulwihteres*): "ond ic secge þæt se god-spellere wæs fæstnung ægþer ge þære ealdan æ, ge þære niwan ge þonne," 163. It is interesting to note that this homily ends with some abrupt anti-Judaism: "Oþþe hu scepede him seo synn þære swigunga þe swa stronglice þa Iudeas þreade, þe to him coman toþon þæt hie his lare gehyrdon; ond he swa cwæþ, 'Ge næddrena cynn, hwylc æteowde eow to fleonne fram ðon toweardan Godes erre'" (Or how did the sin of silence affect him who so strongly rebuked the Jews who came to hear his lore? And thus he spake, "Ye race of vipers, who hath showed you to flee from the wrath of God to come?"; 169).

30 Bede, *Homeliae* II.19.5–7: "Horum ultimus et quasi limes quidam legis et euangelii figurae et ueritatis Iohannes" (The last of them [i.e., last of the witnesses and heralds of Christ's coming under the Old Law] and, as it were, a boundary between law and gospel, figure and truth, was John). This entire homily is a fascinating discussion of John the Baptist; Bede obviously senses that John is a potentially puzzling character who calls out for explication.

31 We might also note here the fact that John makes his home in the liminal world of the desert wasteland as a border-dweller: "Witodlice iohannes on westene wunode betwux eallum deorcynne ungederod ond betwux dracan ond aspidum ond eallum wurm-cynne ond hi hine ondredon" (Indeed John dwelt in the desert unhurt among all the beast-kind, and among serpents and asps, and all the worm-kind, and they feared him; *CH* 1.32.177–9).

defined by alterity and proximity.[32] The Fifth Age of the world was the last age of the Jews and of their Old Law. It ran from the exile in Babylon to the coming of Christ, the beginning of the Sixth Age. As the last of the prophets of the Old Law, a man greater than any other man, and a final human evolutionary point of the Fifth Age before the advent of Christ, John the Baptist stands on the threshold of a new age, and for all these reasons he naturally calls up a connection to Jews in Bede's advent homily when he explicates the significance of John's diet of flighty locusts.[33] The ultimate transitional moment in salvation history, the movement from darkness to light heralded by the birth of Christ in the Advent season, begins with John; and it is no coincidence that in the figural explication of this moment, the Jews have a spectral presence at his side.

Christmas, St Stephen, and Innocents

Advent prepares the way to Christmas and the Nativity, for which Bede and Ælfric both composed various homilies.[34] Here, again perhaps unexpectedly, the Jews appear. In one of his Christmas homilies, Bede addresses

---

32 John also poses a potential theological problem because of his "seniority": if he baptizes Jesus, it might be construed that he is somehow greater that Jesus (i.e., has more authority) and / or that Jesus might be somehow deficient because he needed to be baptized (see Connell, *Eternity Today*, vol. 1, 153–4).

33 We might also note the connection between Advent and the Second Coming in Christian tradition; this would also be another way to associate Jews with John the Baptist, given the role assigned to the conversion of the Jews in Christian eschatological thought.

34 Bede, *Homeliae* I.5, 6, 7, 8; Ælfric, *CH* 1.2 and *CH* 2.1. For a general discussion of Christmas and its history see McArthur, *Evolution of the Christian Year*, 31–57; Horn, *Christian Year*, 66–81; Susan K. Roll, *Toward the Origin of Christmas*; Borgehammar, "Monastic Conception," 29–30; Connell, *Eternity Today*, vol. 1, 88–146. The date of Christmas was perhaps chosen to rival the Roman feast of *Dies natalis soli invicti* (Birth of the Unconquered Sun), a pagan festival held on 25 Dec. because it generally coincided with the winter solstice, the shortest day of the year and after which the daylight would begin to get longer: see Horn, *Christian Year*, 22, 67; Adam, *Liturgical Year*, 122–5; Nardone, *Story of the Christian Year*, 16–19; Roll, *Toward the Origin*, 107–64; Connell, *Eternity Today*, vol. 1, 100–6; and Beckwith, *Calendar and Chronology, Jewish and Christian: Biblical, Intertestamental and Patristic Studies*, 72–3 (71–9 for the entire discussion of the date of Christmas). For an analysis of the Anglo-Saxon liturgy of Christmas and vernacular homilies associated with this day see Bedingfield, *The Dramatic Liturgy*, 25–38; on the Christmas Octave and Epiphany see 38–41 and 42–9.

potential disbelief in Christ's incarnation: how can God be born as a man?[35] For Bede, the example of the Jews helps to illustrate and foster understanding of any potential scepticism at the Nativity. In this homily he explicates John 1:11 ("He came unto his own, and his own did not accept him") in the following way (*Homeliae* I.8.170–9):

Quem enim in potentia dietatis cuncta creantem regentemque non cognouerant ipsum in carnis infirmitate miraculis coruscantem recipere noluerunt. Et quod grauius est sui eum non receperunt homines scilicet quos ipse creauit. Iudaei quos peculiarem sibi elegerat in plebem quibus suae cognitionis reuelauerat archanum quos mirificis patrum glorificauerat actis quibus suae legis doctrinam contulerat ex quibus se incarnandum promiserat et in quibus se incarnatum ut promiserat ostenditipsi eum recipere uenientem magna ex parte recusarunt.

(Indeed, the one whom the Jews had not recognized as creating and reigning in all the power of his divinity, this same one they would not receive shining with miracles in the infirmity of the flesh. And, what is more grievous, "his own did not accept him," namely the men whom he himself created. The Jews, whom he had chosen as his own special people, among whom he had revealed the mystery of knowledge of himself, whom he had glorified by the wondrous acts of the fathers, to whom he had brought the doctrine of his Law, from whom he had promised to incarnate himself, and among whom, as he also had promised, he showed himself incarnate – these Jews for the most part refused to accept him at his coming.)

Thus at the Nativity, the miraculous moment of Christ's birth and the beginning of the Sixth Age of the world, the Jews are depicted as having missed the point, unable to grasp this all-important moment when the world, time, and history changed forever. Standing by unaware that a great temporal threshold has been crossed, they are, for Bede and for Christianity in general, the natural example of unthinking scepticism.

Christmas is followed by the feast of St Stephen the Protomartyr on 26 December. St Stephen's martyrdom in the book of Acts is essentially

---

35 Connell, *Eternity Today*, vol. 1, 114: "Christmas sermons throughout the Middle Ages took up the Christological issues, perhaps because the object of the feast, the infant son, was incommensurate with the lofty theology predicated upon him."

a re-enactment of the crucifixion and has some florid examples of anti-Judaism. In Ælfric's homily for this day (*CH* 1.3), the "disbelieving Jews" (*ungeleaffullan iudei*) set out to quell Stephen's message of the gospel; in a vehement re-enactment of the crucifixion scene, they stone him as Stephen curses them (*CH* 1.3.43–7):

> "Ge wiðstandað þam halgum gaste mid stiðum swuran ond ungeleaffulre heortan; ge sint meldan ond manslagan ond ge þone rihtwisan Crist niðfullice acwealdon. Ge underfengon æ on engla gesetnysse ond ge hit ne heoldon." Hwæt þa iudeiscan ða wurdon þearle on heora heortan astyrode ond biton heora tetð him togeanes.

> ("You oppose the Holy Spirit with stiff necks and unbelieving hearts; you are betrayers and murderers and you maliciously killed the righteous Christ. You have received the law by the decree of angels and you have not kept it." Lo, then the Jews became greatly disturbed in their hearts and gnashed their teeth against him.)[36]

Ælfric speaks of the malice (*teona*) of the cruel, raging Jews and the earthly wickedness (*seo eorðlice arleasnyss*) they represent. This intense anti-Judaic narrative is celebrated and explicated the very day after Christmas; so the joyous moment of Christ's birth, the culmination of Advent, is immediately paired with a reminder of the crucifixion to come at the hands of the Jews in the Christian imagination. In the modern world, we perhaps do not think of the Jews as having much of a presence at the Christmas season, but for the Anglo-Saxons, both 25 and 26 December would have been celebrated in tandem with the rhetorical presence of the Jews.

The next major feast day, 28 December, is the commemoration of the Holy Innocents, the children murdered by Herod in an attempt to kill Christ; it is not too difficult to guess how Herod might be interpreted figurally, and sure enough, Bede makes the connection: "In fact, the death of Herod suggests the end of the malicious intention with which Judaea then raged against the Church. The death of the little ones designates the death of the ones humble in spirit whom the Jews destroyed when they had killed Christ" (Obitus quippe Herodis terminum intentionis malitiosae

---

36 On Stephen the Protomartyr and anti-Judaism in Anglo-Saxon England see Scheil, *The Footsteps of Israel*, 40–1, 208–9, 224, 289–90. Also see ch. 6 by Anlezark below.

qua nunc contra ecclesiam Iudaea saevit insinuat. Occisio paruulorum mortem humilium spiritu quos fugato a se Christo Iudaei peremere designat; Bede, *Homeliae* I.10.86–9). So if we step back and examine this temporal sequence as a unit, we see that the disbelief of the Jews on Christmas day leads to a proleptic representation of their direct murderous intent on the feast of the Protomartyr, and then on to their figural presence as the vengeful Herod. In the Christian imagination, therefore, the great joy that suffuses the tone of the days from 25 December to 28 December is woven together inextricably with the darker spectral presence of the Jews.

What we have so far is the striking presence of the Jews as part of the figural undercurrent to the seasonal narrative that proceeds from Advent through Christmas; this is a typical, multifaceted use of the Jews as hermeneutic tools *in situ*, as the rhetorical situation shifts. Yet from a broader perspective, the simple presence of the Jews proceeding in tandem with the rites and themes of the calendar is significant and has ramifications for the place of the Jews in the Christian sense of time. The liturgy and the liturgical year are acts of *anamnesis*, of remembrance: the ritual, cyclical nature of liturgical thought is designed to recreate the mysteries of Christianity and its history, perpetually at every hour, day, month, year.[37] As the Christian believer moves through the circuit of the Christian year and re-experiences first the voice of John in the wilderness during Advent, then feels the joy of the nativity at Christmas, and witnesses the horrors of St Stephen and the Innocents in the following days, the Jews are there as well, every step of the way, dwelling on the edge of the narrative at each of these moments, incorporated into the understanding of the action, part of the great sacramental unity fostered by the liturgical calendar.[38]

---

37 On the liturgy as remembrance see Horn, *Christian Year*, 8; Stookey, *Calendar: Christ's Time for the Church*, 28–33; Connell, *Eternity Today*, vol. 1, 3–5: "Although the Liturgy of the Word focuses on the proclamation or animation of texts mostly about *past* events, the liturgical event itself, in which these events are proclaimed and heard in the gathered community of faith, is a *present* and *sensory* experience that enables human lives to be wedded, reimagined, and transformed," 5; emphases his.

38 On the communal bonding and unity of the Church through the liturgy and the sacraments see Connell, *Eternity Today*, vol. 1, 4: "… for the baptized the sacraments – and the liturgical year during which the rites unfold – are the privileged and familiar moments when God's presence shows forth and human beings are knitted together in the name of Christ." On sacramental bonding see also Morrison, *"I Am You": The Hermeneutics of Empathy in Western Literature, Theology, and Art*, 8–11.

122   Andrew P. Scheil

This entire period is charged with associations of rebirth and new beginnings. The season moves across the winter solstice, when the long night ceases and the day begins to grow again, an image used in the Old English poem *Christ I* (the *Advent Lyrics*).[39] As part of the rhythms of everyday life, the Anglo-Saxons would experience, year after year, in the dead of winter, the story of John, the last of the prophets, and the forlorn people behind him with their Old Law; each year, the Jews would be part of a great process of transition and renewal as the old world began to give way to the New Dispensation of a new spring while the very light around them grew stronger, day by day. It is a powerful, moving trope. Ælfric himself made this seasonal connection in his homily for the birth of John the Baptist (celebrated in June); there he notes that John was born when the day begins to grow shorter (the summer solstice) because his role was ending, as was the fifth age of the world; and Christ was born when the light began to grow stronger (the winter solstice) because his power was dawning into the world at the start of the sixth age.[40]

The New Year

We move now to 1 January, New Year's Day in the Julian calendar. The two-faced Roman god Janus presided over gates, thresholds, and beginnings, and the deep association of this day with initiation remained throughout the Middle Ages, as the day on which the border between the old and the new is crossed. In the liturgical calendar 1 January commemorates the circumcision of Jesus.[41] Jewish circumcision, of course, was normally understood to prefigure Christian baptism: both were ceremonies of initiation and rebirth. Inevitably, therefore, in his homily for this day (*Homeliae* I.11) Bede discusses the nature of time and the historical difference between the Jewish age of the law and the Christian age of grace, represented by

---

39 On light symbolism in Epiphany see McArthur, *Evolution of the Christian Year*, 67–8; Horn, *Christian Year*, 83; for imagery of darkness transitioning to light in *Christ I* see, e.g., lines 26b–7, 42–6, 104–18, 203–6a, 230–5 (*Christ* in *The Exeter Book*, ed. Krapp and Dobbie, ASPR III, 3–49).

40 Ælfric, *CH* 1.25.118–34; see also Bede, *Homeliae* II.20.61–78 and II.23.189–97. See Kroll, *Toward the Origin*, 50, for this traditional connection.

41 See Horn, *Christian Year*, 79–81; Nardone, *Story of the Christian Year*, 43–4. On the understanding of circumcision in Anglo-Saxon England see Zacher, "Circumscribing the Text." For further reflection on the significance of circumcision and its relation to Christian temporality see Biddick, *Typological Imaginary*.

circumcision and baptism respectively. He also works in a discussion of time and the six ages of the world. Citing Ephesians, Bede urges his brethren to "put off the old man of the former way of life" and "put on the new man, created in justice and the holiness of truth" – this verse traditionally being interpreted as the Jews and the Law giving way to Christianity and the New Covenant.[42] Bede ends the homily by quoting with approval the speech of St Stephen Protomartyr against the "stiff-necked Jews" and explicates its relevance for living the Christian life from day to day.[43] One can observe in this homily the now familiar concatenation of elements: time, the understanding of history, Jews, and moments of transition.

In Ælfric's homily for 1 January, he gives a quick history of circumcision focused upon Abraham, and explains that the Jews circumcised their children on the eighth day after birth "until Christ was born in human form, who established baptism, and changed the signification of the old law to spiritual truth" (oþ ðæt Crist on menniscnysse acenned wearð, se þe fulluht astealde, ond þære ealdan æ getacnunge to gastlicere soðfæstnysse awende; *CH* 1.6.46–8). He then begins a more detailed explanation of circumcision asserting that the ritual was "as great among believing men as is now the holy baptism"; he notes that Christ himself "was subject to the holy law that he had established" so that he could free those who had been "necessarily (*neadwislice*) subject to the same old law."[44] In the Julian calendar, 1 January had been associated with rites of passages and new beginnings; the Christian liturgical calendar retained some of the spirit for that day in the linked pairing of circumcision and baptism. Again, the Jews are present, in a fundamental way, in the delicate overlapping play of Christian time and rites of passage.[45]

---

42 Bede, *Homeliae* 1.11.171–5: "Deponamus secundum pristinam conuersationem ueterem hominem qui corrumpitur secondum desideria erroris; renouemur spiritu mentis nostrae et induamus nouum hominem qui secundum Deum creatus est in iustitia et sanctitate ueritatis" (Ephesians 4.22–4).

43 Bede, *Homeliae* 1.11.179–83.

44 Ond þæt tacn wæs ða swa micel on geleaffullum mannum swa micel swa nu is þæt halige fulluht (*CH* 1.6.53–5) ... Ond he sylf wæs þære halgan æ underþeod þe he gesette, þæt he þa alysde þe neadwislice þære æ underþeodde wæron (*CH* 1.6.66–8).

45 Ælfric was also aware that this day, celebrating the initiation of Christ, had a further significance as the first day of the year; but the matter is somewhat troubling for him, as he digresses on the various traditions for beginning the first day of the year, and the unfortunate propensity of unlearned folk to engage in heathen divination on this day. He was aware that beginning the year on 1 January was a widespread Anglo-Saxon

Epiphany

The last feast day in this section of the calendar is 6 January, the Epiphany; the word derives from the Greek verb *epiphainein*, "to manifest or show forth"[46]; Ælfric thus correctly calls it *swutelungdæg* (manifestation-day).[47] This feast day is also charged with a sense of renovation and renewal. It is the twelfth day after Christmas; Twelfth Night, of course, is the eve of the Epiphany and was known for its customs of revelry, transformation, and renewal.[48] One of the standard readings for this day is the visitation of the Magi, but another is the baptism of Jesus in the Jordan. Bede's homily for the occasion and Ælfric's in the *Second Series* both return us to John the Baptist (and his liminal Judaic associations); John, whom we first met at Advent, now closes out the calendar sequence at the Epiphany. Ælfric's homily for this day in the *First Series* centers on the Magi, but he also discusses the Jews. The shepherds tending their flock are "from the Jewish country" (*on iudeiscum earde*); these good shepherds symbolize the apostles, similarly chosen from the Jewish people to form the primitive church with select gentiles, represented by the magi.[49] Ælfric explains the

---

practice based on Roman custom yet also notes the competing custom of beginning the year at Christmas. Using Bede's *De temporibus* and *De temporum ratione* as sources he also notes the varied practices of the Hebrews, Greeks, and Egyptians. Ælfric is generally uneasy with beginning the year on 1 January due to its association with pagan practices and makes the case for the vernal equinox (which he places on 21 March – the feast of St Benedict) as the appropriate start of the calendar year. I derived all this from Malcolm Godden's article "New Year's Day in late Anglo-Saxon England," 148–50; and his commentary on the appropriate homilies in the *CH*. For the general complexities and history of the issue see Kenneth Harrison, "The Beginning of the Year in England, c. 500–900," 51–70.

46 For general discussions of Epiphany see McArthur, *Evolution of the Christian Year*, 31–76; Horn, *Christian Year*, 82–94; Adam, *Liturgical Year*, 144–7; Nardone, *Story of the Christian Year*, 19–21; Borgehammar, "Monastic Conception," 29–30; Connell, *Eternity Today*, vol. 1, 147–98; and Merja Merras, *The Origins of the Celebration of the Christian Feast of Epiphany*. On the date of Epiphany, see Beckwith, *Calendar and Chronology*, 71–9 and Merras, *Origins of Epiphany*, 10–17.

47 *CH* 2.3.1.

48 See Billington, *Mock Kings in Medieval Society and Renaissance Drama*, 30–54; Hutton, *The Rise and Fall of Merry England*, 7–16; *The Stations of the Sun*, 9–53. The evidence for Twelfth Night revelry in these studies is generally post-1100, however.

49 Ælfric, *CH* 1.7.48. He later notes: "Ða iudeiscan þe on Crist gelyfdon wæron him gehendor stowlice, ond eac þurh cyððe þære ealdan æ; we wæron swiðe fyrlyne æigþer ge stowlice ge þurh uncyððe; ac he us gegaderode mid anum geleafan to þam healican hyrnstane, þæt is to annysse his gelaðunge" (The Jews who believed in Christ were

importance of clear manifestation or evidence for faith and belief on this day, and engages in a digression about the Jews that calls to mind Bede's similar passage for the Christmas day homily cited above (*CH* 1.7.92–102):

Ealle gesceafta oncneowon heora scyppendes tocyme, buton þam arleasum iudeiscum anum. Heofonas oncneowon heora scyppend, þa ða hi on his acennednysse niwne steorran æteowodon. Sæ oncneow þa ða Crist mid drium fotwylmum ofer hyre yþum mihtelice eode. Sunne oncneow þa ða heo on his þrowunge hyre leoman fram middæge oð non behydde. Stanas oncneowon þa ða hi on his forðsiðe sticmælum toburston. Seo eorþe oncneow þa ða heo on his æriste eall biuode. Hel oncneow þa ða heo hyre hæftlingas unþances forlet. Ond þeah ða heardheortan iudei noldon þurh eallum þam tacnum þone soþan scyppend tocnawan, þe ða dumban gesceafta undergeaton and mid gebicnungum geswutelodon.

(All created things acknowledged their Creator's advent, except for the impious Jews alone. The heavens acknowledged their Creator, when they at his birth revealed a new star. The sea acknowledged him, when Christ with dry footsteps miraculously passed over its waves. The sun acknowledged him, when it hid its beams from mid-day till the ninth hour during his passion. The stones acknowledged him, when they burst into pieces at his death. The earth acknowledged him, when it all trembled at his resurrection. Hell acknowledged him, when it unwillingly released its captives. And yet the hardhearted Jews would not for all those signs acknowledge the true Creator, whom unwitting created things perceived, and whom they revealed by manifest signs.)[50]

Christ's public manifestation is the conclusion of our calendrical narrative sequence from Advent to Epiphany and it lends the story a sense of universality: from the Christian perspective all of Time is organized around this moment – the recognition of Christ's divinity at his birth – and all of creation, time, and history stand now clearly ordered around the manifestation,

---

nearer to him locally, and also through knowledge of the old law: we were very remote, both locally and through ignorance; but he gathered us with one faith to the high cornerstone, that is to the unity of his church; *CH* 1.7.66–70).

50 Ælfric here follows Haymo of Auxerre, and through him, Gregory the Great (Godden, *Introduction*, 57).

the Epiphany, of the Lord. The pattern behind time is suddenly revealed to human eyes.[51] Yet, there is a need to construct this vision *through* the Jews, by including them yet setting them apart from the revelation as unbelieving and isolated outsiders. One senses that when presenting such an over-arching, all-encompassing claim about time and history, sublimated doubt must abide within the fabric of Christian ideology; that doubt is expressed through the proximate figure of the Jews.[52] Christianity makes claims for all time and space; perhaps it is almost inevitable that doubts about totalizing claims should surface, embodied in an intimate human proxy.[53] In the traditions of medieval Christian rhetoric, such doubts were represented through the Jews, placed astride fissures in the ideological fault-lines of Christianity.

We can now see the whole story, from Advent to Epiphany, a calendrical narrative glossed and understood, in part, by using the Jews. What is the effect of building into the very structure of Christian time the endless iteration of the Jews at these key moments of transition and renewal? One thing I would suggest is that the writing of the Jews into the DNA of the Christian liturgical calendar should be examined as part of the broader story of world-conspiracy theories involving Jews.[54] Given the anti-Judaism present in the iteration of the Jews in the Christian seasonal calendar and liturgy; given the pervasiveness of the Christian liturgy in Europe and

---

51 As Borgehammar eloquently explains, "The fundamental fact about the liturgical year is that it is a sanctification of time. Certain key events in the history of salvation, and certain key elements of faith, have become attached to certain dates of the calendar like gems on a bracelet. This bracelet is like a magnificent rosary. We cannot handle it without encountering those gems, each of which carries a distinct message. In this way, as the earth spins around its axis and around the sun, creating the recurrent cycle of seasons which we call a year, we learn to experience not a ceaseless progression of days and nights but a pattern of meanings. Events from the past keep returning to us, giving days and seasons character and profile, bequeathing to us an inheritance from our ancestors, and inviting us to add to that inheritance for the future" ("A Monastic Conception," 13). See also the excellent discussion of liturgical time in Roll, *Toward the Origin*, 15–56.

52 Cf. the anti-Judaic invective in *Andreas* (557–65a) when God, in disguise, asks Andrew how the disbelieving Jews could possibly reject Christ, when all of creation recognized his power.

53 Cf. Kruger, *Spectral Jew*, 5–6.

54 The secondary literature on anti-Semitism and conspiracy theory is large; one could start with Cohn, *Warrant for Genocide: The Myth of the Jewish World-Conspiracy*; Laqueur, *The Changing Face of Antisemitism*, 95–101; and *Antisemitism: A History*, ed. Lindemann and Levy.

elsewhere in the world, from the fourth century to Vatican II and beyond; given the universalizing and totalizing claims of Christian ideology; and given the firm place of the "rhetorical Jew" within these currents, it is thus perhaps not surprising to find the concept of Jewish conspiracy theories in later ages and derived traditions, where Jews seem suspiciously present at all key world events.[55] To cite one infamous example of this pathology from the twentieth century:

> What soon gave me cause for very serious consideration were the activities of the Jews in certain branches of life, into the mystery of which I penetrated little by little. Was there any shady undertaking, any form of foulness, especially in cultural life, in which at least one Jew did not participate? On putting the probing knife carefully to that kind of abscess one immediately discovered, like a maggot in a putrescent body, a little Jew who was often blinded by the sudden light.[56]

It is possible that the conceptual foundations of this conspiracy pathology were inaugurated and normalized very early in the Christian tradition through phenomena such as the spectral presence of the Jews in the revolving *transit* of the Christian liturgical year.[57]

---

55 See Aaronovitch, *Voodoo Histories: The Role of the Conspiracy Theory in Shaping Modern History*, 19–49.

56 Adolf Hitler, *Mein Kampf*, trans. James Murphy, accessed at http://gutenberg.net.au/ebooks02/0200601.txt (27 January 2011).

57 My thanks to Samantha Zacher and my fellow participants at the original Cornell conference in which this paper first saw light. This essay was also delivered in slightly different form as a plenary lecture at Purdue University and at the University of Iowa: my thanks to David Nirenberg, Michael Johnston, Robyn Malo, Dorsey Armstrong, Paul Whitfield White, Shaun Hughes, Charles Ross, Kathy Lavezzo, Alvin Snider, Jon Wilcox, Steven Kruger, Lindsay Kaplan, and Jonathan Freedman for their thoughts and hospitality on those occasions.

Literary Types and Anglo-Saxon Audiences

6 Abraham's Children: Jewish Promise and Christian Fulfilment

DANIEL ANLEZARK

The patriarch Abraham appears in the literature of the Anglo-Saxons in a variety of contexts, ranging from his role as a historical figure briefly mentioned in Orosius' world history, to his place marking the turning point between ages of the world, as a type of God in the sacrifice of Isaac, to a discussion of the physical details of circumcision.[1] His pre-eminent status among the patriarchs is reflected in Bede's choice to end his commentary on Genesis at a turning point in Abraham's life (the expulsion of Ishmael), and a similar choice by the poet of *Genesis A* to end his poem immediately after the sacrifice of Isaac, in the same place where Ælfric ends his prose translation of Genesis.[2] By the early eleventh century, then, full versions of Abraham's wandering life were circulating in Old English in both poetry and prose. Abraham is discussed across the Old English homiletic corpus, where the significance of his life and dealings with God are explained to Anglo-Saxon audiences. Abraham was important to the Anglo-Saxons, and to all medieval Christians, as their "father," as he is called in the Canon of the Mass.[3] By identifying themselves as Abraham's children, Anglo-Saxon Christians believed themselves to be the heirs to the promises

---

1 See *The Old English Orosius*, ed. Bately, 133; *The Old English Heptateuch and Ælfric's Libellus de veteri testamento et novo*, ed. Marsden, 205–6; *CH 1, Octabas et circumcisio Domini nostri*, 224–31. Abbreviations have been expanded and punctuation modified.

2 See Bede, *Libri quatuor in principium Genesis usque ad nativitatem Isaac*, ed. Jones; Jones, "Some Introductory Remarks on Bede's Commentary on Genesis," 159; *Genesis A: A New Edition*, ed. Doane, 324–5; *Old English Heptateuch*, ed. Marsden, 3; Clemoes, "The Chronology of Ælfric's Works," 224–5.

3 *Patriarchae nostrae*; see *Missale Romanum*, Editio juxta typicam Vaticanam, 324.

made to him by God. This belief incorporated them into a tradition of reading the Jewish scriptures as texts with Christian meaning, a process initiated by the apostle Paul, and given an influential theoretical articulation by Augustine of Hippo, among other patristic authors. As medieval Christians, the Anglo-Saxons not only read the Old Testament, but also inherited a way of reading Jews. This essay will trace the history of reading Abraham as the "father" of Christian gentile nations, rather than of the Jewish people, and examine the development of this idea in Anglo-Saxon literature. I will begin with a brief survey of the background to the promises made to Abraham and his offspring in scripture, and their interpretation by Christian writers beginning with the gospels through various patristic works. These ideas had a particular impact on two Old English authors. Ælfric of Eynsham, the most prolific writer of Old English prose, reveals a strong interest in the theological role of Abraham and the promises made to him in the formation of Christian identity. This interest is shared by the anonymous author of the Old English poem *Exodus*, who frames his narrative of the flight from Egypt in terms which make the question of who can claim Abraham as father the key to a Christian reading of a foundational event in Jewish history.

Biblical Background

The series of promises to Abraham that begin at Genesis 12, and continue throughout his story, are crucial not only to the structural unity of the narrative of Genesis, but also of the Old and New Testaments.[4] His migration from Chaldea is followed by a divine command to Abram (as he is still called) to leave his homeland, a command which is accompanied by a promise of blessing (Gen. 12:2–3):

faciamque te in gentem magnam et benedicam tibi et magnificabo nomen tuum erisque benedictus; benedicam benedicentibus tibi et maledicam maledicentibus tibi atque in te benedicentur universae cognationes terrae

(And I will make of you a great nation, and I will bless you, and magnify your name, and you will be blessed. I will bless those who bless you, and curse those who curse you, and in you all the kindreds of the earth shall be blessed)

---

4 See Wenham, *Genesis 1–15*, 258, 274–8. The biblical text cited is *Biblia Sacra, Iuxta Vulgatam versionem*, ed. Weber, 4th ed.; punctuation has been added.

This first promise, and its potential implication for the gentile nations, would be given great weight by Christian writers. Abram goes into the land of Canaan, which is subsequently promised to his seed (Gen. 12:7). A further set of promises, immediately after Abram's separation from Lot, again guarantees this land to him and his seed, who will be as numerous as the dust of the earth (Gen. 13:15–16):

omnem terram quam conspicis tibi dabo et semini tuo usque in sempiternum faciamque semen tuum sicut pulverem terrae; si quis potest hominum numerare pulverem terrae, semen quoque tuum numerare poterit

(All the land which you see, I will give to you, and to your seed for ever. And I will make your seed like the dust of the earth: if anyone is able to count the dust of the earth, he shall be able to number your seed also.)

This promise of a multitude of descendants (into eternity) is renewed with a fresh metaphor in response to Abram's prayer for an heir (Gen. 15:1–3), assuring him that one will be provided, and that his descendants will also be as numerous as the stars of the heavens (Gen. 15:4–5).

After the birth of Ishmael and the initiation of the covenant sealed with the sign of circumcision, the promise of offspring is renewed, but for the first time this is extended, assuring Abraham not only that he will become a great nation, but the father of many nations. This is the significance of the new name given to him: "erisque pater multarum gentium nec ultra vocabitur nomen tuum Abram, sed appellaberis Abraham quia patrem multarum gentium constitui te" (and you shall be a father of many nations. Neither shall your name be Abram any more, but you shall be called Abraham, because I have made you a father of many nations. Gen. 17:2–5).[5] This covenant includes the renewal and extension of earlier promises: Abraham's descendants will include kings, they will live in the land promised to him, and they too must live in accordance with the covenant (Gen. 17:6–9). The final renewal of these promises to Abraham himself follows the sacrifice of Isaac, where Abraham's obedience to God's command occasions one final reformulation of the earlier promises: "benedicam tibi et multiplicabo semen tuum sicut stellas caeli et velut harenam quae est in

---

5 The name change is ignored by the author of *Genesis A*, who calls the patriarch *Abraham* from the outset; see *Genesis A*, line 1710.

litore maris; possidebit semen tuum portas inimicorum suorum et benedicentur in semine tuo omnes gentes terrae quia oboedisti voci meae" (I will bless you, and I will multiply your seed as the stars of heaven, and as the sand that is by the sea shore; your seed shall possess the gates of their enemies and in your seed shall all the nations of the earth be blessed, because you have obeyed my voice; Gen. 22:17–18).

Following Abraham's death the promises made to him form the basis of the identity of the people who understand themselves as his seed and heirs. The promises are a key feature of the blessing that Jacob wins from Isaac, and chief among these is the promise of land (Gen. 28:10–22). In Jacob's vision of the heavenly ladder, God renews the promises made to Abraham (Gen. 28:13–14). The concern for the possession of the land dominates interest in the promises throughout the Jewish scriptures.[6] The prophets use the promises in their preaching, condemning the people for their infidelity to the covenant, and point to a fulfilment of the promises that will include the nations in a future Messianic age. Isaiah condemns the evil of his own time and looks forward to an age when the God who redeemed Abraham will redeem his people (Isa. 29:22). Elsewhere in Isaiah, these people are described as being called from the ends of the earth: "et tu Israhel serve meus Iacob quem elegi, semen Abraham amici mei in quo apprehendi te ab extremis terrae" (But you Israel, are my servant, Jacob whom I have chosen, the seed of Abraham my friend, in whom I have taken you from the ends of the earth; Isa. 41:8–9).[7] Ezekiel prophesies the loss of the land given to Abraham as a consequence of the nation's sin (Ezek. 33:24–8). The song of Azarias in the furnace prays for national forgiveness, calling on God to remember his covenant with Abraham, and the promise of a multitude of descendants (Dan. 3:35–6).[8]

The promises made to Abraham were interpreted by the authors of the New Testament as being fulfilled in Jesus, who was interpreted literally and uniquely as the promised seed of Abraham who would bless the nations. Luke's gospel, in words echoing the canticle of Azarias, interprets Christ's

---

6 See Gen. 50:23; Exod. 3:6, 15–16; 32:13; 33:1; Deut. 1:8; 6:10; 30:2; Num. 32:11; 2 Chron. 20:7; Ps. 104:1, 6–12, 42; 2 Esdras (Nehemiah) 9:7–8.

7 See also Isa. 51:2; 63:16.

8 This canticle is included in the poems *Daniel* (lines 283–332) and *Azarias* (lines 5–48); *Daniel and Azarias*, ed., Farrell; references to Christ in both poems (*Daniel* line 401, *Azarias* line 103), reveal a thorough appropriation of the stories by Christian authors.

birth as the fulfilment of the ancient promises in both the *Magnificat* and the *Benedictus* (Luke 1:55, 73–5).[9] The genealogy which opens Matthew's Gospel, and so the New Testament canon itself, emphasizes Jesus' descent from both Abraham and David: "Liber generationis Iesu Christi, filii David, filii Abraham. Abraham genuit Isaac ..." (The book of the generation of Jesus Christ, son of David, son of Abraham. Abraham begot Isaac ...; Matt. 1:1–2). The New Testament re-interpretation of the identity of the seed of Abraham, and consequently of the heirs to the promises of blessing made to him, begins with John the Baptist, who warns the people of Israel: "dico enim vobis quoniam potest Deus de lapidibus istis suscitare filios Abrahae" (For I tell you that God is able from these stones to raise up children for Abraham; Matt. 3:9; see also Luke 3:8). After the cure of the centurion's servant, Jesus himself warns that many will come from east and west to rest with Abraham, Isaac, and Jacob, when the children of the kingdom will be cast out (Matt. 8:11–12).

The clearest explication in the New Testament of the Christian understanding of the promises made to Abraham is found in the letters of Paul to the Romans and Galatians. In Romans 4:1–25, Paul develops an allegorical interpretation of the circumcision, and in his shift away from literal interpretations made "according to the flesh" to reading "in the spirit," he argues that Abraham's true children are so according to faith and grace: "ideo ex fide ut secundum gratiam ut firma sit promissio omni semini, non ei qui ex lege est solum sed et ei qui ex fide est Abrahae qui est pater omnium nostrum" (Therefore is it by faith, so that according to grace the promise might be made firm for all the seed; not for that only which is of the law, but to that also which is of the faith of Abraham, who is the father of us all; Rom. 4:16).[10] In this way not all who are the seed of Abraham according to the flesh are his true children according to God's promise: these children of the promise are his true seed (Rom. 9:7). Naturally enough, Paul allows that Jews as well as gentiles can be Abraham's true children. The epistle to the Galatians (3:1–29) extends this idea of the redundancy of the Law, and develops the concept that blessings are given to believers

---

9 Both canticles were used daily in the monastic liturgy; see Korhammer, *Die Monastischen Cantica im Mittelalter*, 2. See also Nolland, *Luke 1–9:20*, 73–4, 87–8.

10 See Dunn, *Romans 1–8*, 194–241; Berger, "Abraham in der paulinischen Hauptbriefen," 63–77. A different perspective on Abraham's faith is found in James 2:21–3, where the importance of Abraham's good works is also discussed; see Martin, *James*, 90–4.

according to the promise made to Abraham, not according to the Law
(Gal. 3:8–9). Christ redeemed believers from the curse of the Law, so that
the blessing of Abraham might come to the gentiles through faith (Gal.
3:13–14). And in a text that was to come to dominate anti-Jewish polemic
in the early patristic period, Paul argues that the promises to be fulfilled in
and by Abraham's seed were made in the singular, referring to Christ (Gal.
3:16).[11] This leads to a new formulation of the identity of Abraham's seed:
"si autem vos Christi, ergo Abrahae semen estis, secundum promissionem
heredes" (And if you are Christ's, then you are the seed of Abraham, heirs
according to the promise, Gal. 3:29). This doctrine is further developed in
the allegory of Abraham's two sons, one the son of the slave Hagar and the
other of the free-woman Sarah (Gal. 4:22–31).

It is clear from this survey that in the preaching of Jesus and his followers a new interpretation of the promises made to Abraham and his
children became a core element of early Christian identity as the Church
emerged from its Jewish roots. Essential to this were both literal and figurative readings of the Jewish scriptures. The roots of the allegorical exegetical tradition extend back to the mystical interpretation of the figure of
Abraham and other patriarchs by Philo of Alexandria, whose figural readings had a far-reaching influence on early Christian authors.[12] The story
of Abraham is, in fact, a *locus classicus* for the discussion of how figurative
reading works.[13] The most important western writer on the theory of the
Christian reading of Jewish scriptures is Augustine of Hippo, who turns
to the example of Sarah and Hagar in his discussion of typology in his *De
Genesi ad litteram*, one of the most influential commentaries on Genesis
of the medieval period.[14] The freedom allowed the Christian reader of
Jewish scriptures is radically defined by Augustine in his *Confessions* (XII.
xviii.27):[15] "As long as each interpreter is endeavouring to find in the holy

---

11 See Siker, *Disinheriting the Jews: Abraham in Early Christian Controversy*, 150–1,
    172–3, 188.
12 See Daniélou, *From Shadows to Reality,* 115; in Philo's *De somniis* I.i.25, Abraham
    represents the virtue derived from application to study; Siker, *Disinheriting the Jews*, 20,
    notes that in Philo's *Quis rerum divinarum heres* the fruit of the Promised Land is "the
    sure and steadfast apprehension of the wisdom of God." Figurative readings include
    allegory and typology, though "typological interpretation always presupposes a literal
    sense; allegory can bypass it," Markus, *Signs and Meanings*, 11.
13 See Daniélou, "Abraham dans la tradition chrétienne," 68–87.
14 *De Genesi ad litteram* libri XII, ed. J. Zycha, VIII.4.8; see Markus, *Signs and Meanings*, 6.
15 Cited Markus, *Signs and Meanings*, 19.

scriptures the meaning of the author who wrote it, what evil is it if an exegesis he gives is one shown to be true by you [God], light of all sincere souls, even if the author whom he is reading did not have that idea and, though he had grasped a truth, had not discerned that seen by the interpreter?" After the time of Jesus, however, this freedom is not enjoyed by Jews themselves. In his *De doctrina christiana* (III.5–6), Augustine quotes Paul in 2 Corinthians 3:6 ("The letter kills, but the spirit gives life"), applying the text to the difference between Christian and Jewish readings of the Old Testament, whereby the Jews are understood to be still in bondage to signs rather than liberated through their meanings. The Christian, who reads in the spirit, can find meanings in typology that Jewish readers cannot see.[16] The Anglo-Saxons adopted this stance fully when reading Abraham.[17] Paul's writings had offered a way of interpreting the promises made to Abraham that saw the inclusion of gentiles in the fulfilment of promises historically made to Jews, but also allowed for an interpretation whereby the Jews themselves might be understood to be excluded. By the middle of the second Christian century, this tendency toward theological exclusion of Jews from the promises of the Kingdom, as exemplified in the writings of Justin Martyr, had become the norm.[18] After this time gentile Christians tended to regard themselves exclusively as Abraham's children, though as we shall see this understanding was not universal. Early patristic commentary dwelt on the significance of the promises re-iterated after the sacrifice of Isaac, and developed Paul's remarks in his Letter to the Galatians (Gal. 3:15–17), which were taken to be a comment on this set of promises.

The standard Christian understanding, derived from Paul, was that the unique, singular descendant through whom the gentile nations were to be blessed was Jesus (the Messiah), the greatest of Abraham's offspring.[19] In Jesus, the descendant of Abraham (Matt. 1:1), the gentiles are engendered children of Abraham by faith (Rom. 4:16, 17). For Irenaeus it is the son of God who delivers by faith a posterity for Abraham as numerous as the

---

16 See Markus, *Signs and Meanings*, 24–5. See also Fredriksen, "*Excaecati Occulta Justitia Dei*: Augustine on Jews and Judaism," 299–324.

17 See Jones, "Some Introductory Remarks," 157; Holder, "Bede and the Tradition of Patristic Exegesis," 407; Ray, "What do we know about Bede's Commentaries?", 18.

18 See Siker, *Disinheriting the Jews*, 172–3, for a discussion of *Dialogue with Trypho* 25–6.

19 See Tertullian, *De carne Christi* 22, *PL* 2:789; Augustine, *Contra Faustum* 12.6, *PL* 42:257; Jerome, *Commentaria in epistola ad Galatas* 1, *PL* 26:378–9; Haymo, *Enarratio in epistolam ad Galatas* 3, 15–17, *PL* 117:680–3.

stars,[20] and Ambrose sees faith as the means by which Abraham's race is propagated.[21] Cyril of Alexandria, developing another theme that became popular among commentators, claims that the Jews have no right to call Abraham father, except according to the flesh, while Christians are his true spiritual children by faith.[22] Rabanus Maurus makes a similar distinction between the carnal posterity of Abraham, equated with the dust of the earth, and the spiritual posterity, who shine like the stars of heaven and aspire to a heavenly inheritance.[23] In regarding themselves as Abraham's heirs, the Anglo-Saxons were no exception. Indeed, it has been pointed out that the idea that the converted English had joined the elect and become Abraham's children of the promise is not only an important theme in Bede's commentary on Genesis, but also explains the structure of the work as a whole.[24] Clearly the Anglo-Saxons were not the only gentile nation to experience conversion to Christianity, nor the only people to include themselves in the blessings promised to Abraham. Within this shared belief, however, the Anglo-Saxons developed their own interpretations of this Christian doctrine.[25]

Ælfric and Abraham's promises

Ælfric, among all writers in Old English, presents the most comprehensive treatment of the subject of the fulfilment of God's promises to Abraham. Indeed, his careful and consistent presentation of the theme suggests that the question was a crucial one in his own theology, one to which he attached lasting importance. In his Old English version of Alcuin's Latin *Interrogationes Sigeuulfi in Genesin*, Ælfric treats the promises made to Abraham in two questions. Question LX closely translates Alcuin's Question CLV, asking how many promises God made to Abraham:[26]

---

20 *Contra Haereses*, 4.7.1–2, *PG* 7:991–2.
21 *De Abraham*, 1.3.20–21, *PL* 14:428.
22 *Glaphyra in Genesim*, 3.2, *PG* 69:113.
23 *Commentariorum in Genesim*, 2.12–17, *PL* 117:533–41.
24 See Jones, "Some Introductory Remarks," 125–31.
25 See now Zacher, *Rewriting the Old Testament in Anglo-Saxon Verse: Becoming the Chosen People*, which examines the earliest examples of English biblical poetry with a view to exploring their artistic and cultural responses to the Old Testament texts and the Jewish laws, practices, and beliefs they adapt and rewrite for their own theologico-political purposes.
26 See Maclean, "Ælfric's Version of the *Interrogationes Sigeuulfi in Genesin*," *Anglia* 6:425–73, and *Anglia* 7:1–59, 42, lines 395–40; Clemoes, "Chronology," 225.

Hu fela behata behet god abrahame? Twa; An wæs þæt he and his ofspring sceoldan agan þone eard iudeisces landes; Oþer þæt he is þurh geleafan manegra þeoda fæder; and ealle þeoda syndon gebletsode on his ofspringe. þæt is on criste;

(How many promises did God make to Abraham? Two. One was that he and his offspring should have a territory in the land of the Jews. The second was that he is the father of many nations by faith, and all nations are blessed in his offspring, that is in Christ.)

From the survey of biblical material above it is clear that this simplified answer is not strictly true, though Ælfric's conciseness stems from the fact that the questions were designed to accompany his Genesis translation. The answer presents a standard Christian reading of the import of the promises as a whole: they promised land to the Jewish people, and blessing and salvation for the nations in Christ. The superior importance of the promise to the nations is signalled by its reiteration in Ælfric's Question LXIX (Alcuin's CCI). In discussing the apparent inconsistency of scripture on the subject of God testing Abraham,[27] Ælfric adds to Alcuin's text the consequence of Abraham's obedience:[28] "swa þæt god him cwæð to; On þinum ofspringe beoð ealle eorðlice mægða gebletsode" (so that God said to him: "In your offspring will all the earthly kindred be blessed"). In his addition, Ælfric makes no mention of the promise of land, as this is irrelevant to the Anglo-Saxon Christian. A similar thematic emphasis is found in Ælfric's *Sermo de memoria Sanctorum*, where in his brief mention of Abraham the theme of the promise fulfilled for Christians dominates:[29] "Abraham for his micclan geleafan to gode. and for his gehyrsumnysse underfeng swilce bletsunge æt gode. þæt eall mancynn ða þe gelyfað on god is gebletsod on his cynne." (Abraham, because of his great faith in God, and because of his obedience, received such blessings from God that all humankind that believes in God is blessed in his nation.) Ælfric's presentation of the promise is formulated in his own words, and draws on no particular biblical passage.[30]

---

27 See Maclean, "Interrogationes," 50.

28 See Maclean, "Interrogationes," 50–2, lines 499–500; compare *PL* 100:516–66, No. CCI.

29 See *Ælfric's Lives of Saints*, ed. Skeat, I, 338, lines 25–7.

30 See Zettel, "Ælfric's Hagiographic Sources and the Latin Legendary Preserved in B.L. MS. Cotton Nero i + CCCC MS.9 and other Manuscripts," 47.

The lines of Ælfric's thought on the relative importance of the promises made to Abraham can be seen in his *Passio Sancti Stephani*, based on a sermon by Fulgentius.[31] As the first Christian martyr, Stephen's death symbolized for Christians an important turning point away from Judaism. For the part of the *Passio* dealing with the promises, Ælfric draws not on Fulgentius, but directly on the account of Stephen's martyrdom found in the Acts of the Apostles (7:2–8). In his summary of Stephen's preaching, Ælfric retains a section on Abraham, quoted in indirect speech. Ælfric removes all reference to the promise of land for Abraham's descendants, and to circumcision, providing instead material of direct interest to an Anglo-Saxon Christian audience. He adds to his source in such a way as to emphasize the lack of faith in the listening Jews (*CH* 1.3.29–34):

Ða wolde se halga wer Stephanus heora ungeleaffullan heortan gerihtlæcan mid heora forðfædera gebysnunge and gemynde, and to soðfæstnysse wege mid ealre lufe gebigan. Begann ða him to reccenne be ðam heahfædere abrahame, hu se heofonlica God hine geceas him to geþoftan, and him behet þæt ealle ðeoda on his ofspringe gebletsode wurdon, for his gehyrsumnesse.

(Then the holy man Stephen wished to correct their unbelieving hearts with the examples and memory of their forefathers, and with all love turn them to the way of righteousness. He then began to recount to them concerning the patriarch Abraham, how the heavenly God chose him as a companion, and promised him that because of his obedience, all nations would be blessed in his offspring.)

Ælfric's recasting of the Acts passage is barely even a paraphrase. Acts contains no reference at this point to the lack of faith among the Jews, or mention of Abraham as a companion of God, and Ælfric simply replaces Stephen's reference to the promise of land with that offering blessing to all nations.[32] The result of this reworking – a striking example of the theology of displacement – is that Stephen talks not about the significance of Abraham from a Jewish perspective, but rather a gentile one. Consequently, the reference in Acts to the old covenant is removed, and

---

31 *CH* 1.3.198–205; see Smetana, "Ælfric and the Early Medieval Homiliary," 163–204, 183; Godden, *Ælfric's Homilies: Introduction, Commentary and Glossary*, 23–8.
32 Compare Acts 7:2–8.

the promise relevant to Stephen's Jewish audience is replaced by the promise meaningful for Ælfric's Anglo-Saxon readers.

Abraham often appears in Ælfric's works in summaries of biblical history. In his second series, homily 1, *De natale Domini*, Ælfric offers a wide-ranging discussion of material, derived from a variety of sources, on several themes associated with Christ's nativity and the Incarnation. The example of Abraham demonstrates the truth of God's promises and prophecy: "Ealle ða ðing ðe crist dyde for us. ealle he wæron ær gefyrn gewitegode. þæt men sceoldon gelyfan þæt he is soðfæst." (All these things that Christ did for us, all of them were prophesied long ago, so that men should believe that he is righteous.)[33] Ælfric articulates the historical and prophetic link between all those who *rihtlice gelyfað* and the promise to Abraham that many nations would be blessed in his seed (*CH* 2.1.127–33):

Se ælmihtiga god behet gefyrn worulde Abrahame þam heahfædere þæt on his cynne sceolde beon eal mancynn gebletsod. and him eac swa gelæste; Of Abrahames cynne com se mære cyning Dauid. and of ðam cynecynne com seo halige maria. and of marian crist wearð acenned. and þurh crist is eal mancynn gebletsod. þa ðe rihtlice gelyfað.

(The almighty God promised the patriarch Abraham in an age long ago that in his kin all mankind would be blessed, and so also it was fulfilled for him. From Abraham's kin came the famous king David, and from that royal kin came the holy Mary, and from Mary Christ was born, and through Christ all humankind, those who believe rightly, is blessed.)

The inheritance of the blessing offered to Abraham is not offered specifically to either Jews or gentiles, but with close adherence to Paul's doctrine, to all who believe. This impartiality becomes a mark of Ælfric's theology of promise: the individual's response in faith to Jesus is what matters. A similar approach is found in *De natale Domini*, Ælfric's homily for the Annunciation of Mary,[34] where again Ælfric takes care to preserve the Pauline emphasis on the singular seed of Abraham, Christ, which is crucial for

---

33 See *CH* 2.1.121–2; see Godden, *Ælfric's Homilies: Introduction*, 346–54.

34 A similar approach is found in *Adnuntiatio sanctae Mariae* (*CH* 1.13.281–9, at 287), where Ælfric again develops Bede's comments on the promises to Abraham; see *Opera Homiletica*, ed. Hurst., I.4, 29–30; see Smetana, "Early Medieval Homiliary," 88; Godden, *Ælfric's Homilies: Introduction*, 101–9.

142   Daniel Anlezark

the recognition and the fulfilment of God's promise to Abraham that all nations would be blessed in this seed. Unsurprisingly, there is no mention of land or of the Jewish people, apart from the implication that they are Abraham's children according to the flesh.

The discussion of Abraham is more detailed in Ælfric's homily for the second Sunday after Epiphany. This homily is structured around the symbolism of the six water jars transformed at Cana as representing the six ages of the world, drawing mostly on Bede's homily for the same occasion.[35] At the beginning of the third age God tested Abraham's obedience in the sacrifice of Isaac, a story described more fully by Ælfric than Bede; Ælfric applies the conventional typological interpretation which saw the episode as a foreshadowing of Christ's crucifixion.[36] Where Bede's original had made only a passing reference to the *perpetuae benedictionis heredi-tate*, Ælfric provides a full version of the promise (*CH* 2.4.152–60):

Ic gebletsige ðe. and þinne ofspring ic gemenigfylde swa swa steorran on heofenan. and swa swa sandceosol on sælicum strande; Þin sæd soðlice geagnað his feonda gatu. and on ðinum sæde beoð gebletsode ealle eorðlice mægðe. for ðan ðe ðu gehyrsumedest minre stemne.

(I will bless you and multiply your offspring like the stars in heaven, and like the sand on the seashore. Your seed truly will gain the gates of its enemies, and in your seed all earthly kindred will be blessed, because you obeyed my voice.)

Ælfric's addition provides a clearer context for the explanation of the importance of the promises for his own audience, though he retains Bede's reference to the "eternal" dimension of the blessing. He returns to Bede's imagery to illustrate the spiritual participation of his audience in the promise.[37] Ælfric adds the key Pauline text (Gal. 3:29), found neither in Haymo

---

35 See *CH* 2.4.29–40; Bede, *Opera Homiletica*, CCSL 122, I.14; see Smetana, "Early Medieval Homiliary," 196; Smetana, "Ælfric and the Homiliary of Haymo of Halberstadt," 463–4, demonstrates that Ælfric draws on Haymo, *PL* 118:126–37, for details which Bede does not include; see Gatch, *Preaching and Theology in Anglo-Saxon England*, 77–8; see also Godden, *Ælfric's Homilies: Introduction*, 370–80.

36 See Daniélou, *Shadows to Reality*, 115–30. The augmenting detail amplifying Abraham's role in the homily is drawn from Haymo; see Smetana, "Ælfric and the Homiliary of Haymo," 463–4; Godden, *Ælfric's Homilies: Introduction*, 376.

37 *Opera homiletica*, CCSL 122, I.14, lines 179–82.

nor in Bede, which emphasizes the particular meaning of these promises to his listeners as gentiles, who are the originally intended beneficiaries of the promises (*CH* 2.4.173–8):

> Ge sceolon eac gelyfan þæt seo bletsung ðe god behet abrahame gæð ofer us. and we sind Abrahames sæd. swa swa paulus þeoda lareow cwæð; Eornostlice gif ge cristes sind. þonne sind ge Abrahames sæd. and æfter behate yrfenuman.

> (You must also believe that the blessing that God promised Abraham extends over us, and we are Abraham's seed, just as Paul the teacher of the nations says: "Truly, if you are of Christ, then you are Abraham's seed, and then called an heir.")

Ælfric is at pains to point out that inclusion in the blessing promised to Abraham is not automatic. The conditional *gif* introduced with the quote from Paul warns against the presumption in the claim that "we are Abraham's seed."

Ælfric's homily on the Circumcision includes further detail on Abraham's promises.[38] The sources for the first part of the homily, on ritual circumcision and its New Testament counterpart (baptism), are Bede and Haymo.[39] The link between the sign of circumcision, the promise of offspring, and the promise that Abraham would be the father of many nations, are all explained by Ælfric, despite the apparent awkwardness that aspects of the subject matter seem to present for him as a preacher.[40] The promise that Abraham is to be "the father of many nations" is given particular prominence, as is the etymological basis of the name change from Abram, *Healic fæder* (exalted father), to Abraham, *manegra ðeoda fæder* (father of many nations). In an addition by Ælfric, Isaac's arrival is interpreted as the occasion of God's promise of blessing for all humanity through Abraham's *cynn* (*CH* 1.6.41–3): "Ðaða him cild com þa com hit mid Godes foresceawunge and bletsunge to þan swiðe þæt God him behet eallum mancynne bletsunge þurh his cynn." (When the child came to him, it came with God's

---

38 See *CH* 1.6.224–31.
39 See Godden, *Ælfric's Homilies: Introduction*, 45–53.
40 Ælfric reveals some anxiety about his audience's reaction to the details of circumcision; the covenant and Law were "god on hire timan" ("good in their time," line 72), and circumcision may seem "dyslic to gehyrenne" ("foolish to hear," line 85). See also Zacher, "Circumscribing the Text."

foreknowledge and great blessing, that God promised him blessing for all mankind through his nation.) This oblique reference, found in neither source, conflates the Lord's reflection on the implications of his promise at Mambre (Gen. 18:17–19), and the confirmation of these promises after the sacrifice of Isaac (Gen. 22:18). Ælfric's reading draws deeply on patristic conventions of reading the Jewish scripture. The covenant of circumcision was kept by all until the birth of Christ, when the "significations" (*getacnunge*) of the old Law were changed to spiritual truth. The bodily circumcision provides a typological foreshadowing of baptism, and beyond this, following Paul, Ælfric develops a moral allegory, whereby gentile believers are properly called Abraham's people (*CH* 1.6.113–17):

> Gif we þas gastlican ymbsnidennysse on urum þeawum healdað þonne sind we Abrahames cynnes æfter soþum geleafan, swa swa se þeoda lareow Paulus cwæð to geleaffullum, Gif ge sind Cristes, þonne sind ge Abrahames sæd, and æfter behate yrfenuman.

> (If we keep the spiritual circumcision in our customs, then we are of Abraham's nation, according to true faith, just as Paul the teacher of the nations said to the faithful: "If you are of Christ, then you are Abraham's seed, and then called heirs.")

Ælfric uses this favourite Pauline text (Gal. 3:29) stressing the conditional nature of the blessing, and the need for the correct spiritual and moral response of the believer. Ælfric is not particularly concerned here with a polemic against Jews or the Law, which preoccupy his sources, but rather the spiritual state of his Anglo-Saxon audience.

Ælfric's own pastoral priorities reveal themselves in his use of the figure of Abraham in his adaptation of sources that concern themselves with the conflict between the Church and the Synagogue. Ælfric sometimes tones down the condemnation and exclusion of Jews, preferring to emphasize the idea of gentile inclusion. The first part of his homily for the third Sunday after Epiphany follows the homily for the same Sunday by Haymo.[41] Haymo's homily is an exposition of three miracles: the cure of a leper (Matt. 8:1–13); the miraculous cure of the servant of the centurion

---

41 *CH* 1.8; see Smetana, "Early Medieval Homiliary," 186.

(Luke 7:1–10); and the cure of the ruler's son (John 4:46–53). The second of these miracles deals with the faith of a gentile (*CH* 1.8.95–101):

> ða wundrode se Hælend þa ða he ðis gehyrde, and cwæð to þære fyligendan meniu, Soð ic eow secge, ne gemette ic swa micelne geleafan on Israhela þeode. Ic secge eow to soþan, þæt manega cumað fram eastdæle and westdæle and gerestað hi mid Abrahame þam heahfædere and Isaac and Iacob on heofenan rice. ða rican bearn beoð aworpene into ðam yttrum þeostrum, þær bið wop and toða gebit.

> (Then the Saviour marvelled when he heard this, and said to the following multitude, "I tell you the truth, I have not met such great faith in the people of the Israelites. I say to you truly, that many will come from the east and the west, and they will rest with the patriarch Abraham, and with Isaac and Jacob, in the kingdom of heaven. The children of the kingdom will be cast into the utter darkness, where there is weeping and grinding of teeth.")

When reworking his source material Ælfric eliminates much of the verse-by-verse commentary, and gives added emphasis to the miraculous cure of the centurion's servant, retelling the story in its essential details. The lack of faith among the people of Israel is not intended to refer to the *heahfæderum oððe witegum* (patriarchs and prophets).[42] In place of Haymo's lengthy condemnation of the "carnal" Israel, which sees Christ's miracles but refuses to believe, Ælfric suggests that the *andwerdan folc* (present people) were not yet (*ða gyt*) of such great faith.[43] Ælfric's comment introduces a further departure from his source, when he cites the example of Martha and Mary as two (Jewish) sisters who *swiðe on God belyfde* (believed greatly in God).[44] His retelling of the miraculous cure of the servant, and Christ's prophecy that many will come from east and west to rest with the three patriarchs follows Haymo's model, but Ælfric's comment is his own (*CH* 1.8.156–9):

---

42 *CH* 1.6.144–5; the explanation is found in Haymo: "Quod non de patriarchis et prophetis dicit" (*PL* 118:145A).

43 *CH* 1.6.145.

44 See Smetana, "Early Medieval Homiliary," 186.

ðas word sind lustbære to gehyrenne, and hi micclum ure mod gladiað, þæt manega cumað fram eastdæle middangeardes and fram westdæle to heofenan rice, and mid þam heahfæderum on ecere myrhðe rixiað;

(These words are joyous to hear, and they greatly gladden our mind, that many will come from the eastern part of the earth, and from the western part, to the heavenly kingdom, and will reign with eternal joy with the patriarchs.)

Ælfric's interest in the inclusiveness of the promised blessing of all nations responds to the tendency in his source to limit the application of this promise, even where this limit is imposed on the Jewish nation. However, Ælfric's care is theologically based – those Jews who lived before and during Christ's time (and believed) are distinguished from those who come later (and do not believe).

Exodus and Promise

The foundational doctrine of the Christian religion is the death and resurrection of Jesus, which coincided historically with the celebration of the Jewish Passover. This convergence had a profound influence on the Christian imagination, so that the historic exodus of the Israelites from Egypt became for Christians a prefiguration of a spiritual liberation in Christ. Christ became the new Moses (John 1:17). The exodus is inseparable from the theology of promise: as Abraham's children, the Israelites are returning to the land promised to him. This association became an important one for Christian writers, and discussions of Easter and the exodus were tied to the question of who Abraham's heirs were. In Byrhtferth of Ramsey's *Enchiridion*, where he discusses the origins of Easter, he explains the mystical significance of the events with comments drawn from Augustine and Bede.[45] Between his translation of the passage from the Book of Exodus and its patristic explication, Byrhtferth comments: "we synt Abrahames bearn, and eac Israeles, his sunu sunu, bearn we synt getealde" (we are the children of Abraham, and we are also considered the children of Israel, the son of his son).[46]

---

45 See Exodus 12:1–11; *Byrhtferth's Enchiridion*, ed. Michael Lapidge and Peter Baker, 122–5.
46 *Enchiridion*, ed. Lapidge and Baker, 122–3, lines 29–30.

Ælfric's treatments of the exodus make the same point in a more complex way. In his *De sex aetatibus huius seculi* Abraham stands at the turning point between the second and third ages of the world, a commonplace in patristic and Anglo-Saxon literature.[47] No source has been suggested, and Ælfric is probably producing his own synthesis from a wide range of reading. He mentions only very briefly the most important aspects of the life of Abraham the *heahfæder*: his faith and the promise of blessing for all nations in his offspring.[48] However, when Abraham is referred to later in the account of the exodus, his association with the Promised Land is made plain – the goal of the six hundred thousand crossing the Red Sea is "þam æðelan earde þe God Abrahame behet" (the noble land that God promised to Abraham).[49] This connection is made again in the description of the Israelites' entry into *Abrahames eard* (Abraham's land), promised to Abraham in the geographic centre of the world.[50] The evocation of this pattern of historical promise and fulfilment is striking in the light of Ælfric's earlier omission of this promise. It would seem that emphasis on the connection between Abraham and blessing is of such importance that it alone is clearly stated, even to the point of unbalancing the thematic development of the text. Ælfric develops this theme of promise and blessing in his account of the entry into the land of Canaan in *De populo Israhel*.[51] The sermon concentrates mostly on Moses and the events of the exodus. Ælfric, however, makes a small but significant addition to the account translated from the Book of Numbers, giving Abraham and his promise a place in the narrative not found in the source (Num. 13:3–4):[52] "and þæt folc gelædan to ðam behatenan lande, swa swa he gefyrn behet þam heahfædere Abrahame" (and led that people to the promised land, just as long before

---

47 See Schmidt, "*Aetates mundi*: die Weltalter als Gliederungsprinzip der Geschichte," 289; Tristram, *Sex aetates mundi: Die Weltzeitalter bei den Iren und den Angelsachsen*, 197.

48 *Sex aetates mundi*, ed. Tristram, lines 71–7. The unique manuscript text is damaged, though reading is not impossible, and the editor has made use of other Ælfrician texts dealing with similar subject matter as the basis of her emendations; see Tristram, *Sex aetates mundi*, 194.

49 *Sex aetates mundi*, ed. Tristram, line 93.

50 *Sex aetates mundi*, ed. Tristram, line 157.

51 See *Homilies of Ælfric: Supplementary Series*, ed. Pope, II, 641–60; on the question of Ælfrician anti-Judaism in this homily, see Scheil, *The Footsteps of Israel*, 295–312.

52 See *Homilies of Ælfric*, ed. Pope, II, 647, lines 140–7; compare Numbers 13:3–4: "Mitte viros qui considerent terram Chanaan, quam daturus sum filiis Israel singulos de singulis tribubis ex principibus. Fecit Moyses quod Dominus imperaverat."

he had promised the patriarch Abraham). Ælfric does not discuss the significance of this promise beyond stating God's desire to keep his word, but it is significant that Ælfric feels the need to tie the exodus to Abraham in a way that his biblical source does not. The same emphasis is found in the writer's *Introduction to the Old and New Testaments* – an original work – which shares elements with the treatment of the promised land in *De populo Israhel*, and *Sex aetates huius saeculi*. In the *Introduction* Abraham inaugurates the third age of the world,[53] and it is in this context that the most significant aspects of his life are presented in summary form. Only one promise is mentioned at this point, that immediately after the sacrifice of Isaac:[54] "þæt þurh his cyn eall mankynn beon gebletsod for his micclan geleafan and for his gehirsumnisse, þe he hæfde to Gode" (that through his nation all humankind will be blessed because of his great faith and because of his obedience which he had towards God). The third age extends down to David, who, Ælfric is careful to point out, is of Abraham's *cynn* and from whom came Christ, who delivered all mankind. The promise of land, again not mentioned in the account of Abraham, is evoked only in terms of its fulfilment. The promise made to Abraham is historically fulfilled in the Exodus, as God wished to bring *Abrahames cynnes* afterwards *to heora earde* (to their land), and Joshua later leads the people of Israel into *Abrahames earde*.[55]

The link between the fulfilment of the historical promise of land in the Old Testament and the promise of salvation in Abraham's seed in the New is again tied to the exodus in Ælfric's Second Series sermon for Midlent Sunday. In this text, Ælfric integrates material from two principal sources, a commentary on the Pentateuch spuriously ascribed to Bede and Alcuin's *De virtutibus et vitiis liber*, within the scheme of the three ages of this world: *ante legem*; *sub lege*; *sub gratia* (before the Law, under the Law, under grace).[56] Neither of these sources has material on the three ages, which Ælfric has introduced to provide structural cohesion. Ælfric's treatment of Abraham, who lived during the first of these ages, often differs significantly from the interpretations in the relevant parts of the Pentateuch

---

53 See *Old English Heptateuch*, ed. Marsden, *Libellus*, lines 134-63.

54 See *Old English Heptateuch*, ed. Marsden, *Libellus*, lines 158–60.

55 See *Old English Heptateuch*, ed. Marsden, *Libellus*, lines 191, 228.

56 See *CH* 2.12, 110–26, at 110; *In Pentateuchum commentarii*, *PL* 91:189–358; *Liber de Virtutibus et Vitiis*, *PL* 101:613–38. The material on Abraham for this sermon is drawn from a wide variety of sources, biblical and non-biblical, some of which Ælfric has used elsewhere; see Godden, *Ælfric's Homilies: Introduction*, 448–66.

commentary.[57] The promise of land merited by Abraham's obedience is referred to in passing: "þa forgeaf se ælmihtiga god him and his ofspringe þone eard" (then the almighty God gave him and his offspring the land).[58] As the sermon unfolds, however, and the spiritual significance of the events of Jewish history is revealed, the thematic importance of the connection between land, exile, and the promise to Abraham becomes the basis of the sermon's structural unity. The exile of his seed in Egypt is prophesied to Abraham (*CH* 2.12.22–7):

> Þa cwæð se ælmihtiga god to abrahame. wite ðu þæt ðin cynn sceal ælðeodig wunian. on oðrum earde feower hund geara. and hi hi on ðeowte gebringað and micclum swencað; Soðlice ic deme ðam folce. and ðin mægð siððan mid micclum æhtum of ðam lande færð. and on ðam feorðan cneowe hi gecyrrað hider ongean;

> (Then said the almighty God to Abraham, "Know that your people shall dwell as exiles in another land for four hundred years, and they will bring them into servitude and they will toil greatly. Truly I will condemn that nation, and then your kinsmen will journey with great possessions from that land, and in the fourth generation they will return here again.")

The fulfilment of the first part of this prophecy follows immediately: "and þær eardodon feower hund geara. swa swa se ælmihtiga god abrahame sæde" (and they dwelled there four hundred years, just as the almighty God said to Abraham).[59] The fulfilment of the second part of the prophecy depends upon the promise of land, which is explained in terms of its allegorical significance (*CH* 2.12.178–82):[60]

> Þæt egypta land hæfde tacnunge þyssere worulde. and pharao getacnode þone ðwyran deofol þe symle godes gecorenum ehtnysse on besett. on andwerdum

---

57 Compare, for example, the treatment of Genesis 15, where the commentary focuses almost exclusively on the allegorical understanding of the beasts of sacrifice, *PL* 91:234–5, whereas Ælfric is interested only in the promise of four hundred years of exile.

58 *CH* 2.12.19–29.

59 *CH* 2.12.36–7; Ælfric translates Alcuin's Question CLXIX, discussing the problems of calculating this length of time, as his Question LXIV; see Maclean, "Interrogationes," 43–7.

60 Some of these interpretations are found in the Pentateuch commentary; for example, the commonplace reading of the Promised Land, "'In terram,' id est in coelum," *PL* 91:230D, 236D, and Egypt, "Ægyptus significat mundum," *PL* 91:231C.

life; Swa swa se ælmihtiga god ða his folc ahredde wið þone cyning pharao. and hi lædde to ðam earde þe he abrahame and his ofspringe behet. swa eac he arett dæghwomlice his gecorenan wið þone ealdan deofol. and hi alyst fram his ðeowte. and fram ðyssere geswincfullan worulde. and gelæt hi to ðam ecan eðele, ðe we to gesceapene wæron;

(The land of the Egyptians had the signification of this world and Pharaoh signified the accursed devil who always besets God's chosen with persecution in this present life. Just as the almighty God then delivered his people from Pharaoh the king, and led them to the land that he had promised to Abraham and his offspring, so also he daily delivers his chosen from the ancient devil, and releases them from his servitude and from this world full of strife, and leads them to the eternal homeland, for which we were created.)

At the beginning of the *Secunda sententia de hoc ipso*, Joshua is the one who leads the people of Israel into the Promised Land.[61] Joshua and the twelve tribes are Abraham's offspring, the nation from which Christ will spring (*CH* 2.12.409–13):

Hwæt ða siððan se sigefæsta cempa þone eard ealne emlice dælde betwux twelf mægðum þæs æðelan mancynnes Abrahames ofspringes ðe hit eal gewann, and hi on ðam lande leofodon siððan oð þæt se ælmihtiga cyning of ðam cynne asprang, Drihten hælend ure sawle to hæle;

(Indeed then the victorious champion evenly divided up the land among the twelve tribes of the noble human race of Abraham's offspring who won it all and afterwards they lived in that land, until the almighty king, the lord and Saviour, sprang from that nation for the salvation of our souls.)

The arrival of Christ brings an end to the historical importance of the Promised Land, which along with the promises made to Abraham are now understood in new terms. This allegorical patterning continues to evolve after the allegorical development of the wars between the people of Israel and the eight nations, understood as eight sins that must be overcome by the soul. In this context the allegorical, and eschatological, significance of the land promised to Abraham again is brought to the fore (*CH* 2.12.542–8):

---

61 *CH* 2.12.377–8.

To ðam earde we wæron gesceapene. ac we hit forwyrhton; Nu næbbe we hit
næfre buton we hit eft gewinnon mid gastlicum gecampe ðurh Godes fultum.
swa swa Israhel ðone eard gewann. ðe abrahame ær behaten wæs;

(For that land we were created, but we have forfeited it. Now we will not
have it ever unless we again strive in the spiritual struggle with God's support, just as Israel won that land that was earlier promised to Abraham.)

In a fully developed example of the kind of reading strategy advocated by
Augustine of Hippo, the Christian spirit reads the Jewish letter. The fulfilment of God's promise of land was not simply a matter of course: only
through warfare, with the help of God, was it fulfilled. The same is true
at the allegorical level for the Christian warrior. Inheritance of the promised heavenly homeland, made possible through Christ, Abraham's seed,
depends on the outcome of the individual's faithful fight against sin. This
allegorical interpretation developed by Ælfric offers a possible ground for
his wider concern for the promise of land, over and above his concern to
demonstrate the past fulfilment of God's promises. The essential element
tying Anglo-Saxon readers to these past events and their spiritual meaning, however, is their inclusion as Abraham's children.

Both the Christian spiritual reading of the Jewish past and the pivotal
role of Abraham are brought together by the poet of the Old English
Exodus, a work written centuries before Ælfric's homilies, according to
scholarly consensus.[62] The poet introduces the Israelites' journey under
Moses in spiritual terms. Moses leads the people in the exodus, while
Abraham provides the underlying rationale for the journey: the land of
Canaan is their destination because of the promise of a homeland (*onwist
eðles, Abrahames sunum*, line 18: to the sons of Abraham a dwelling in a
homeland). Abraham is referred to at two other key moments in the poem.
As the Egyptian army bears down on the terrified Israelites, Moses exhorts
the people not to be afraid, as the "the eternal God of Abraham" (*se ecea
Abrahames god*, line 273) will protect his people. The shift from history to
eternity attunes the Christian ear to the spiritual meaning of the historical
events, but even more precisely to the eternal promise of blessing made
to Abraham's offspring. The shift to Christian modes of reading the Old
Testament is crucial for understanding the significance of the account of
Abraham which follows the recollection of Noah's flood in the so-called

---

62 *Exodus*, ed. Lucas, 69–72; this edition is cited.

"patriarchal digression" at the beginning of the crossing of the Red Sea (lines 353–61). Here a genealogy of the tribes jumps from Israel (line 358), back to Noah (lines 362–76), then forward to Abraham.[63] The poet introduces Abraham as a man given a new name by God (lines 380–3):

> Þæt is se Abraham   se him engla god
> naman niwan asceop;   eac þon neah and feor
> halige heapas   in gehyld bebead,
> werþeoda geweald.   He on wræce lifde.

(That is the Abraham for whom the God of angels created a new name; furthermore, near and far holy multitudes were given into his protection, the power of the nations; he lived in exile.)

The poet's allusion to Abraham's new name evokes his paternity of the nations for the Christian reader, and the reference to the patriarch's historical exile, a parallel to that of the Israelites in Egypt, develops the shift to allegory.[64] The poem's account of Abraham culminates in the promise made after the sacrifice of Isaac (lines 419–25):

> "Ne sleh þu, Abraham,   þin agen bearn,
> sunu mid sweorde.   Soð is gecyðed,
> nu þin cunnode   Cyning alwihta,
> þæt þu wið Waldend   wære heolde,
> fæste treowe,   seo þe freoðo sceal
> in lifdagum   lengest weorðan,
> awa to aldre   unswiciendo.
> …
> He að swereð,   engla Þeoden,
> wyrda Waldend   and wereda God,
> soðfæst sigora,   þurh his sylfes lif,

---

63 See Hauer, "The Patriarchal Digression in the Old English *Exodus*, Lines 362–446," 77–90; Anlezark, "Connecting the Patriarchs: Noah and Abraham in the Old English *Exodus*," 171–88; Abraham, originally called Abram, first appears in the Genesis narrative at Gen. 11:27 in the context of a genealogy describing descent from Noah's blessed son Shem.

64 See Earl, "Christian Traditions and the Old English *Exodus*," 541–70 (reprinted in *The Poems of MS Junius 11: Basic Readings*, ed. Liuzza, 137–72.); Irving, Jr, "New Notes on the Old English *Exodus*," 314.

þæt þines cynnes   and cneowmaga,
randwiggendra,   rim ne cunnon,
yldo ofer eorðan,   ealle cræfte
to gesecgenne   soðum wordum,
nymðe hwylc þæs snottor   in sefan weorðe
þæt he ana mæge   ealle geriman
stanas on eorðan,   steorran on heofonum,
sæbeorga sand,   sealte yða;
ac hie gesittað   be sæm tweonum
oð Egipte   ingeðeode
land Cananea,   leode þine,
freobearn fæder,   folca selost."

("Abraham, do not slaughter your own child, your son with the sword. The truth is made known, now that the king of all things has tested you, that you keep your covenant with the ruler, which will become an enduring peace-pledge for you in your life-days, unfailingly forever to the ages … He, the prince of angels, ruler of fates, and God of hosts, righteous in victories, swears an oath on his own life, that men across the earth will not be able with all their skill, to count in true words your people, generations of descendants, of shield-bearing warriors, unless someone become so wise in mind that he alone might count all the stones on earth, stars in the heavens, sand of the sea-shores, the salty waves; but between the two seas, as far as hemmed-in Egypt they will be established in the land of Canaan, your people, the free-born of the father, most excellent of nations.")

The poet carefully develops the promise of land to Abraham and his off-spring on two levels of meaning. The fulfilment of the promise of land shows God's fidelity, but for his Christian heirs more importantly this rep-resents the hope of heaven "forever to the ages" (*awa on aldre*, line 425). The themes of genealogy, promise, and inheritance are woven through not just the account of Abraham and the sacrifice of Isaac, his son and heir, but throughout the whole poem. The Israelites' destination is the land of Canaan because it was promised to their forefathers, a point the poem re-turns to after the crossing is successfully completed (lines 558–64):

"wile nu gelæstan   þæt he lange gehet
mid aðsware,   engla Drihten,
in fyrndagum   fæderyncynne,
gif ge gehealdað   halige lare,

þæt ge feonda gehwone   forð ofergangað,
gesittað sigerice   be sæm tweonum,
beorselas beorna.   Bið eower blæd micel.”

(“now the Lord of angels will fulfill what he long ago promised with sworn
oaths, in ancient days to your paternal ancestors – if you keep the holy teaching – that henceforth you will overrun each enemy, occupy a victorious realm
between the two seas, the beer-halls of men. Your glory will be great.”)

The theme of promise is key, and the meaning of “paternal ancestors” is
to be heard literally by the Israelites, but spiritually by the Anglo-Saxon
reader. As in Ælfric’s homily for Midlent Sunday, the spiritual meaning
trumps the historical. The poet overtly draws his readers’ attention to how
the scriptural text must be read and understood (lines 526–35):

run bið gerecenod,   ræd forð gæð,
hafað wislicu   word on fæðme,
wile meagollice   modum tæcan
þæt we gesne ne syn   Godes þeodscipes,
Metodes miltsa.   He us ma onlyhð,
nu us boceras   beteran secgað
lengran lyftwynna.   Þis is læne dream,
wommum awyrged,   wreccum alyfed,
earmra anbid.   Eðellease
þysne gystsele   gihðum healdað …

(The mystery is explained, counsel flows forth; he has wise words in the bo-
som, wishes earnestly to teach minds, so that we might not be lacking God’s
nationality, the creator’s mercy. He enlightens us more – now scholars explain to us better concerning longer lasting life-joys. This is a transitory happiness, cursed with sorrows, granted to exiles, a tarrying for wretched ones.
Deprived of the homeland we keep this guesthouse with sorrows …)

The poet’s emphasis on “mystery” (*run*) is the key to reading both the
action of the poem and the Old Testament as a whole. The “true” exile is
the exile from the “homeland” of heaven, a truth which is explained by
Christian scholars – a clear appeal to authoritative early Christian authors.
The poet’s shift to the mystical meaning of the exodus serves to redefine
the promised “homeland” as heaven, and logically realigns the meaning “your paternal ancestors.” The poet simply assumes Anglo-Saxon

Christians will understand this reference as pointing to Abraham as the ancestor of the Christian nations, and that they will identify themselves as his children.

Nicholas Howe has argued that the Anglo-Saxons incorporated the myth of the exodus into their imaginative interpretation of their own historical experience as migrants into Britain. *Exodus* provides evidence that for the Anglo-Saxons this was one way in which they read the Jewish past into their own story as a nation. However, the belief that they had been chosen by God for salvation has other, less exclusive, roots. The Christian tradition of rereading Abraham lies at the heart of the new identity the early Church created for itself, appropriating the patriarch as the father of all Christians, to the exclusion of those who did not believe in Christ. This appropriation is grounded in a strategy of reading scripture that was well developed in Jewish circles by the first century of the Christian era, and indeed, the first great Christian author, Paul, was well trained as a Jew in the kind of allegorical exegesis developed by Philo of Alexandria. As the Church moved away from its Jewish roots, this tendency to read the Jewish scriptures as Christian texts became more marked and often aggressive. Augustine of Hippo provided a full rationale for this approach, and those who read like him were free to find the Christian spirit in Jewish letters. The Anglo-Saxons inherited this tradition with their conversion to Christianity. It is evident that across the centuries of Anglo-Saxon Christianity, from the *Exodus* poet to Ælfric, the adoption of Abraham as an ancestor was a crucial element in this Christian identity. As believers in Christ, the Anglo-Saxons believed along with all Christian gentile nations that they became children of Abraham, and would enjoy the benefits of the eternal blessing promised to him. The Jewish people, the nation that did not know how to read Abraham according to the spirit, but which clung to the letter, not only had lost the land promised to him,[65] but also their identity – they were regarded as children no more.

---

65 The Jewish loss of the promised land is emphasized by Ælfric in his account of the destruction of the Temple in his *Letter on the Old and New Testaments*, where it serves as a postscript to biblical history; see *Old English Heptateuch*, ed. Marsden, *Libellus*, 229–30; see Anlezark, "Understanding Numbers in London, British Library, Harley 3271," 149–50.

7 Time, Liturgy, and History in the Old English *Elene*

THOMAS D. HILL

I

Any discussion of the Old English poetic *Elene* necessarily involves some consideration of the *Inventio crucis* tradition, and the editorial and scholarly work of Stephan Borgehammar has made it much simpler to discuss the poem in the context of the legendary and liturgical tradition of the *Inventio crucis* as a whole.[1] The poem is clearly based upon some version of the A version of the *Inventio* legend, and yet it elaborates distinctively upon this narrative.[2] Constantine's adversaries, for example, are Germanic warriors, not the followers of a rival Roman general. Again, the sea voyages, which are passed over quite briefly in the Latin legend, are elaborated at some length in the Old English poem. In other words, while Cynewulf followed his Latin source at least reasonably closely, he felt free to elaborate upon it, to change it in some respects, and to develop aspects of it which are only suggested in the Latin *Vorlage*. Even if we wish to assume that Cynewulf himself simply followed some version of the *Inventio crucis* legend, which differed from the well-known text which Borgehammar

---

1 Borgehammar, *How the Holy Cross Was Found: From Event to Medieval Legend*, 47. On the sources of the Old English *Elene* see Biggs et al., eds., *The Sources of Anglo-Saxon Literary Culture*, 264–7. The entry "Iesus Christus, Inventio santae crucis" was written by Biggs and Whatley.
2 It is, of course, possible that some of the differences we can observe between the Old English poem and the A text of the *Inventio crucis* legend reflect the influence of some mediate text either Latin or vernacular. For the sake of simplicity, I am assuming that the single individual Cynewulf was responsible for the differences between these two texts.

has edited, someone made the changes which we can discern in contrasting *Elene* with the A version of the legend. These changes are meaningful and affect our understanding of the narrative.[3]

One paradox of the *Inventio crucis* legend is that the narrative involves a kind of counterpoint between a legendary narrative, historically problematical in a variety of ways, and the quite true historical fact, that the conversion of Constantine and Constantinian policy in the years after the battle of Milvian Bridge, profoundly affected the history of the Christian church in the Mediterranean world and in Europe as a whole for millenia. Indeed one could argue that the conversion of Constantine was the most important historical event in the history of the church since the apostolic age.

The *Inventio crucis* legend states that Constantine's mother, Elene, through the agency of Judas, found the true Cross on which Jesus had suffered and the nails which pierced his hands and feet. Obviously these claims are suspect historically – how can one know which cross is the true Cross or which nails are the real relics of the passion? According to the legend there are miracles that identify the true Cross and the true nails, but these relics are immediately reworked and reshaped, so the question inevitably rises as to how one can be sure that a given fragment of the Cross is from the true Cross. During the reformation, John Calvin, in particular, was utterly scathing in his contempt for these claims and his doubts were shared by Erasmus.[4] In the modern church the feast of the *Inventio crucis* is no longer celebrated. While the objections that occurred to the sixteenth-century reformers and modern church authorities might not be relevant to an earlier age, the historical questions which have been raised must at least have occurred to Christians during the medieval period. At the same time, while the historical claims implicit in the *Inventio crucis* legend are suspect at best, the legend marks a crucial juncture in the real history of the Church. Until the conversion of Constantine, the Christian Church in the Mediterranean world had been at best tolerated and had on occasion been the subject of active persecution. After the conversion of Constantine (with some exceptions), the Church was supported by secular power as it has continued to be in the West until the present time. But the

---

3 For a more extended version of this argument, see Hill, "Literary History and Old English Poetry: The Case of *Christ I, II, III*," 3–22.

4 Borgehammar, *How the Holy Cross Was Found*, 2.

western Church, at least, does not commemorate or celebrate Constantine as a saint; the feast and religious commemoration that is associated with the conversion of Constantine is the feast of the *Inventio crucis,* which was traditionally celebrated on 3 May. Thus the liturgical celebration of the *Inventio crucis* celebrates simultaneously a historical event which is at best problematical – the finding of the True Cross – and another historical event, which is quite real and was of tremendous political and cultural importance, the emergence of the Church from its position as an institution which was tolerated but still marginal, to an institution which was of central importance in the Roman and then Byzantine empire and in the various states which emerged in Europe after the fall of the Western empire.

II

Some years ago I wrote a paper arguing that the Old English *Elene,* and by implication the hagiographic text or texts which are the sources of the Old English poem, should be understood as essentially symbolic rather than as historical narratives. Medieval Christians or at least some medieval Christians may have believed that Elene, the mother of Constantine, had discovered the "True Cross" in the holy land during the imperial rule of her son Constantine, but the narratives about the *Inventio crucis,* as they are told in *Elene* and the Latin sources of the poem, are essentially symbolic narratives about the finding of the Cross as a figure for conversion. My argument was essentially a literary critical one and was based on a number of episodes and details in the text that cannot be understood historically. There was, for example, no substantial Jewish community in Jerusalem in the age of Constantine. The character Judas cannot be the brother of Stephen the Proto-martyr, as he is explicitly identified in the poem, since the poem is (erroneously) dated to the early third century; and there are other such discrepancies. Again, the language and imagery of the poem conform to such an interpretation.[5]

As far as the sources of the poem were concerned, I limited myself to the Latin *Inventio crucis* legend and to the tradition of Christian-Latin literature generally as the "source" for such motifs and themes in the poem, such as the contrast between the letter and the spirit and the role of the *Judaei* who are witnesses and *confessores* without understanding the full

---

5 "Sapiential Structure and Figural Narrative in the Old English *Elene,*" 159–77. This paper was reprinted in Bjork, ed., *Cynewulf: Basic Readings,* 207–28. The reprint corrects an error in the original and is currently the preferred text.

meaning of their witness. But an important source for our understanding of the poem – one which I did not explore when I wrote that paper, and one which has been ignored by later scholars interested in the poem – are the prayers, invocations, and other texts which are associated with the liturgical celebrations of the feast of the *Inventio crucis* on 3 May and the feast of the Exaltation of the Cross on 15 September.[6] While these texts are not directly echoed or quoted in the Old English poem, they do suggest how the *Inventio crucis* legend was "read" and understood in the early medieval world generally and in the Anglo-Saxon Church specifically. We do not know to what extent the Old English *Elene* or the Latin *Inventio crucis* legends were read and circulated, but we do know that, by the later centuries of the Anglo-Saxon period, the liturgical feasts of the *Inventio crucis* and of the *Exaltatio crucis* were celebrated in English churches and monasteries and in the rest of Christian Europe as well. If we assume – and there are reasons for doing so – that these feasts were celebrated in England in the ninth century (the earliest date which has been proposed for the poems of Cynewulf), every year Cynewulf and his auditors would have heard or would themselves have recited the prayers and other "proper" texts associated with these feasts. The understanding of the legend that is implicit in these texts is thus relevant to the poem and its reception. And it is clear from reading these texts that the *Inventio crucis* legend was understood not as a straightforward historical event, but as a symbolic event in which the history of the fourth century, the passion of Jesus, and the ongoing tradition of Christian worship and praxis in the medieval world were linked together.

Any discussion of Anglo-Saxon liturgical practice has to begin with the admission that, particularly for the earlier period, it is very hard to know precisely which liturgical texts were in use in the ongoing tradition of worship at any specific church or monastery. But there are a number of service books preserved from the later Anglo-Saxon period, and we may assume a given Anglo-Saxon Christian would normally have occasion to travel from time to time and thus to be exposed to different liturgical traditions. The practice of Anglo-Saxon royal itineraries, of the king and his court moving from estate to estate throughout the realm, meant that upper class Anglo-Saxons might have travelled quite widely as they sought the king's

---

6 Some of the texts associated with the "Inventio Crucis" are simply repeated in the liturgy of the exaltation of the Cross later in the liturgical year.

court and that they would have brought servants and retainers with them. I would thus argue that it is legitimate to cite "Cross" texts from different liturgical traditions, as potentially relevant to *Elene*, without necessarily claiming that Cynewulf or his original audience must have known any particular text. Whether or not Cynewulf knew these specific texts in exactly the form in which I cite them, these texts are evidence for how the *Inventio crucis* and the related feast of the *Exaltatio crucis* were understood in the early medieval, and, to some extent, specifically in the Anglo-Saxon Christian community.

Let me illustrate this claim by quoting and explicating the clauses for the proper of the mass for the *Inventio crucis*. I quote from the additions to the *Gregorian Sacramentary*, and the prayer that I quote was widely disseminated:

> Deus qui in praeclara salutiferae crucis inuentione,
> passionis tuae miracula suscitasti, concede ut uitalis ligni
> pretio, aeternae uitae suffragia consequamur.[7]

> (Oh God, who in the glorious discovery of the health-giving Cross, reawakened the *miracula* (miracles/amazing events) of your passion, grant that by the worth of the life-giving tree, we may reach the safety of eternal life.)

This is a rich text and a full analysis of its phrasing would involve an extended explication. Instead, I concentrate on those aspects of the prayer, which seem relevant to *Elene* and the *Inventio crucis* tradition. To begin with, the event of the *Inventio crucis* is *praeclara* – glorious. The definition of the *inventio* as *praeclara* corresponds to the account of the finding of the Cross in the legend tradition and in the poem. Judas recovers the Cross while Elene, her court, and presumably the inhabitants of Jerusalem look on. The miraculous signs occur before a crowd of faithful Christians and of amazed Jews. There are divine signs to indicate where Judas should dig for the Cross and there is no question as to whether he will find it. The next clauses of the prayer are more problematic. By the invention of the

---

7 Deshusses, ed., "Le Sacramentaire Grégorien," II, 306 (no. 3499). For another instance of this prayer in a sacramentary with Anglo-Saxon affiliations, see Orchard, ed., *The Sacramentary of Ratoldus* (Paris, Bibiothèque Nationale de France, lat. 12052), 268, no. 1287.

Cross, God "roused" or "awakened" the amazing events, the *miracula*, of the passion. While the A text of the *Inventio crucis* legend includes a resurrection miracle, such miracles are common in hagiographic tradition and the prayer seems to make a much larger claim. The meaning of *suscito* is important. The core meaning is "to cause to move from a recumbent position" and the extended meanings "to rouse" or "to waken" derive from this meaning. This phrasing might be taken to allude to the resurrection miracle which serves to distinguish the true Cross from the crosses on which the thieves died, but it also corresponds to the history of Christianity implicit in the poem and in the *Inventio crucis* tradition generally. In these texts, the Roman emperor Constantine is not the heir and indeed the protégé of the persecutors, and someone who had known about Christianity since his youth, as in fact the historical Constantine had, but a man who is profoundly ignorant of the claims and the nature of Christian faith. His ignorance and the ignorance of his counsellors are exculpatory. The *miracula* of the passion (and the word is in the plural) were reawakened on this (liturgical) day.

The Old English *Elene* and the *Inventio crucis* legend generally serve to celebrate the spiritual authority of secular rulers, specifically Constantine and Elene,[8] and to obscure the historical fact that the greatest impediment to the dissemination of Christianity was for generations the hostile secular authority of the *imperatores* of the Roman empire. This complicates the clarity of the hagiographic narrative. The events of the age of persecution are simply elided in the *Inventio crucis* tradition. The good news of the passion and resurrection of Jesus Christ was not rejected by the secular authorities and yet affirmed and vindicated by the heroism of the martyrs; it was hidden and then found – "invented" in the etymological sense in the age of Constantine. From this perspective, the truths of Christianity could be said to have been dormant until they were "wakened" or "aroused" by the discovery of the true Cross.

The final clauses of this prayer are less relevant to the *Elene* and the *Inventio crucis* tradition, but are interesting nonetheless in that they associate the Cross with the tree of life and implicitly with the tree of the knowledge of good and evil whose fruit was the occasion of the fall.

---

8 On this problem see Whatley, "The Figure of Constantine the Great in Cynewulf's *Elene*," 161–202.

Another liturgical text associated with the feast of the *Inventio crucis*, which in effect both glosses and summarizes the *Inventio crucis* narrative, occurs in the *Bobbio Missal*:

Uenerabilem totum mundo de inuencione sancte crucis sacratissimum diem sollemniter celebrantes gracias agamus diuine potenciae qui tante salutis uixillum, quod iudaica nobis abscondibat malicia, celestis hodie reuelauit clemencia nam, etsi gens perfida dominum nostrum in sepulcrum retenere non potuit vel ipsa ✠ [crucis]⁹ indicia uoluit sub fossa celare quid enim illa mens perfida poterat excogitare de cruce que iam sacrelegium conmiserat in auctorem itaque, sicut in christi resurreccione calliditas iudeorum damnata est, ita est in cruces manifestacione uirtutis confusa.¹⁰

(Solemnly celebrating the venerable and most holy day of the invention of the holy Cross over all the world, we give thanks for the divine power – because a *vexillum* (a military standard) of such health-giving power, which Jewish wickedness was hiding from us – heavenly mercy today revealed; for just as the people of false faith could not keep our lord in the sepulchre and wished to conceal the traces of the cross in a ditch; for (that was) what that unfaithful intention was able to devise concerning the Cross, (that intention) which already had committed sacrilege against its author; and thus, as in the resurrection of Christ the deceit of the Jews was condemned, so (the deceit of the Jews) was *confusa* (upset/confused) by the manifestation of the power of the Cross.)

This prayer is both a gloss and an interpretation of the *Inventio crucis* legend. Interestingly, as in the previous prayer, the *Inventio crucis* is associated with the resurrection of Jesus. The author of the prayer associates the Matthean account of the Jews who condemned Christ, demanding that his tomb be guarded after the execution lest his disciples steal his body and claim that he was resurrected (Matthew 27:63–5 and 28:12–15), with the "burial" of the Cross. The *Inventio* recapitulates as it were the resurrection. An implicit claim in this narrative is that the resurrection was in a sense not fully complete until the holy Cross was found in the vicinity of Jerusalem.

---

9 The manuscript has a cross symbol, not the word "crucis,"
10 Lowe, ed., *The Bobbio Missal: A Gallican Mass-Book*, 86–7.

This claim corresponds well with the *Inventio crucis* legend and the Old English *Elene* in that the finding of the Cross (and the nails) marks a crucial transition – the end of the hidden Church. After the reign of Constantine, Christianity is no longer a private hidden cult; it is the religion of the state and, from the perspective of an Anglo-Saxon churchman, the age of the public, political dominance of the Christian church that began under Constantine and continued until the historical present. Medievalists are so used to the idea of the association of the authority of the king and the authority of God that we tend to forget that the office of the Roman *imperator*, like that of the Anglo-Saxon *cyning*, was originally a secular one with strong pagan associations. One of the crucial issues for early Christians was that the *imperator* demanded sacrifice to the reigning emperor as to a divinity as a sign of political conformity; and Anglo-Saxon and Germanic kingship is closely associated with the cult of Woden/Oðinn, an association which was maintained throughout the Anglo-Saxon period in the genealogies such that even Christian kings like Alfred claimed to be descended from pagan gods. I do not want to press the argument too hard since it is a speculative one, but the suggested date of *Elene*, a poem which celebrates the religious authority of Constantine, who was the recipient of divine revelation, and of his saintly mother Elene is generally situated in the ninth century, just about the time when we have evidence for the first English coronation rituals.

To return to the problem of these liturgical texts, another point of contact between these prayers – or to be more precise, the narrative implicit in these prayers – and the *Inventio crucis* legend is the emphasis on resurrection. The *Inventio crucis* completes and fulfils the resurrection of Jesus Christ, but, interestingly, even the *Inventio crucis* is not complete until a further resurrection unfolds. Guided by divine signs, Judas excavates Golotha and finds not just the Cross, but also the crosses on which the two thieves were crucified. And, for the moment, the quest for the true Cross is frustrated since the three crosses are apparently indistinguishable. So Judas waits and prays until a widow grieving over the death of her only son comes by and Judas resurrects the dead youth by touching the body with each one of the three crosses. As one might expect in the context of medieval hagiography, when Judas touches the body of the youth with the third Cross, the wood of the true Cross resurrects the youth and the identity of the true Cross is thus dramatically demonstrated in a *praeclara* way.

This episode in the narrative has not attracted much critical attention, but it is worth asking what function it serves in the larger *Inventio crucis* narrative. The recovery of the crosses involved direct divine intervention:

if God is willing to guide Judas to the place where the crosses were buried, why would He not immediately show Judas which of the three crosses was the true relic? And indeed the Cross on which Jesus suffered was marked with a sign, the trilingual inscription, Jesus of Nazareth, King of the Jews. If the true Cross was preserved, why was the sign lost? One version of the legend of the recovery of the true Cross deals with the problem of the identity of the true Cross in contrast to the thieves' crosses by specifying that the true Cross was so marked,[11] and this would seem a simple solution to the problem of its identity. And if the sign were somehow lost, a further divine miracle would seem a simple solution.

But if the *Inventio crucis* is a legend closely associated with the resurrection, recapitulating in a sense the resurrection of Jesus, then it is deeply appropriate that the true Cross be revealed as truly what it is by manifesting its power in a new resurrection miracle. Again, the prayer text speaks of the invention of the Cross as the final (*confusio* "confusion," "defeat") deceit of the Jews in a clause which most modern readers would find offensive. But in the context of the larger narrative, the emphasis in these prayers on the final *confusio* of the Jews corresponds to the narrative implicit in these liturgical texts. One interesting contrast between the Old English *Elene* and its Latin source is that the *Inventio crucis* legend specifies that after the Cross and the nails have been found, Elene banished from the holy land those Jews who were not converted.[12] In this version of the narrative the historical Roman exile of the Jews from Israel is recapitulated and completed by the Christian empress Elene. The Old English poem, however, says nothing of such an event. After the recovery of the nails, which completes and fulfils the process of the invention, the Jews in *Elene* are all converted:

> Leode gesawon
> hira willgifan   wundor cyðan,
> ða ðær of heolstre,   swylce heofonsteorran
> oððe godgimmas,   grunde getenge,
> næglas of nearwe   neoðan scinende
> leohte lixton;   leode gefægon,
> weorud willhreðig,   sægdon wuldor Gode

---

11 Borgehammar, *How the Holy Cross Was Found*, 39.
12 *Inventio Crucis A*, ¶ 15, ed. Borgehammar, 271.

ealle anmode,   þeah hie ær wæron
þurh deofles spild   in gedwolan lange,
acyrred fram Criste;   hie cwædon þus,
Nu we seolfe geseoð   sigores tacen,
soðwundor Godes,   þeah we wiðsocun ær
mid leasingum.   Nu is in leoht cymen,
onwrigen wyrda bigang;   wuldor þæs age
on heannesse   heofonrices God.   (1110–24)[13]

(The people saw
Their ruler make known a miracle,
Then there from the hiding place like the stars of heaven,
Or divine jewels near to the ground,
Nails from the enclosed place shining from below
The light gleamed – The people rejoiced.
The host was exultant; they said, "Glory to God,"
All of one mind, though they previously were
By the deceit of the devil long in error,
Turned away from Christ. They spoke thus
"Now we ourselves see the sign of victory
The true glory of God, though we rejected it previously,
With lies. Now is come into the light,
The outcome of events revealed. May he possess glory for that,
On high, God of the kingdom of heaven.)

This is yet another instance of the unhistorical aspect of the *Elene* narrative. Just as such basic historical facts as the exile of the Jews from Israel, the imperial persecution of the Christians, the date of Constantine's reign, or the span of years which can conceivably separate two brothers are elided or ignored, Cynewulf in effect elides the continued presence of Jews in Christendom. Some of these errors might be the result of ignorance or carelessness, but Cynewulf was a literate and in some ways a learned man and it is hard to imagine that he was unaware of all of these historical difficulties. And indeed in this final detail his narrative differs from his known source.

---

13 Gradon, ed., *Cynewulf's Elene*, rev. ed., 66–7. I have followed Gradon's text but have romanized the script of the poem in certain respects, printing "w" for "wynn" and "g" for "yogh."

I would argue, again, that the narrative of *Elene* is symbolic rather than "historical" and I would also argue that one of the sources for the reception of the legend in *Elene* are the various liturgical texts associated with the *Inventio crucis* legend. A common liturgical formula – for various prayers and blessings associated with the *Inventio crucis* and the *Exaltatio crucis*, and indeed numerous other feasts – begins "Deus qui nos hodierna die / God who on this day" has revealed the Cross or manifested himself in a variety of ways, suggests something of the ahistorical and paradoxical character of liturgical time. Literally the formula simply means that on this day of the year, the event that is celebrated in a given feast occurred. But the formula is a suggestive one that implies that divine time exists on a different plane than mundane historical time as we experience it. In history, Jews, persons practicing rabbinic Judaism, continued to live in the Mediterranean world and perhaps even in northern France during Cynewulf's lifetime. But in liturgical time, the day on which the Cross was found and the *miracula* of the resurrection were awakened, and the day in which the "false faith" of the Jews was diffused and confused – this was a day in which the story had to end happily – or at least happily from Cynewulf's Christian perspective. In history Jews and Christians lived separately and continued to live separately as indeed they still do. But in the imagined "liturgical" and symbolic space of the *Inventio crucis* narrative, a narrative of which Cynewulf's *Elene* is arguably the most aesthetically rich version, a reconciliation which has never occurred in real history is, at least for a moment, imagined.

8 Jewish Magic and Christian Miracle in the Old English *Andreas*

CHARLES D. WRIGHT

In the Old English *Andreas*,[1] the apostle Matthew is allotted to journey to the island[2] of Mermedonia to preach to the heathen cannibals who dwell there. Immediately upon his arrival Matthew is imprisoned, drugged, and blinded by the Mermedonians, who intend to kill and eat him after fattening him for thirty days. Matthew's apostolic immunity to poisons (cf. Mk 16:18) enables him to retain his faculties and his faith intact after being forced to drink the magical potion that the Mermedonians administer to render their victims docile. Still able to pray, he beseeches God to preserve him from the mockery of his captors and from the terrible death they intend to inflict upon him. In response, the voice of God penetrates the darkness of the prison, assuring Matthew that in twenty-seven days he will send Andreas to rescue him along with his fellow captives. When the Mermedonians throng into the prison to check the runic inscriptions that determine each captive's date for slaughter,[3] they find that Matthew has just three days left. The Lord is then mindful of Matthew's suffering and faithful service:

---

1 Quotations from *Andreas* and other Old English poems are from the *ASPR*, by line numbers. See also *Andreas and the Fates of the Apostles*, ed. Krapp, and *Andreas and the Fates of the Apostles*, ed. Brooks. Unless otherwise noted, translations are from Gordon, *Anglo-Saxon Poetry*, 181–210, with some minor modifications. I wish to thank Lisa Lampert, Samantha Zacher, and Dov Weiss for their corrections and suggestions.

2 On the poet's unique representation of Mermedonia as an island, see Wright, "*Insulae Gentium*," which discusses the lexicographal evidence for the meanings of OE *igland/ ealand* but for *Andreas* posits the influence of the "biblical sense" of *insulae* as the homelands of the Gentile nations.

3 On this scene see now Battles, "'Contending Throng' Scenes."

Þa wæs gemyndig,   se ðe middangeard
gestaðelode   strangum mihtum,
hu he in ellþeodigum   yrmðum wunode,
belocen leoðubendum,   þe oft his lufan adreg
for Ebreum   ond Israhelum;
swylce he Iudea   galdorcræftum
wiðstod stranglice.   (lines 162–7a)

(Then he who had established the world with mighty powers forgot not how he dwelt in misery among strange people, bound with fetters, he who had often showed forth his love in the presence of[4] the Hebrews and Israelites; also he had sternly withstood the magic arts of the Jews.)

This passage, occurring just before Christ informs Andreas that he must journey to Mermedonia to rescue Matthew, does not correspond to anything in the poet's source, the *Acta Andreae et Matthiae apud anthropophagos*.[5] Thomas D. Hill has explicated the "onomastic crux" in this passage, which distinguishes between the love Matthew showed in the presence of "Hebrews and Israelites" and his opposition to "Jews." As Hill observes, patristic authorities often (though not consistently) used the terms *Hebraei* and *Israelitae* in reference to the Jews as God's chosen people, reserving the term *Iudaei* for pejorative contexts when castigating them for unbelief or for crucifying Christ.[6] Here, however, the charge against the Jews is that they practised "magic arts." Following a suggestion by G.P. Krapp, Kenneth Brooks translates *galdorcræftas* as "evil

---

4 I follow the glossaries of Krapp and Brooks in translating *for* as "in the presence of" rather than "for." In the phrase *his lufan* it is not clear whether *his* refers to Matthew's or Christ's love.

5 The poet's immediate source is unknown, but it can be reasonably closely reconstructed by comparing the Greek *Praxeis* and the Latin *Casanatensis* versions of the *Acta*, both edited by Blatt, *Die lateinischen Bearbeitungen*. Both are translated by Boenig, *The Acts of Andrew*. I cite the translation of the *Casanatensis* in Allen and Calder, *Sources and Analogues*, 14–24. For the Old English prose version of the legend, see Cassidy and Ringler, *Bright's Old English Grammar*, 205–19. It is reasonable to attribute substantive differences from both the Greek and Latin to the *Andreas* poet. While it is always possible that a particular difference reflects a lost variant version of the legend, we should not privilege evidence we do not have over evidence we do have and needlessly foreclose a productive avenue of interpretation. Old English poets were often far more free in adapting their sources than were, for example, Old English homilists.

6 Hill, "Hebrews, Israelites, and Wicked Jews."

machinations," on the assumption that "the word … is here generalized to include evil customs of any kind, especially those practised by heathen peoples, with whom the Jews, as the enemies of Christ, are sometimes equated."[7] Hill similarly argues that "the poet is referring here to the negative aspect of Jewish history in the Old and New Testaments, notably such Old Testament episodes as the worship of the Golden Calf and the final apostasy (in Christian terms) of the crucifixion of Christ." He suggests that "blasphemous deceits" would better capture these larger associations of *galdorcræftas*. J.P. Hermann, however, believes that the *galdorcræftas* are to be understood literally as "magic arts," which Hermann productively relates not only to the sorcery (*gedwolcræft*) of the Mermedonian magicians (*dryas*) who concoct potions, but also to the "white magic" of Christianity, "reconceptualized as miracle or mystery."[8] As Don C. Skemer has observed, in the Middle Ages "Jews enjoyed a reputation for the magical arts, even as they themselves decried 'foreign magic.'"[9] The *Andreas* poet, however, seems to have something more concrete in mind relating specifically to Matthew. Yet what kind of Jewish *galdorcræftas* might the poet have thought that Matthew opposed?

According to standard patristic and medieval exegesis, a particular kind of Jewish "magic" was in fact explicitly condemned in the gospel of Matthew. In Matthew 23:5 – a passage not parallelled in the other gospels – Jesus berates the Pharisees for false piety in the form of a distinctive devotional practice: "omnia vero opera sua faciunt ut videantur ab hominibus dilatant enim phylacteria sua et magnificant fimbrias" (And all their works they do for to be seen of men. For they make their phylacteries broad and enlarge their fringes).[10] From patristic times to the present, this passage has occasioned a good deal of commentary, much of it focusing on what "phylacteries" were and why Jesus condemned their use by the Pharisees (or the way that the Pharisees used them). According to E.R. Goodenough, who cites a comment in the fourth-century *Panarion* of Epiphanius of

---

7 Brooks, *Andreas*, 69 (note to line 166); compare Krapp's note, *Andreas*, 89.

8 Hermann, *Allegories of War*, 133. Cf. also Thormann, "The Jewish Other," 9. *DOE*, s.v. *galdorcræft*, cites the passage from *Andreas* under sense 1., "art of enchantment, occult art, incantation" http://tapor.library.utoronto.ca/doe/, accessed 2 April 2013.

9 Skemer, *Binding Words*, 25. A classic study is Trachtenberg, *Jewish Magic and Superstition*; see also Bohak, *Ancient Jewish Magic*.

10 Quotations from the Vulgate are from *Biblia Sacra iuxta Vulgatam versionem*, ed. Gryson; translations are from the Douay-Rheims version. For the "fringes" on the prayer shawl cf. Nm 15:38.

Salamis, Matthew was referring to the purple stripes on the prayer shawl, in which case Jesus was simply criticizing an ostentatious elaboration of a holy vestment affected by the Pharisees.[11] The alternative view – one that Epiphanius explicitly rejects, showing that it was current at his time – is that Matthew was referring to *tefillin*, "small leather capsules containing certain passages of Scripture that were bound on the upper forehead and on one's left arm."[12] A recent analysis by Maurice Casey of the Aramaic substrate of Q (the putative common source of the gospels of Matthew and Luke) confirms that the Greek word *phylakteria* in this passage refers to *tefillin*, which were sometimes rectangular in shape and could therefore have been "made broad"; Casey concludes that "Orthodox scribes and Pharisees wore broader *tefillin* than normal, and Jesus objected to their overt display of religiosity ...."[13] There is, moreover, abundant evidence that *tefillin*, though originally intended as reminders to obey the Torah, eventually also came to function as amulets conferring protection and long life, accounting for Matthew's use of the word *phylakterion*, literally "means of protection," "amulet." According to Yehudah B. Cohn, this "invented tradition" of *tefillin* as amuletic artefacts probably arose in the late Second Temple Era under the influence of Hellenic culture, facilitated by a literalist interpretation of the verses in Exodus (13:9, 16) and Deuteronomy (6:8; 11:18) that enjoined a "sign" on the hand and between the eyes. These verses were among the ones most often inscribed on the small folded pieces of parchment enclosed in separate compartments within the *tefillin*.[14]

Whatever the historical origins of the amuletic function of *tefillin*, and however Matthew himself may have understood Jesus's criticism of the

11 Goodenough, *Jewish Symbols*, 209–10; see Skemer, *Binding Words*, 110. For the passage in Epiphanius, see *The Panarion of Epiphanius*, trans. Williams, 41. According to Williams, Epiphanius conflated phylacteries with the purple fringes by folk etymology ("φυλακτήριον from ἀλουργοῦφεῖς, 'purple woven,' by a rearrangement of its letters").

12 Lincicum, *Paul and the Early Jewish Encounter with Deuteronomy*, 40; Lincicum provides an up-to-date survey of early archaeological and literary evidence for *tefillin*, which are still worn by observant Jewish men at morning prayers.

13 Casey, *An Aramaic Approach to Q*, 83–7 (quotation from 87). Alternatively, "broad" may refer to the straps that attach the *tefillin* to the head. According to Tigay, "On the Term Phylacteries (Matt 23:5)," 49, the Hebrew equivalent of Greek *phylakteria* was *qemîʾîn* (singular *qamiaᶜ*).

14 Cohn, *Tangled up in Text*, 88–96; on the four "tefillin verses" see Cohn's detailed commentary, 33–48. In the Vulgate the crucial parts of these verses read: *et erit quasi signum in manu tua et quasi monumentum ante oculos tuos et ut lex Domini semper in ore tuo* (Ex 13:9); *erit igitur quasi signum in manu tua et quasi adpensum quid ob*

Pharisees, in the early Middle Ages this passage from Matthew's gospel was consistently read by Christian exegetes as condemning the use of phylacteries as a superstitious form of protection, that is, as magical amulets worn on the forehead. Jerome's commentary on Matthew was decisive in establishing this interpretation. According to Jerome,

> Dominus cum dedisset mandata legis per Moysen ad extremum intulit: *ligabis ea in manu tua et erunt inmota ante oculos tuos* [Deut. 6:8]; ... Hoc Pharisaei male interpretantes scribebant in membranulis decalogum Moysi, id est decem legis uerba complicantes ea et ligantes in fronte et quasi coronam capiti facientes ut semper ante oculos mouerentur quod usque hodie Indi et Babylonii faciunt, et qui hoc habuerit quasi religiosus in populis iudicatur.... Pictaciola illa decalogi phylacteria uocabant quod quicumque habuisset ea quasi ob custodiam et munimentum sui haberet, non intellegentibus Pharisaeis quod haec in corde portanda sint non in corpore, alioquin et armaria et arcae habent libros et dei notitiam non habent.[15]

(The Lord, when he gave the commandments of the Law through Moses, added at the end: "You will bind these on your hand and they will be unmoved before your eyes." ... The Pharisees, interpreting this perversely, wrote on small parchments the Decalogue of Moses, that is, the ten words of the Law. Folding them up, they even bound them to their forehead and made a crown, so to speak, on their head, so that they would always be moving before their eyes. The Indians and the Babylonians do this up to the present day, and among the people the one who has this crown is judged as righteous.... [The Pharisees] called those little depictions of the Decalogue "phylacteries" because whoever had them had his own protection and fortification as it were. Now the Pharisees did not understand that these things need to be carried in the heart, not in the body. But chests and boxes hold books and do not have the knowledge of God.)[16]

---

recordationem inter oculos tuos (Ex 13:16); *et ligabis ea quasi signum in manu tua eruntque et movebuntur inter oculos tuos* (Dt 6:8); *ponite haec verba mea in cordibus et in animis vestris et suspendite ea pro signo in manibus et inter vestros oculos conlocate* (Dt 11:18).

15 *In Matheum*, ed. Adriaen, 212–13. For a recent commentary on this passage see Itzkowitz, "Jews, Indians, Phylacteries."

16 *Jerome: Commentary on Matthew*, trans. Scheck, 259–60. Jerome suggests that the Pharisees did not take to heart the injunction of Dt 11:18, *ponite haec verba mea in cordibus et in animis vestris.*

Jerome's explication of the phylacteries of the Pharisees was often quoted by later Christian writers,[17] including, *inter alia*, Smaragdus of St Mihiel,[18] Hrabanus Maurus,[19] Christian Druthmar,[20] Pseudo-Bede,[21] Agobard of Lyon,[22] Otfried of Weissenburg,[23] and Sedulius Scottus.[24] Broadly paraphrasing Jerome, Heiric of Auxerre adds a remarkable macaronic etymology for the Latin loanword *phylacteria*: Greek *phylaxe* "seruare" and Hebrew *thorath* "lex."[25]

That the word *phylacteria* in the Vulgate text of the passage was understood by some Anglo-Saxon readers as referring specifically to magical amulets is shown by the gloss *lybesn* ("charm," "amulet") in batch glosses from Matthew in the Cleopatra Glossaries. According to Greg Waite, these glosses "refer to the Hebrew *tefillin* from the *Vulgate* Matthew 23:5,"[26] which indeed seems likely in view of the wide dissemination of Jerome's comment; yet even a glossator unfamiliar with Jerome's comment (or a similar one) and therefore with *tefillin* would still be likely to understand *phylacteria* as referring to amulets, since that was the word's primary meaning through the Carolingian period, and continued to be its meaning with reference to Jewish or pagan "phylacteries" even after it developed a positive meaning with reference to Christian reliquaries, including reliquary and pectoral crosses.[27] A curious allusion in Byrhtferth's *Enchiridion*

---

17 For a survey of Greek and Latin commentary on Mt 23:5 see Bartelink, "Phylakterion-phylacterium," 29–32 and 47–8.

18 *Collectiones in epistolas et evangelia*, PL 102: 474.

19 *Expositio in Matthaeum*, ed. Löfstedt, 592–3.

20 *Expositio in Matthaeum*, PL 106: 1447.

21 *In Matthaei evangelium expositio*, PL 92: 98 (ninth century).

22 *De picturis et imaginibus*, ed. van Acker, 175.

23 *Glossae in Matthaeum*, ed. Grifoni, 287.

24 *In euangelium Mathaei*, ed. Löfstedt, 2:513–14.

25 *Homiliae per circulum anni* I.37, ed. Quadri, 324.

26 Waite, "Old English *lybesn*" (quotation from 18). Other terms used to gloss the word include *æ-becn* ("sign of the Law"), *þwænga* ("straps"), *wrædas* ("bands"), and *h(e)als-bæc* ("neck books"); the notion that Jews hung phylacteries from their necks is found in canon 36 of the Council of Laodicea: "Pittatiola decalogi collis suis suspendentes Iudaei filacteria vocabant" (cited by Bartelink, "Phylakterion-phylacterium," 51) .

27 See Bartelink, "Phylakterion-phylacterium," 55–60. According to Bartelink, who dates the "Christian sense" of the word to the ninth century, Gregory the Great's use of *filacta* [v.l. *filacteria*] to designate a reliquary cross is an isolated early example attributable to Byzantine influence: *Registrum* 14.11.12, ed. Hartmann, 2:431–2. On Cross phylacteries see now Hahn, *Strange Beauty*. On the range of meaning of Latin *phylacterium* see also the *Thesuarus Linguae Latinae* 10/1:2060–1; online version

refers to "nonnulli <clerici> imperiti … qui non habere desiderant philacteria sua" (ignorant clerics … who do not want to keep their phylacteries with them), thereby making a mess of their computistical calculations, and then admonishes the reader that "Intuend<a> est soller<ter> uia phariseorum et saduceorum, et respuenda uelut peripsima doctrina eorum" (One should observe carefully the ways of the Pharisees and Saducees, and reject their doctrines like rubbish).[28] Rebecca Stephenson is surely right to associate this passage and the use of the word *philacteria* with Mt 23:5,[29] but she does not explain why Byrhtferth contrasts the doctrines (and implicitly the phylacteries) of the Pharisees with good "phylacteries" that the ignorant clerics wrongly dispense with. The answer, I believe, lies in a passage from Byrhtferth's computus that refers to Pachomius receiving the authentic Easter tables (in the form of the mnemonic decennovenal verses "Nonae Aprilis norunt quinos") from an angel "in uno philacterio."[30]

In having Christ commend Matthew for sternly resisting Jewish *galdorcræftas*,[31] therefore, the *Andreas* poet is alluding to the "phylacteries" condemned uniquely in Matthew's gospel, which the poet believed was first written in Hebrew expressly for the Jews (*Wæs hira Matheus sum,/se mid Iudeum ongan godspell ærest wordum writan wundorcræfte*, lines 11b–13; Matthew was one of them, who by wondrous power first began among the Jews to write the gospel in words).[32] Since in this context the poet

---

http://www.degruyter.com/databasecontent?dbid=tll&dbsource=%2Fdb%2Ftll, accessed 2 April 2013; *Novum glossarium mediae latinitatis*, ed. Dolbeau, cols. 104–6.

28 *Byhrtferth's Enchiridion* i.3.3, ed. Baker and Lapidge, 46.

29 Stephenson, "Scapegoating the Secular Clergy," 132.

30 *Byrhtferth's Enchiridion*, ed. Baker and Lapidge, 420. Here the word is apparently used in its positive sense "portable reliquary" and by metonymy designates the text by the container that held it. Alternatively, it may be a rare example of the sense "band de parchemin, par ext. petit texte," illustrated with just a single attestation in the *Novum glossarium mediae latinitatis*, ed. Dolbeau, col. 106 (sense C 3 e). On the legend see Jones, "A Legend of Saint Pachomius." Anglo-Saxon illustrations of this scene show an angel conferring a scroll upon Pachomius: see Wormald, *English Drawings*, plates 24(a) and 34(a); pl. 34(b) shows Christ giving the scroll to an angel.

31 OE *galdor/galdorcræft* most often refers to oral incantations, but these are of course often based on written texts, such as the gospel of John, which *Bald's Leechbook* refers to as *Iohannes gebed & gealdor* (*DOE* s.v. *galdor* 2.a. "specifically in medical texts and charms"). The word *galdor* also glosses Latin *praestigia(e)* (sense 2.b.) and *necromantia* (sense 2.c.). In *Riddle* 48.6, *galdorcwide* refers specifically to an inscription on a paten or chalice. The word *phylacteria*, moreover, was sometimes glossed as *carmina*, as in *The Corpus Glossary*, ed. Lindsay, 137: "philactaria, carmina uel decem praecepta legis."

32 See Wright, "Matthew's Hebrew Gospel."

also refers more broadly to *Iudea*, the term may reflect his understanding that the wearing of phylacteries was not confined to the Pharisees; or, since Christian writers often did characterize the practice as specifically Pharisaical, *Iudea* may be synecdochic. As Jonathan Elukin has shown, Jerome came to identify the Pharisees as a sect with the Jews as a people, an identification that was perpetuated by Bede and later Carolingian writers: "Bede blurred the distinctions between the Jews and the Pharisees by emphasizing that the Jewish people shared in some of the Pharisees' meaningless traditions. Bede's language is often imprecise, and oscillates between references to the Pharisees and references to the Jews."[33] The *Andreas* poet similarly generalizes a Pharisaical practice as common Jewish one, using the more pejorative term, and the alliteration of *Judea/galdorcræftum* neatly mirrors that of *Pharisaei / phylacteria*.

As distinctive devotional artefacts, *tefillin* were markers of Jewish identity whose rejection by Christ (in Jerome's reading of Mt 23:5) created an oppositional marker of Christian identity by their very absence. A remarkable illustration of a forehead phylactery occurs in the famous portrait of Ezra in the Anglo-Saxon Bible known as the Codex Amiatinus, based on the Codex Grandior from Vivarium, where the figure represented was Cassiodorus (Figures 1–2).

According to Elisabeth Revel-Neher, "A thin strap holds [Ezra's] hair together and falls behind his neck; it broadens over his forehead and there is a small cube beneath his hair like a bulge. Though seldom recognized as such, this little cube is the *tefilla shel rosh*, the frontlet phylactery worn on the forehead."[34] The phylactery, then, is not the elaborate golden headgear (which represents the *lamina aurea* of a Jewish High Priest, as Paul

---

33 Elukin, "Judaism: From Heresy to Pharisee," 60.

34 Revel-Neher, *The Image of the Jew* 60, citing Roth, "Jewish Antecedents," 24–44. See also Revel-Neher, "A Judeo-Christian Dialogue, 501–34. For an alternative iconography for *tefillin* in the later Middle Ages see Mellinkoff, 'Round-Topped Tablets." Mellinkoff recognizes one unmistakable example of *tefillin* in the form of round-topped tablets from the fourteenth-century Holkham Bible (London, BL Add. 47692, fol. 27v; see her Fig. 20), where the Pharisees have miniature round-topped tablets attached to their foreheads, recalling Jerome's definition of phylacteries as "little depictions of the Decalogue." This raises the possibility that some earlier representations of the tablets may also have been intended to represent *tefillin*. While no other example known to me is so clear as the one in the Holkham Bible, it is probably not an accident that Jews who hold round-topped tablets in medieval Christian images almost always hold them in their *left* hand, as Jewish tradition prescribed. According to Mellinkoff, the iconography of the "round-topped" tablets may have originated in England, and the earliest

Meyvaert has argued), but the inconspicuous square below it, highlighted by a red stroke or dot (forehead *tefillin* often were marked with a dot in Byzantine iconography).[35] In this context the phylactery does not have the negative associations it does in Jerome's exegesis of Matthew 23:5, since Ezra's role here relates to his restoration of the Law after the destruction of the Temple (Ezra 7–10, Neh 8).[36] The well-known relationship between the Ezra portrait and the Matthew portrait in the Lindisfarne Gospels (Figure 3) is indirect – according to Paul Meyvaert, the Matthew portrait was also made from a drypoint outline of the Cassiodorus portrait.[37] Nonetheless, the contrast between the two neatly illustrates how *tefillin* (added to the Ezra portrait along with the four pieces of clothing proper to the Jewish *pontifex*) could iconographically index Jewishness.

The *Andreas* poet does not allude to the material form of Jewish *tefillin* but rather to their magical function as designated by the word *phylacteria*, just as the Anglo-Saxon Matthew glossator translated *phylacteria* as *lybesn* ("charm," "amulet"). The poet's representation of phylacteries as *galdorcræftas* bears directly on his manifest concern with the distinction between pagan and Jewish "magic" and Christian "miracle." The most explicit manifestation of that concern comes during the account of the (non-biblical) miracle in which Christ commands a stone statue of one of the Cherubim and Seraphim to leap from the wall of a temple and witness to the Jews that Christ is the eternal son of God who was known to the patriarchs Abraham, Isaac, and Jacob (lines 706–810). Christ subsequently dispatches the stone angel to Mamre to awaken the three patriarchs from their graves to bear witness themselves to him as the creator of heaven and earth. He does so only after the "eldest (leaders)" (*þa yldestan*) at

---

examples she was able to locate are from the Old English Hexateuch, where the tablets occur in three scenes. In one of these (Mellinkoff's Fig. 10) Moses does hold the tablets in his left hand, but in another (Fig. 9) he holds one tablet in each hand, and in a third (Fig. 11) he holds them in his right hand, with his left hand holding instead a banner.

35 In the black and white detail of Fig. 2 the stroke is clearly visible. I have not seen the manuscript itself, but in the colour reproductions I have been able to consult it shows as dark red or red. Though quite small, the red stroke can be seen in the reproductions in Marsden, "Job in His Place" (pl. 6) and Brown, *The Lindisfarne Gospels* (fig. 21a, p. 57). For examples in Byzantine iconography see Revel-Neher, *The Image of the Jew*, 62–3 with Plates VI and VII and Fig. 13; 65 with Fig. 17; 68 with Fig. 25; Revel-Neher, "By Means of Colors," 513–14 with Figs. 9–11.

36 See Fried, *Ezra and the Law*.

37 Meyvaert, "The Date of Bede's *In Ezram*."

the temple claim that he had made the statues speak through "magic arts" (*drycræftum*) and "devilish enchantments" (*scingelacum*) (lines 761–7a). The corresponding passage in the Greek *Praxeis* version of the *Acta* has Christ being accused of using magic by "the Jews," referring to the laity and "high priests" who had accompanied Christ to "the desert of the gentiles" where the miracle was performed.[38] In the Latin *Casantanensis* version – where the scene of the miracle is "the temple of the gentiles" – there is no charge of magic; instead we learn that "the chief priests (*principes sacerdotum*) of the law saw and knew all that had happened and yet they did not believe in Him."[39] The *Andreas* poet imagines the scene to have taken place at the Temple in Jerusalem, drawing on I Kings 6:29 for the detail that images of the Cherubim were carved on the Temple wall, *quasi prominentes et egredientes de pariete*.[40] The term *þa yldestan* may therefore correspond to *principes sacerdotum*; yet in an earlier passage in which the Latin refers to the *principes sacerdotum*, the poet distinguishes among "bisceopas ond boceras / ond ealdormenn" (lines 607–8), where *bisceopas* presumably corresponds to *principes sacerdotum* and *boceras* certainly to Scribes. The word *ealdormenn* elsewhere in Old English sometimes designates *principes sacerdotum* but also (in Northumbrian and Mercian) Pharisees;[41] yet if it referred here to the *principes sacerdotum* there would be no plausible correspondence left for *bisceopas* (which, when used of Jewish "bishops," always refers to high priests).[42] In *Andreas*, then, the *ealdormenn* and *yldestan* are probably the Pharisees, who were often designated by forms of *eald* as well as by *ealdormenn*.[43]

---

38   *The Acts of Andrew*, trans. Boenig, 8–9.

39   *Die lateinischen Bearbeitungen*, ed. Blatt, 61; *Sources and Analogues*, trans. Allen and Calder, 23 (their translation "chief priests of the law" corresponds to the apparently corrupt phrase "principes sacerdotorum lex," taking *lex* as an error for *legis*).

40   See Szittya, "The Living Stone," 169.

41   MacGillivray, *The Influence of Christianity*, 7–10.

42   The *DOE* cites Jn (WSCp) 7.45: "þa þenas comon to þam bisceopum & to þam Phariseon & hig cwædon to him, for hwi ne brohton ge hine hider," where instead of *Phariseon* the Lindisfarne Gospels has *aldormonnum* and the Rushworth Gospels has *aldormen*.

43   See the *DOE*, s.v. *eald* I.A.1.ci. and II.B.1.c.; *ealdormann* I.A.3.1.a. See also Boyd, "Aldrediana VII," 23–6; Fleming, "The Most Exalted Language," 193 (citing *DOE* and Boyd). The *Andreas* poet's usage would be consistent with other features that suggest an Anglian origin, for which see Fulk, *A History of Old English Metre*, 315.

The earlier allusion to Jewish *galdorcræftas* of course sharpens the irony of the Pharisees' charge that Christ's miracle was accomplished by magic.[44] Yet it also brings into sharper focus the similarity between the magical and the miraculous. Hermann has eloquently analysed how the poet demonizes Jewish as well as pagan magic as a strategy for constructing Christian identity against the Other.[45] Jewish magic was especially threatening to this discourse of difference because Christ and the apostles were themselves Jews, and because their "miracles" are formally indistinguishable from magic: Christ makes a stone statue speak and trees spring up from blood (lines 1146–9); Andreas makes himself invisible (lines 986–9) and calls forth a flood of water from a pillar (lines 1503–9a). Calling such supernatural manipulations of the natural world "miracles" (*wundra*) differentiates them on a semantic level, but in itself does little to justify how they differ from making magic potions, as did the Mermedonians *dryas þurh dwolcræft* (lines 33–4), or from using magic amulets, as the Pharisees did according to Matthew's gospel.[46]

Taking a cue from his source, the poet conjures up that difference by having the stone angel, and then the patriarchs, witness to the Jews not just that Christ is the eternal son of God, but also that he had created heaven and earth, sea and sky (lines 746b–50). The entire episode is prefaced by a statement that, through the many miracles (*wundra feala*) he performed both secretly and openly, Christ "made known that he was king by right over the earth … the ruler and maker of heavenly glory, one eternal God

---

44 Their accusation that Christ's miracles were accomplished through "devilish enchantments," while corresponding to the charge of magic in the *Acta Andreae*, inevitably evokes the Pharisees' charge in the gospel of Matthew that Christ cast out demons through the prince of demons: *Pharisaei autem dicebant in principe daemoniorum eicit daemones* (Mt 9:34); *Pharisaei autem audientes dixerunt hic non eicit daemones nisi in Beelzebub principe daemoniorum* (Mt 12:24); in Mk 3:22 it is instead the "scribes" who make this charge and in Lk 11:15 more vaguely "certain persons."

45 See Hermann, *Allegories of War*, 133–9: "the expulsion of Jewish magic serves to purge Christianity of the difference it bears within itself" (133).

46 Current scholarship does not, of course, accept a facile distinction between "magic" and "miracle." My concern, however, is not with the validity or the grounds of the etic distinction but rather with the emic distinction as articulated in the poem and in patristic and early medieval sources. On "emic" vs. "etic" approaches to the problem of magic and miracle see Reimer, *Miracle and Magic*, 16, and Eve, *The Jewish Context of Jesus' Miracles*, 363–5. Cohen, *Tangled up in Text*, 23–5, invokes the distinction in relation to the "magical" function of *tefillin*.

of all created things" (lines 600–703). The implication is that the manipulation of the natural world is not *drycræft* or *galdorcræft* if it is performed by or through the *cræft* (cf. lines 584b–5) of the one who created the world itself and marked it out into earth, sea, and sky.[47] Yet since the Jews also believe that God created the world, they must also be shown to have failed to recognize that Christ as *godes ece bearn* is the one who "established" (*staþolode*, line 799b) and "marked out" (*amearcode*, line 750a) all creation – despite the *wundra* performed by him in their presence and even after the testimony of the patriarchs whom they do acknowledge.[48] The purpose of this episode, therefore, is not just to castigate Jewish unbelief, but also to show why Christ's *cræft* is not magic, but miracle (*wundor*).

The verb *amearcode* echoes Christ's statement that the form (*hiw*) of the stone statues had been "marked" (*amearcod*) and "written by the skill of hands" (*þurh handmægen awriten*) on the wall of the temple (lines 724b–6), suggesting an analogy between the "written" statue that Christ made to speak and the natural world that he had "marked out with his hands" (*amearcode mundum sinum*, line 750). Creation is thus a divine form of writing visible to all, just as Christ's *wundra* were performed publically. The Jews are characterized as *modblinde menn* (line 814a) because, though Christ had made known many miracles, they still "did not believe their own teachings" (*ne gelyfdon larum sinum*, lines 812–13), that is the teachings of the Old Testament patriarchs who had foreknown Christ and who have just proclaimed to their former co-religionists (for the patriarchs are refashioned into Christians *avant la lettre*) "the original works of the father" (*frumweorca fæder*, line 804a) and who have "praised with words the prince of glory" (*wordum weorðodon wuldres aldor*, line 806). The refusal to "imbibe" the teaching of Christ, even after he performed so many miracles while they looked on (*Haliges lare / synnige ne swulgon, þeah he soðre swa feala / tacna gecyðde, þær hie to segon*, lines 709a–11), places the "blind" Jews in stark opposition to Matthew, a Jew who wrote a gospel in Hebrew "with wondrous power" (*wundorcræfte*, line 13b) and who is still

---

47 This is the essential criterion by which other Anglo-Saxon writers distinguished magic from miracle. See Jolly, *Popular Religion*, 86.

48 As Szittya ("Living Stone," 173) has noted, in Mt 21:31–2, Christ rebukes the Pharisees for not having believed in the resurrection of the dead, invoking these three patriarchs: *non legistis quod dictum est a Deo dicente vobis ego sum deus Abraham et deus Isaac et deus Iacob?*

able to praise Christ in his heart after being blinded by his Mermedonian captors and forced to imbibe their magic potion (lines 48–53).[49]

The problem of the relation between divine writing and right reading brings us back to Jewish *galdorcræftas* as phylacteries. Jerome had insisted that the Pharisees "perversely interpreted" the verse in Deuteronomy which they (according to Jerome) took to enjoin the literal use of *tefillin* as protective amulets. Since rabbinic tradition consistently prescribed that *tefillin* should contain a set of verses from Exodus (13:1–10; 13:11–16) and Deuteronomy (6:4–9; 11:13–21),[50] Jerome's claim, frequently repeated by medieval writers,[51] that the Pharisees used the Decalogue (Ex 20:1–17; Dt 5:4–21) is sometimes assumed to have been an error.[52] The discoveries at Qumran proved, however, that *tefillin* of the Second Temple period often did contain the Decalogue.[53] Now the Decalogue was the key Old Testament text in Paul's polemic against the Jews and the Old Law:

---

49 On the metaphorics of Jewish blindness in *Andreas* see Scheil, *The Footsteps of Israel*, 234–6. A closely similar passage occurs in *Christ II*, lines 640b–4.

50 See Cohn, *Tangled up in Text*, 124–7.

51 In addition to the citations of Jerome cited above, see *Liber questionum in euangeliis*, ed. Rittmueller, 360; Pseudo-Jerome, *Expositio in quattuor euangeliis*: "phylacteria, id est, X verba Legis in chartula conscripta portantes pharisaei in fronte" (*PL* 30:557). An addition to the *Vita III Boethii* in the eleventh-century English manuscript Oxford, Corpus Christi College 74, after referring to Jerome's characterization of phylacteries as *pictaciola*, adds the following concise explanation: "Faciebant enim breuicula in quibus scribebant decalogum, id est x uerba legis, et circumligabant capiti suo in modum corone, quasi recordationem ut uiderentur illud preceptum complere, *et erit quasi signum in dextera tua, et uelut appensum quid, ob recordationem, ante oculos tuos* [Ex 13:16]"; ed. Esposito, "Miscellaneous Notes," 113. The manuscript is no. 671 in Gneuss and Lapidge, *Anglo-Saxon Manuscripts*. Two ninth-century glossaries from Reims transmit the following definition: "Philacteria, id est, decem verba legis vel scriptura vana, quod ligat homo aut super caballum [= *capellum*, 'cap,' so Pitra] aut super caput suum' (Reims, Bibliothèque Municipale 671 (s. ix in., Reims), fol. 196v, ed. Pitra, *Spicilegium solesmense*, 1:504; Paris, BnF lat. 12445 (s. ix³⁄₄, Reims), fol. 12v, ed. Flach, *Études critiques*, 173).

52 Jerome makes this claim not only in his commentary on Matthew but also in his commentary on Ezechiel, ed. Glorie, 330); compare Pseudo-Jerome, *Quaestiones hebraicae in libros Regum et Paralipomenon* (*PL* 23:1394).

53 Photographs of nine phylactery capsules from Qumran Cave 4Q can be seen at the website *National Treasures: Selected Artifacts from the Shelby White and Leon Levy Center for National Treasures* http://www.antiquities.org.il/t/search_en.aspx?q=phylactery+capsule. Qumran caves yielded a number of phylacteries containing the Decalogue. See Stemberger, "Der Dekalog im frühen Judentum," 149–50. According to Cohn (126), in the tannaitic period the Decalogue was no longer included in *tefillin* (and had also been excluded from the liturgy), so Jerome's understanding was apparently outdated by his time but was historically accurate.

180   Charles D. Wright

manifestati quoniam epistula estis Christi ministrata a nobis et scripta non atramento sed Spiritu Dei vivi non in tabulis lapideis sed in tabulis cordis carnalibus ... qui et idoneos nos fecit ministros novi testamenti non litterae sed Spiritus littera enim occidit Spiritus autem vivificat. (2 Cor 3:3, 6)

(Being manifested that you are the epistle of Christ, ministered by us, and written not with ink, but with the Spirit of the living God; not in tables of stone, but in the fleshly tables of the heart. ...Who also hath made us fit ministers of the new testament, not in the letter, but in the spirit. For the letter killeth, but spirit quickeneth.)

Paul goes on to refer to the veil on the face of Moses, which he understands as a "veil upon the heart" of the children of Israel "in the reading of the Old Testament," one that will not be taken away until the conversion of the Jews (vv. 13–16).[54] Jerome's criticism of phylacteries had been couched in similar language – the Pharisees, he said, failed to understand that the Decalogue must "be carried in the heart, not in the body." As a material embodiment of the letter of the Law, phylacteries are contrasted with a spiritualized "writing" that transcends signification.[55] In *Andreas*, the statue "written" on the wall of the Temple and made to bear witness to Christ already invokes the metaphor of "dead" writing on stone that must be vivified by the spirit and carried in the heart;[56] the charge by the Pharisees that the statue spoke through "devilish enchantments" is for the poet further evidence that they bear in their hearts, not the truth of their own scripture, but a fire-breathing, poisonous serpent (lines 767b–79) – a conventional patristic image, as Thomas D. Hill has shown, of the *malitia* of the Jews who rejected Christ.[57]

---

54 See the discussion of this Pauline image in Boyarin, "The Subversion of the Jews."

55 See Hermann's discussion (*Allegories of War*, 126–34) of how Christian miracle operates semiotically in *Andreas*, erasing the distinction between signifier/signified, accident/ essence, and letter/spirit. On the opposition of carnal and spiritual forms of writing in *Andreas* see also Fee, "Productive Destruction," 51–62; Godlove, "Bodies as Borders," 146–7.

56 As Szittya ("The Living Stone," 171–2) has argued, the statue is typologically the living stone of 1 Peter 2:4–5. The image of the "tables of the heart" is itself from the Old Testament, cf. Prv 7:2–3 (*serva mandata mea et vives et legem meam quasi pupillam oculi tui liga eam in digitis tuis scribe illam in tabulis cordis tui*).

57 Hill, "Two Notes," 156–60. According to Filastrius, *Diversarum hereseon liber* (ed. Marx, 9–10), Jews who worshipped the brazen serpent carried images of the serpent on neck-amulets along with incantations "uelut phylacteria," which they carried on their

The Decalogue itself as writing on stone figures explicitly later in the narrative when Andreas discovers marble columns supporting a wall in Mermedonia. Much as Christ had endowed the stone statue with speech, Andreas now commands the marble pillar to emit streams of water from its pedestal. Addressing the pillar, Andreas says that God himself had written the Decalogue upon it (i.e., upon marble):

On ðe sylf cyning

wrat, wuldres god,   wordum cyðde
recene geryno,   ond ryhte æ
getacnode   on tyn wordum,
meotud mihtum swið.   Moyse sealde,
swa hit soðfæste   syðþan heoldon,
modige magoþegnas,   magas sine,
godfyrhte guman,   Iosua ond Tobias.   (lines 1509a–16)

([T]he King himself, the God of glory, wrote upon thee, set forth in words, awful mysteries, and in ten words[58] the Lord strong in might set a sign of his just law; to Moses he gave it, as truthful men have afterwards kept it, brave followers, his kinsmen, God-fearing men, Joshua and Tobias.)

The Decalogue is here represented as both "just law" (*ryhte æ*) and "awful mysteries" (*recene geryno*), that is, both as the Old Law and as the New. The poet's statement that "Joshua and Tobias" later kept the Decalogue that had been given to Moses is his own rather cryptic addition to his source. Efforts to justify his invocation of these two seemingly random and unrelated Old Testament figures have focused on various spiritual qualities or figural meanings associated with each,[59] but have failed to account for what the poet actually says about them – that each was a custodian of the Decalogue after Moses. The allusion bridges the gap between the Giving of the Law (written on stone) to Moses[60] and the *traditio legis*

---

bodies as protective amulets. This work was known to Bede; see Lapidge, *The Anglo-Saxon Library*, 208.

58 The designation "ten words" corresponds to the Vulgate "decem verba" and Septuagint "deka logoi," where "words" literally translates Hebrew *divarim*, "words," "statements."

59 Trahern, "Joshua and Tobias"; Hieatt, "The Harrowing of Mermedonia," 49–51; Walsh, "The Baptismal Flood," 146–50; Bishop, "*Þyrs, ent, eoten, gigans*," 269.

60 See Leone, "Divine Dictation."

by which Christ transmits the New Law (written on the heart) to Peter and Paul, who represent all the apostles.[61] The relevance of Joshua to the immediate context can be more concretely explained by his role as custodian of the ark of the covenant (Jo 3–8) and by his writing of the Mosaic law on stones and his reading of "all things that were written in the book of the law" (Jo 8:34) before the people of Israel as they stood on both sides of the ark.

The reference to Joshua can be thus be accounted for satisfactorily, yet it should not be overlooked that the name *Iosua* is editorial: the Vercelli Book reads *iosau*, and while the emendation is eminently plausible paleographically, the scribal corruption raises the possibility that a different name has been obscured. Restoring *Iosias* yields an alternative Old Testament figure – Josiah – who was famous for his rediscovery in the Temple of "the book of the law" (2 Kings 22), which book Jerome identified as Deuteronomy, one of the two books containing the Decalogue. Josiah had the book read publically (2 Kings 23:2) and was inspired to undertake a sweeping program of religious reform, destroying the idols that the Jews had been worshipping (2 Kings 22–3).[62] Josiah also ordered that the ark of the covenant containing the two tablets of the Law be placed in the sanctuary of the Temple (2 Chr 35:3). Eucherius of Lyon recorded a tradition according to which Josiah, forseeing the Babylonian Captivity, later caused the ark to be removed and hidden:

> Arcam Domini in qua erant duae tabulae testamenti quo ablatam esse credendum est? Legimus in Paralipomenon Iosiam regem Iuda, cum in Hierusalem faceret pascha Domino, ad leuitas ita locutum esse: *Ponite arcam in sanctuario templi, quod aedificauit Salomon filius Dauid rex Israhel; nequaquam enim eam ultra portabitis* [2 Chr 35:3]. Hoc loco ita intellegere quidam uolunt, quod Iosias futuram praeuidens captiuitatem arcam Domini, incertum tamen quo tunc loco, curarit abscondi.[63]

---

61 See Hvalvik, "Christ Proclaiming his Law." Anglo-Saxon respresentations of the motif are discussed by Hawkes, *The Sandbach Crosses*, 56–60.

62 See Monroe, *Josiah's Reform*.

63 *Formulae spiritalis intelligentiae*, ed. Mandolfo, 111–12. This tradition, which contradicts the biblical statement (2 Mc 2:4) that Jeremiah hid the ark, is rabbinic: see Davila, "Scriptural Exegesis," 47.

(By whom are we to believe that the ark of the Lord containing the two tablets of the covenant was removed? We read in Chronicles that Josiah, king of Judah, when he was observing the passover for the Lord in Jerusalem, said thus to the priests: "Put the ark in the sanctuary of the temple, which Solomon the son of David king of Israel built: for you shall carry it no more." In this passage some would thus understand that Josiah, foreseeing the future captivity, had the ark of the Lord hidden, yet it is not clear in what place at that time.)

Josiah was therefore custodian of the Decalogue quite literally, and in two written forms: as the stone tablets themselves, contained in the ark of the covenant, which he secured at the Temple and then hid; and as a scroll containing the book of Deuteronomy, which had previously been lost.

There is little to choose between Josiah and Joshua, who might equally be said to represent the literal custody and transmission of the stone tablets of the Decalogue as well as the oral teaching of the Law as the basis for establishing religious community.[64] As Jean Daniélou has noted, for Origen "Joshua's renewal of the Covenant and rereading of the Law is a type of the New Covenant" and "of Jesus explaining the Law and the Prophets to his disciples at Emmaus," revealing its true significance.[65] Josiah did not have a comparable typological resonance, yet he was prominently invoked as a precedent for Charlemagne's religious reforms in the *Admonitio generalis*, written probably by Alcuin.[66] Andreas's destruction of heathen idols following his discovery of the stone pillar representing the Decalogue and his establishment of the Mermedonian church (lines 1687–8) recalls Josiah's similar act following his discovery of the tablets of the Law and restoration of the Temple.

As for Tobias, the book that bears his name shows him faithfully observing many of the Ten Commandments – to the extent that a modern commentator has characterized the book of Tobit as "the Decalogue in action."[67] More importantly, according to Bede – author of the only early commentary

---

64 Joshua and Josiah are implicitly connected in the Old Testament; see Nelson, "Josiah in the Book of Joshua."

65 Daniélou, *From Shadows to Reality*, 282.

66 *Admonitio generalis*, ed. Boretius, 54. See McKitterick, *The Frankish Church*, 2–3. On Alcuin's role in drafting the *Admonitio* see Scheibe, "Alcuin und die *Admonitio Generalis*."

67 Auneau, "Écrits didactiques," 353–87.

on the book – Tobias also received and passed on the Decalogue in the allegorical form of the ten talents of silver that he lent to his friend Gabelus in exchange for a chirograph, and then had his son and namesake Tobias take back:

> Tobias Gabelo contribuli suo egenti dedit sub chirographo decem talenta argenti. Et populus Dei gentibus per septuaginta interpretes diuinae legis quae in decalogo continetur scientiam commisit ut per hoc eas ab infidelitatis egestate liberaret; sub chirographo autem dedit, id est sub conditione restituendi postquam ipse ditesceret uel qui dederat repeteret. Acceperunt autem gentes uerbum Dei a populo Israhel per interpretationem quod post incarnationem dominicam etiam spiritaliter nunc intellegunt et ad conquirendas uirtutum diuitias exercent; reddunt uero faeneratori cum credentes in fine saeculi Iudaeos in unitatem ecclesiae recipiunt eis que saluandis Christi sacramenta committunt et scripturarum quoque reserant archana.[68]

> (Tobias gave ten talents of silver to his needy tribesman Gabael under his signature. Likewise the people of God through seventy translators entrusted the knowledge of the divine law contained in the Ten Commandments to the Gentiles to free them from the poverty of unbelief. Now Tobias gave it under his signature, that is, under the condition that it be repaid when the debtor gets rich or when the creditor asks for it back. Likewise, the Gentiles borrowed God's word from the people Israel through a translation. Now after the Lord's incarnation they understand (God's word) spiritually and practise it so as to acquire the riches of virtues. Surely they will repay back the moneylender at the end of the age when they welcome believing Jews into the unity of the church and entrust Christ's sacraments and open Scripture's mysteries to those who are to be saved.)

For Bede, then, Tobias represents the Jews' custody of the Decalogue as well as their transmission of the Law to the Gentiles, who are able to understand it spiritually "under translation," and who will give it back to the

---

68 Bede, *In Tobiam*, ed. Hurst, 4; *Bede: A Biblical Miscellany*, trans. Foley and Holder, 59. This passage has been cited and discussed (without reference to *Andreas*) by Scheil, *The Footsteps of Israel*, 60. Trahern, "Joshua and Tobias," 332, cites a passage from Isidore of Seville that contrasts the father and son as representing the Old Law and Christ respectively.

Jews converted in the last times. In *Andreas*, as James W. Earl has argued, the conversion of the pagan Mermedonians is also a type of the eschatological conversion of the Jews,[69] making Tobias the ideal Old Testament figure for the transmission of the Law as *ryhte æ* from the Jews to the Gentiles and ultimately back again to the Jews as *recene geryno*.

When Andreas says that the Decalogue was written upon the Mermedonian pillar, he presumably means that it had been written on the same kind of stone (marble, for that reason the most noble of stones, lines 1517–19), not that it was actually engraved upon the pillar itself – whether as a copy or as *spolia* from the ark of the covenant.[70] Yet by virtue of Andreas's association of the material and the text, the pillar symbolizes the transmission of the Decalogue to the Gentiles through the mediation of the apostles. The church erected upon that spot at Andreas's command incorporates the Decalogue into its very fabric – at once a material and a metaphorical enactment of that transmission.

If, as seems likely, the poet believed that Jewish phylacteries contained the Decalogue, its custodianship as both *ryhte æ* and *recene geryno* by *Iosau* (whether Joshua or Josiah) and by Tobias is implicitly contrasted with its superstitious misuse as *galdorcræftas* imputed to the Pharisees by Matthew. Moreover, Matthew's gospel, which alone transmits the Sermon on the Mount, is precisely the one in which Christ reinterpreted the Decalogue spiritually (Mt 5:17–48). Matthew, then, had "showed forth his love" in the presence of the Hebrews and Israelites by writing for them the gospel that taught the Decalogue as "awful mysteries," even as he had resisted Jewish *galdorcræftas* (containing the Decalogue as "just law") by recounting Christ's condemnation of phylacteries.

Yet the *Andreas* poet was surely aware that the "Jewish magic" condemned in Matthew's gospel had its Christian counterpart. For the wearing of scriptural "phylacteries" was widespread among Christians from late Antiquity through the Middle Ages, including in Anglo-Saxon England. Jerome himself had turned his invective against the phylacteries of the Pharisees into a reprimand of superstitious Christian women who wear amulets made from the gospels or the wood of the Cross:

---

69 Earl, "The Typological Structure of *Andreas*," 74–8.

70 Earl ("Typological Structure," 74) assumes that the pillar is actually made from the stone of the ten commandments. See also Ferhatovic, "Spolia-Inflected Poetics."

Hoc apud nos superstitiosae mulierculae in paruulis euangeliis et in crucis ligno et istiusmodi rebus, quae habent quidem zelum Dei sed non iuxta scientiam, usque hodie factitant, culicem liquantes et camelum glutientes.[71]

(Among us there are superstitious little women who keep doing this up to the present day with little Gospels and with the wood of the Cross and with things of this sort. They have a zeal for God, to be sure, but not according to knowledge. Straining out a gnat, they swallow a camel.)

Caesarius of Arles cited Matthew 23:5 in sternly warning his congregation against the use of "phylacteries," meaning of course amulets:

… quod dolendum est, sunt aliqui, qui in qualibet infirmitate sortilegos quaerunt, aruspices et divinos interrogant, praecantatores adhibent, fylacteria sibi diabolica et caracteres adpendunt. … Etiam si vobis dicatur, quod res sanctas et lectiones divinas filacteria ipsa contineant, nemo credat, nemo de illis sanitatem sibi venturam esse confidat … Qui enim filacteria facit, et qui rogant ut fiant, et quicumque consentiunt, toti pagani efficiuntur; et, nisi dignam egerint paenitentiam, non possunt evadere poenam. … Hos enim filacterarios in phariseis ipse arguit christus, dicens: *dilatant enim filacteria sua, et magnificant fimbrias.* Melius est in corde verba dei retinere, quam scripta in collo suspendere.[72]

(What is deplorable is that there are some who seek soothsayers in every kind of infirmity. They consult seers and divines, summon enchanters, and hang diabolical phylacteries and magic letters on themselves. … Even if you are told that phylacteries contain holy facts and divine lessons, let no one believe it or expect health to come to him from them. … Anyone who makes these phylacteries or asks to have them made, as well as all those who consent to it have become pagans, and unless they perform sufficient penance they cannot escape punishment. … Christ himself rebuked the Pharisees who wore phylacteries when He said: "For they widen their phylacteries and enlarge their tassels." It would be better to keep the words of God in one's heart than to wear them in writing on one's neck.)

---

71 *In Matheum*, ed. Adriaen, 212; *Commentary on Matthew*, trans. Scheck, 260.

72 *Sermo* 50, ed. Morin, 225–6; trans. Mueller, *Caesarius of Arles*, 254. On Caesarius's use of the term see Bartelink, "Phylakterion-phylacterium," 50–2.

These amulets were Christian in that they contained Christian texts, but Caesarius regarded them as pagan in their magical function and therefore analogous to the Jewish phylacteries condemned by Christ. Similar warnings against phylacteries were sounded by Eligius of Noyon and Boniface,[73] and were echoed in canonical legislation – often characterizing them as pagan but sometimes comparing them to Jewish phylacteries.[74]

Learned Anglo-Saxon ecclesiasts were also alarmed by the proliferation of phylacteries among Christians. In his *Historia Ecclesiastica*, Bede recounted that Cuthbert had combatted the use of phylacteries against the plague:

Nam et multi fidem quam habebant iniquis profanabant operibus, et aliqui etiam tempore mortalitatis, neglectis fidei sacramentis quibus erant inbuti, ad erratica idolatriae medicamina concurrebant, quasi missam ad Deo Conditore plagam per incantationes uel fylacteria uel alia quaelibet daemonicae artis arcana cohibere ualerent.[75]

(For many of them profaned the creed they held by wicked deeds and some of them, too, in times of plague, would forget the sacred mysteries of the faith into which they had been initiated and take to the false remedies of idolatry, as though they could ward off a blow inflicted by God the Creator by means of incantations or amulets or any other mysteries of devilish art.)

Alcuin, writing to Æthelhard, bishop of Canterbury, condemned the wearing of *ligaturae* with gospels verses as a "pharisaical superstition":

Multas videbam consuetudines, que fieri non debebant. Quas tua sollicitudo prohibeat. Nam ligaturas portant, quasi sanctum quid estimantes. Sed melius

---

73 *Vita Eligii*, ed. Krusch, 707); Boniface, *Letter 50*, ed. Dümmler, 301.

74 In a series of canons against Judaizing, the Council of Laodicea (ca. 364) forbade clerics from making phylacteries (*amuleta* in the Latin version): Mansi, *Sacrorum conciliorum nova*, 2:570 (canon 36). See Simon, *Verus Israel*, 361. Cf. also *Concilium Aquisgranense* (816) (canon 94), ed. Werminghoff, 372–3 ("Nolo te dilatare fimbrias et ostentui habere filacteria et conscientia repugnante pharisaica ambitione circumdari").

75 *Bede's Ecclesiastical History*, ed. and trans. Colgrave and Mynors, 432–3. As Waite ("Old English *lybesn*," 15) notes, this passage repeats almost verbatim one in Bede's earlier *Vita Cuthberti* 9, but with the substitution of *fylacterium* for *(al)ligatura*. In the Old English Bede, the phrase *per incantationes uel fylacteria* is rendered *þurh heora galdor oððe lefesende* (see Waite's discussion).

est in corde sanctorum imitare exempla, quam in sacculis portare ossa; evangelicas habere scriptas ammonitiones in mente magis, quam pittaciolis exaratas in collo circumferre. Haec est pharisaica superstitio; quibus ipsa veritas improperavit philacteria sua.[76]

(I saw many improper customs practised, which it is your duty to stop. For they are carrying amulets, thinking them something sacred. It is better to copy the examples of the saints in the heart than to carry them in bags, to have gospel teachings written in one's mind than to carry them round one's neck written on scraps of parchment. This is the superstition of the Pharisees, whom Christ himself reproached for their phylacteries.)

Material evidence for Anglo-Saxon amulets is abundant, and their use was by no means restricted to superstitious women or unsophisticated clergymen.[77] It is difficult to say whether surviving Anglo-Saxon cross pendants[78] were simply devotional or in some sense "magical"; the apotropaic power of the Cross against demons, however, was universally accepted (including by Jerome) and would not have been regarded by Christians themselves as a form of magic. Still, anyone familiar with Jerome's comment on Jewish phylacteries would know that he had also scorned the use of cross-amulets and amuletic gospels by Christians. From Jerome's perspective wearing such amulets was Judaizing, while for Caesarius and Alcuin amulets were strictly forbidden to Christians as pagan and "pharisiacal."[79]

The *Andreas* poet never directly acknowledges that the "Jewish magic arts" opposed by Matthew had their Christian counterparts. Indeed, he suppresses acts of Christian magic in his source, notably the magical use of the sign of the Cross or *crux usualis*;[80] for he twice omits references in the *Acta* to Andrew making the sign of the Cross as an offensive weapon.[81] In the *Praxeis*, *Casanatensis*, and OE prose *Andreas*, when Andrew

---

76 *Letter 290*, ed. Dümmler, 448; trans. Allott, *Alcuin of York*, 69.

77 See Meaney, *Anglo-Saxon Amulets*; Cain, "The Apocryphal Legend," 387–90.

78 These are surveyed by de Vegvar, "*In Hoc Signo*," 106–11.

79 Neither Caesarius nor Alcuin refers to cross-amulets, perhaps because of the ambiguity that obtained regarding the kinds of powers that might legitimately be attributed to the sign of the Cross. For examples of amuletic gospels see Skemer, "Written Amulets," 253–305.

80 See Johnson, "The *Crux Usualis*."

81 This is one of the categories of the apotropaic use of the *crux usualis* discussed by Johnson, 92–5.

frees Matthew from the prison he forces open the door by making the sign of the Cross.[82] In *Andreas*, however, the door opens "through the touch of the Holy Spirit" (*þurh handhrine haliges gastes*, line 1000), with no reference to the sign of the Cross.[83] Again, in the Greek, Latin, and Old English prose versions Andrew makes the sign of the Cross when he commands the pillar to emit a flood of water,[84] but not so in *Andreas* (lines 1495–1508). Evidently the poet objected to the use of the Cross like a magic wand. He does, however, explicitly endorse an alternative to cross-amulets as protection against demons. After Andreas has been tortured and confined in the Mermedonian prison, the devil enters, taunting him that Herod had defeated his master (*lareow*), the king of the Jews (*cyning Iudea*), and consigned him to the (actual) Cross (lines 1320–7). When the devil orders his six companions to kill Andreas, they are warded off by a sign that Andreas bears on his body:

Syððan hie oncneowan   Cristes rode
on his mægwlite,   mære tacen,
wurdon hie ða acle   on þam onfenge,
forhte, afærde,   ond on fleam numen.   (lines 1337–40)

---

82 *Praxeis*, trans. Boenig, 12; *Casanetensis*, trans. Allen and Calder, 25 (here the prison guards are also killed by the sign of the Cross; in the *Praxeis*, they die as a result of Andrew's prayer); OE Prose *Andreas*, ed. Cassidy and Ringler, *Bright's Old English Grammar*, 212.

83 Here there is probably some influence from the scene in *Beowulf* in which the door of Heorot is forced open at the touch of Grendel's hand: *Klaeber's Beowulf*, ed. Fulk et al., lines 721b–2. (I thank Jill Fitzgerald for this suggestion.) As incongrous as it may be to have the action of the Holy Spirit mimic that of Grendel, the *Andreas* poet probably did have this passage in mind, as the parallel *Duru sona onarn* (*Andreas* line 999b, *Beowulf* line 720b) suggests. I agree with those who argue that the *Andreas* poet drew on *Beowulf*. See Friesen, "Visions and Revisions," 150–1.

84 *Praxeis*, trans. Boenig, 20 (where Andrew also invokes the "image of the Cross at which the heavens and earth tremble"); *Casanatensis*, trans. Allen and Calder, 31 (where Andrew invokes the power of Christ "before whose power heaven and earth tremble"); and the OE Prose *Andreas*, ed. Cassidy and Ringler, 216 (where he invokes the Lord and the sign of the Cross "before whom heaven and earth are afraid"). In *Andreas* the sign of the Cross is not made, nor is the Cross invoked; instead, Andreas invokes the "commands" (*rædum*) of the Lord "before whose sight all creation will become afraid when they see the Father of the heaven and earth seek mankind with a great host," an allusion to the Last Judgment not paralleled in the *Acta*.

(After they perceived the Cross of Christ, a glorious token, on his countenance, then they grew terrified, timid, fearful, and took to flight.)

Learning of his minions' failure, the devil accuses Andreas of dealing "in magic arts" (*aclæccræftum*, lines 1362–3a), as if Andreas had used the Cross as an apotropaic weapon – as indeed it *was* regarded by many pious Anglo-Saxon Christians.[85] Yet unlike the "superstitious little women" mocked by Jerome, Andreas does not bear a cross-amulet. As Thomas D. Hill has shown, the *tacen* that Andreas bears on his countenance is the *sphragis* (seal), the sign of the Cross made on the forehead of the newly baptized.[86] Hill quotes Jean Daniélou's statement that "one of the points most frequently brought out by the Fathers of the Church concerning the *sphragis* is that it makes the Christian fearful to demons."[87] Like the Jewish phylactery, the *sphragis* is carried on the forehead; but unlike Jewish or Christian amulets, it is not a material artefact, but an immaterial (sacramental) sign.[88]

This scene in which the *sphragis* preserves Andreas from death reprises an earlier one in which the Mermedonians had entered the prison with the intent of killing Matthew but were prevented from doing so by a sign that he bears:

Hæfdon hie on rune   and on rimcræfte
awriten, wælgrædige,   wera endestæf,
hwæne hie to mose   meteþearfendum
on þære werþeode   weorðan sceoldon. ...
Hie ða gemetton   modes glawne,
haligne hæle,   under heolstorlocan
bidan beadurofne   þæs him beorht cyning,
engla ordfruma,   unnan wolde.
Ða wæs first agan   frumrædenne
þinggemearces   butan þrim nihtum,
swa hit wælwulfas   awriten hæfdon ...   (lines 134–7, 143–9)

---

85 See Johnson, "The *Crux Usualis*."
86 Hill, "The Sphragis." See also Lampe, *The Seal of the Spirit*, 275.
87 Daniélou, *The Bible and the Liturgy*, 59.
88 It may be significant that the poet does not specify how or where those runic inscriptions are applied. In the *Praxeis* and *Casanatensis*, we are told that tablets are attached to the hand of each victim; in *Andreas*, the possibility is left open that the runes are hung around the neck, like an amulet, or even written on the forehead, like the *sphragis*.

(Greedy for slaughter, they had set down with writing and reckoning the doom of men, when they must become food for those lacking meat among the people. ... Then they found the holy man, wise-minded, boldly awaiting in prison that which the bright King, the Prince of angels, willed to grant him. Then the term of time had passed save for three nights, the appointed space, as the warriors had set it down in writing ...)

The runic inscriptions that track how many days each prisoner has left to live make for a ghoulish parody of "releasing letters":[89] they do indeed protect the life of the bearer, but only for thirty days, and then they just as surely condemn him to death. Matthew's inscription has a pseudo-apotropaic effect, preventing the Mermedonians from killing and eating him, but only temporarily. The allusion to Jewish *galdorcræftas* – which I have argued the poet understood as pseudo-apotropaic phylacteries containing written inscriptions – comes just a few lines later.

The poet's disapproval of Christian magic – with a special exemption for Christian miracle – can also be gauged by his treatment of the apostolic lottery in the *Acta*. The *Praxeis*, *Casanatensis*, and OE prose *Andreas* all represent the apostles as casting lots to determine where each would go to preach the gospel, with Matthew receiving the lot for Mermedonia:

In illo tempore erant apostoli simul in unum congregati, et dividebant inter se regiones, mittentes sortes, quatenus agnoscerent unusquisque, qualis pars ad eum ad predicandum devenirent. Devenit namque beati mathei in sortem provincie que dicitur mermedonia ... (§1, ed. Blatt, 33)

(At that time all the apostles were gathered together and they divided the regions among themselves, casting lots to see which area each was to be assigned for preaching. The province called Mermedonia ... fell in the lot to the blessed Matthew.)

The poet significantly alters this description. In *Andreas* the apostles no longer cast lots themselves; instead, God simply assigns Matthew his "lot": "þam halig god hlyt geteode/ut on þæt igland ..." (Holy God appointed

---

89 The locus classicus for "releasing letters" (*litterae solutoriae*) is the story of Imma, *Bede's Ecclesiastical History* 4.22, ed. Colgrave and Mynors, 402–3 (Imma's bonds are loosened when his brother, the priest Tunna, says masses said for him, but his captors assume he must be in possession of "releasing letters"). See the discussion by Lerer, *Literacy and Power*, 30–60, who refers (53) to the Mermedonian writing "[that] attempts to bind and destroy rather than release and revive."

him his lot out on that island …). Not a form of divination, even of a divinely sanctioned kind, the "lot" received (not cast) by Matthew is nothing more than his predetermined marching orders, and the expression *hlyt geteode* is nothing more than a dead metaphor.[90] It is not hard to see why the *sortes apostolorum*[91] tradition should have been objectionable. Lot-casting was among the most frequently condemned "pagan" magical practices,[92] and it was also perceived as a Jewish practice that, according to Bede, was licit under the Old Law, but not under the New. The potentially embarrassing episode in Acts in which apostles cast lots to choose a replacement for Judas (1:26) was confronted head-on by Bede, arguing resourcefully that, because it took place before the Pentecost, the lot-casting was still under the old dispensation and thus lawful.[93] The apocryphal tradition of the *sortes apostolorum* could not be justified this way, and while the authors of the Greek and Latin texts of the *Acta Andreae* were unconcerned, the *Andreas* poet was unwilling to countenance post-Pentecostal apostolic cleromancy.

Rather than simply omitting any reference to the *sortes*, however, the poet re-represents it as a "lottery" in name only. The advantage of retaining the term "lot" (*hlyt*) is that the misnomer heightens the contrast between the salvific "lottery" of the apostles and the malefic lot-casting conducted by the Mermedonians after Andreas has deprived them of their foreign victims in order to determine which one of their own will be killed and eaten:

> Leton him þa betweonum   taan wisian
> hwylcne hira ærest   oðrum sceolde
> to foddurþege   feores ongyldan;
> hluton hellcræftum,   hæðengildum
> teledon betwinum.   (lines 1099–1103a)

---

90 Compare the use of the verb *hleotan* in line 480b, where the sense is simply "receive." Like OE *hleotan*, Latin *sortior* could mean "to allot" or "be allotted" without implying lot-casting. Compare Lantfred of Winchester, *Translatio et miracula S. Swithuni*, Praefatio: "bis senas sortiti [*scil.* didascali] prouincias," ed. Lapidge, *The Cult of St Swithun*, 256–7. The poet's alteration of the apostolic *sortes* has been noted in passing by Shaw, "Translation and Transformation," 166, and Scheil, "Space and Place," 202; also Godlove, "Apostolic Discourse," 311–12.

91 See Czachesz, *Commission Narratives*, 226–31.

92 See Chardonnens, *Anglo-Saxon Prognostics*, 124, quoting the *Poenitentiale Theodori*, with reference (n. 139) to similar condemnations in other penitentials.

93 *Expositio Actuum apostolorum*, ed. Laistner, 14–15; Martin, trans., *The Venerable Bede*, 21.

(Then among them they let the lot direct which of them should first yield his life as food for the others; they cast lots with hellish arts, they made count with idolatries among them.)

The poet here represents lot-casting as a scapegoating form of divination, but with a human victim rather than the goat of Leviticus 16:7–11, creating a demonic parody of the self-sacrifice of Christ.

As Hermann has argued, the poet's condemnations of magic construct Christian identity by scapegoating both pagans and Jews, legitimizing the suppression of the former and the supersession of the latter.[94] What Jews and pagans perceive as Christian *drycræft* and *scinlac* is transformed before our very eyes into *wundor* by appeal to Christ's power as creator over the elements that he brought into being. Forms of Christian magic that cannot be justified in this way are made to disappear from view by textual legerdemain. The lot-casting of the apostles in the *Acta*, too close to pagan and Jewish lot-casting for comfort, is palmed as an empty metaphor of the apostolic commission. The sign of the Cross, which twice performs an open-sesame in the *Acta* (opening prison doors and floodgates) is in the first case silently switched for the direct action of the Holy Spirit and in the second case just as silently ditched. And in a more complex kind of misdirection, Christian phylacteries are simulated through the devil's charge that Andreas had protected himself through *aclæccræft*, but only after they have been replaced by the baptismal *sphragis*.[95]

In *Andreas*, the Christian "hermeneutics of supersession"[96] operate on multiple levels, but are epitomized by the written sign: the books of the Old Testament are superseded by Matthew's gospel, the first book of the New Testament and the only one originally written in Hebrew; the marble tablets of the Decalogue, preserved by Josiah/Joshua and Tobias, are superseded spiritually as *recene geryno* written on the heart; and the phylacteries (*galdorcræftas*) on the foreheads of Jews are superseded by the *sphragis* (*tacen*) on the foreheads of Christians.[97]

---

94 Hermann, *Allegories of War*, 122–5, 139–40, 147.

95 Skemer, *Binding Words*, 84–9.

96 See Boyarin, "The Subversion of the Jews."

97 Collins, *Crisis and Catharsis*, 125, suggests that the "mark of the beast" that the Antichrist places on the right hand or forehead of his followers in Rv 12:16–17 "may be a parodying allusion to the Jewish practice of wearing phylacteries on the forehead and left hand or arm" in contrast to the *sphragis*, "a guarantee of protection from the natural and demonic plagues of the end time" in Rv 3:10, 7:3, 9:4.

Visual Media: Representations of Jews and Jewish Spaces

9 Hagar and Ishmael:
The Uncanny and the Exile[1]

CATHERINE E. KARKOV

Hagar and Ishmael occupy an ambivalent and problematic place in both biblical history and Anglo-Saxon culture. They are mother and son, but they are not the legitimate mother and son, that status being accorded to Sarah and Isaac. They are exiles cast out into the wilderness by Abraham and doomed to inhabit the desert wastes, but it is a curious sort of exile. They are, in effect, exiles from exile as they are forced out of the life of willing exile that Abraham has accepted from the Lord, and their exile is also a form of return to Hagar's homeland of Egypt. They are symbolic of the Jews, but they are also interpreted as signifying the Muslims, a double identity addressed but never successfully resolved in exegesis.[2] Moreover, Hagar is also denied by both peoples, and this is part of what makes her a particularly troubling figure. She is both absent and present, denied and doubled, and made to merge with a number of other figures in the sources in a way that makes her a truly uncanny figure. The uncanny can take many forms, but it is at heart a disturbance of the personal, something – a presence – at once both familiar and foreign. It can include stories like E.T.A. Hoffman's "The Sandman" (and Freud's interpretation of it) in which characters are doubled, deformed, or made to blend into one another.[3] Sometimes they are mirror opposites, sometimes it is

---

1 I would like to thank Eric Prenowitz for his helpful comments on an earlier draft of this paper. On the perceptions in Anglo-Saxon England of Ishmael and his descendants, see Hall, ch. 2, above.

2 Scarfe Beckett, *Anglo-Saxon Perceptions of the Islamic World*, 98.

3 On the uncanny and its history see Freud, "The Uncanny"; Royle, *The Uncanny*. See ibid., pages 39–50 for a summary of the difference between Freud's interpretation of "The Sandman" and E.T.A. Hoffman's original story.

impossible to disentangle one from the other, as is also the case with the biblical pair Hagar and Sarah. This essay argues that the Genesis narrative situates Hagar within a series of exiles, doublings, and divisions, and that the Anglo-Saxon retellings of her story take those processes even further.

Hagar is above all a slave and concubine, but she is also an Egyptian princess. The Vulgate also makes her a wife, not only at the moment that Sarah gives her to Abraham to wife (*uxorem*), but also by identifying her with, and hence doubling her by, Ketura, Abraham's second legitimate wife, the mother of Zimran, Jokshan, Medan, Midian, Ishbak, and Shuah (Gen. 25:1–2). Jerome seems to have accepted that the two names referred to the same woman, but he did not accept Ketura's status as wife, glossing her name with *copulata* or *uincta*.[4] The author of a commentary on the Pentateuch composed at the Canterbury of Theodore and Hadrian had a clearer opinion: "*Cethura* [XXV.1] alia uxor Abraham, non Agar, ut multi arbitrantur."[5] Whatever his opinion on the matter, his words indicate that the confusion of the two women was known in Anglo-Saxon England, and they signal the start of an Anglo-Saxon insistence on Hagar's status as a concubine and slave and not a wife. Ælfric omitted all mention of Ketura from his late tenth-century translation of Genesis, beginning Genesis 25 with verse 5, the verse in which Abraham gives all his possessions to Isaac.[6] The Vulgate Genesis also says of Sarah that "Tulit Agar ægyptiam ancillam suam post annos decem quam habitare coeperant in terra Chanaan, et dedit eam viro suo uxorem (She took Agar the Egyptian her handmaid, ten years after they first dwelt in the land of Channa, and gave her to her husband to wife; Gen. 16:3), but both the Old English poem *Genesis*, a poem arguably composed – or at least a version of it was composed – in the eighth century, and Ælfric's translation of Genesis omit the verse entirely.[7] In the Anglo-Saxon version of the story, Hagar emerges more clearly as the deformed double of Sarah, a figure who, along with her son, must be permanently banished from Abraham's line,

---

4   Scarfe Beckett, *Anglo-Saxon Perceptions of the Islamic World*, 120. Ketura has also been identified with Hagar in the Hebrew tradition, though more controversially (Friedman, *Commentary on the Torah*, 85).

5   "*Cetura* [XXV.1]: another wife of Abraham; not Agar, as many suppose." Bischoff and Lapidge *Biblical Commentaries from the Canterbury School of Theodore and Hadrian*, 330–1 (trans. Lapidge).

6   Neither Bede's commentary on Genesis nor the Junius 11 *Genesis* extends as far as Genesis 25.

7   See further below. See also Anlezark, "An Ideal Marriage," 198.

from his home, and from the narrative. Her very absence, however, continues to haunt the story, an absent presence, and most especially it haunts those parts of the story from which she has been excised.

In his *In Genesim*, written sometime ca. 717–25, Bede accepted that Sarah had given Hagar to Abraham "to wife"; nevertheless he was quite clear that in begetting a child by Hagar Abraham was only fulfilling his duty to his wife. He divides Hagar from Abraham, even at the moment of Ishmael's conception by stipulating that Abraham felt no lust, and thus implying that Hagar did. His division between Hagar and Sarah, however, was far more blurred. The Vulgate states that Sarah gave Hagar to Abraham in the hope that she would be able to have children by her.[8] If Hagar is Sarah's property, presumably her children would also be Sarah's property, and if Abraham is Sarah's husband, then his children are also hers. But Bede, quoting from Augustine's *De civitate Dei*, accepts a phrasing of events in which the two women eerily seem to become one. Sarah, "suae sterilitatis credidit esse solatium si fecundum ancillae uterum quoniam natura non poterat uoluntate fecerat suum … uteretur mulier ex altera ad pariendum, quod non poterat ex se ipsa" (believed that it would be a consolation for her own sterility if she voluntarily made her handmaid's fertile womb her own, since she could not be fertile by nature … in order to give birth from another because she could not from herself).[9] The wording underscores the doubled maternity of the two women, but it also silences the biblical statement that Sarah gave Hagar to Abraham "to wife" by effecting a union that makes it unclear as to exactly how the two "wives" are to be separated. What is the effect of the metaphorical on our reading of the physical? Does Sarah simply accept Hagar's womb as her property just as Hagar herself is her property, or is Hagar's womb to be transposed into Sarah's body, or Sarah into Hagar's body? However the words are to be understood, Hagar's body and motherhood here disappear within the figure of Sarah, causing her in effect to be cast out from the family long before she is cast out of the household. For Freud, the mother's womb was the ultimate *Heim*, and the most *unheimliche* of places, the home that we all share but to which we can never return,[10] and Hagar's lack of home, in

---

8 Genesis 16:2, "si forte saltem ex illa suscipiam filios."

9 Bede, ed., *In Genesim*, 200; Bede, *On Genesis*, 278. See also Augustine, *De civitate Dei*, 48, 529.

10 Freud, "The Uncanny," 245.

terms of household, homeland, and her own body, trap her in a series of internal exiles, and figure her again and again as cipher for the uncanny.

It was Hagar and Ishmael's status as outcasts and unwilling exiles that seems to have been Bede's main concern, undoubtedly because it was that status that gave rise to what he perceived to be a much larger religious threat. Yet here again, the division between social and religious bodies is as blurry as that between the physical bodies of Abraham's wives. Just as Hagar's almost identification with Ketura led to her doubling by and disappearance within a second legitimate wife, and just as the idea that Sarah could give birth through Hagar led to her doubling by and disappearance within the first wife, the transforming of the Hagarenes and Ishmaelites (names identified with various pre-Islamic and Arab peoples) into the Saracens effecting her disappearance yet again behind the legitimate wife and mother Sarah. The term "Saracen" was unique to the Christian West, and as Katharine Scarfe Beckett notes, "Biblical exegetes seem simply to have assumed that the northern Arabs were descendants of Hagar's son Ismael and knew themselves to be congenitally inferior to Isaac's descendants because their ancestor was a slave and, furthermore, not the mother of the Chosen People. Consequently, the logic goes, Ismaelites began to call themselves Saracens in a rather feeble attempt to make it appear that they were descended from Abraham's free wife Sarah, and not from her handmaid."[11] The Ishmaelites and Hagarenes, like Hagar herself, are thus made to be willing participants in their own disappearance. They choose their name just as Hagar chooses sex and wickedness, and like Hagar they were viewed as inferior peoples, changeable and deceptive. The identification of the pre-Islamic peoples of the desert as the Saracens was popularized by Jerome,[12] who went on to describe the Saracens as nomadic raiders who attacked and were attacked by all the desert peoples. This description was "updated" by Bede in his *In Genesim*, where he describes Jerome's words as referring to a time long past. He writes that "Nunc autem in tantum manus eius contra omnes, et manus sunt omnium contra eum, ut Africam totam in longitudine sua ditione premant, sed et Asiae maximam partem, et Europae nonnullam omnibus exosi et contrarii teneant" (Now the Saracens hold the whole breadth of Africa in their sway, and they also hold the greatest part of Asia and some part of Europe, hateful and

---

11 Scarfe Beckett, *Anglo-Saxon Perceptions of the Islamic World*, 95.
12 *Liber quaestionum hebraicarum in Genesim*, 21.

hostile to all).[13] But Bede also repeats the ambivalent relationship that both Hagar and Ishmael have with the Muslim and Jewish peoples. He states clearly in his commentary on Genesis 16:12 that Ishmael is the father of the Saracens, but he is equally clear in his commentary on Genesis 16:1–4 that "Notandum autem quia hic primus antequam nasceretur secondus Isaac a Domino nomen accepit, certi utique gratia mysterii, quia et ueteris testamenti, quod significatur in Ismahel, et noui quod in Isaac, haeredes ante secula fuetunt in diuina electione praecogniti" (Moreover, it should be observed that the first son Ishmael received his name from the Lord before he was born, as did the second son Isaac, undoubtedly for the sake of a settled mystery, because the heirs both of the Old Covenant, which is signified by Ishmael and of the New, which is signified by Isaac, were foreknown among the divinely elected before their times).[14]

Bede was also concerned to make it clear that Hagar and Ishmael were entirely deserving of their fate, as he devoted more space in his commentary on Sarah's ordering Hagar and Ishmael to be cast out (Gen. 21: 9–10) than to any other part of Genesis with the exception of the scattering of the people of Babel. In his commentary on Genesis 21:9–10, the blending of Hagar and Sarah that took place in the passage concerning the bodies and wombs of the two women cited above is turned into a violent cleavage. Hagar and Ishmael become the persecutors of Sarah and Isaac, *carnales sensu* (carnal in understanding),[15] base, and signifying an attachment to the wealth and pleasures of this world. Citing Galatians 4:29, Bede describes Ishmael's play with Isaac as persecution.[16] In the act of persecution it is possible to equate Ishmael once again with the Saracens as described by Bede, but here Bede is emphatic that Hagar and Ishmael represent the Old Covenant and the Jews. God, he writes, "reprehendit qui sufficere sibi ad salutem litteram legis absque gratia iuuante confidunt, quod est Iudeorum proprium."[17] As such, they become symbols of corruption within the contemporary church, and a lesson in the need for it too to be cast out.

---

13 Bede, *In Genesim*, 201; *On Genesis*, ed. and trans. Kendall, 279.
14 Bede, *In Genesim*, 200; *On Genesis*, ed. and trans. Kendall, 279.
15 Bede, *In Genesim*, 241; *On Genesis*, ed. and trans. Kendall, 321.
16 Bede, *In Genesim*, 240; *On Genesis*, ed. and trans. Kendall, 318.
17 Bede, *In Genesim*, 240; *On Genesis*, ed. and trans. Kendall, 319: "reproves those who trust that the letter of the Law is sufficient for their salvation without the aid of grace, which is characteristic of the Jews."

Sunt et hodie nonnulli in ecclesia noui quidem testamenti sacramentis imbuti, sed per intentionem animi carnalis ad uetus testamentum atque ad figuram Agar et Ismahel pertinentes – non quod uere ueteris testamenti mandata sectentur … sed quia temporalia a Domino beneficia neglectis aeternis requirunt … qui siue in actibus nequam inter bonos catholicos ad mortem usque perdurent, siue propter haereses et aperta schismata sacerdotali iudicio de ecclesia tamquam ancillae filii per Saram liberam expellantur.[18]

(There are some in the Church even today who are steeped indeed in the sacred truths of the New Covenant, but adhere by the volition of their carnal mind to the Old Covenant and to the figure of Hagar and Ishmael – not that they are truly following the commandments of the Old Covenant … but because they seek temporal benefits from the Lord to the neglect of eternal ones … These are persons who either persist until the time of their death in wicked deeds among good Catholics, or are expelled from the Church by episcopal decree, like sons of a bondwoman by the free woman Sarah, on account of their heresies and open schisms.)

Bede's worry over Hagar and Ishmael, and their uncanny doubling and disappearance are taken up by the later *Genesis* poet and the producers of the ca. 1000 Junius 11 manuscript (Oxford, Bodl. Lib., MS Junius 11), by Ælfric, and by the artists of the late tenth- or early eleventh-century Old English Hexateuch (London, BL, MS Cotton Claudius B.iv). The *Genesis* poet was not concerned, at least not explicitly so, with the identification of Hagar and Ishmael with a particular people or peoples, but he (or she) was concerned with issues of social status and legitimacy. In terms of narrative content, the poem does not expand on what is stated in the biblical Genesis, indeed, as noted above it eliminates verses that might be read in any way as problematic, but it does expand greatly on the biblical text in its description of the emotional and psychological states of the characters, and in the language used to describe their status in relation to each other. This is particularly evident in the words chosen to describe Hagar and Sarah, words that affect the relationship between and social standing of the two.

Aside from the reference to Sarah giving Hagar to Abraham as a wife (*uxor*) in Genesis 16:3, the Latin of the Vulgate establishes a clear division

---

18 Bede, *In Genesim*, 242; *On Genesis*, ed. and trans. Kendall, 321–2.

between Hagar and Sarah. In both Genesis 16 and 21 Hagar is always the *ancilla* (handmaid, servant) and Sarah the *uxor* (wife) or *dominae* (mistress). The Old English poem, while refusing to grant Hagar the status of wife, complicates that relationship by varying the words used to refer to the two women. Hagar is *mæg* (line 2228b), *ides* (lines 2229a, 2271b, 2806a), and *fæmne* (lines 2228a, 2264a, 2304b), while Sarah is *ides* (line 2234b), *wif* (lines 2244a, 2778b), *cwen* (line 2261b), *hlæfdige* (line 2275a), *bryd* (lines 2784a, 2799a), and *mæg/mæged* (lines 2783b, 2798b). With the exception of *hlæfdige*, these are all words that can mean simply "woman," and certainly the need for poetic variation and the constraints of metre must have been partially responsible for the poet's choice of words. Yet even given these considerations it is clear that Sarah's nobility and legitimacy, especially the latter, are paramount. In addition to being the *wif*, a word which can mean "wife," and thus be used to distinguish a married from an unmarried woman, she alone is the *cwen*, the *hlæfdige*, and the *bryd*, words which all imply an exalted status of one kind or another. *Hlæfdige* is the word Hagar uses to refer to Sarah when she tells the angel who meets her in the desert that she has fled from the wrath of her mistress, and it can be taken as a literal translation of the Latin *domina*. *Cwen*, according to the *Dictionary of Old English*, is a term that can mean simply "woman," but also carries the meanings of "noblewoman," "wife," or "queen." It is used in the poem at the point at which Abraham tells Sarah that she may deal with Hagar as she wishes, and Sarah turns from being the persecuted to being the persecutor.

Ða wearð unbliðe   abrahames cwen,
hire worcþeowe   wrað on mode,
heard and hreðe.   higeteonan spræc
fræcne on fæmnan.[19]

(Then Abraham's wife became unfriendly to her servant, hostile in mind, hard and cruel. She spoke severely to the woman; 2261–4a.)

In this context the term distinguishes Sarah as not only noble in comparison to Hagar her servant (*worcþeowe*), but also distinguishes her as the noble

---

19 All passages are taken from Doane, *Genesis A*. All translations are my own unless otherwise noted.

wife of Abraham, the syntax of the lines causing her to stand quite literally in this passage between him and Hagar. *Bryd*, again according to the *DOE*, can mean bride or spouse, and can carry mystical or religious connotations. Daniel Anlezark has argued convincingly that the *Genesis* poet repeatedly uses this word to refer to Sarah as a way of underscoring the fact that she and she alone is the legitimate wife,[20] but in this particular section of the poem it also functions as a subtle reference to the typological relationship between Sarah and the Virgin Mary. It is used twice for Sarah shortly after she has given birth to Isaac, the first time introducing the passage in which she, the prince's wife, speaks to Abraham and instructs him to send Hagar and Ishmael away, and the second when the Lord instructs Abraham to listen to Sarah, his wife.

>   þa cwaeð drihtlecu mæg,
> **bryd** to beorne: "forgif me, beaga weard,
> min swæs frea: hat siððan
> agar ellor   and ismael
> lædan mid hie   ne beoð we leng somed
> willum minum   gif ic wealdan mot.
> næfre ismael   wið isace,
> wið min agen bearn   yrfe dæleð
> on laste þe   þonne þu of lice
> aldor asendest."   Þa wæs abrahame
> weorce on mode   þæt he on wræc drife
> his selfes sunu.   Þa com soð metod,
> freom on fultum.   wiste ferhð guman
> cearum on clommum.   cyning engla spræc
> to abrahame,   ece drihten:
> "læt þe aslupan   sorge of breostum,
> modgewinnan   and mægeð hire,
> **bryde** þinre."

(Then the noble **bride** said to her lord, "grant my request, guardian of treasure, my beloved lord. Order Hagar to go away and to take Ishmael with her. No longer shall we dwell together if I might have my will. Never shall Ishmael with Isaac, with my own son, divide inheritance after you, when you

---

20 Anlezark, "An Ideal Marriage."

send forth your spirit from your body." Then Abraham was afflicted in his heart, that he must drive his own son into exile. Then came the just Lord to help him. He knew that the heart of the man was bound with cares. The king of the angels, the eternal Lord, spoke to Abraham. "Let sorrow and cares disappear from your breast, and listen to the woman, your **bride**"; 2782b–99a)

In both lines it is Sarah's position as Abraham's wife that gives her the right and authority to order Hagar and Ishmael to be banished, and to have her instructions followed, but the passage as a whole also works to highlight the connection between Sarah and Mary, as it is only now after the birth of the miraculous son (a type of Christ), that the parallel between the two women is firmly established. The passage also plays on the act of doubling and division, exile and home. The sending out of Ishmael is mirrored in/ opposed by the sending forth of Abraham's spirit after his death, and both are necessary so that lineage and inheritance may pass intact to Isaac.

In a similar act of doubling and division, the Old English poem, like the Vulgate, conveys a clear mistress/servant relationship between the two women, yet the Old English gives Sarah and Hagar a common bond that the Latin does not. They are united by the use of the words *mæg* (woman, maiden, virgin, wife) and *ides* (woman, wife, virgin, queen, lady) to refer to them both at different times. The points at which the poet uses the word *mæg*, which can imply a maiden or virgin may be significant. For Hagar it is used only before she conceives Ishmael, when in giving her to Abraham Sarah says, "Her is fæmne." While in this section of the poem it is used for Sarah only after the birth of Isaac (lines 2783 and 2798),[21] where her typological relationship to Mary is most clear. The poet's paralleling of the two women, Sarah and Hagar, is strengthened by the use of the phrases *freolecu mæg* (free [freeborn, noble, or beautiful] maiden) for Hagar and *drihtlecu mæg* (lordly [or noble] maiden) for Sarah (lines 2218b and 2782b). Again, the prefix *driht-* conveys a sense of religious or mystical nobility that *freo-* does not, nevertheless the phrases do blur the division between the two women. Is Hagar freeborn, or beautiful, or noble, or is she all of these things? Certainly the tradition that she was a freeborn Egyptian princess suggests that she could be all of these things. The confusion is doubled by a second paralleling between Hagar, the *freolecu mæg*,

---

21 See Anlezark, "An Ideal Marriage," 196 for its use in reference to Sarah elsewhere in the poem.

and the *bearn … freolic to frofre* (child … nobly [or freeborn or beauti-
ful] as a comfort, lines 2218b–19a) that Sarah believes herself unable to
produce, a parallel that also, of course, foreshadows the doubled pair of
Ishmaël and Isaac.

The poetic doubling of Hagar and Sarah both mirrors and effectively
conveys the fact that they are a mirrored pair in the biblical story. They are
both mothers, they are both mothers to sons of Abraham, they are both
the persecuted and the persecutor, and they both feel sorrow because of
the doubling of their situations. This latter mirroring is brought out in
the *Genesis* poem through the poet's attention to the emotional or psychological states of the two women. Sarah is *sar on mode* (sad in her heart,
line 2216b) because she cannot conceive; Hagar's heart swells with pride
when she conceives (*hire mod astah*, line 2237a); Hagar's pride and insolence again lead Sarah to speak to Abraham her *modes sorge* (heart's
sorrow line 2245b); and when Hagar escapes Sarah's cruelty by fleeing
into the desert, the angel finds her sitting *geomormode* (sad at heart, line
2270a). The emotions the two women feel in *Genesis* do make them seem
more human, more like the poem's readers than does the sparse biblical
narrative, and an interest in the emotional or psychological depth of key
characters is evident in all the poems of the Junius manuscript, especially
Genesis. As I have argued elsewhere, the *Genesis* poem does seem to have
an interest in legitimacy and queenship (or at least noble motherhood) that
may reflect the problems with excess wives and heirs that was so much a
part of Anglo-Saxon politics from the reign of Edgar (959–75) through to
the Norman Conquest.[22] Tenth- and eleventh-century queenship may be a
digression from the topic of this paper and the subject of this volume, but
true lineage and their status as a "chosen people" were very much on the
minds of the Anglo-Saxons. Just as Bede made his commentary on Hagar
and Ishmael relevant to his contemporary audience, so it seems did the
Genesis poet.[23] The *Genesis* poet also followed Bede in making it clear to
his audience that Hagar was to be equated with carnality and the desires
of this world rather than the next. Thus Hagar's arrogance, pride in her

---

22 Karkov, *Text and Picture in Anglo-Saxon England*, 142–58.

23 The *Genesis* poem may have its origins in the eighth century, but the written version
   of the poem that comes down to us is firmly dated to the late tenth or early eleventh
   century.

pregnancy, refusal to obey and scorn for Sarah are emphasized in a notable expansion of the Vulgate's statement that she simply "despised" (*despexit*) her mistress.

> hire mod astah   þa heo wæs magotimbre
> be abrahame   eacen worden.
> ongan æfþancum   agendfrean
> halsfæst herian,   higeþryðe wæg,
> wæs laðwendo.   lustum ne wolde
> þeowdom þolian   ac heo þriste ongan
> wið sarran   swiðe winnan.

(Her heart became arrogant when she became pregnant with a son by Abraham. The proud woman began to scorn her mistress, to be arrogant, insolent, and hateful. She would not suffer servitude according to her desires, but she shamelessly began to cause great strife with Sarah; 2237–43)

Hagar and Ishmael are ultimately cast out, and in turn they give rise to the outcast peoples of the Old Testament. Sarah and Isaac, on the other hand, are obedient and voluntary exiles, and they will give rise to the chosen people who will inhabit the promised land. Yet the death, or in this case disappearance of the double, is also the death or disappearance of the self.[24] Sarah too will ultimately disappear, as the casting out of the illegitimate mother and son is also the moment at which the maternal is replaced by the paternal, as will be discussed further below.

In the Junius 11 manuscript Hagar's disappearance is mirrored accidentally, but quite appropriately, in her non-representation, an effect due entirely to the artists' failure to complete the planned cycle of illustrations any further than Abraham leading his people into Egypt on page 88. Judging from the content of the poem and the distribution of the spaces left for the drawings, it is likely that Hagar would have been depicted being offered to Abraham (p. 101), in Abraham's bed (p. 102), fleeing Sarah's persecution (p. 103), in the desert (p. 104), and returning to Abraham and giving birth to Ishmael (p. 105). In addition, Ishmael playing with Isaac and Abraham banishing Hagar and Ishmael may have been intended for the blank spaces

---

24 For a cogent summary of the double and the self, see Royle, *The Uncanny*, 187–202.

on pages 133 and 134 respectively.[25] Something of what these missing drawings might have looked like can be gleaned from the surviving images in the roughly contemporary Cotton Claudius B.iv, although we should certainly not assume that the cycle of illustrations in the two manuscripts would have been identical.

The Old English text of Claudius B.iv generally follows the Vulgate very closely, although again there are some significant omissions and changes in the sections with which this paper is concerned. As Daniel Anlezark has noted, Ælfric omits the verse in which Sarah gives Hagar to Abraham as a wife (Gen. 16:3), and describes Hagar as Abraham's *cyfese* (concubine) rather than *ancilla* (serving girl) shortly before she and Ishmael are cast out (Gen. 21:12), focusing our attention again on her transgressive body.[26] As was the case with the Junius 11 *Genesis*, it is reasonable to assume that Ælfric made these changes in order to make the text more relevant to his contemporary audience for whom the issue of concubines and illegitimate sons could be a problem.[27] In contrast to the Junius 11 *Genesis*, the reader of Claudius B.iv is given no information about the characters' thoughts or emotions; Sarah is a *hlæfdige* throughout, Hagar a *ðinen* (handmaid), *wielen* (female slave or foreign woman), or *cyfese*, and Ishmael a *fostorcild* (foster-child), a word which implies a disavowal of his paternal descent from Abraham as it suggests the bringing up of a child not one's own.[28] But the story in Claudius B.iv is told primarily through the accompanying miniatures, which consist of nine scenes spread over five folios (27v–8r and 35v–6v). Two of the most remarkable features of the cycle are the literal doubling of the figures of Hagar and Sarah in the drawings up to the point at which Hagar and Ishmael are forced out into the wilderness, and the way in which the characters are either united or separated within the individual compositions as a means of indicating the physical or emotional bonds or states of isolation through which the narrative progresses. Benjamin Withers has noted that the architectural frames in Claudius B.iv

---

25 On the cycle of illustrations, see Karkov, *Text and Picture in Anglo-Saxon England*, 203–4; Henderson, "The Programme of Illustrations in Bodleian MS Junius XI." There is a lacuna in the manuscript after page 134, and the missing pages may well have included images of Hagar and Ishmael in the desert.
26 Anlezark, "An Ideal Marriage," 195, 196, 198.
27 Anlezark, "An Ideal Marriage," 196.
28 All passages from Cotton Claudius B.iv are taken from Ælfric, *The Old English Heptateuch*. All translations are my own.

serve as more than just a theatrical backdrop, they can serve to both clarify and carry narrative content,[29] but they can also be used (as they are in Figures 4 and 5) to suggest the inner thoughts and emotions that the text omits. Both the use of varied architectural framings, and the visual doubling of Hagar and Sarah throughout the illustrations make manifest the *unheimliche*, literally un-homely, nature of this story. The home divides as well as unites, excludes as well as includes. Hagar is never at home in Abraham's home. It is never her home, but neither is the wilderness – the home which is not one – into which she is eventually banished.

In the first episode of the story, on the top of folio 27v, Sarah offers Hagar to Abraham. The two women, the one in the control and possession of the other, are united within one architectural frame, while Abraham sits by himself under a second. Sarah kneels before Abraham, her head slightly violating the frame, pointing back at her handmaiden. Her body and her gesture serve to suggest both the physical separation of Abraham from Hagar at this point, and the fact that she is offering her handmaiden to him. Sarah as wife both intrudes and negotiates between them, her pose indicating at once that Abraham is her lord and that she is the one in control of the situation. Aside from the colour of their robes the women are virtually identical. One kneels, and the other appears to bow; the angle of their heads, the way in which they both direct their eyes towards Abraham, and the gesture they make with their left hands are all quite similar. However, Hagar's open and raised hands might be read in a number of different ways. They could indicate acceptance, prayer, even astonishment. Abraham himself stands in a similar pose in the drawing at the top of folio 26v as the Lord tells him that his children shall be as numerous as the stars. Alternatively, her stance could represent shock or disbelief, as it may do in the pose of the man who moves away from Noah's ark at the lower left of the miniature on folio 15v. It is repeated again in the two scenes of Hagar in the wilderness (Figures 5 and 7), where both interpretations would be appropriate. Its ambiguity adds some depth to Hagar's role in the visual narrative, while at the same time making her an enigmatic figure. On the one hand, she is Sarah's double, acquiescing to her wishes, but on the other she is literally the "other," the one who will eventually

---

29 Withers, *The Illustrated Old English Hexateuch*, 40. On the relationship between Sarah and Hager in Cotton Claudius B.iv, see also Mellinkoff, "Sarah and Hagar: Laughter and Tears," although Mellinkoff's view that the manuscript does not reveal anything of Anglo-Saxon society's views of the women is untenable.

stand apart, the one who is powerless and has no voice within Sarah's plans for herself and her husband.

In the central drawing on folio 27v (Figure 4) it is Sarah who is isolated within a simple gabled structure. Only her head is visible, her chaste body being hidden from our view by the green curtains that surround her bed; however her wide open eyes indicate that she remains not only knowledgeable, but in control of the events unfolding in the adjacent chamber. Indeed the detail turns her into an invisible presence in her husband's chamber. The image, like Bede's text, creates an uncanny blending of the two women. Hagar's body is present in Abraham's bed, but Sarah is uncannily present as well,[30] both by proxy of her handmaid and as an observer along with the readers of the manuscript. The bulk of the space of the drawing is devoted to the figures of Abraham and Hagar, curtains drawn back to reveal their bodies lying together on a single bed in marked contrast to the lone and covered body of Sarah. Hagar's body is positioned closer to the viewer, allowing it in effect to shield the body of Abraham from our gaze. Abraham's innocence and how to explain it to his readers was clearly something that concerned Ælfric, as it had Bede before him. In his *Interrogationes Sigeuulfi in Genesin*, Ælfric wrote:

Hu mihte Abraham beon clæne. þæt he nære forligr geteald þa þa he hæfde cyfese under his riht wife? Abrahames wif wæs untymende oð hire ylde 7 þa bæd heo hire were. þæt he wið hire wylne tyman sceolde. 7 he swa dyde. swiþor for bearnteame. þonne for galnysse. 7 eac seo ealde æ þe þa stod. næs swa stið on þam þingum swa swa cristes godspel is þe nu stent. 7 tæcð to anum wife.[31]

(How can Abraham be clean, so that he is not considered guilty of adultery when he had a concubine in addition to his lawful wife? Abraham's wife was infertile until her old age, and she told her husband to have a child with her servant. And he did so, more for procreation than for lust. Also, the Old Law then held, and it was not as strict about these things as is Christ's Gospel which holds now and teaches monogamy.)

---

30 One of the definitions of the uncanny is "the presence of what ought to be absent." See further Bearn, "Wittgenstein and the Uncanny," 33.

31 Maclean, "Ælfric's Version of the *Interrogationes Sigeuulfi in Genesin*," LXV–VI, 439–46. Quoted in Anlezark, "An Ideal Marriage," 195–6.

In Claudius B.iv the text is arranged in order to make clear Abraham's obedience to his wife, and his "cleanness" in contrast to Hagar's wickedness. The text running between the upper and central images reads, "Abram ða dyde swa swa him dihte Sarai. 7 Agar ða geeacnode, 7 eac forseah hyre hlæfdian" (Abraham then did just as Sarah told him. And Hagar then became pregnant and scorned her lady). The composition of the Claudius B.iv miniature helps to make this point clear to the reader visually. It not only allows the viewer to understand that the conception of Ishmael has occurred, but also makes the point that it is Hagar's body and not Abraham's that is to be identified with lust and copulation. The artists have used similar compositions elsewhere in the manuscript to indicate the sexualized and transgressive potential of the female body. The bodies of the daughters of Lot having sex with their father are revealed in much the same manner on folio 33v. By contrast, the conception of the legitimate heir by the legitimate bride is never shown, and Sarah's body throughout the episodes with Pharaoh and Abimelech remains concealed from our eyes. In the latter episode (folio 34v), the artist has conveyed Abimelech's desire and Sarah's chastity by representing Sarah as a ghostly figure, a disembodied presence whose head rests on the pillow beside that of Abimelech. Her body remains absent. The contrast not only heightens our awareness of the chastity of the legitimate bride, it also serves to make the miraculous and divinely ordained conception of Isaac all the more notable.

The drawing of the conception of Ishmael again makes clear the doubling and division of Hagar and Sarah. The arrangement of their bodies and the covering or masking of all but their heads (the one by a curtain the other by bedclothes) make them literally mirror images of each other, and indicate that they are now set firmly in opposition to one another. Hagar sleeps passively while Sarah's eyes are wide open, making it clear that she is still actively in control. Hagar's body has been sexualized, while Sarah's remains chaste.

The miniature at the bottom of the page depicts Sarah complaining to Abraham of Hagar's insolence and cruelty, and conveys Hagar's guilt in a clear and unequivocal manner. Abraham and Sarah are joined in animated conversation at left, while Hagar stands isolated beneath a gabled structure. The picture reverses the grouping of the figures at the top of the page. Sarah is positioned not only as one part of a couple alongside her husband, but also as a figure standing between and separating Abraham from Hagar in an image reminiscent of the syntax of the line describing the same moment in the Junius 11 *Genesis*.[32] The empty chamber that separates Hagar from Sarah and Abraham, and the fact that her body moves away from them signify both the gulf that now separates her from them, and foreshadow her eventual banishment. Hagar's posture with her head leaning back towards the talking couple, suggests that she is listening in on their conversation – perhaps a visual means of conveying the lack of obedience that brought that conversation about. In front of her is a small door, a sign of her coming flight. Drawing and text are arranged so that the image breaks up the text of Genesis 16:6. The text above the picture ends with Abraham telling Sarah that Hagar is her own and she may do with her what she will. The following line describing Sarah afflicting Hagar and Hagar fleeing into the desert is written at the top of folio 28r, the same folio on which these are events are depicted.

Sarah and Abraham's prominence and favoured position in the biblical narrative are in part conveyed by the number of images that are devoted to telling their story in comparison to the number devoted to that of Hagar. On folio 28r (Figure 5), the last line of Genesis 16:6 and the whole of Genesis 16:7 through 16:16 are compressed onto one page and into two miniatures. The upper drawing is placed after verse 14 in which Hagar names the well at which the angel appeared to her, compressing the entire story of her flight and return into one half of the drawing, and neatly separating the verbal and pictorial account of her experience from that of Abraham and the birth of his *fostorcild* at the bottom of the page. On the left Sarah sits spinning and chastising Hagar, while at right the angel, bearing a scroll representing his words, greets her at the well.

The lower drawing depicts the birth of Ishmael at left and Sarah and Abraham enthroned at right. The plants in the spandrels of the arches that frame the scene of Hagar and Ishmael provide a link to the representation of Hagar's flight above, and also foreshadow the wilderness into which they will eventually be banished, and the wild places in which Ishmael is destined to live. The scene is also a doubling and a mirroring (an image in reverse) of the birth of Isaac depicted on folio 35r. In that scene Sarah, facing to the left rather than the right – in other words, in the opposite direction from Hagar – reclines beneath an elaborate domed roof, her pillow forming a halo around her head. This is obviously a much more special and blessed event, the birth of a child of the spirit rather than a

---

32 See above p. 207.

child of the flesh. Ishmael is also doubled by Isaac, the pose of the two boys and the midwife on the left being virtually identical, although the second midwife who fills Ishmael's bath with water is missing from the depiction of Isaac. Abraham is also shown giving thanks to an enormous hand of God for the birth of Isaac, something he does not do for the birth of Ishmael. In fact Hagar's pose, reclining on her bed while looking and reaching out towards her child to the right, is also doubled by the bodies of Lot's two daughters who are shown giving birth on folio 34r. The poses in which they lie and the gestures they make are nearly identical to Hagar's, and the artists are again signalling the link between these wicked women and their outcast sons, something the text could never do so clearly and which such economy.

Folios 27v and 28r must also be read as a double-page opening, the way an Anglo-Saxon reader would have encountered them. The two pages are linked by a series of repeated motifs: thrones, beds, the pairing and isolation of figures. At upper left Sarah sits enthroned, as Abraham had been enthroned on the previous page, and at bottom right the couple are shown enthroned together. All three figures are reclining in beds on folio 27v and the bed is repeated in the drawing of the birth of Ishmael. The motifs are repeated, but the images are not identical, setting up an uncanny play of mirrored or almost mirrored imagery. But the *mise en page* of the opening also works subtly to reinforce the message that Hagar represents the carnal body, wickedness, and the outcast. Reading from left to right across the centre of the opening, Hagar's sleeping with Abraham (and the consequent conception of Ishmael) lead directly to Sarah's persecution of Hagar and her flight. The arrangement implies visually that it is Hagar's sleeping with Abraham for which she is punished. Sarah's wifely virtue, her chastity as well as her spinning – a proper duty of all wives – make a stark contrast to Hagar's sexualized and disobedient body. But the arrangement of imagery also reinforces Sarah's control. Her wide-open eyes watch over both the pages, while her spinning is a sign of both her position as wife and her control of the household. Hagar is effectively trapped between the watchful control of her mistress at left and the heavenly control of the angel that swoops into the drawing from the right. A similar message is conveyed by the drawings at the bottom of the two pages. Hagar's disobedient body (she is eavesdropping on Sarah and Abraham's conversation), and her body just after having given birth to the illegitimate Ishmael, are framed by and contained within the legitimate union of Abraham and Sarah.

On folio 35v (Figure 6) the focus is on the impropriety of Ishmael rather than Hagar. At the top of the page is a depiction of the feast in celebration of the weaning of Isaac, with Isaac himself awkwardly depicted floating in mid-air beside his father. His presence in this drawing, however, is important. First, it helps the viewer to identify him as the child to the right, the child standing on lower ground in the scene of him playing with Ishmael below. The text accompanying the lower drawing says simply that "Sarra beheold hu Agares sunu wið Isaac plegode," but this is a construction that can be understood in two different ways. It is at first sight a simple translation of the Vulgate statement that Sarah saw the son of Hagar the Egyptian playing with her own son,[33] but the Old English, like the Latin (*ludentem*), can be understood different ways. It can mean that Sarah saw Ishmael playing together with Isaac, or that she saw Ishmael playing in the sense of "toying with" or "mocking" Isaac; but *wið* can also mean "against," so the phrase carries the ghostly suggestion that Sarah saw Ishmael playing *against* Isaac. The drawing picks up on this by placing Ishmael on higher ground, an indication that he has put himself above Isaac through pride and persecution, just as his mother had grown proud and persecuted Sarah. While it could be a purely coincidental detail, the red arch beneath which Abraham stands as the hand of God instructs him to listen to his wife and cast out Hagar and Ishmael echoes that under which Sarah sits as she is about to cause Hagar to flee.

The second reason Isaac's presence in the upper drawing is important is that it places Isaac beside Abraham. He has now become his father's son, separated from his mother both physically by weaning and socially in anticipation of the coming testing and triumph of both himself and his father. Like circumcision, weaning is then a cutting off that creates a new attachment, in that it becomes a sign of the reaffirmation of lineage, paternity, inheritance, and covenant. This pairing of father and legitimate son is opposed in the drawing on the facing page by the pairing of the exiled Hagar and Ishmael as they are forced out into the wilderness. Hagar's maternal body is here cast out, but it is again doubled uncannily by the body of Sarah whose maternal bond with Isaac is replaced by the new bond created with his father. The connection between the two women is made apparent visually by the depiction of their clothes as virtually identical, and the mirroring of Sarah's pose at the bottom of folio 35v by that of Hagar at the top of folio 36r (Figure 7).

Themes of opposition also serve to unite the drawings across the two pages. Abraham's family has an abundance of food, a feast, while Hagar

---

33 Genesis 21:9: "vidisset Sarra filium Agar Aegyptiae ludentem."

and Ishmael suffer thirst and hunger as their meagre portion of bread and water runs out. Abraham's family dwells in a lavish architectural setting, while Hagar and Ishmael inhabit an empty wilderness. Again, the bodies of the two women work to highlight their differing circumstances. The reversal of their poses on the lower left and upper right of the opening is balanced by their differently doubled bodies at upper left (Sarah) and lower right (Hagar). In this case both women sit in similar postures, but Sarah holds a drink and has a table full of food while Hagar has none. Both also gaze up into the faces of the one responsible for supplying them with food: Abraham whose wealth has provided the feast,[34] and the angel of the Lord who is in the process of revealing to Hagar the well that will save her and her son. Sarah and Abraham are here associated with civilization and social structure, while Hagar is associated with wilderness and waste. Sarah's reason and control, moreover, contrast with Hagar's emotion and despair. She appears here as the stereotypical female body – sexualized, open and maternal, emotional, and aligned with nature rather than culture. Ishmael is in turn embraced by both the feminized body and the wild. On the left side of the drawing he is literally embraced by the mother's body, the curve of his form both echoing and contained within that of his mother, while at left his reclining form is contained within the drooping leaves of the plant on which he rests his head. Ishmael, like his mother, is weak and fallen, in every way the opposite of the boy who placed himself above Isaac on the facing page. The permanent cleaving of Hagar and Ishmael from Sarah and Isaac is underscored by both the confining trees and the scroll-bearing angel who swoops in from the left, the latter a reversal of the angel on folio 28r who appeared in order to send Hagar back to Sarah and the paternal home.

The story of Hagar and Ishmael ends with the text and miniature in the upper half of folio 36v (Figure 8). The wilderness is represented much as it was in the preceding miniature, although more lush. It provides game for Ishmael's bow, but Ishmael's catch of a few birds cannot of course compare with the herds of sheep and oxen that Abraham presents to Abimelech on the facing page. On the left Hagar and Ishmael's Egyptian wife sit enclosed by plant-scrolls, looking on as Ishmael takes aim with

---

34 "Þæt cild soðlice weox 7 wearð gewened, 7 Abraham worhte, swa swa heora gewuna wæs, micelne gebeorscipe to blisse his mannum on þone dæg, þe man þæt cild fram gesoce ateah." (And truly that child grew and was weaned, and Abraham made, as it was the custom, a great feast for the happiness of his people on the day that that child was taken from suck.) Crawford, *The Old English Version of the Heptateuch*, 137–8.

his bow and arrow. Hagar the Egyptian is again doubled, this time by Ishmael's wife, while Ishmael stands apart. Ishmael's isolation, his wild nature, and his profession of archer contrast with the fortified city and kingly attributes of Abimelech and his court below. The *mise en page* once again serves to highlight the otherness of both mother and son. Genesis 21:20 has been split so that the opening words *7 heo wunode mid him* (and God dwelt with him) are written just above the lower drawing on folio 36r. Turning the page, the reader sees and reads not God's dwelling with Ishmael, but Ishmael's isolation, along with that of his mother and wife. The single line of original text above the image reads "He weox þa, 7 wearð on þam westene scytta, 7 hys modor him genam wif on Egypta lande" (He grew then and became an archer in the wilderness, and his mother took a wife for him from the land of Egypt). Text and drawing bring the doubling of Hagar and Sarah full circle. Hagar presents Ishmael with an Egyptian wife just as Sarah had presented Abraham with her Egyptian handmaid, and Hagar and her daughter-in-law sit apart from Ishmael, just as Sarah and Hagar had stood apart from Abraham. The body of Ishmael's wife intervenes between him and his mother just as Sarah's figure had been placed between Hagar and Abraham.

Conclusion

The hierarchical pairing of figures – Martha and Mary, Rachel and Leah, Hagar and Sarah, Ishmael and Isaac – is a common biblical trope, however few figures double or haunt each other to the extent of Hagar and Sarah or Ishmael and Isaac, and few are as comprehensively figured as outcast. It is not just their pairing, but the ways in which they are paired, the insistence on their presence as a means of instigating their absence, and the qualities and peoples for which they may or may not stand that make Hagar and Ishmael truly uncanny. Even at her most physically present moment in the narrative, the conception of Ishmael according to the flesh, Hagar is doubled by, or a double for, Sarah. As this paper has shown, Anglo-Saxon authors and artists from Bede to Ælfric complicated this moment further by suggesting a physical blending of the two women, and thus the disappearance of the one within the other (Bede), or by figuring Sarah as an uncanny presence controlling the events taking place within her husband's bed (Ælfric and the artists of Claudius B.iv). The conception of Ishmael also leads to a role reversal between the two women. Hagar becomes arrogant and proud, improperly assuming the role of mistress and thus becoming a deformed double of Sarah, and when Sarah regains her rightful position

Hagar must flee. For Hagar's wickedness towards Sarah, and for Ishmael's assuming a similar position towards Isaac, they are ultimately banished for good, disappearing into the desert, into the desert tribes, and eventually into the Saracens. In their identification with the Saracens, they return to Sarah only to be subsumed within her again – at least in terms of a western European imaginary. But if Hagar and Ishmael disappear in the merging of the Hagarenes and Ishmaelites into the Saracens, Sarah also disappears in the creation of the Saracens as an outcast people, and especially in Bede's portrayal of them as an outcast people who are hateful and hostile to all. In this same slippage and merging of identity, the Jews, biologically the descendants of Isaac, disappear with and into the Saracens as, for Bede, Hagar and Ishmael represent the Synagogue and the Old Covenant, just as Sarah and her son Isaac represent the Church and the New Covenant.[35] The uncanny relationship between Hagar and Sarah becomes a metaphor for the uncanny relationship between Jews and Christians.

It is clear that the Anglo-Saxons were troubled by Hagar and Ishmael, and especially by Hagar. Bede, the *Genesis* poet, Ælfric, and the artists of the Claudius B.iv manuscript all changed the biblical story in ways that foregrounded their sins, their wickedness, and their deceit. Sometimes the changes were blatant, the omission of entire biblical verses, for example; sometimes they were more subtle, such as the choices of words used to describe Hagar in *Genesis*, but all were designed to make Hagar and Ishmael more knowable – more familiar to, and thus more like the Anglo-Saxons themselves. The Anglo-Saxons had concubines, illegitimate sons and corrupt clerics, and Hagar and Ishmael could be used to exemplify the evils and the dangers of all of them. But there was also a larger more historic and political danger. Hagar and Ishmael represented the Old Covenant, the Synagogue and the Jews cast out in favour of the New Covenant, the Church and the Christians, and the Anglo-Saxons famously figured themselves as the new Chosen People. The Anglo-Saxons had "cast out" and replaced the Britons, as the Jews had been cast out and replaced by the Christians. But there was always the fear of a return of those who had been cast out, the fear that contemporary sin and corruption would bring about a return of the old order that haunted the margins and wildernesses of the island, its uncivilized i.e., non-Christian places, as Hagar and Ishmael haunted the biblical wilderness. In this respect the Anglo-Saxons

---

35 See above p. 201. See also Scheil, *The Footsteps of Israel*.

became their own uncanny doubles for Hagar and Sarah. For the moment they were the chosen, but there was always the possibility that that order could be overturned and they could become the outcasts. Moreover, like the Jews, the Britons were an "other in our midst," not easily distinguished from the Anglo-Saxons among whom they might pass undetected. But perhaps even more troubling were the Saracens who troubled the borders of Europe and, at least during the time at which Ælfric was writing, inhabited some of its most holy places. Anglo-Saxons could, and did, end up as slaves within the Islamic world. How aware the Anglo-Saxons were of the slave trade and the fate of those who were sold into it is unclear, and certainly varied over time,[36] nevertheless it raises the possibility that whether they knew it or not, the Anglo-Saxons themselves were threatened by a return to captivity and bondage, the threat that they themselves might disappear within the doubled figuration of Hagar and Sarah.

---

36 See Pelteret, *Slavery in Early Medieval England*; Lavezzo, "Gregory's Boys: the Homoerotic Production of English Whiteness."

10 King Edgar Leaping and Dancing before the Lord[*]

ADAM S. COHEN

One of the most famous pictures from Anglo-Saxon England is the representation of King Edgar in the so-called New Minster Charter (London, British Library, MS Cotton Vespasian A. viii, fol. 2v; Figure 9).[1] Not only is it a relatively rare example of a royal image from tenth-century England, and thus a logical springboard for any discussion of Anglo-Saxon kingship, but it also appears as the introduction to a document, probably written by Bishop Aethelwold of Winchester, that details the king's involvement in the refoundation of the New Minster as a monastery, making this "one of the most important surviving contemporary records of the Benedictine Reform of the reign of King Edgar."[2] As such, the image and charter have been treated extensively by art historians, historians, and

---

[*] Versions of this essay were presented at the 47th International Congress of Medieval Studies (Kalamazoo, 2012) and at the Hebrew University, Department of the History of Art (Jerusalem, 2015); I thank the audiences at both for their helpful feedback. I am especially grateful to Ben Withers for his original encouragement with this work, to Beth Tovey, Erika Loic, Julia Bolotina, Elisabeth Trischler, and Samantha Chang for research assistance, and to Julian Harrison at the British Library for generously permitting me to examine the New Minster Charter itself. Finally, Jennifer O'Reilly has not only long been a model scholar to me, but she has also shown her support for my research, and I humbly dedicate this essay to her in gratitude for both.

1 Temple, *Anglo-Saxon Manuscripts*, 44 (no. 16); Karkov, *Ruler Portraits*, 85–93.

2 Rumble, *Property and Piety*, 65–97, provides an overview of the charter in addition to the text, translation, and copious notes; this quotation from 65. For King Edgar in general, see most recently the collection of essays edited by Scragg, *Edgar, King of the English 959–975;* and the articles by Pratt, "The Voice of the King in 'King Edgar's Establishment of Monasteries,'" 145–204, and "Kings and Books in Anglo-Saxon England," 297–377.

philologists, all of whom have contributed to our visual and textual appreciation of this remarkable document. Although the contours of what is generally thought about the frontispiece will be well known, it is worth giving a summary sketch of the image nonetheless before offering a new interpretation that adds one more layer of complexity to it and to our understanding of the late tenth-century religious and intellectual milieu of Anglo-Saxon England.

Framed by a rich acanthus foliate border of the type associated with Winchester artistic products,[3] King Edgar stands flanked by Mary and Peter and looks up to Christ, held up in a golden mandorla and acclaimed by four angels. Edgar, the largest figure on the page, offers a golden book – the charter itself – to Christ. Mary, holding a golden palm and cross, and Peter, with a golden key, act as intercessors for the king. The page, although now faded, was originally stained purple (and the entire charter text written in gold ink), an indication of the book's luxuriousness and a reference to the theme of kingship that is essential to the meaning of the picture.[4] Kingship is also expressed in the elegiac couplet on the recto facing the image: SIC CELSO/RESIDET SO/LIO QUI CON/DIDIT ASTRA REX VENE/RANS EADGAR/PRON[US] ADORAT E[UM] (Thus he sits on his lofty throne, who created the stars; King Edgar, inclined to veneration, worships him;[5] Figure 10). On the basis of several studies by Robert Deshman we can conclude that the image (in conjunction with the facing titulus and charter text itself) communicates that through the presentation of the charter, which signifies the replacement of secular canons with Benedictine monks at the New Minster, Edgar acts like Christ and thus merits the intercession of Mary and Peter for his ultimate acceptance into heaven at the Last Judgment.[6] This is not to suggest that the image has only a single meaning. Catherine Karkov, for instance, has argued recently

---

3 Deshman, *Benedictional of Aethelwold*, 232–50.

4 On the significance of purple, see Henderson, *Vision and Image,* 122–35. The charter is the only extant Anglo-Saxon manuscript written entirely in gold. For the theme of kingship, see Deshman, *Benedictional*, 195–200, and Deshman, "*Benedictus Monarcha*," esp. 118–20.

5 On the distich and its translation, see above all Teviotdale, "Latin Verse Inscriptions," esp. 101–2, and Karkov, "Frontispiece," esp. 226 and n. 15. Although I agree on the whole with Karkov's reading, my own translation differs slightly from those that have been offered previously.

6 Deshman, "*Benedictus Monarcha*," "*Christus Rex*," and *Benedictional*, esp. 184–97.

that Edgar should be compared to Christ also in the way he incorporates an ecclesiastical body within himself.[7] In the current essay, I propose an interpretation that complements existing ideas by suggesting that the frontispiece also embeds ideas about Edgar that are grounded in early medieval notions of Davidic kingship.

Despite general scholarly agreement about the overall contours of the image, there is one feature that has never been satisfactorily explained: the pose of King Edgar. The position of his arms and hands clearly indicates that he is seen from behind, so his head would be turned up and to the side in order for the viewer to see his face, which is an adequate demonstration of Edgar's veneration of Christ above. But close inspection of Edgar's feet shows that something is amiss: if he is being seen from behind, then his feet cannot be in the position they are. (The best way to demonstrate this is by physically trying to mimic Edgar's position; one can be successful only by breaking a hip, knee, or ankle.) If Edgar is being portrayed with his back to the viewer, then his right leg – seen on the viewer's right – would fit organically with his torso, but that foot is turned precariously forward. More to the point, the foot on the left leg, with the heel clearly visible to the inside of the pose, simply cannot turn at that angle. The alternative is to conclude that we are seeing Edgar's legs from the front (such that his problematic left leg is actually his right leg), but this results in a bifurcated Edgar whose top half is seen from behind while his feet are seen from the front; his legs could belong more or less comfortably with either his torso or his feet, but not both.

It might be thought that Edgar's awkward pose represents the artist's attempt to give visual form to the words *adorans* and *pronus* in the facing titulus, but this is dissatisfying on at least two counts. First, as Elizabeth Teviotdale has indicated, although the vocabulary might indicate supplication, the prominent use of gold and Edgar's relatively upright position indicate more the prevailing attribute of majesty for the king.[8] Second, Karkov has pointed out that while scholars have translated *pronus* as "prostrate" (perhaps with the image of Edgar in mind, I would add), there is

---

7 Karkov, "Frontispiece."

8 Teviotdale, "Latin Verse Inscriptions," 102: "Notwithstanding the characterization of Edgar as supplicant and prostrate in the poem, in this instance grandeur of presentation is paramount, as is apparent not only in the large gold letters of the inscription but also in the pose of King Edgar in the painting."

no compelling reason for doing so; "inclined" is preferable.[9] Although Karkov adduced no specific evidence for her reading, it seems quite correct. In the Vulgate, for example, of the twenty times that *pronus* appears (all in the Old Testament), in eighteen instances it is modified by a form of *in terram* or *in faciem* to make explicit that the individual so described is on the ground or on his face (or both). In the other two instances, Exodus 32:22 and Proverbs 22:9, *pronus* is used to indicate a characteristic – an inclination in one case to evil and in the other to mercy, but in neither case a physical description. Given Edgar's upright stance, there is thus no reason to see *pronus* in the New Minster titulus as a description of his pose, but rather as an adjective that works in concert with *adorans* to indicate the king's proclivity to venerate Christ.[10]

That still leaves the problem of Edgar's awkward pose, which begs the question of how, in a composition of such artistic mastery, it was possible to render the figure of the king so awkwardly. Was the artist simply incompetent when it came to the figure of Edgar? There are contemporaneous examples of Anglo-Saxon artists struggling with the organic rendering of unusual poses, as can be seen, for example, in the representation of the bound personification of Avarice on folios 28r and 29v of the Parker Library's illustrated copy of Prudentius's *Psychomachia* (Figure 11).[11] Yet the unknown artist of the charter picture was in most respects quite adept – note, most pointedly, his otherwise very careful treatment of the feet, such that Mary's are obscured *behind* the foliage-entwined gold border, Peter is delicately perched on top of it, while Edgar assumes an intermediary position with one foot on top and the other *in front* of the border, making him the only figure who shares the (earthly) space of the viewer. We are forced, therefore, to ask once more what motivated the desire to render Edgar in an unusual and perhaps artistically challenging pose, especially if we agree

---

9 Karkov, "Frontispiece," 226, n. 15. Among those who translate *pronus* as "prostrate" are Gameson, *Role of Art*, 7, and Teviotdale, "Latin Verse Inscriptions." Rumble, *Property and Piety*, 70, opted for "inclined in reverence."

10 An analysis of the couplet's linguistic sources will be offered below.

11 Cambridge, Corpus Christi College, Parker Library MS 23. See Budny, *Corpus Christi College*, 275–437, and http://parker.stanford.edu/parker/actions/page.do?forward= home, with full bibliography. Note, too, the very awkward position of the middle Magus on fol. 18r of the Bernward Gospels of ca. 1015 (Hildesheim, Cathedral and Diocesan Museum MS 18), where the artist seems to be grappling with a problem similar to the New Minster Charter artist. For a reproduction, see, for example, Brandt, *Kostbare Evangeliar*, pl. 8.

with Karkov that the picture is meant to complement, not illustrate, the adjectives of the facing titulus.

Several scholars have signalled the direction of the solution, but by glossing over the intricacies of Edgar's figure they have not fully explicated its meaning. Teviotdale stated the matter most directly: "The king is shown from behind and with knees bent, features that point to his humility as he offers the charter to Christ,"[12] and humility is indeed a leitmotif of both the charter text and the image. It appears first in the charter's historical preamble that couches Edgar's actions in refounding the New Minster by situating them in the grand sweep of sacred history. The charter opens with a short account of creation and the fall of the rebel angels and, in section two, the creation of man who, in contrast to the rebellious angels, flourished in paradise because of his humility and virtue.[13] After several sections recounting the temptation, fall, and the redemption that comes through Christ, three sections detail Edgar's motivations for and actions towards replacing the canons of the New Minster with Benedictine monks, whom he enjoins specifically to worship Christ with humility (contrasting them with the "rebellious" canons). In the penultimate section, in which Edgar sums up the essence of his gifts to the New Minster, he refers to himself explicitly as making the donation "through our humility."[14] It is therefore not surprising that the frontispiece would depict Edgar in a way that communicates his humility, but it is worth noting that the specific pose does not conform to earlier pictorial models expressing this idea. Teviotdale contrasted Edgar's pose with that of the diminutive figure of Abbot Dunstan, who, in a slightly earlier Anglo-Saxon manuscript, is represented near Christ's feet, kneeling almost horizontally with his face in his hands (Figure 12).[15] As Teviotdale argued, such a humble pose, itself based on the Carolingian model established by Hrabanus Maurus in his *De laudibus sanctae crucis*, would not be appropriate for a king. But this was precisely the attribute of humility that King Charles the Bald adopted

---

12 Teviotdale, "Latin Verse Inscriptions," 102.

13 Rumble, *Property and Piety*, 76. On the cosmological and theological bases of the text and Edgar's actions, with special emphasis on the theme of the rebel angels, see Johnson, "Fall of Lucifer."

14 Rumble, *Property*, 91.

15 On this manuscript, "St. Dunstan's Classbook" (Oxford, Bodleian Library, MS Auct. F.4.32, fol. 1r), see Temple, *Anglo-Saxon Manuscripts*, 41 (no. 11), and Budny, "St Dunstan's Classbook."

as an expression of *imitatio Christi* in his own prayerbook, where the king is depicted prostrate before Christ on the cross.[16] So although humility could be a royal attribute and is an important aspect of the New Minster Charter, the specificity of Edgar's pose suggests that there is something more at work here.

The next hint comes from Elżbieta Temple, who offered a very precise description of Edgar's pose and claimed that it "suggests inspiration from the Court school of Charles the Bald (cf. Bible of San Paolo)."[17] While it is not clear to which of the many figures in the San Paolo Bible she was referring, her description of Edgar as "precariously poised on tip-toe in a 'dancing' posture on the edge of the frame," is decidedly on the mark, for there is no better explanation for the twist between the upper and lower halves of Edgar's body than by seeing it as a way to represent a dancing figure. Not only does this account for the pose itself, but it also expands our iconographic understanding of the humility of Edgar, who has been rendered thus in the guise of the Old Testament King David leaping and dancing as described in 2 Samuel 6. In this chapter, David has decided to bring the Ark of the Lord, which had been in Kiryat-Yearim for twenty years, to his capital, Jerusalem. The critical passage is verses 14–16:

> David danced with all his might before the Lord, and David was girded with a linen ephod. And David and all the house of Israel brought the ark of the covenant of the Lord with joyful shouting, and with sound of trumpet. And when the ark of the Lord was come into the city of David, Michal the daughter of Saul, looking out through a window, saw king David leaping and dancing before the Lord: and she despised him in her heart.

That the episode is an expression of David's humility is made clear in the subsequent verses when Michal criticizes the king for acting like a buffoon,

---

16   Munich, Residenz, Schatzkammer, fols. 38v–39. On this manuscript, see Deshman, "Exalted Servant," who explicated the fundamental role of humility for the picture's conception of the ruler. It is important to note, moreover, that despite the charter's emphasis on humility, it is not one of the characteristics by which Edgar expresses his *imitatio Christi*, which is based more on themes of kingship and judgment, as is clearly expressed in the equation made between God's cleansing of the rebellious angels and Edgar's cleansing of the "depraved canons." See Deshman, "*Benedictus Monarcha*," 118–20, and Karkov, *Ruler Portraits*, 88–93.

17   Temple, *Anglo-Saxon Manuscripts*, 44.

to which he responds that he would play music and belittle himself even more for God, who had transferred the crown to him from Michal's father, Saul.[18] This is understood as a validation of David, while Michal herself is said in the concluding verse to have remained childless all her days, which was certainly a punishment for her unwarranted rebuke of David.

Images of King David dancing before the ark appeared frequently in the later Middle Ages, and several examples depict David with upraised arms and a tilted head in ways very reminiscent of Edgar's pose in the New Minster charter, including a representation in a fourteenth-century copy of Dante's *Divina Commedia* where the episode is used as an exemplar of humility (Figure 13).[19] The scene was less frequent in early medieval art, but its appearance in several Byzantine manuscripts, including the ninth-century Sacra Parallela, suggests that it may have been more common in the earlier period than extant examples reveal (Figure 14).[20] Kurt Weitzmann has shown convincingly that the scene was depicted in the third-century frescoes of the synagogue at Dura-Europos; although the fragmentary nature of the fresco makes it possible to question the identification, the wide step taken by the lead figure and seen in many of the representations of

18　Although dancing was generally frowned upon in the Middle Ages, related, as it was, to such cases as Salome or classical heathen practice, David's action of course was viewed favorably. On medieval attitudes to dance, see for example Hausamann, *Die tanzende Salome*; Carter, "Celestial Dance"; Rohmann, "Invention of Dancing." On David specifically, see Zimmermann, "Histrio fit David."

19　For Dante's use of David as a topos for humility, see Heimann, "Manuscript from Winchcombe," esp. 104–6. On the manuscript, New York, Morgan Library, MS M. 676, fol. 59v, see Puhle and Hasse, eds., *Heiliges Römisches Reich*, v. 1, 403 (no. V.24), with further literature. Another image to note is in the Morgan's 'Weigel-Felix' *Biblia Pauperum* of ca. 1435, MS M. 230, fol. 16r; on this manuscript, see Frühmorgen-Voss, Ott, and Bodemann, *Deutschsprachigen Illustrierten Handschriften*, v. 2, 4, 301–5. The *Biblia Pauperum* page with the image of David dancing is discussed by Susan Smith in relation to the nakedness of Christ, in Smith, "'Bride Stripped Bare." Neither Morgan picture is found in the otherwise convenient list of images in Hourihane, ed., *King David*, esp. 118–21 for David dancing before the Ark. Also useful is Wittekind, *Kommentar mit Bildern*.

20　For a catalogue and consideration of early medieval David cycles, see Suckale-Redlefsen, *Bilderzyklen zum Davidleben*. See also Weitzmann, *Sacra Parallela*, 83, 97. The Byzantine images of David dancing can be found easily in Kessler, *Bibles from Tours*, 158–62. For an extensive consideration of pictures of David dancing, see Heimann, "Twelfth-Century Manuscript."

this scene seems decisive.[21] Less certain is an even more fragmentary fresco from the top of the west wall of the Carolingian church of St John in Müstair, which most likely represented the bringing of the ark to Jerusalem and Michal's ridicule of David.[22] Unfortunately, the state of the evidence does not make it possible to be certain of the identification or to discern anything about what David might have looked like if he was, indeed, in this scene.[23] A contemporary Carolingian image in the so-called Folchart Psalter, which was produced in the monastery of St Gall between 872 and 883, certainly relates David to the transfer of the ark.[24] In addition to numerous sumptuous title pages and initials in gold, silver, and purple, the manuscript opens on pages seven to fourteen with eight decorated pages for the litany, whose contents are arranged in double arcades reminiscent of canon tables. On six of the pages, each column is surmounted by an image of an apostle (for a total of twelve figures), while page nine depicts David as a seated author in one lunette and, in the other, eight figures who represent the Psalm co-authors and scribes. Page twelve has a second representation of David, who is the large, crowned figure in the left lunette, leading a group of people and holding a lyre, while the right lunette shows the ark being transported on the ox-cart (Figure 15). There is some dispute

21 Weitzmann and Kessler, *Frescoes*, 94–8, figs. 6, 134–5. Weitzmann thus refuted
    Carl Kraeling, who identified the scene as the Transfer of the Ark into the Tabernacle
    (1 Kings 8:3–4). I am less convinced by Weitzmann's contention that the Dura fresco
    is a conflation of the two scenes. More problematic is the hesitation articulated by
    Kraeling: "Whether the unpleasant association of David's 'dancing before the Ark'
    would have deterred the artist from depicting the scene described in II Sam. is hard to
    say" (in his preliminary report of the sixth season [1932–1933, New Haven, 1936, 355],
    cited by Weitzmann, 96). As we hope to show, medieval artists did not share Kraeling's
    attitude that there was an "unpleasant association" to this David scene.
22 The scenes were so identified by Birchler, "Karolingischen Architektur," esp. 180,
    an interpretation accepted by Wütrich, *Wandgemälde von Müstair*, 29. More recently,
    Goll, Exner, and Hirsch, *Müstair*, 122–3 seemed inclined to accept Birchler's interpreta-
    tion but recognize the difficulty in being certain.
23 Although it does not include a discussion of the scenes in question (which are simply
    listed as "Return of the Ark of the Covenant" and "Mockery of David by Michal"), see
    the important essay by Cwi, "Study." I was not able to consult her 1979 Johns Hopkins
    University PhD dissertation, "St. John, Müstair and St. Benedict, Malles: a Study in
    Carolingian Imperial Iconography."
24 On this manuscript, St. Gall Stiftsbibliothek MS. 23, see Eggenberger, "Illustration,"
    von Euw, *St. Galler Buchkunst*, vol. 1, 394–9, and the magnificent website http://
    www.e-codices.unifr.ch/en/description/csg/0023, with numerous colour illustrations.

about whether the smaller, uncrowned figure who follows the ark in a dancing posture reminiscent of the Sacra Parallela manuscript is a second representation of David, Uzzah who was killed for improperly touching the ark earlier in the narrative (2 Samuel 6:2–7), or simply another rejoicing Israelite.[25]

The Folchart Psalter, admittedly, is not explicit about showing David dancing before the ark (though this picture still will play an important part in our argument below), but a second St Gall manuscript, the Golden Psalter (*Psalterium aureum*) of 883–8, indicates that Carolingian artists and theologians were familiar with and explored the iconography of David dancing in many ways (Figure 16).[26] Herbert Schade has pointed out how David, although ostensibly on his throne, is in fact springing up in a dancing posture to participate in the song and dance of his four co-Psalmists; the co-Psalmists represent the four evangelists, while David is a type for Christ himself.[27] The Golden Psalter image is thus implicated in the many strands of patristic and Carolingian commentary that interpreted David dancing not only as a type of Christ, but also as a representation of the harmony of the spheres (through the music) and as a demonstration of the sacramental function of the Church (through David's linen *ephod*).[28] More to the point, David, as is well known, was understood as an exemplar for contemporary Carolingian rulers, who in particular were reminded by such exegetes as Hrabanus Maurus, Smaragdus, and Hincmar of Reims that it was David's humility that underscored God's choice of him as king.[29] Hugo Steger, Herbert Kessler, Paul Dutton, and Isabelle Marchesin have demonstrated that several Carolingian representations of David the

---

25 For a discussion of the different positions, see Steger, *David Rex et Propheta*, 171, where he concluded that the figure is indeed David. von Euw, *St. Galler Buchkunst*, 394, also saw this figure as David.

26 St. Gall Stiftsbibliothek MS. 22. See Eggenberger, *Psalterium aureum*, esp. 39–53, von Euw, *St. Galler Buchkunst*, vol. 1, 400–8, and http://www.e-codices.unifr.ch/en/ description/csg/0022.

27 Schade, "Bild."

28 Schade, "Bild." Although Schade conveniently summarized the key ideas in early medieval writing on David's dance, in my opinion he read too many of these into each individual image, including that of the Golden Psalter, without sufficient discrimination among several possible meanings.

29 See above all Anton, *Fürstenspiegel und Herrscherethos*, esp. 420–30, and Deshman, "Exalted Servant." David's humility was also a topos for Byzantine rulers. See, for example, Maguire, "Davidic Virtue," and Meyer, "Daughters of Israel." Both authors discuss images of women dancing in acclamation of the Old Testament/Byzantine king.

Psalmist were predicated on the notion of his dancing and that these in turn informed pictures of the Carolingian kings themselves.[30] The most obvious example is in the First Bible of Charles the Bald from 845 (Paris, BnF, MS lat. 1, commonly called the Vivian Bible), where the frontispiece to the Book of Psalms shows the crowned David strumming his lyre and crossing his legs while turning his head back to look over his shoulder (Figure 17). This dancing motion and, most critically, David's explicit nakedness, indicate that the picture is drawing on the theme of humility as expressed specifically in the passage from Samuel. Furthermore, by making several subtle links between the representation of David and that of Charles the Bald at the end of the manuscript, Audradus Modicus, the intellectual force behind the First Bible, communicated that David should be seen as a model for Charles.[31]

With these images of David in mind, we can turn again to the picture of King Edgar in the New Minster Charter. Although Edgar's pose is not exactly like that of David in the First Bible of Charles the Bald and other Carolingian works, the king's dynamism alone, as Temple discerned, should be enough to support our reading of the king as being in a dancing posture. The representation of Edgar is especially striking in contrast with its most important, and only extant, Anglo-Saxon manuscript antecedent of a royal depiction, in which a decidedly static and reserved King Aethelstan is shown offering a book to Saint Cuthbert (Figure 18).[32] In addition, it has not been sufficiently appreciated that the skin of Edgar's legs is visible between his leggings and his tunic, which is also a departure from the Aethelstan image. This daring exposure of Edgar's skin is somewhat

---

30 Steger, *David Rex et Propheta*, 75–98; Kessler, *Illustrated Bibles*, 96–100; Dutton and Kessler, *Poetry and Paintings*, 81–4; Marchesin, "Corps musical." All of these references include images from the relevant manuscripts.

31 Kessler, *Illustrated Bibles*, 96–110; Dutton and Kessler, *Poetry and Paintings*, 83–4. For other ways that Carolingian imagery was manipulated to make associations with Old Testament rulers, see also Diebold, "Verbal, Visual, and Cultural Literacy," and Diebold, "Ruler Portrait."

32 Cambridge, Corpus Christi College, Parker Library MS 183, fol. 1v. For the most important literature on this key manuscript, see above all Rollason, "St Cuthbert and Wessex"; Budny, *Corpus Christi College*, 161–85; Karkov, *Ruler Portraits*, esp. 55–63; https://parker.stanford.edu/parker/actions/manuscript_description_long_display. do?ms_no=183 with full bibliography. Although she does not mention this image, Julia Smith's recent consideration of Aethelstan's gifts of relics in light of Carolingian and Ottonian tradition and contemporary political concerns should be consulted for the broader context of Aethelstan's actions; "Rulers and Relics."

minimized because the colourist did not follow the lines of the hem on the leg to the viewer's left; if he had been more careful we would have seen halfway up Edgar's thigh. Whether or not we may see in the New Minster Charter and other Anglo-Saxon manuscripts faithful records of contemporary dress,[33] it must be pointed out that the artists, especially for representations of the king, were making ideological as much as sartorial statements. We must assume, therefore, that the choice of the short tunic in the New Minster Charter was made precisely to reveal the king's legs as a way of linking him to the nude David.

Interpreting Edgar as a David figure suggests, as I have indicated, that the validation of Edgar's rule is due to his humility, as was articulated by Carolingian exegetes well known to such Anglo-Saxon theorists as Aethelwold,[34] who was most likely responsible for the text of the Charter and can be presumed to have had a part in the visual iconography as well. In the earlier Anglo-Saxon period, it seems that Edgar's great-grandfather, King Alfred, who himself had translated the first fifty Psalms into English, identified himself closely with David.[35] In a Winchester hymn from the late tenth century, the supplicant prays to Christ the highest creator and says, "Let us lift up our minds and hands just as David commanded us to do at night," underscoring David's importance as a model for prayer; the contemporaneous antiphon before Lyric 2 of the Exeter Book refers to Christ himself as the "key of David."[36] Most important, Anglo-Saxon coronation *ordines* make multiple references to David.[37] Specifically, the *consecratio* in

---

33   Owen-Crocker, *Dress in England*, 149–68.

34   Deshman, *Benedictional*, 196–200; Deshman, "*Benedictus Monarcha*," esp. 124–31.

35   Davidic elements in Anglo-Saxon England have not been explored thoroughly, but see Nelson, "Political Ideas of Alfred," esp. 138 (repr. in Nelson, *Rulers and Ruling Families*, IV); O'Neill, "Old English Introductions"; Stanton, *Culture of Translation*, 121–9. These authors emphasize David's dual role as king and author as being most important for Alfred.

36   The hymn, "O optime creator rerum," is printed in Gneuss, *Hymnar*, 287 (no. 20). For the antiphon, see Muir, ed. *The Exeter Anthology of Old English Poetry*, v. 1, 44; v. 2, 386–7.

37   For the various texts, see Schramm, *Kaiser, Könige und Päpste*, v. 2, 140–248. Schramm notes the connections to continental *ordines*, but his conclusions have been challenged by several scholars, most notably Janet Nelson in a series of essays reprinted in her *Politics and Ritual*: "Inauguration Rituals" (283–307, esp. 300), with a reference to David as a model for inauguration with anointing, though here and elsewhere she emphasizes the importance of Solomon as well; "The Earliest Surviving Royal *Ordo*: Some Liturgical and Historical Aspects" (341–60); "The Second English *Ordo*" (361–74).

the *ordo* for Edgar's coronation of 973, which most manifestly expressed the sacral nature of his rule,[38] lists a series of Old Testament figures and their virtues, with which the king was also to be imbued, and this included "being exalted with the humility of David"; later the *benedictio* essentially concludes with a short prayer that Edgar rule like David and Solomon.[39]

David dancing before the ark is especially suitable as an ideological model for the New Minster picture, because embedded within the iconography is the idea of dedication central to the charter. In the vita of the sixth-century Eligius, the saint is explicitly said to have danced before the translation of the relics of St Martial just as David did before the ark.[40] And in the Folchart Psalter, the picture of David and the procession of the ark on page twelve is paired with a representation, above the lunettes, of the dedication of the book by Folchart on the left and Abbot Hartmut on the right, both of whom turn to Christ in the centre (Figure 15). In theory, such a dedication image, with Folchart holding the book, would make more sense at the beginning of the litany, which is not only a more prominent place in the volume but also logically shows David as the author of the Psalms (which Folchart in turn has copied). Rather, Folchart has deliberately chosen to associate his act with the relatively rare representation of David and the ark precisely in order to suggest that making and dedicating the book to Christ is analogous to David's own activity. Similarly,

---

38 Edgar's coronation at Bath in 973 has long been the object of intense historical speculation. For a concise summary of her position (as laid out in more detail in the articles cited in the previous note), see Nelson, "Coronation Rituals and Related Materials," 114–30, esp. 123–5. For a contrary view, see Jones, "The Significance of the Royal Consecration of Edgar in 973," 375–90. Most recently, Smith has approached the matter from another perspective in "The Edgar Poems and the Poetics of Failure in the *Anglo-Saxon Chronicle*," 105–37, esp. 117–22. In keeping with most scholarship, all these authors agree about the heightened religious and Christological nature of the event, which also applies to legal documents associated with Edgar; see Whitelock, ed. *English Historical Documents I, c. 500–1042*, esp. 442, and Wormald, *The Making of English Law*, esp. 313–20, and n. 246.

39 "David humilitate exaltatus" (Schramm, "Der 'Edgar-Ordo'" [973], p. 236); for an English translation, see Legg, *English Coronation Records* (Westminster, A. Constable & Co., 1902), 24, 27. As far as I can tell, the continental versions cited by Schramm, whatever their precise connections to the 973 *ordo* (as per Nelson), do not use this particular phrase, which would thus have originated with the Edgar *ordo*. See also Kleinschmidt, *Untersuchungen über das englische Königtum*, esp. 153–60.

40 Krusch, ed., "Vita Eligii," bk. 1, chap. 18, 684, as discussed by Rohmann, "Invention," 23, who conveniently provides the original Latin text.

Edgar is depicted in the guise of David dancing to communicate that his act of rededicating the New Minster should be understood as a kind of re-enactment of David's humble transfer of the ark to its new, sanctified home in Jerusalem.[41]

As Nicole Guenther Discenza has demonstrated, however, humility for ninth- and tenth-century Anglo-Saxon rulers needed to be calibrated carefully to indicate that the king was humble before God alone and not before his own subjects.[42] Unlike David, Edgar does not rejoice with his people. Carefully positioned with one foot extending into the viewer's space and the rest of his body in the celestial realm, Edgar in the charter image demonstrates that the king uniquely mediates between the terrestrial and heavenly realm, where the object of dedication is not the ark but Christ. In a further contrast to David, who dared not touch the ark directly after the episode of Uzzah's death, the elongated – and twisted – fingers of Edgar's right hand just touch the angel's robe (similar to the way the angels touch Christ's mandorla), suggesting the king's ability to connect more directly with the Saviour. The accessibility of Christ in contrast to the God of the Old Testament was a fundamental point of Christian theology that was constantly and variously expressed in medieval art.[43] In the case of the New Minster Charter, this is accomplished by changing the object of David's worship from the ark – a closed container whose contents were hidden – to a depiction of Christ elevated in full visual majesty.[44] Replacing the ark with

41 I am grateful to Prof. Richard Layton, University of Illinois at Urbana-Champaign, for discussing this aspect of the picture with me. For a linguistic consideration of Anglo-Saxon attitudes to dancing, which includes attention to the passage from 2 Samuel 6, see Stanley, "Dance, Dancers and Dancing."

42 Discenza, "Paradox of Humility." See also McClure, "Bede's Old Testament Kings," for a more general analysis of the way Old Testament kingship was understood in Anglo-Saxon England.

43 See, above all, the various essays by Kessler collected in *Spiritual Seeing*.

44 The ark and its relationship to Christ had long been the subject of patristic exegesis and it was interpreted in many, sometimes overlapping, ways – as Christ, the Virgin Mary, the Church, or the Crucifix. Augustine, for example, in his exposition of Psalm 131 (on verses 8–9), wrote that the ark of holiness could be understood either as Christ's resurrection and the body of his church or as the incarnate body of Christ himself. See Augustine, *Exposition*, 165 (15). The first Augustinian view would lend support to Karkov's reading ("Frontispiece") in the New Minster page of an ecclesiastical layer that sees Christ present in the church and among the congregational body represented by Edgar. For interpretations of the ark as related to medieval image theory, see Kessler, *Seeing Medieval Art*, 66–9.

Christ was in keeping with Bede's position: "It is appropriate that the ark ... designates the incarnation of our Lord ... [It] was made of acacia wood because the Lord's body is composed of members free from every stain of imperfection."[45] The equivalence of the ark and Christ was made manifest both textually and visibly by Theodulf of Orléans, the theorist and bishop who authored the *Opus Caroli Regis Contra Synodum* (often called the *Libri Carolini*), which codified the Carolingian position against the iconophile decisions of the Second Council of Nicea of 787 (although the document was never promulgated).[46] Despite his hardline position against the fashioning of images, Theodulf not only allowed that the holy vessels of the tabernacle (and Temple) were important as divinely sanctioned material works, but also designed a mosaic of the ark and cherubim for his own oratory apse at Germigny-des-Prés (Figure 19).[47] In so doing, Theodulf communicated that it was Christ himself who emerged from between the cherubim and whose sacrifice on the cross – the basis of the Eucharistic ritual performed at the altar beneath the mosaic – was the fulfilment of the promise represented by the notably empty ark depicted above. The New Minster Charter takes this idea one step further not by juxtaposing ark and Christ, but by literally replacing the ark with a depiction of Christ in Majesty, before whom Edgar dances as David did before the ark.

Unlike the ark, of course, which was transported along the ground by oxen and cart, Christ in an elevated mandorla is supported and adored by angels; he is also seated on an orb and rainbow representing the heavens he created. This common iconographic detail gives visual representation to the words in the facing couplet: SIC CELSO/RESIDET SO/LIO QUI CON/DIDIT ASTRA REX VENE/RANS EADGAR/PRON[US] ADORAT E[UM] (Thus he sits on his lofty throne, who created the stars; King Edgar, inclined to veneration, worships him; Figure 10). Although

---

45 *Bede: On the Tabernacle*, trans. Holder, 1, 3 (11). In the subsequent chapter, 4, Bede elaborated at length on his exegesis of the ark as an expression of Christ's incarnation, among other things. The great English typological work of ca. 1200, the *Carmen in Pictor*, included David Dancing Before the Ark as a type for the Communion to the Apostles; a marginal note makes specific reference to David's nudity. See Wirth, ed., *Pictor in Carmine*, 220.

46 See the edition of the treatise by Freeman, *Opus Caroli Regis*, and the essays conveniently collected in Freeman, *Theodulf of Orléans*, which includes an English version of the extensive MGH introduction (I, esp. 33–53 for Theodulf's attitude toward images).

47 Freeman and Meyvaert, "Theodulf's Apse Mosaic," with further literature [this essay is not in the Variorum volume].

Michael Lapidge has suggested, with all due caution because of the brevity of the text, that the author [Aethelwold] "was apparently familiar" with the poetry of Vergil, Prudentius, Caelius Sedulius, and Alcimus Avitus (all known in Anglo-Saxon England),[48] I would suggest that the closest parallel to the first line is from Boethius's *The Consolation of Philosophy*, which thus casts the poem and the image in a different light. Book 1, metre 5 opens:

O stelliferi **conditor** orbis
Qui perpetuo nixus **solio**
Rapido caelum turbine uersas
Legemque pati **sidera** cogis

O Maker of the circle of the stars,
Seated on your eternal throne,
Spinner of the whirling heavens,
Binding the constellations by your law –

and continues in lines 29–36:

.... Premit insontes
Debita sceleri noxia poena,
At perversi **resident celso**
Mores **solio** sanctaque calcant
Iniusta vice colla nocentes.

The innocent endure the pains
That are the proper penalties of crime,
And evil ways sit in the thrones of kings,
And wicked men in unjust recompense
Trample beneath their heels the necks of the good.[49]

---

48 Lapidge, "Aethelwold as Scholar," esp. 96, n. 53. The references are to Vergil, *Eclogues* II.61 (*condidit arces*); Prudentius, *Psychomachia* line 875 ("Hoc residet solio pollens Sapientia"); Caelius Sedulius, *Carmen Paschale* II.193 ("pronus adorat, cuius super aethera sedes"), and Alcimus Avitus, *De spiritalis historiae gestis* I.143 ("factorem pronus adorat").

49 Text and translation from Boethius, *Theological Tractates*, 158–61. See also Langston, ed., *Consolation Of Philosophy*, 12, for a modern prose rendering of the poem.

234   Adam S. Cohen

This treatise, which had been translated into Old English by King Alfred, was known to the tenth-century Benedictine reformers in Aethelwold's circle,[50] and the highlighted words alone suggest that Boethius is at least as likely a textual source as Vergil or Prudentius. More important is the whole tenor of the text, a heartfelt prayer by Boethius, which shares with the couplet a grandiose view of the Creator, a focus on kingship and, with the charter text overall, a concern with vice and its judgment.[51] It provides a richer literary and philosophical backdrop to the opening sentence of the charter proper as well: OMNIPOTENS TOTIVS MACHINAE CONDITOR ineffabili pietate uniuersa mirifice moderator qu[a]e condidit (THE ALMIGHTY CREATOR OF THE WHOLE SCHEME OF THINGS guides marvelously with ineffable love everything which He has created; note the repeated use of *conditor* and related verbs).[52] By drawing on this passage from the *Consolation*, the couplet author, presumably Aethelwold himself, cast the picture of Edgar dancing before the Lord and the facing poem as a kind of Boethian prayer. He also enhanced dramatically the sense of the cosmic stage for Edgar's actions and underscored the virtue of the king's reform of the New Minster.[53]

---

50 Bolton, "Study," and Kleist, *Striving with Grace*. See, in general, Payne, *King Alfred & Boethius*; Discenza, *King's English*; Godden and Irvine, eds., *Old English Boethius*.

51 Johnson, "Fall of Lucifer," 518 noted the emphasis on thrones in the language of the Charter and its literary parallels, the *Genesis A* poem and Peniarth Diploma. Although the couplet has *condidit astra* rather than *conditor orbis stellifera*, *astra* does appear elsewhere in the *Consolation* (as does the verb *conditor*). I thank Professor Fabio Troncarelli for entertaining positively my suggestion of the link between the charter couplet and Boethius and for his helpful suggestions.

52 The text, which reproduces somewhat the orthography of the charter, and the translation are taken from Rumble, *Property and Piety*, 74.

53 I have not found a better source for the *pronus adorat eum* in the second line of the couplet than Sedulius and Avitus as suggested by Lapidge, "Aethelwold as Scholar." The passage in Sedulius, *Carmen Paschale*, II.193 (*PL* 19:618A), is about Lucifer's Temptation of Christ, while the Avitus passage, *De spiritalis historiae gestis* I.143, is about God's command to Adam to take possession of the materials of the world, but not to worship them and instead to adore the Creator (*PL* 59:327 and Shea, *Alcimus Ecdicius Avitus*, 75). Could either or both of these passages be some kind of warning to Edgar? Neither source seems as compelling to me as the Boethius for the first line of the couplet and the charter preamble. The phrase also makes a brief appearance in a vita of St Neot, but this too does not strike me as a meaningful comparison; on the complicated history of this saint's Lives, see Godden, "The Old English Life of St Neot," 193–225. Professor Patrick McBrine was most generous in discussing these matters with me and I thank him sincerely for his assistance.

The formal structure of the New Minster picture demonstrates not only Edgar's subservience to Christ but also the alignment of the two rulers on the central vertical axis, which is echoed in the facing text page. As many scholars have noted, the composition and layout of the couplet mirror the image, with the line about Christ enthroned coming first and above that devoted to the description of Edgar's worship below. As Mechthild Gretsch has suggested, the use of *Rex* as the first word on the second line can be taken to refer simultaneously to Edgar and Christ, further emphasizing the kingly aspect of Christ and the Christ-like aspect of Edgar.[54] While it is true that the text of the charter suggests that Edgar acts on the model of Christ in reforming the New Minster, the image, in the interpretation advanced here, is less explicit about drawing a parallel between the two. Instead, it focuses on Edgar's humility before the glorious Creator. In a second Edgar image, however, the topos of humility is switched, such that Edgar takes the central place normally reserved for Christ. This is the frontispiece to an eleventh-century copy of the *Regularis Concordia*, the monastic compact promulgated by Edgar around 970 and probably written by Aethelwold; the image likely replicates a tenth-century Winchester original (Figure 20).[55] Here Edgar is co-enthroned with two ecclesiastics who represent Bishop Aethelwold and Archbishop Dunstan, another principal Benedictine reformer. Deshman has demonstrated in great detail how the crowned Edgar is assimilated to Christ as ruler, judge, and abbatial shepherd.[56] But what is of particular note here is the figure of the anonymous monk below who, girded with a scroll, represents all the monks of England who accept the *Regularis* (and the Rule of Benedict) co-authored and held by Edgar and

---

54 Gretsch, *Intellectual Foundations*, 309–10. Deshman has explored thoroughly the multiple ways that Anglo-Saxon thinkers expressed in both texts and pictures a theory of Christocentric kingship, especially among works associated with Aethelwold of Winchester and Edgar. See his "Benedictus," "*Christus rex*," and *Benedictional*, esp. 192–214 ("Following the venerable precedent of the Carolingians, Aethelwold justified the king's role in ecclesiastic and monastic affairs by wrapping his secular power in the spiritual mantles of Christ and Saint Benedict. Both were regalized to represent interrelated heavenly exemplars for King Edgar who, like a Christ-like abbot, could legitimately exercise his authority over the monasticized Church," 214)

55 British Library, MS Cotton Tiberius A.iii, fol. 2v. On this manuscript, see Temple, *Anglo-Saxon Manuscripts*, 118–19 (no. 100). Despite the acknowledged dependence on a tenth-century exemplar, Withers, "Interaction of Word and Image," properly reminds us not to forget the eleventh-century context in which this particular manuscript was viewed and understood, though that is not our concern here.

56 Deshman, "*Benedictus Monarcha*," esp. 104–9, with further literature.

the bishops. In contrast to the static and frontal king directly above him, the monk lunges or strides to the left while twisting his head to the right to look at Edgar above. The *Regularis* frontispiece thus recapitulates in essence the relationship of Edgar and Christ in the New Minster Charter. This time, however, it is Christocentric Edgar who is the recipient of the reverence and the monk whose "dancing" posture indicates the attribute of humility fundamental to the monastic profession.[57]

The frontispiece of the *Regularis Concordia* indicates that the New Minster Charter was not the only manuscript of the tenth-century Benedictine reform that supplemented its texts with images that manipulated formal and iconographic components to articulate important messages about the sacred nature of the reform. In both cases, the figure at the bottom of the composition twists his body to reveal not only his subservient position but also the specific attribute of humility. In the New Minster Charter, the fact that this figure is the king himself could have been potentially awkward, but by cloaking Edgar in the guise of King David leaping and dancing before the Lord, the composer of the picture, presumably Bishop Aethelwold, demonstrated at one and the same time the theological substitution of the ark by Christ and the divine sanction of the Anglo-Saxon king through his humility.[58]

---

57 See, in general, Leclercq, *Love of Learning*, and Asad, "On Discipline and Humility in Medieval Christian Monasticism," in Asad, *Genealogies of Religion*, 125–67.

58 The association of the English monarch with the ark of the Lord continues into the present. The second verse of "God Save the Queen," dating back at least into the eighteenth century, reads: "O Lord, our God, arise, Scatter her enemies, And make them fall," which is a reference to Numbers 10:35, "And whenever the ark set out, Moses said, 'Arise, O Lord, and let the enemies be scattered; and let them that hate thee flee before thee.'" I thank Charles Heller for bringing this to my attention.

11 "In those days": Giants and the Giant Moses in the Old English Illustrated Hexateuch

ASA SIMON MITTMAN

Introduction: Giants in Those Days

The eleventh-century Old English Illustrated Hexateuch, probably produced in the second quarter of the eleventh century, in or near St Augustine's Abbey, Canterbury,[1] houses a wealth of imagery, including several images of giants that appear throughout the manuscript's approximately 400 images and 156 folios. These giants form a primary point of contrast for both the Jewish protagonists within the narrative and for Anglo-Saxon readers/viewers, helping the latter in their process of identity formation. Images of Moses, the great Jewish prophet, as not only horned but also gigantic complicate what might otherwise have been a simplistic dichotomy of "us" and "them," thereby creating a more fertile basis for contemplative viewing.

Anglo-Saxon readers, associating themselves with the ancient Israelites of the narrative, would be able to see themselves in the role of the giant-slayers, and would perhaps in doing so have reflected on legends of more recent conquests of giants, including those believed to have been the autochthonous inhabitants of Britain. The figure of Moses, however, would have challenged the reader/viewer to reconsider his position with respect

---

1 London, British Library, Cotton Claudius B.iv. See most recently Withers, *The Illustrated Old English Hexateuch*, chap. 2, esp. 85, for an extended discussion of the dating and provenance of the Hexateuch, as well as a CD-ROM of the full manuscript. He places it ca. 1020–1040. The manuscript has been digitized and is available freely at the *British Library Digitized Manuscripts* (no date) http://www.bl.uk/manuscripts/SetupFullDisplayHandler.ashx?ref=Cotton_MS_Claudius_B_IV (accessed February 2015). This essay is dedicated to my old friend Cliff, who is something of a giant.

to the giants, and thus to their ancient Jewish adversaries: as we turn the folios, we find the figure of Moses enlarging until he, too, is one of the giants on the earth in those days.

About halfway through this manuscript, we come upon a series of illustrations containing a massive, oversized figure of Moses. On folio 139v, for example, at the lower left edge of the full-page illustration, he towers over the crowd before him (Figure 21). He holds a staff and two large, curving blue horns protrude from his brow. Ruth Mellinkoff has admirably explored the Anglo-Saxon image of Moses's horns,[2] which in this manuscript often appear to be a headdress rather than genuine horns. Moses – the central figure of the manuscript[3] – is here also depicted in hieratic scale, so that his pictorial size reflects his relative importance within the image. While this use of scale is conceptually clear, and served as a relatively common device in Anglo-Saxon art, the figure clearly resembles a horned giant, creating a provocative ambiguity among the giant figures of the narrative.

The 400 images in the manuscript usually adjoin the texts that they illustrate. Richard Gameson cites this manuscript as one of a handful of examples of "integrated imagery," in which the images are fully integrated with and placed in close proximity to their texts, such that meaning is produced through the intersection of text, image, and context.[4] These three factors should help explain the images of Moses as not only horned but also gigantic. The Hexateuch's images of literal giants – and other Anglo-Saxon perspectives on them – will be examined first, as the primary context for the image of Moses as a horned giant.

Giants in Anglo-Saxon England

Giants enter the narrative near the very beginning of Genesis, a biblical book often reproduced and illustrated in Anglo-Saxon England.[5] In the

---

2 Mellinkoff, *The Horned Moses*, and "More about Horned Moses," 184–98.

3 Withers, *The Illustrated Old English Hexateuch*, 134–49.

4 Gameson, *The Role of Art in the Late Anglo-Saxon Church*, 35–6, 54. Of the two Old English examples, the Hexateuch and Oxford, Bodleian Library, Junius 11, Gameson, 37, cites the former as being far better coordinated.

5 Gneuss, "A Preliminary List of Manuscripts Written or Owned in England up to 1100," lists ten Bibles, two Old Testaments, and one Genesis-Judges volume, as well as the Old English Genesis poem in Junius 11. There are also seven surviving copies of the paraphrase, leaving at least twenty known copies.

Old English paraphrase of the Hexateuch, as in the Vulgate, we read that "Entas wæron eac swylce ofer eorðan on ðam dagum" (there also were giants on the earth in those days).[6] This verse merited an illustration in the Hexateuch, to be discussed at length below (Figure 22). There are numerous other references to giants in the Bible, with Goliath providing the most familiar example.[7] Perhaps modern readers would be tempted to assume that these references were always interpreted metaphorically, as surely was the giant with his arms outstretched at the far left of folio 10v of the contemporary Harley Psalter.[8] However, Augustine – the influential bishop of Hippo in the fifth century – explicitly asserted the reality of giants, doubting not their existence but their humanity.[9] Augustine also elaborated at length in *The City of God* on the presence of giants in the world, both before and after the flood. In his summation, he writes:

Igitur secundum scripturas canonicas Hebraeas atque Christianas multos gigantes ante diluvium fuisse non dubium est, et hos fuisse cives terrigenae societatis hominum; Dei autem filios, qui secundum carnem de Seth propagati sunt, in hanc societatem deserta iustitia declinasse. Nec miranda est, quod etiam de ipsis gigantes nasci potuerunt. Neque enim omnes gigantes, sed magis multi utque tunc fuerunt, quam post diluvium temporibus ceteris.[10]

(Therefore, following the canonical scripture, Jewish and Christian, there is no doubt many giants existed before the flood, and were citizens of the

---

6 OE Genesis 6:4, f. 12v. For a critical edition of this text, see Marsden, *The Old English Heptateuch and Ælfric's "Libellus de veteri testamento et novo."* This and all other texts from the Hexateuch, which vary slightly from Marsden's edition, are based on transcription from Claudius B.iv. Translations, unless otherwise noted, are my own. Verses from the Old English paraphrase will be designated "OE." This text is a translation of the Vulgate Genesis 6:4: "Gigantes erant super terram in diebus illis." For the Vulgate text, I have relied on *Biblia Sacra Iuxta Vulgatam Versionem*, ed. Fisher, Gribomont, and Weber (designated "Vulgate").

7 See the following Vulgate passages, some of which have been omitted from the OE: Genesis 6:4, Numbers 13:33, Deuteronomy 2:11, 2:20, 3:11, 3:13, Joshua 12:4, 13:12, 15:8, 17:17, 18:16, 2 Samuel 21:16, 21:18, 21:20, 21:22, 1 Chronicles 20:4, 20:6, 20:8.

8 London, BL, Harley 603. Temple, *A Survey of Manuscripts Illuminated in the British Isles*, 81, no. 64.

9 Augustine, *De Civitate Dei Libri XII*, ed. Kalb and Dombart, *Bibliotheca Scriptorum Graecorum et Romanorum Teubeneriana*, 16:8, 135.

10 Ibid., 15:23, 112. For discussion of this passage, and Augustine's role in establishing that "the sons of man" were the offspring of Seth, see Orchard, *Pride and Prodigies*, 76.

earthly society of the men, while the sons of God, who are descended from the flesh of Seth, having deserted righteousness, declined into this society. Nor is it to be marvelled at that those (descended) from the same were able to be born giants. Nor indeed were they all giants, but rather, at that time there were more than at all other times after the flood.)

Augustine therefore confirms the presence of giants in ancient times, both antediluvian and postdiluvian. He also confirms the continued presence of giants in the world, including a giant Goth woman living in Rome "[a]nte paucos annos" (a few years ago).[11] Augustine even verifies the reality of giants through personal experience, writing:

Vidi ipse non solus, sed aliquot mecum in Uticensi litore molarem hominis dentem tam ingentem, ut, si in nostrorum dentium modulos minutatim concideretur, centum nobis uideretur facere potuisse. Sed illum gigantis alicuius fuisse crediderim. Nam praeter quod errant omnium multo quam nostra maiora tunc corpora, gigantes longe ceteris anteibant; sicut aliis deinde nostrisque temporibus rara quidem, sed numquam ferme defuerunt, quae modum aliorum plurimum exederent.[12]

(I have seen, myself, not alone, but with several others with me, on the beach at Utica, the molar tooth of a man, so huge that, if it were cut up into small pieces, it could be seen to be able to make one hundred of our standard teeth. Indeed, I would believe it to have been from a giant, for, the giants of old exceeded by far the bodies of all the others back when others were bigger than we are.)

The apocryphal Book of Enoch, popular in Anglo-Saxon England, also verified the presence of giants, providing four accounts of their creation.[13] As Elizabeth Coatsworth notes, "the influence of The Book of Enoch on Anglo-Saxon poetry ... has been strongly argued."[14] The Hexateuch (together with Junius 11) has an "otherwise unique" image of the translation

---

11 Augustine, *De Civitate Dei*, 15:23, 109.
12 Ibid., 15:9, 75. Stephens, *Giants in Those Days: Folklore, Ancient History, and Nationalism*, 91, explains Augustine's reference to times when men were larger. See book 7 of Pliny's *Natural History* and 7.155 and 7.211 of Homer's *Illiad*, which claim that humans are decreasing in stature over time.
13 Black, ed. and trans., *The Book of Enoch, or Enoch I*, chapters 7, 9, 15 and 106.
14 Coatsworth, "The Book of Enoch and Anglo-Saxon Art," 135–50, at 50.

or ascension of Enoch.[15] The Book of Enoch repeatedly clarifies the somewhat ambiguous Biblical account of how giants came into being, presenting the generation of the giants as the result of the union of angels and human women. In chapter seven, we learn that the two hundred Watchers, or Angels, chose wives from among the "beautiful and comely daughters" of men.[16] The women then "bore great giants of three thousand cubits," bloodthirsty and rapacious.[17] Relying on the authority of the Bible, Augustine, and the Book of Enoch, Anglo-Saxons Christians would have had no reason to doubt the existence of giants, whether they descended from Seth (according to Augustine) or from angels (according to the Book of Enoch). Indeed, following Augustine, Ælfric assumes the reality of giants but condemns their worship as gods.[18]

The Hexateuch's description of the genesis of the giants is somewhat ambiguous. It reads:

Entas wæron eac swylce ofer eorðan on ðam dagum, æfter ðan ðe godes bearn tymdon. wið manna dohtra ⁊ hi cendon ða synd mihtige fram worulde. ⁊ hlis fulle weras. ða geseah god ðæt micel yfelnys manna wæs ofer eorðan. ⁊ eal geðanc manna heortena wæs awend on yfel on eallum timan. Gode ofðuhte ða ðæt he mann geworhte ofer eorðan. He wolde ða warnian on ær. ⁊ wæs gehrepod mid heortan sarnysse wið innan. ⁊ cwæð ✠ ic adylgie ðone man ðe ic gesceop fram ðære eorðan ansyne fram ðam men oðða nytenu fram ðam slincendum oðða fugelas. me ofðingð soðlice ðæt ic hi worhte.[19]

(Giants were over the earth in those days, after which the sons of God propagated with the daughters of man, and they conceived. They are the mighty ones from ancient times, and men of renown. Then God saw that great wickedness of man was over the earth, and all thought of men's hearts was perverted toward evil at all times. God grieved then that he had made man over the earth. He wished then that he had taken caution beforehand and was touched with grief of the heart from within. And he said: ✠ I henceforth will obliterate that man whom I created from the surface of the earth, from that

---

15 Ibid., 139.
16 *The Book of Enoch*, chapter 6, page 27.
17 *The Book of Enoch*, chapter 7, page 28.
18 Ælfric, *The Homilies of the Anglo-Saxon Church*, 1, ed. Thorpe, 366.
19 OE Genesis 6:4–7, f. 12v.

man to the animals, from the creeping [creatures] to the birds. I am truly grieved that I made them.)[20]

In this passage, close to the Vulgate version, the biblical narrative switches from giants to men, and it is in the men that "God saw … great wickedness." From this point on in the passage, God explicitly condemns "man," not giants. But the passage as a whole also allows for, even encourages, a conflation of men and giants. Giants are described in terms that must have rung with a positive tone in the ears of an Anglo-Saxon audience, particularly the lay audience that has been posited for this vernacular manuscript.[21] "They are the mighty ones from ancient times, and men of renown." And yet, dominant exegetes such as Cassiodorus blamed the flood on the giants.[22]

The Book of Enoch, more detailed than the Vulgate's account, informs us that "the giants, who have been produced from spirits and flesh, shall be called mighty spirits upon the earth."[23] Here, it is the giants, not men, by whom "much blood was spilled upon the earth, and the whole earth was filled with wickedness," and who are therefore to blame for the Flood.[24] In the Old English paraphrase of the Hexateuch, there is a further linguistic tie between giants and wicked men. Unlike the Vulgate, which positions the giants *super terram* and mankind *in terra*, the Old English locates both giants and man *ofer eorðan*.[25] This is a subtle distinction, but one which serves in the Old English paraphrase to cement the ties between the giants and the wickedness of the men who follow them, gigantic or otherwise.

The Giants of the Hexateuch and their Placement in the Text

The depiction of giants illustrating Genesis 6:4, immediately preceding the coming of the flood, is the Hexateuch's earliest representation of giants

---

20 My thanks to Roy Liuzza for his thoughts on a portion of this translation.
21 Withers, *The Illustrated Old English Hexateuch*, 178–9, argues that the manuscript might have been for older laymen retiring to a monastery, visiting laymen or laymen visited out outside of a monastery, and that lay and monastic audiences, as well as male and female audiences, were not as separate as they are often made out to be.
22 Harris, *Race and Ethnicity*, 148; and Cohen, *Of Giants: Sex, Monsters, and the Middle Ages*, 19.
23 *The Book of Enoch*, chapter 15, page 34.
24 Ibid., chapter 9, page 30.
25 Vulgate, Genesis 6:4–5.

(Figure 22).[26] These figures fill their half-page frame, dominating the page; after the preceding images, their size is startling. They are the largest among the thousands of figures in this volume, twice the height of those on the surrounding folios and because of the way in which their feet are positioned, they appear weightier. They seem as if drawn to scale with the rest of the figures in the manuscript. Still, they gesture to one another as if they were engaged in polite conversation. Their styles of dress, hair, and beard in no way distinguish them from the rest of the biblical characters. Indeed, the second giant from the left is quite similar to the figure of Noah on the facing folio (Figure 23). Both wear forked beards, face to their left and have their cloaks clasped at their left shoulders and draped over their right shoulders and chests. Both wear dark shoes, and have decorative gold trim along the lower edges of their knee-length robes.

Still, there are very slight visual differences between the image of Noah (the one man deemed worthy of salvation from the impending flood) and the monstrous giant (conceptually linked to the evil that precipitated it). The giant's facial expression is as questioning as Noah's is compliant, and in the context of this manuscript, in which even sorrowful figures are shown smiling, he seems mournful. While both raise their hands, palms out, Noah's gesture is open, accepting of God's commandment. In contrast, the giant's hands, oversized even by Anglo-Saxon standards, seem grasping.[27]

The giants of Genesis 6:4 are, of course, antediluvian, and they ought to be, therefore, the only ones to appear in the Bible. However, by folio 118, we find that others have survived the great flood, and are more fearsome (Figure 24). As Cohen recounts:

The Hebrew Bible overflows with stories of postdiluvian giants: Og of Bashan, the aboriginal inhabitants of Canaan, David's mighty nemesis, Goliath. Only Noah and the contents of his ark were supposed to survive God's celestial wash cycle, and yet giants were still walking the earth after the divinity purged its dirtied landscape. Some theologians speculated that

---

26 Dodwell and Henderson both note that, while the Byzantine Octateuchs also contain images for this passage, there seems to be no connection between them and the Hexateuch. See Dodwell and Clemoes, *The Old English Illustrated Hexateuch*, 66; Henderson, "Late-Antique Influences in Some English Mediaeval Illustrations of Genesis," 175, and "The Joshua Cycle," 215.

27 Gameson, *The Role of Art*, 146–7, among others, notes the importance of representations of hands in Anglo-Saxon art.

these monsters survived by climbing the tallest mountains and thrusting their nostrils above sea level for forty days and forty nights, or that one of them, Og, had simply ridden atop the roof of the ark.[28]

Fabulous though this sounds, Mellinkoff cautions us that "we should not doubt the reality of that belief."[29] The giants of folio 118, for example, are the Sons of Anak, described by the spies of Israel. This passage is from Numbers, which may be significant since "less than a third of Numbers has been rendered by the Old English translators."[30] If the translators cut more than two-thirds of this book, they must have seen this passage as highly important to have retained it. Caroline Lousia White notes, "the principle of omission with Ælfric is here unmistakable. He wishes to furnish a practical, easily-understood rendering of the parts which are most important for the laity to know. All else he passes over."[31]

This passage is a translation of Numbers 13:33–4; because the verses are reversed in the paraphrase, though, it is far more ambiguous in its meaning than the Latin of the Vulgate. The passages from the Vulgate and Old English paraphrase are as follows:

Detraxeruntque terrae quam inspexerant apud filios Israhel dicentes terram quam lustravimus devorat habitatores suos populum quem aspeximus procerae staturae est. Ibi vidimus monstra quaedam filiorum Enach de genere giganteo quibus conparati quasi lucustae videbamur.[32] (Vulgate)

(And they have slandered the land they had examined, saying to the sons of the house of Israel, "The land which we have inspected devours its inhabitants. Its people, whom we have seen, are of great stature. There we have seen certain monsters who are the sons of Anak, of the race of Giants, by whom we were seen as if we were locusts.")

---

28 Cohen, *Of Giants*, 20. Mellinkoff discusses the same legends at length in "Cain's Monstrous Progeny in *Beowulf*," 183–97, at 183, 187–8.
29 Mellinkoff, "Cain's Monstrous Progeny," 183.
30 Marsden, "Old Latin Intervention in the Old English *Heptateuch*," 229–64, at 258.
31 White, *Ælfric: A New Study of his Life and Writings*, 146. Scholarly consensus would now replace "Ælfric," here, with "the translators."
32 Vulgate Numbers 13:33–4.

⁊ we ðær gesawon of ðam ent cynne. Enachys bearna micelra wæstma ðam we ne synd ðe gelicran ðe lytle gærstapan. ⁊ hi tældon ðæt land mid heora teon wordum.[33]

("And we saw there among them the race of giants, Anak's descendants, greatly increased. To them we were not like them, but like little grasshoppers." And they slandered that land with their harmful words.)

Since there are no quotation marks in medieval manuscripts, passages of speech must be distinguished by context.[34] Still, the boundaries of the quotation are clear in the Vulgate because it identifies the quote with *dicentes*. In the Old English, while the preceding line establishes that a quotation has begun (*cwædon*), there is no indication of when the spies of Israel have finished speaking.[35] In the Old English paraphrase, it is perfectly possible to read the passage to mean that the giants, rather than the spies, slandered the land with harmful words. This shifts a burden of guilt away from the Israelites and onto the giants.

Curiously, this image does not appear directly preceding nor immediately following the passage it presumably illustrates. Perhaps this is because the panel is a composite image, representing multiple points in the narrative.[36] These passages all appear on the facing folio, where the image could certainly have been placed.[37] However, the image instead immediately follows

---

33 The Old English is a paraphrase of Numbers 13:34–3, f. 117v.

34 Parkes, *Pause and Effect: An Introduction to the History of Punctuation in the West*, 171. The Hexateuch contains a variety of punctuation, including *distinctions*, but the *puncti* do not clarify the matter (Parkes, *Pause and Effect*, 27–8, 303–4).

35 OE Numbers 13:32, f. 117v.

36 Dodwell, *The Old English Illustrated Hexateuch*, 37, cites OE Numbers 13:24 and 29 in addition to 13:34, thereby accounting for the representation of the cutting of the grapes and the presence of the giant descendants of Anak inside a city with high walls: "⁊ of ðam winbogum mid berium mid ealle ⁊ æpplum ⁊ ofætum eft mid him brohton" (And from that grape vine they brought back with them the grapes and all the fruit and food) and "Micele burga ðær synd ⁊ mærlice geweallode." (Their cities are great and splendidly walled.)

37 BL, Cotton Claudius B.iv, fol. 117v, lines 19–20 of 38. There was ample room for the image below this line. David Johnson observes that "the final layout of Claudius B.iv is highly regular," and that "each picture must follow the text it illustrates," but clearly they need not do so directly. See Johnson, "A Program of Illumination in the Old English Illustrated Hexateuch," 169–99, at 175.

Numbers 14:32–4, in which God prophesizes doom for those among the Israelites who *murmurat contra* (murmur against) Moses:[38]

Eowre bearn beoð worigende on þisum westene feowertig wintra ⁊ eower forligr berað oð ðæt heora fædera hreaw beon fornumene. æfter ðæra feowertigra daga getæle þe ge ðæt land besceawodon. Ger bið for dæge geteald. ⁊ on foewertigum gearum. ge underfoð eowre unriht wisnyssa þæt ge witon mine wrace.[39]

(Your children will be wanderers in this wilderness for forty winters, and will bear your fornication, until the carcasses of their fathers will be consumed. After, you will bear this for forty days counting, with you having seen that land, each day for a year, and in the fortieth year you will accept your iniquity, and you will know my vengeance.)

The illustrations, as Withers points out, were the driving force behind the layout of the manuscript.[40] The reordering of the text illustrated by the image – which has the potential to cast the Sons of Anak not only as gigantic but also as slanderous – and the juxtaposition of the image with this later passage on punishment for iniquity combine to extend the condemnation of the giants well beyond the implications of the Vulgate,[41] and therefore to shift it away from the Israelites.

The earlier image of the giants from Genesis 6:4 is likewise slightly distanced from the text it illustrates. The relevant verse appears on the facing folio, directly below the image of Noah discussed above (Figures 22 and 23). Here, reasons of layout might have been more germane, since there would not have been space below this image for another of larger size.

---

38 The Vulgate passage, Numbers 14:27 ("Usquequo multitudo haec pessima murmurat contra me querellas filiorum Israhel audivi"), in which the congregation is said to murmur against Moses, does not appear in the Old English paraphrase contained in the Hexateuch. Instead, it runs directly from Numbers 14:22 to 14:30.

39 OE Numbers 14:33–4, f. 118.

40 Withers, *The Illustrated Old English Hexateuch*, 17, 86, 105.

41 Cohen, *Of Giants*, 18, notes a related phenomenon regarding Anglo-Saxon interpretations of The Book of Wisdom, not contained in the Hexateuch: "The Book of Wisdom unites the giants and the 'despotic princes' only by narrative proximity, but in early medieval England, the two episodes in salvation history (the destruction of the giant, the promulgation of idols) became conjoined into a newly hybrid foundational narrative that bridged classical, biblical, and northern traditions."

However, the placement of the second image of giants could imply that the placement of the first was more deliberate. Since sketches for the images were drawn before the text was added, their placement was certainly of great concern to the designer.[42] The oversized image of the giants on folio 13 is neatly framed above and below by the text of Genesis 6:11 and 6:12. Here, the text of the Hexateuch reads: "Ða wæs eall seo eorðe gewemmed ætforan gode. ⁊ afylled mid unriht wis nysse. Ða geseah god ðæt seo eorðe was gewemmed. for ðan ðe ælc flæsc gewemde his weg ofer eorðan. ✠" ("Then was all the earth defiled before God, and filled with iniquity. Then God saw that the earth was defiled, because all flesh defiled its way on the earth.✠")[43] Walter Stephens notes that this passage immediately precedes a passage "in which God repents of having created mankind, whose evil thoughts and deeds have polluted the earth … and thus decides to destroy the world in a flood."[44] In both cases, the images illustrate texts explicitly referring to giants, but are directly juxtaposed with verses about the sinfulness of men and their resultant punishment. The designer's page layout thus links the monstrous giants with the sins of man. The giants are thereby rendered inherently wicked, so that their bodily abnormality is linked to moral depravity. As beholders, we are therefore encouraged to read the "great wickedness of man" in Genesis 6:5 as a reference not to the Israelites, but to the giants they strive against.[45]

Within the line at the end of the text of Genesis 6:12 is a cross (✠) most likely drawn by a twelfth-century annotator who added a number of Latin comments in the margins.[46] The cross is a *signe de renvoi* that directs the reader to a comment in the lower margin of both folios in this opening (see

---

42 Johnson, "Program of Illumination," 175, 182.

43 OE Genesis 6:11–12, f. 13r.

44 Stephens, *Giants in Those Days*, 74.

45 OE Genesis 6:5. See n21.

46 Dodwell, *The Old English Illustrated Hexateuch*, 15. For a thorough edition and commentary on these annotations, see Doane and Stoneman, *Purloined: The Twelfth Century Reception of the Anglo-Saxon Illustrated Hexateuch (British Library, Cotton Claudius B. iv)*. Doane and Stoneman discuss the script at length in chap. 4. They note that "[the] style of script belongs to the late twelfth century; it, or variations of it, appear on almost every page of the book on a massive scale – the approximately 360 discrete annotations amounting to nearly half the bulk of the main Old English text itself." Similar crosses are commonly found in many types of manuscripts from the period, including biblical and liturgical manuscripts. Also see Budny, *Insular, Anglo-Saxon, and Early Anglo-Norman Manuscript Art*, lxvii.

Figures 22 and 23).[47] The comment is heavily abbreviated and somewhat damaged but may be reconstructed as follows:

> ✠¶✠ Potuit *etiam* esse uero [ut] incubi demones genuer*unt* gigantes. a magnitudine corp*orum* sic dictos denominatos | a geos q*uod* est *terra* ... *sed* etia*m* i*n*manitate corp*orum* respo*n*debat inmanitas a*n*imor*um*. Post diluuiu*m* *tamen* nati sunt· || alii gigantes in ebron. ⁊ post fuer*unt* in thani, ciuitate. egypti. a qu*a* tytanes dicti s*unt* de | quor*um* stirpe fuit enachi*m*. cui*us* filii habitauer*unt* in ebron. de q*u*ibus ort*us* *est* golias· ⁊ q*u*ida*m* alii. | ¶ Iratus (...) d*eus* peccatis hominu*m* dixit.

> (✠¶✠ It is possible, however (that) incubi (or) demons begot the giants, so called (and) named from the great size of their bodies for [Greek] "geos," that is, "earth" ... but the monstrousness of their bodies corresponded to the monstrousness of their souls. But after the flood other giants were born in Hebron and they were later in the Egyptian city of Than, from which ... they are called "Titans." From their race were the Enakim whose sons have inhabited Hebron from whom was born Goliath and certain others. ¶ God has said he was angry at the sins of men.)[48]

Through this exegetical addition, the original giants of Genesis 6:4 are placed in a nexus of gigantic sins. The giants referred to in this annotation as the "Enakim" are the sons of Anak depicted on folio 118. The commentator, perhaps responding to the program of juxtaposition observed above, has rather forcefully linked this image of giants with sin, and with God's scorn. In this comment, the giants are not merely wicked, outsized men; they are demon-spawn. As the result of the interbreeding of demons with incubi – demons that mate with and impregnate sleepers – they must be wicked beings. Here, they are not merely large, but monstrous in their bodies. This exterior flaw is immediately tied to an interior failing:

47 Budny, "The Vivian Bible and Scribal, Editorial, and Organizational Marks," 199–239, at 206.

48 BL, Cotton Claudius B.iv, fol. 12v–13, lower margin. Transcription and translation from Doane and Stoneman, *Purloined Letters,* 36–7, with expanded abbreviations denoted with italics. Note that Doane and Stoneman do not indicate the *signe de renvoi,* and omit the pilcrows in their translation. My thanks to Sidney Tibbetts for help with this heavily abbreviated transcription, and to Jim Tschen-Emmons for his thoughts on the translation, both of which were useful prior to the publication of Doane's now-invaluable study. The commentator may be relying on Isidore's *Etymologies,* XV.1.24.

monstrous minds. This marginal comment therefore associates the antediluvian giants with the postdiluvian, ties them to sin, renders them of evil disposition, and constructs them as the ancestors of Goliath himself, the adversary not only of the Jews in general, but of David – a key ancestor of Christ and the purported author of the Psalms. Further, the references to the Titans and the Sons of Anak serve to damn these giants. Of course, in Greek mythology, the Titans strove against the Olympian gods.[49] This reference casts the giants of Genesis as essentially opposed to divine order. The comment may have been inspired by Bede's *In Genesim*, where he connects Genesis 6:4 with the same classical myths and biblical passages.[50]

This commentary, and the location of the image in the Hexateuch, may also point towards the Book of Enoch, which links the giants not only to sin but directly to the great Flood. In chapter 106, we read:

> Exalted ones of heaven transgressed the word of the Lord and violated the covenant of heaven. And behold, they committed sin and transgressed the law, and they had intercourse with women and committed sin with them and have married some of them, and from them begotten children, and they bore children on the earth, the giants, not beings like spirits, but like creatures of flesh. And there will be great destruction for one year ... and the earth shall rest and be cleansed of great corruption.[51]

This account may have influenced the marginal comment, and also the careful relocation of the Hexateuch's illustration of the giants of Genesis 6:4. The wickedness of giants, implied in the original passage, is therefore stressed by the image placement and further pressed by this marginal commentary.

This comment serves in one further way to forge a connection between the giants and the destruction of sinful men. The cross serving as a *signe de renvoi* following Genesis 6:12 bears a minuscule "a" beneath it. The marginal comment bears the same mark, clarifying that this comment relates to this passage. However, on folio 12v, there is another cross with an "a"

---

49 Bulfinch, *Bulfinch's Mythology*, 122.
50 Bede, *Bedae Venerabilis Opera, Libri Quatuor in Principium Genesim*, ed. Jones, 100: "Gigantes dicit homines inmensis corporibus editos ac potestate nimia praeditos, quales etiam post diluuium, id est temporibus Moysi uel Dauid multos fuisse legimus ... illos iuxta fabulas poetarum terra genuerit."
51 The Book of Enoch, chapter 106, page 100.

beneath it. This mark is between the second and third words of Genesis 6:8, suggesting that perhaps the comment applies to both 6:12 and 6:8:

Gode ofðuhte ða ðæt he mann geworhte ofer eorðan: he wolde ða warnian on ær ⁊ wæs gehrepod mid heortan sarnysse wiðinnan. ⁊ cwæð ✠ ic adylgie ðone man ðe ic gesceop fram ðære eorðan ansyne fram ðam men oðða nytenu fram ðam slincendum oðða fugelas. me ofðingð soðlice ðæt ic hi worhte.[52]

(God regretted that he made man on earth. He wished that he was on guard earlier, and was crying out with pain within his heart. And he said ✠ I henceforth will obliterate that man whom I created from the surface of the earth, from that man to the animals, from the creeping [creatures] to the birds. I am truly grieved that I made them.)

Through this trio of signs, the commentator has linked the giants of Genesis 6:4 to two instances of mankind's sinfulness and God's resultant regret. In this way, the twelfth-century commentator reinforces the eleventh-century designer's choice to link these concepts through juxtaposition.

The illustration of Numbers 13:33–4 discussed above, depicting the giant Sons of Anak, merits careful attention, as it is one with little artistic precedent. It is one of the many unfinished illustrations in the Hexateuch.[53] The faces of the crowd of Israelite onlookers have been filled in, fleshed out by a later hand. They look at the bountiful grape vines around them, and across the image at the giants who barely fit beneath their high yellow arch. The central figure, wearing blue robes, boldly gestures towards the giants, with his knees bent as if in motion towards their city. A second figure reaches around to caution or restrain him, pointing away from the giants as if to suggest a hasty retreat. The giants seem wholly unaware of or unconcerned with the Israelite *gærstapan* (grasshoppers) in the fields behind them.[54] As if to emphasize their height, the giants are drawn within an archway that is not quite tall enough for them. Their heads scrape its lower edge, and the feet of the giant in the middle of the arch extend beyond the edge of the frame of the image.

---

52 OE Genesis 6:7–8, f. 12v.

53 Dodwell, "Techniques of Painting in Anglo-Saxon Manuscripts," 652 and 657. The image bears several obvious, later additions. See also Dodwell, *The Old English Illustrated Hexateuch*, 61.

54 OE Numbers 13:34, f. 117v.

The Land of Canaan – promised to the Israelites two folios earlier in Numbers 13:2 on a full text page – is depicted as a land of abundance: the vines hang heavy with their bounty, doubling over to form an arch that mimics on a smaller scale the masonry arch of the giants and, in doing so, serves yet again to emphasize the disparity in size between the Israelites and the Anakim. The spies return with the fruit of these vines[55] from Canaan, the land that "fluit lacte et melle," the land which "flewð witodlice meolce. ⁊ hunie" (flows with milk and honey).[56] One branch of grapes is mentioned in the text of the Vulgate (though the Old English paraphrase omits this verse), but the image on the following folio shows the Israelites laden with four.[57] The grape vines here in both images serve to stress the bounty of the land and also the terror caused by the Anakim. Only truly terrifying opponents would keep those who have wandered in the desert from a land of such richness.

The Hexateuch's Anglo-Saxon readers might have been more predisposed to associate themselves with the Israelites in these images than readers elsewhere. Through the writings of Gildas and Bede, among others, the Anglo-Saxons came to see themselves as analogous to, indeed as modern-day versions of, the "Old Testament" Jews, as Nicholas Howe, Patrick Wormald, and Benjamin Withers have argued. Howe writes:

> Like the Jews, the Anglo-Saxons were a people (according to their own myth of migration) that had been chosen by God to possess a promised land. Home was thus not simply a site of long settlement, a matter of territory or geography, it was also – for both Israelites and Anglo-Saxons – a place blessed by a divine covenant.[58]

This perceived affinity would perhaps have prepared readers conceptually to slip into the Jews' position within the images and narrative. This would not be an unmixed blessing. The Israelites are frequently forced into contact with these giants, who occupy the land promised to them, much as the

---

55 Numbers 13:24 and 27.
56 Vulgate Numbers 13:28 and OE Numbers 13:28, f. 117v.
57 Vulgate Numbers 13:24: 'Palmitem cum uva.'
58 Howe, "Looking for Home in Anglo-Saxon England," 157. See also Howe, *Migration and Mythmaking in Anglo-Saxon England*, 33–7, Withers, *The Illustrated Old English Hexateuch*, 138, and Wormald, "*Engla Lond*: The Making of an Allegiance," 1–24, at 14.

Anglo-Saxon's myths of origin filled Britain with giants in need of eradication before the land could be settled.[59]

In both of the images discussed here, the giants of the Hexateuch are connected with passages describing the destruction of sinful humans. In both cases, the biblical text seems to connect the sins and ensuing destruction with men, rather than with these giants. However, the proximity of text and image, conjoined with exegesis and marginal commentaries creates meaning, in both cases rendering the giants as sinful, suspect, and, notably, on the verge of destruction. This rendering is in keeping with an Anglo-Saxon view of giants that, according to Cohen, "represent[s] the unassimilated remnant of [the] past," as seen in *The Ruin*.[60] Indeed, the commentator not only added a note connecting the Tower of Babel on folio 19 with the giant Nimrod, perhaps following commentaries by Bede, Isidore, and Petrus Comestor,[61] but also restored a line omitted in the paraphrase on folio 125, describing "Og rex basan. Gigas. ⁊ potens" (King Og of Bashan, the giant, and powerful; Figures 25 and 26).[62] Again and again, the translators, designer, illuminators, and commentator stress the vital role played by giants as figures against which the Israelites (and therefore the Anglo-Saxons) might struggle and thereby define themselves.

The Crown of Horns

In the image on folio 124v, above the commentator's note about the giant Og, a hieratically enlarged, horned figure of Moses violently collides with the literal giants of Genesis (Figure 25). In the chaotic, unfinished image, the Israelites at last redeem themselves for their cowardice in the face of the Sons of Anak. Here, "Israhel ofsloh. og þone cyninge. ⁊ his suna ⁊ his folc eall to forwyrde" (Israel slew King Og and his sons and all his people to death).[63] In this image, however, an interesting inversion occurs. While Og is the giant, according to the Vulgate and the marginal comment on folio

---

59 See, for example, Geoffrey of Monmouth, *The Historia regum britannie of Geoffrey of Monmouth*, I, ed. Wright, 13: "Erat tunc nomen insule Albion que a nemine exceptis paucis hominibus gigantibus inhabitabatur."
60 Cohen, *Of Giants*, 5 and 8–9.
61 Dean, "The World Grown Old and Genesis in Middle English Historical Writings," 548–68, at 566.
62 BL, Cotton Claudius B.iv, fol. 124, lower margin.
63 OE Numbers 21:35, f. 124r.

124v, the combatants in the image all seem roughly the same size and can be distinguished only by their headgear. Meanwhile, Moses stands at the far left edge of the image, erect and oversized, filling the frame from top to bottom. He appears somewhat estranged from his followers, horned and majestic. Moses is very similarly posed and placed on the facing folio (Figure 25). In both images, violent chaos rages before him, and on both folios a figure at the exact centre of the image – perhaps the giant King Og, himself – is beheaded.[64] The corpses of the Ogites already litter the base of the image so thickly that the troops must stand upon them to battle on-ward. And while this occurs, Moses, otherworldly in his stature, wearing his prodigious horns, converses calmly with God, whose immense hand emerges from a bloody red cloud above the image's frame to deliver the promise of victory.[65] Below, the disparity in size is even more apparent, as Moses leads his followers towards Moab. Here, the mighty warriors who have just annihilated Og and his army seem like schoolchildren, like "grasshoppers" behind their leader's towering presence.

While horns are an emblem of monstrosity, Moses's horns seem to be removable, thereby marking Moses as different without rendering him in-human. Thus, Mellinkoff and others have shown that the horns of Moses, represented "as horns on a hat or headdress, not as organic growths," were viewed as a positive symbol when first represented, rather than as the symbol of ignominy they have since become.[66] His hieratic scale is likewise surely honorific. On folio 105v, Moses ascends the mountain as a normal man, but returns altered after his direct, "face to face" contact with God (Figure 28). This is the first appearance of the horned headdress in the manuscript.[67] He is also larger. If placed side by side, the first figure of Moses would reach only to the shoulder of his own later self, suggesting

---

64 Cohen, *Of Giants*, 64, discusses this image.

65 OE Numbers 21:34, f. 124r.

66 Mellinkoff, *Horned Moses*, 17. Mellinkoff, *Horned Moses*, 13, called the Hexateuch "the earliest artistic representation thus far found of horns on Moses" in 1970, and held to this belief in 1986 (see "More about Horned Moses," 184). The image of Moses with a single horn in the Uta Codex is also dated to the middle of the eleventh century, and Uta may predate the Hexateuch by a few decades. Regardless, as Adam Cohen notes, "whether the horned Moses in the Uta Codex precedes or follows the Old English Hexateuch, the two depictions have nothing to do with one another." See Cohen, *The Uta Codex*, 126.

67 Mellinkoff, *Horned Moses*, 17, notes that this is the first original occurrence, though previous images have horns added by a later hand.

that he has suddenly grown in importance at this moment.[68] Because direct contact with God could be disfiguring or even deadly, the image must contain a visual representation of such change.[69] The emphasis on images of a giant, horned Moses by both the designer and commentator emerge out of the context of medieval English cultural interests. Throughout the Hexateuch, the texts and the images with which they are conjoined make clear that the giants are evil, sinful creatures in need of eradication. The horned Moses stands in stark contrast to these monstrous representations. To align him directly with these beings would be a misunderstanding of the illuminators' intent. And yet, he is unquestionably presented on a grand scale, larger than any other figures save the antediluvian giants of Genesis 6:4, larger even than the figures of God in the Creation cycle at the beginning of the manuscript. In the images of folios 124v and 125, Moses's violent conquest of the giants allows his own form of grandeur to supplant theirs. Perhaps this was analogous in the minds of Anglo-Saxon readers to the conquest of the gigantic aboriginal inhabitants of Britain.

The Grandeur of Moses

Returning to the image on folio 139v with which I began my discussion (see Figure 21), we see Moses, at the lower left, blessing the Israelites with his right hand, shortly before his death (depicted at the top of the image).[70] Because of the Anglo-Saxon identification with the "Old Testament" Israelites, Moses is here also, in a sense, blessing the intended readers/ viewers. As Withers notes regarding an image of Moses reading to the Israelites on folio 100v, the Old English text of the Hexateuch informs us that Moses is said to speak to the *folc*, and in doing so "joins the reader and the hearer into a community based on the reading and public display

---

68   In other simultaneous narrations in the Hexateuch, such as the sacrifice of Isaac in fol. 38, the main figure (Abraham) remains consistent throughout his three appearances, suggesting that the enlargement of Moses was a conscious choice.

69   Propp, "The Skin of Moses' Face – Transfigured or Disfigured?" 375–86, at 384, notes that "the Bible is replete with tales of men killed by contact with the divine sphere. Accordingly, we might suppose that the unusual condition of Moses' skin after meeting Yahweh was in fact an injury or disfigurement." Propp, 384, continues to assert, following Eerdmans, that "the function of the *masweh* [the veil he holds before his face, depicted on folio 105v] was to spare the people the gruesome sight." See Eerdmans, *The Covenant at Mount Sinai Viewed in Light of Antique Thought*, 20–2.

70   The relevant texts are Vulgate Deuteronomy 33:1 and 34:7.

of text."[71] Behind him, slipping in from the left edge of the image's frame is the right hand of God, likewise in a traditional, two-fingered gesture of blessing. Moses's extended hand is tremendous, but larger still is the hand of God, which reaches down to the gigantic Moses just as his hand in turn reaches out to the huddled crowd before him. The hands are different in scale and orientation, but nearly identical in form. The implication is clear: In the most basic terms, Moses is greater than ordinary men, but God is greater still. In more metaphorical terms, this image is no doubt a reference to the role of Moses, alluded to above, as God's special representative to the people of Israel. The Vulgate prefaces the blessing given here as follows: "Haec est benedictio qua benedixit Moses homo Dei filiis Israhel ante mortem suam" (This is the blessing with which Moses, the man of God, blessed the sons of Israel before his death).[72] The paraphrase omits the remainder of chapter 33, so that while the Vulgate provides individual blessings for each of the tribes, the paraphrase simply informs us that "Moyses ða gebletsode ær his deaðe israhela bearn. ða twelf mægða ælce mid syndrigre bletsunge" (Moses then blessed before his death the children of Israel, then the twelve tribes, each separately with blessings).[73] Here, the specificity of the individual blessings is lost in favour of one group blessing, though perhaps the dative singular *mid syndrigre bletsunge* echoes the original Vulgate formulation.[74] The tribes are huddled together as a tightly bound mass, awed before the figure of Moses who towers over them. His figure has steadily (if not quite consistently) increased in size throughout the manuscript so that now, just before his death, the Israelites reach only to his waist. He appears more massive now than even the Anakim. Moses is positioned so that his left arm, extended in a gesture of blessing, stretches forward to overshadow the head of the foremost of the Israelites in a pose that emphasizes his height.

At the upper right of the image, we see Moses walking with a youthful, cross-nimbed figure labelled *D[omi]n[u]s* (Lord) by the commentator.[75] The two figures gaze across the opening of the manuscript at the facing

---

71 Withers, *The Illustrated Old English Hexateuch*, 162.

72 Vulgate Deuteronomy 33:1. While this image also recalls the image of Moses as the *manum robustam* (mighty hand) (Vulgate Deuteronomy 34:12), this phrase is also omitted from the paraphrase. Nonetheless, this may have informed the production of this image. My thanks to George Hardin Brown for bringing this to my attention.

73 OE Deuteronomy, 33:1, f. 139.

74 My thanks to an anonymous peer reviewer for this grammatical insight.

75 BL, Cotton Claudius B.iv, fol. 19. Comment in upper margin.

folio where they see the Promised Land and Gilead. At the left, the same divinity receives Moses's corpse, wrapped in a winding sheet. In the centre of the image, the Israelites mourn the death of Moses. The chronology of these scenes is somewhat confusing. Like the image of the sacrifice of Isaac on folio 38, we begin at the lower left and move upward, but if we are to follow the order of the narrative, we must move from lower left to upper right, then back to upper left and finally down to the central mourners. Although chronological, this pattern is rather complex, and in late Anglo-Saxon art, chronology does not always indicate the intended viewing order.[76]

In this image, rather than following the chronological conundrum outlined above, the eye flows in accordance with the visual pattern created by the layout of the image, moving in a zigzag up from Moses, through the Israelites, to the mourners, to the death scene, and finally ends with the walking pair, whose gazes in turn lead us towards the vision on the facing folio. As Withers writes, "Unlike the mourning Israelites, the readers and viewers of Claudius B.iv have been permitted to clamber up to the summit of Mount Nebo, where [Moses] is granted a view of the cities of the Land of Milk and Honey."[77] Enhanced by the presence of the cross-nimbed figure – Christ in the place of God the Father[78] – this pattern results in a vision of a resurrected Moses, a Moses so great that he has even triumphed over death; he appears to exceed the normal bounds of humanity. Cohen writes of "the body of the giant, the monstrous being that is undeniably both human and something Other (prehuman, posthuman)."[79] The giants of Genesis 6:4 are explicitly prehuman. Moses, following his direct contact with God atop Mount Sinai, has become posthuman, something beyond and above his followers, and his body is marked with the signs of his difference.[80]

This image has been compared several times with a somewhat similar composition in the Bible of San Paolo fuori le mura, which also shows

---

76 For example, see S. Lewis, *The Rhetoric of Power in the Bayeux Tapestry*, 63–4. See also Mittman and Kim, "Locating the Devil 'Her' in MS Junius 11."

77 See Withers, *The Illustrated Old English Hexateuch*, 266, for discussion of this image.

78 This substitution is also noticed and commented on by Withers, *The Illustrated Old English Hexateuch*, 266.

79 Cohen, *Of Giants*, 11.

80 For discussion of the posthuman monstrous, see MacCormack, "Post-Human Teratology."

the Blessing of the Tribes and the Death of Moses in three tiers (Figure 27).[81] Though not directly related to the Hexateuch, the San Paolo Bible provides an excellent point of comparison.[82] At the most basic level, the figure of Moses in the San Paolo image is neither horned nor gigantic.[83] He is of normal human scale, but haloed to indicate his sacred status. While the halo does set him apart from the majority of humanity, it does not denote Moses's intimate relationship with God, as the one man to view even a portion of his radiance. Further, the role of Moses as mediator between God and man – a prime focus of the Hexateuch image – is not nearly as prominent in the San Paolo image, as he speaks from the centre of the image, without the authoritative hand of God in blessing over him. He neither strolls with God, nor is his corpse personally received by him. Finally, while the compositions appear quite similar, the position of the Israelites alter the visual flow, so that in the San Paolo image, the vision of the Promised Land arrives before the death of Moses, rather than after it, as in the Hexateuch. This arrangement is more logical, surely, but does not visualize as directly or powerfully the greatness, the grandeur, of Moses.

Conclusion

The original audience for such manuscripts was expected to look beyond their outer appearance to their inner meaning. On one level, the hieratic representation of Moses is simply intended to convey his importance. Mellinkoff argues against a metaphorical reading of the horns, asserting that the illuminators were "probably unaware of the symbolical and

---

81 Gaehde and Mütherich, intro., *Carolingian Painting*, 27, places this manuscript at Reims ca. 870. It was made for Charles the Bald by Ingobertus, *scriba fidelis*.

82 Swarzenski, *Monuments of Romanesque Art*, 21; Mellinkoff, *Horned Moses*, 14–15; and Withers, *The Illustrated Old English Hexateuch*, 269. Withers provides an excellent discussion of the image throughout his final chapter and, at 269–77, provides an extended and useful comparison of the two images, with points of overlap with my current discussion, though his focus is largely on the image of the Land of Milk and Honey on the facing folio.

83 Later English manuscripts, such as the Lambeth Bible (also most likely from St Augustine's, Canterbury, ca. 1140–50) contain giant images of Moses. For the Lambeth Bible, London, Lambeth Palace Library MS 3 (vol. 1) and Maidstone Museum (vol. 2), see Kauffman, *A Survey of Manuscripts Illuminated in the British Isles*, 99, no. 70.

metaphorical aspects of biblical language. Thus they translated *gehyrned* into a literal image, a horned Moses."[84] This conjecture assumes a lack of oversight by a learned cleric, though other images in the manuscript would clearly have required exegetical input. Nonetheless, a literal image need not be devoid of further meaning. The designer of the image could have understood the presumed metaphorical intent of "horned" and still chosen to represent him as such. At a similar level of comprehension, Moses's scale may be both literal and symbolic at the same time. I believe that an Anglo-Saxon audience would have read in these images some of the qualities that are associated with giants – tremendous power ("They are the mighty ones from ancient times, and men of renown"),[85] but also an ontological complexity, a status as not quite human. Unlike some biblical characters, Moses possesses great ambiguities. He alone converses directly with God, and is marked by the experience (explicitly, here) with features that set him apart.[86] Indeed, he even requires a curtain to separate himself from his followers at certain moments, as on folio 105v (Figure 28).[87]

The figure of Moses in the Old English Hexateuch complicates the notion that giants are pure representations of sinfulness. Such an analysis would have been too simplistic, and would also not have accounted for the human-like appearance of some of the giants in this manuscript. Indeed, further into his commentary on Genesis, Bede states that "'gigans' aliquando in bono, ut est istud de Domino, *Exultauit ut gigas ad currendam uiam*" (the "giant" at times is in accordance with good, when they descend from God, *like a giant rejoicing to run the course*).[88] He therefore ties Genesis 6:4 to Psalm 18:6, where the racing giant is generally interpreted as a symbol of Christ. This is the passage illustrated in the Harley Psalter, mentioned above. Bede provides an analogy to help his readers, pointing out that symbols can stand for two diametrically opposed concepts. In relation to the giants, he writes, "sicut etiam 'leo' aliquando Dominum, aliquando diabolum designat. Sed diabolum propter superbiam et ferocitatem, Dominum propter potentiam" (just so, "the lion" sometimes symbolizes

---

84 Mellinkoff, *Horned Moses*, 26.

85 OE Genesis 6:4–7, f. 12v. See n21.

86 Vulgate and OE Deuteronomy 34:7 and Exodus 34.

87 Vulgate and OE Exodus 34:33. Moses holds a curtain on a rod before him on several folios of the Hexateuch, including fol. 105v, depicting the moment he descends from the mountaintop.

88 Bede, *Libri Quatuor in Principium Genesim*, 101.

the Lord and sometimes the devil. But the devil on account of pride and savageness, [and] the Lord on account of power).[89] Bede is, as usual, subtle and sophisticated. He is willing to accept the possibility of giants that are "in accordance with good," so long as "they descend from God." Surely this language could be applied to Moses as he appears in the Hexateuch.

The giants and the giant Moses demarcate opposing poles, bounding humanity between them. They show the power of the enemies of God's "chosen people" (Israelite or Anglo-Saxon), but also the means to overcome them. The key images in the sequence of the life of Moses – his transformation upon direct contact with God, his death, marked by the receipt of his corpse by God, as well as over a dozen images between these two – depict Moses conversing with God, who appears as a hand emerging from the clouds; these images stress time and again that Moses's power does not come from within. The otherworldliness of Moses's power source is reinforced in the image of the battle with Pharaoh's magicians on folio 81v where, through God's power, Aaron's staff turns into a snake to swallow those created by the magicians.

The depiction of Moses's death on folio 139v follows a series of folios in which nineteen out of twenty-two contain no image (Figure 21). This is the by far the longest sequence of text-only folios in the manuscript, and it consequently focuses increased attention on the full-page, boldly coloured image of the blessing, vision, and death of Moses. Furthermore, there are only six other full-page images out of the 400 in this manuscript, another indicator of the great importance of the scene. This image, then, was central to the designer's understanding of the story of the Hexateuch.

On this folio, we confront one of the most impressive images of Moses in the manuscript, horned and gigantic. Moses's horns are clearly part of a headdress, indicating that they are not organic parts of his body, but there is no way to separate the figure's size from the presentation of the great Jewish prophet. Above Moses's giant form, though, is the indication of a being far greater. The hand of God looms over him, blessing him with precisely the same gesture he blesses his followers. This correspondence is further emphasized by the nearly identical poses of the figures of Moses and Christ at the upper right of this image. They both stand with their bodies pointed to the right, their knees bent, their left feet raised higher than their right, their hands up and open. Even the hems of their drapery

---

89 Ibid.

are nearly identical. Through this visual echo, the image stresses the continuity of God's presence from "Old Testament" to "New," in accordance with the notion of the Anglo-Saxons that they were a new "chosen people," like the Jews of antiquity.[90] The most notable differences between the figures are the substitution of horns for halo, suggesting the honorific intent of the horns, and the position of the heads. Instead of facing out to the Promised Land, Christ turns back to look at Moses. Here, in this final scene, Moses returns to normal stature. While in previous images he towered over all the earthly figures around him, even including the giant Og, in the presence of Christ he is brought down to size.

The presence of the giant hand of God behind him, at the left edge of the image here, and hovering over him throughout the Hexateuch, clarifies that Moses is being conceived of as an instrument of the greatest of powers. He mirrors God's gesture, below, and his pose, above, and in so doing, demonstrates his accord with God. In this way, the designer of the Hexateuch recasts the Jewish Bible as a prefiguration of the Christian concept of *fortissimus Christi*. For the monastic creators of this manuscript, Moses could have been seen as following the imperative of Saint Benedict, in the second sentence of his Rule, under which they lived: "Domino Christo vero regi militaturus, oboedientiae fortissimo atque praeclara arma sumis" (Take up the most strong and bright weapons of obedience, to fight for the Lord Christ, the true king).[91] Moses is continually shown as obedient to the directives of the hand of God, and also as a fighter for him, and his gigantic size makes him the visual equal of the giants he must oppose.

The giants of the Hexateuch are neither biblical nor medieval, in their entirety. They are hybrid monsters, a fusion of biblical text and Anglo-Saxon interpretation. As a result, it is difficult to summarily dismiss them all as monstrous Others. A reader identifying with the Israelites would see himself both violently overcoming giants, and led by one as well. Unlike other monsters, like dragons or gryphons, giants look more or less like we do. The massive figures of Genesis 6:4, for example, are only subtly distinguished in appearance from the family of Noah on the facing folio (see Figures 22 and 23). They are greater and more terrible, and yet not wholly Other. Such monsters were a vital component of the worldviews

---

90 Howe, "Looking for Home in Anglo-Saxon England," 157 and Howe, *Migration and Mythmaking in Anglo-Saxon England*, 33–7 and n58 above.
91 Butler, *S. Benedicti Regula*, 1.

of their creators and, as such, were pointedly included in the Hexateuch by its original eleventh-century translators, designer, and illuminators, and emphasized again by the twelfth-century commentator. Where, then, do viewers sit in the world presented by the Hexateuch? Neither evil giant nor prophetic giant, Anglo-Saxon viewers become like the Israelites depicted in the manuscript: fascinated, fearful spectators, watching the mightiest members of creation battling for dominance. In doing so, they would be reminded of their own modest scale, their own small place in what the Anglo-Saxons saw as the universe's divine order.

Epilogue: Pre- and Post-Conquest Identifications: Continuity and Difference

12 Reading Ælfric in the Twelfth Century: Anti-Judaic Doctrine Becomes Anti-Judaic Rhetoric

HEIDE ESTES

In the decade before he became Abbot of Eynsham in 1005, Ælfric wrote voluminous saints' lives and homilies in Old English for use throughout the liturgical year. Two generations later, England changed dramatically, with the Norman Conquest and the subsequent upheavals in leadership and language use. However, Ælfric's work survives in numerous manuscripts from the eleventh and twelfth centuries, and some of the manuscripts were extensively annotated in the thirteenth century, demonstrating that they were used among English-speaking clerics and lay people for centuries after Ælfric's death.

After the Norman Conquest, Jewish communities were established across England, becoming numerous by the twelfth century. In 995, Ælfric's comments about Jews would have been understood as pertaining to Jews who lived far away, geographically and probably also temporally. After 1066, when Jews were living in England, however, these same offhand comments about Jewish wickedness, faithlessness, and hard-hearted slaughter of Jesus would have been understood as referring to the neighbours and community members of those who were hearing the sermons. The legal status of Jews was tenuous, and the preaching of the first Crusade encouraged violence against Jewish communities across northern Europe. In conjunction with these historical realities, when lay people regularly heard in sermons such as those by Ælfric that Jews were perfidious and treacherous people who had plotted collectively to kill Jesus, suspicions about the actions of their neighbours would have been a fairly unsurprising result. In fact, the first known accusation of Jewish ritual murder in northern Europe occurred in Norwich in 1142. Additional accusations followed in the subsequent decades, and riots against Jews began to occur in 1189 during the coronation of Richard I. Rereading Ælfric's homilies and saints' lives in the twelfth century results in meanings very different from those available to readers and auditors at the time of their conception at the beginning of the eleventh century.

Pre-Conquest England

Cecil Roth surveyed the evidence compiled by Joseph Jacobs and agreed that Jews did not live in England before the Norman Conquest. "Whether or no individuals visited the country, it may be stated with confidence that no permanent settlement was formed, no community established, and no synagogue built."[1] Roth's conclusion has been widely accepted by subsequent scholars of medieval Judaism.[2] In the tenth century, pilgrims and other travellers from England might well have come into contact with Jews in Rome or Aachen, but the numbers of individuals who would have made journeys to such places was limited, and such journeys would not likely have resulted in prolonged contact. The vast majority of the Anglo-Saxon people would not have travelled far from their home communities and would have had no contact with Jews and no knowledge of Jewish communities, religion, ritual, or daily life.

Stephen Harris argues that ethnicity in early medieval Europe, including Anglo-Saxon England, was tribal rather than national, and that one of the distinguishing features was a "common tongue, a shared language, … the material for a shared compendium of songs and stories."[3] Harris argues that it is important to investigate notions of race and ethnicity as observable from written Anglo-Saxon texts, rather than mapping onto the period modern notions of race or ethnicity.[4] He notes, further, that the ontological problem in dealing with difference is that outsiders must be understood through one's own language. "Querying the foreign via a complex of implication and metaphor inherent in one's native tongue was (and is) an important function of literary culture."[5] In Anglo-Saxon textual sources, "foreigners and outsiders are sometimes spoken of as monstrous or as fearsome variations on existing creatures … Whatever or whoever is described as new or alien, if not too terrible, may be accommodated into

---

1 Roth, *A History of the Jews in England*, 2.
2 Ben-Sasson, ed., *A History of the Jewish People*, 394; Scheil, *The Footsteps of Israel*, 3.
3 Harris, *Race and Ethnicity*, 10.
4 Ibid., 8.
5 Ibid., 10.

domestic categories."[6] He points out, however, that describing a group of non-Anglo-Saxon people as a category is distinct from describing individual foreigners, and "applying that category to the real world is another story entirely."[7] He observes, moreover, that ethnicity is a cultural rather than a biological construct: "Ethnic origins and racial particularity may derive not from any fact of race, but from the semantic demands of a matrix of metaphors, a model, locked in language and in books."[8]

Post-Conquest Jewish Settlement

Following the establishment of Norman rule, Jews fairly rapidly established communities in England, and by the twelfth century lived in London as well as in numerous towns across the Southwest and the Midlands. References to Jewish communities begin to appear in documentary sources in the early twelfth century. A "Street of the Jews" is recorded in London by 1128, and the Pipe Roll contains references to Jewish financial activity in 1130.[9] In 1141, Jews had established a community in Oxford.[10] By the start of Henry II's reign in 1154, official records made reference to Jewish communities in London, Norwich, Lincoln, Winchester, Cambridge, Thetford, Northampton, Bungay, Oxford, and Gloucester (in order of decreasing financial significance and probably numerical size)[11] as well as in Bristol and York.[12] The Jew Aaron of Lincoln, who died around 1186 as the wealthiest person in England, had recorded financial transactions with "private individuals"[13] among whom were the Archbishop of Canterbury and the Abbot of Westminster, the bishops of Bangor and Lincoln, and numerous earls and other members of the aristocracy, as well as with the towns of Winchester and Southampton.[14] Jews in other communities across England also served as bankers.[15] Jews journeyed together with clerics, and used St Paul's Cathedral in London to seek out debtors.[16] By the end of Henry's

---

6 Ibid., 12.
7 Ibid., 11.
8 Ibid., 36.
9 Roth, *History of the Jews*, 7.
10 Ibid., 8.
11 Ibid., 11.
12 Ibid., 12.
13 Ibid., 15.
14 Ibid., 15–16. See also Ben-Sasson, *History of the Jewish People*, 473.
15 Roth, *History of the Jews*, 15.

rule (1189), there were also Jewish communities in Exeter, Stamford, Lynn, Bury, Bedford, Devizes, Ipswich, Canterbury, Hereford, Dunstable, Chichester, and Newport – as well as small communities or isolated families in other places including Nottingham, Winchester, Worcester, and Leicester.[17] Including the communities already established earlier, by 1189 Jews are known to have lived in communities of varying size in 28 towns and cities as far west as Hereford and as far north as York.[18] In other words, there would have been frequent and regular contact between Christians and Jews at various social levels.

With the establishment of identifiable Jewish communities, anti-Jewish activity and sentiment developed. Gavin Langmuir points out that hostility towards Jews was greatest in northern Europe, where communities were newly established rather than of long duration.[19] In England, claims that Jews ritually slaughtered Christian children were made in 1144, 1168, 1181, and 1183, though there is no evidence that Jews committed any such atrocities. During the coronation of Richard I in 1189, residents of York rioted against Jews, who took refuge in the castle where they faced the choice of death by starvation or baptism. Instead, they committed suicide en masse.[20] In the following year there were additional riots against the Jews in several other cities.

In 1144, a boy named William was found dead in the woods outside Norwich. Rumors arose that he had been crucified by Jews, but the Sheriff of Norwich protected the Jewish community. Nevertheless, Thomas of Monmouth wrote a *Life of William* in which he dubbed him a saint and invented a tale of ritual murder. Thomas's work was written over a long period, but Langmuir uses internal evidence to date the first book in the *Life* to about 1149–50, four to five years after the events occurred.[21] Thomas's

---

16   Ibid., 11.

17   Ibid., 12.

18   Ibid., 11–12.

19   Langmuir, "Anti-Judaism as the Necessary Preparation for Antisemitism," in *Toward a Definition of Antisemitism*, 57–62.

20   Ben-Sasson, *History of the Jewish People*, 420.

21   Langmuir, "Thomas of Monmouth: Detector of Ritual Murder," in *Toward a Definition of Antisemitism*, 209–36, at 223–4. See also Bennett, "Towards a Revaluation of the Legend of 'Saint' William of Norwich," 119–39, at 120. Langmuir's conclusions are generally accepted, but have been challenged by Israel J. Yuval, as summarized by McCulloh, "Jewish Ritual Murder," 698–740, who argues for a later date of composition for Thomas's legend, 700–1 and passim.

legend is then summarized in the Peterborough Chronicle entry for 1155.[22] Accusations of ritual murder of Christian children by Jews then crop up repeatedly in medieval English literature; in the twelfth century there were accusations at Gloucester (1168), Bury St Edmond's (1181), and Winchester (1192), with several additional such claims made in several English communities in the thirteenth century.[23] Chaucer's *Prioress's Tale* is probably the best-known version. Norwich was the third-wealthiest city in England in the early Middle Ages, and with 200 Jews had the second-largest Jewish community; only London was home to a larger number of Jews.[24]

Gillian Bennett argues that, rather than being the source of anti-Jewish sentiment, claims about ritual murder grew out of existing antipathy towards Jews. "I think it is very probable that, in England at least, accusations of Jewish child-murder were part of anti-Jewish feeling rather than a primary cause of it."[25] Bennett further notes that scholars have tended to view Thomas of Monmouth's tale of ritual murder in Norwich as an "aberration," but, pointing to the attacks on Jews by Crusaders towards the end of the twelfth century, argues that, in fact, the Jewish political situation in England was complex and potentially difficult, and relationships with Christians may generally have been difficult.[26]

Anti-Judaism and Anti-Semitism

In this context, the copies of Ælfric's homilies, with their many negative references to Jews, would have been read and heard very differently than in the context in which they were originally written, and could possibly have enabled a climate of political and social antipathy towards actual Jews. A typical example is the homily for Palm Sunday, copied in four twelfth-century manuscripts,[27] which concerns Jesus' final journey to Jerusalem. Jesus asks his disciples to go and get him a donkey:

---

22 Langmuir, "Thomas of Monmouth," 210.
23 Heng, "Jews, Saracens, 'Black Men,' Tartars," 247–68, at 252. See also Depres, "Adolescence and Sanctity," 33–62, at 33.
24 Bennett, "Towards a Re-Evaluation," 123.
25 Bennett, "William of Norwich and the Expulsion of the Jews," 311–14, at 311.
26 Bennett, "Towards a Re-Evaluation," 123–4; "Thomas of Monmouth," 313.
27 Bodley 343 (second quarter of twelfth century); CCCC 302 (late eleventh/early twelfth century); CCCC 303 (first quarter of twelfth century); BL Cotton Faustina A.ix (first quarter of twelfth century).

euntes autem discipuli fecerunt sicut praecepit illis Iesus et adduxerunt asinam et pullum et inposuerunt super eis vestimenta sua et eum desuper sedere fecerunt plurima autem turba straverunt vestimenta sua in via alii autem caedebant ramos de arboribus et sternebant in via. (Matthew 21:6–8)

(Then the disciples went and did as Jesus had directed, and brought the donkey and her foal; they laid their cloaks on them and Jesus mounted. Crowds of people carpeted the road with their cloaks, and some cut branches from the trees to spread in his path.)[28]

In the Homily for Palm Sunday, Ælfric has quite a bit to say about the donkey:

"Se getigeda assa ⁊ his fola getacniað twa folc þ[æt] is iudeisc. ⁊ hæþn … Hi wæron getigede for ðan þe eal mancynn wæs mid synnum bebunden."

(The tied donkey and his foal betoken two people, that is, Jews and heathens … They were tied, because all mankind was bound with sins.)[29]

A few lines later, Ælfric adds more:

Assa is stunt nyten ⁊ unclæne ⁊ toforan oðrum nytenum ungesceadwis; … Se getemede assa hæfde getacnunge þæs iudeiscan folces. þe wæs getemed under þære ealdan .æ.; Se wilda fola hæfde getacnunge ealles oðres folces þe wæs þa gyt hæðen ⁊ ungetemed.

(The donkey is a stupid beast and unclean and more irrational than other beasts … The tame donkey betokens the Jewish people, who were tamed under the old law; the wild foal betokens all other peoples, who were as yet heathen and undomesticated.)[30]

---

28 *The Holy Bible Douay-Rheims Version*, with revisions and footnotes (in the text in italics) by Bishop Richard Challoner, 1749–52, Taken from a hardcopy of the 1899 Edition by the John Murphy Company. Web. www.drbo.org. Accessed 17 August 2012. Translation is from *The Oxford Study Bible*, ed. Suggs, Sakenfeld, and Mueller.
29 *CH* 1.14.42, 45–6, *Dominica Palmarum*.
30 *CH* 1.14.54–5, 61–3.

In the gospel account, Jesus celebrates Passover with his disciples, and is then betrayed to the Roman authorities by Judas, acting alone.[31] According to Ælfric, however, the Jewish leaders conspired to bring about his death:

Þa namon þa heafodmen. andan. ongean his lare. ⁊ syrewydon mid micelre smeagunge. hu hi mihton hine to deaðe gebringan; ... þeahhwæðere ne nydde he na þ[æt] iudeisce folc to his cweale. ac deoful hi tihte to ðam weorce.

(Then the leaders took enmity against his teaching, and plotted with much thinking how they might bring him to death ... nevertheless, he did not compel the Jewish people to kill him, but the devil incited them to that deed.)[32]

In this frequently copied sermon, Ælfric goes beyond the language of the Biblical text in assigning culpability for Jesus's death to a conspiracy among the Jewish leaders, rather than attributing it to the betrayal of a single individual followed by the actions of a rioting crowd.

Ælfric's comments about Jews fall into a category of discourse often referred to as "anti-Judaic," as distinct from "anti-Semitic," a term generally applied to later and more virulent anti-Jewish sentiment. Gavin Langmuir defines anti-Judaism as "a total or partial opposition to Judaism – and to Jews as adherents of it – by people who accept a competing system of beliefs and practices and consider certain genuine Judaic beliefs and practices as inferior."[33] He points out that anti-Judaism can arise, and has arisen, in pagan and communist contexts, but "the Christian has been the most intense because of the intimate dependency of Christianity on Judaism."[34]

Langmuir distinguishes "three aspects" of Christian anti-Judaism: "the doctrinal, the legal and the popular."[35] Doctrinal anti-Judaism refers to Christological readings of the Hebrew Bible that claim that good Jews anticipated Christians and Christianity, but that most pre-Christian Jews and all Jews since the advent of Christianity are "at the least inferior to Christians and, at the strongest, the polar enemies of Christianity."[36] Under legal anti-Judaism, Langmuir refers to laws restricting Jews from various

---

31 See, e.g., Matthew 26.
32 *CH* 1.14.159–61, 163–5.
33 Langmuir, "Anti-Judaism," 57.
34 Ibid., 57.
35 Ibid., 58.
36 Ibid.

activities that would allow them control over Christians, whether via public office or slave ownership.

Langmuir argues that "popular" anti-Judaism arose only in the eleventh century and only in northern Europe, where Christian identity and Jewish communities were both more recent developments. Under these circumstances "indoctrination in Christianity and its attendant anti-Judaism had here proved more explosive than its propagators had intended."[37] In the thirteenth century, "popular" anti-Judaism – which Langmuir defines as based in realities that Jews were involved in money-lending and rejected Christianity – gave way to anti-Semitism, which he distinguishes from anti-Judaism because it is based on "new accusations of ritual murder, host desecration and well-poisoning [that] were not faulty and inflexible generalizations but false fantasies unsupported by evidence."[38]

In the interval between the period of Ælfric's composition in the late tenth century, and the re-inscription and reuse of his words in the twelfth century, after Jews had settled England, a transition from "doctrinal" to "popular" anti-Judaic sentiment occurs. This shift occurs between the time that Ælfric was writing, shortly before 1000 when no Jews lived in England and his anti-Judaic writings were purely doctrinal, and the twelfth century, when the copyists, readers, and hearers of his sermons lived in a society in which Jews were present. The twelfth century in England also saw the creation of a legal atmosphere that punished Jews, with disproportionately high taxation[39] and limits on Jewish participation in economic and social life.[40]

The inscription of the texts in the twelfth century, then, carries a significance different from that borne at the time of their composition at the end of the tenth century or of their transmission in seven surviving manuscripts of the eleventh century. In a discussion of reader response to texts, Jane Tompkins points out a major shift since the Middle Ages in the significance of reading a text (or hearing one read). Classical rhetoric takes the text as "the instrument of a social transaction."[41] For the medieval period, "[t]he text remains an object rather than an instrument, an occasion for

---

37 Ibid., 60.
38 Ibid., 61.
39 Roth, *History of the Jews*, 16–17.
40 Ibid., 7–8.
41 Tompkins, "The Reader in History," 201–32, at 211.

the elaboration of meaning rather than a force exerted upon the world."[42] In the past century or so, however, literary scholars have read texts as sites of interpretation, whether they locate meaning(s) within the text itself or in the individual reading selves. Ælfric wrote his homilies not for modern critics to interpret or analyze, but to persuade his audience to follow Christian ideals; those who copied the homilies and read them aloud in the twelfth century had the same purpose. In a document designed, then, to persuade hearers of the truth of the Christian religion, comments about the perfidy of the Jews take on significant social power.

The transmission of anti-Jewish ideas in a time and place devoid of Jews is problematic in the willingness to scapegoat an entire community and to use depictions of that community in the projection of unity and identity within one's own community. But the transmission of such ideas in a context of coexistence with actual Jews may have created a climate that enabled violence against the Jewish community. The continued inscription and annotation of Ælfrician texts implies their continued use in preaching contexts; the anti-Judaic ideas in them, then, might well have encouraged those who perpetrated violence against the Jews. Richard I's failure to punish those who had rioted against Jews during and after his coronation may well have been related to the transmission of such anti-Judaic claims. The lack of punishments inflicted on those who participated in violence against Jews – to whom the rioters were also often indebted for outstanding loans – would have amounted to tacit encouragement for further acts of violence.

After the arrival of Jews in England, then, Ælfric's sermons have the potential to be read as anti-Jewish rather than anti-Judaic. They have the potential to be heard as referring to one's neighbours or the family living in the next town, rather than being heard as directed against the non-Christian religious practices of a group that lived elsewhere, far away in space and in time. Ælfric's habit of collapsing the Jews that lived at the time of Christ with Jews everywhere, at all times, would have very different meaning when people were living side by side with Jews, depending upon Jews for business and personal loans, drawing upon Jewish transactions for tax purposes.

---

42 Ibid., 225.

Ælfric's Anti-Judaic Rhetoric

In the tenth century, Ælfric was using models of racial and ethnic belonging to attempt to unite Danes and Angles and other tribal groups of memory, asserting Christian unity against Jewish and pagan otherness, including against the pagans of the Anglo-Saxons' own past. When Jews came to England, they had to be conceived of according to these existing categories of unity and otherness. Harris's observations on how new members of a community need to be named and described using existing linguistic paradigms helps to explain why this was so: Ælfrician sermons and saints' lives created a framework in the English language for the absent Jew that associated Jews with terms like "bloodthirsty" and "savage." When the Jews arrived into England and were inserted into existing linguistic paradigms, the results couldn't really be anything but problematic.

As Andrew Scheil has argued, anti-Judaic discourse was widespread in Anglo-Saxon England as "a meditative vehicle for exegesis" used in "a variety of representational strategies built into the very structure of medieval Christianity."[43] While travellers might have encountered Jewish people in Rome or Aachen, most people's knowledge of Jews would have been limited to what they learned within a Christian context: from hearing the Bible read, or listening to commentaries on it; from hearing sermons or lives of saints. Jews were presented as the other, as a figuration that consolidated Christian identity in a time of gradual conversion from paganism, but they were an abstract other, demonized in abstract form. Ælfric's sermons were anti-Judaic rather than anti-Semitic: directed at the Jewish people as a group, and in terms of religious practice, rather than at Jewish individuals in terms of individual ethnic identity.

For Ælfric and other pre-Conquest writers, "the Jew" was an absent "other" opposed to English Christians as a function of doctrine. Ælfric was dealing with textually, rather than personally, transmitted ideas about Jews. His notion of "the Jew" as deicide was a religious construct, a more or less abstract aid to the idea that several formerly pagan kingdoms of England could combine in Christian community and unity. In Ælfric's homilies and saints' lives, by far the greatest number of negative comments about Jews involve the claim that the Jews killed Jesus. As noted above, these comments echo, but also go beyond, the language in the Gospels.

---

43 Scheil, *The Footsteps of Israel*, 3.

The Gospel accounts describe Judas acting alone to betray Jesus. In the homily for Palm Sunday quoted above, Ælfric blames the Jewish leaders; in *De Initio Creaturae* he writes that the Jewish people plotted collectively with Judas to find a way to put Jesus to death:

Ða nam þ[æt] iudeisce folc micelne andan ongean his lare. ⁊ smeadon hu hi mihton hine to deaðe gedon; Ða wearð an þæra twelfa cristes þegena se wæs Iudas gehaten þurh deofles tyhttinge beswicen. ⁊ he eode to ðam Iudeiscan folce ⁊ smeade wið hi hu he crist him belæwen mihte.[44]

(Then the Jewish people had much anger against his teaching, and conspired how they might do him to death. Then one of the twelve thegns of Christ who was called Judas was seduced by the devil's enticement, and he went to the Jewish people and conspired with them how he could betray Christ to them.)

It is important here for the twelfth-century reception of this passage that the Jews are twice identified as *þæt iudeisce folc* (the Jewish people) – not a handful of individuals, but the people as a whole. The idea that the Jews conspired collectively to kill Jesus is repeated in several of Ælfric's homilies.[45]

Even more frequent, appearing in at least ten homilies, is the claim that Christ "from iudeum on rode ahanged wæs" (was hanged on the cross by the Jews).[46] In some of Ælfric's examples, the devil is supposed to have incited the Jews to violence. More problematic once Jews have settled England is the additional comment about the Cross, "þæt com us to hæle and to ecere alysednysse and heom to forwyrde" (that [the cross] brings us [Christians, English people] to health and to eternal redemption, and them [the Jews] to destruction, *Forty Soldiers*, lines 319–20).[47] This comment suggests that the perfidy with which Ælfric identifies the Biblical Jews is not seen as a fact of the past, but is understood to have contemporary

---

44 *CH* 1.1.265–9, *De Initio Creaturae*.

45 Examples include "Natale Innocentium Infantum," "Natale Sancte Pauli," "In Festivitate Sancti Petri Apostoli," and "Dominica Palmarum." *CH* 1.5, and 27; *CH* 2.24, and 14.

46 *CH* 2.27.23 See also *CH* 2.4; *CH* 1.10, 20, 27, 31, 38; and Pope, ed., *Homilies of Ælfric*, 4, 7, 21.

47 Skeat, ed. *Ælfric's Lives of Saints*, vol. 1, 256 and 258.

and ongoing resonance. For Ælfric, writing at a time when Jews were a geographically distant people, this comment has a doctrinal significance, but for readers and auditors of the same homilies 150 or 200 years later, it may contribute to the development of what Langmuir calls "popular" anti-Judaic sentiment.

In addition to accusations of direct involvement in deicide, Ælfric regularly charges the Jews with lack of faith, and specifically with failure to recognize the divinity of Jesus (a claim that makes sense if one assumes that Jesus is in fact divine), assertions frequently in conjunction with the statement that Jews are hard-hearted (*heard-heortan*)[48] and bloodthirsty (*wælhreow*),[49] and that they act with malice (*teona*)[50] or with blasphemy (*hosp*).[51] Like the comment quoted above about the significance of the Cross, such accusations are frequently made in contexts which elide past and present, equating Jews at the time of Gospel events with Jews in Ælfric's present. In one example:

> Ða Iudeiscan noldon urne Drihten oncnawan / mid soðum geleafan, þæt he Godes Sunu is, / ac mid anwilnysse his wordum wiðcwædon, / and nabbað nu naðor ne þone Fæder ne hine, / swa swa he sylf sæde on sumum oðrum godspelle: / Se ðe me hata, he hatað minne Fæder.[52]

> (The Jews would not acknowledge our Lord with true belief, that He is God's son, but with obstinacy they contradicted His words, and now they have neither the Father nor Him, just as He Himself said in some other Gospel: He who hates me, he hates my Father.)

In not accepting Christian doctrine that Jesus was the son of God, Ælfric argues that Jews forfeit any relationship with God (as "Father"). The conflation of past with present would have been of little local significance in a place where Jews lived far away and could have been taken to belong in the distant past. However, when practising Jews lived in the same communities in which the homilies were being preached, the message would have the effect of vilifying the neighbours and their beliefs rather than simply

---

48   *CH* 1.15.180; 1.25.219–20; Pope, ed., *Homilies of Ælfric* 4, vol 1, 278, line 258.

49   *CH* 2.14.235, 310; Skeat, ed., *Ælfric's Lives of Saints*, XXXII (Edmund), 322, line 105.

50   *CH* 1.3.65 (Stephen).

51   *CH* 1.10.158; 22.55; *CH* 2.13.148.

52   Pope, ed., *Homilies of Ælfric*, vol. 1, 388, Homily 9, lines 201–6, *Dominica post Ascensionem Domini*.

asserting one's own faith in contrast to a theologically, geographically, and chronologically distinct people.

Several other insults to the Jews occur in one or more of Ælfric's homilies that were copied in the twelfth century, indicating their ongoing use by clerics and relevance to the population of England. The Jews are, for example, *reðe* (cruel, savage, wild,)[53]; they are *arleas* (worthless, dishonorable, impious),[54] *earm* (wretched),[55] and *þwyr* (perverse, depraved, bent).[56]

Meanwhile, Ælfric, like his contemporary Christian commentators, insists that the Hebrew Bible no longer has validity, but has been superseded by the "New Testament," and that the Jews fail to understand correctly their own bible. In *CH* 2.8, for instance, Ælfric writes of Christians, "We hedað þæra crumena ðæs hlafes. and ða Iudeiscan gnagað þa rinde. for ðan ðe we understandað þæt gastlice andgit þæra boca. and hi rædað þa stæflican gereccednysse buton andgite" (We heed the crumbs of the loaf, and the Jews gnaw the rind, because we understand the spiritual meaning of the books, and they read the literal narrative without understanding).[57] In the last decade of the tenth century, this claim would not have particular local relevance. In the twelfth century, however, when Jewish communities existed in England alongside Christian ones, the idea that the Jews misinterpreted the Hebrew Bible would have direct importance to relationships between individual Jews and Christians as well as between the two communities.

Like other Christian writers before him, Ælfric projects the construct of evil Jews backwards onto the Hebrew Scriptures or "Old Testament" so that any heroic Jewish figure is seen as anticipating Christianity, while negatively portrayed members of the Jewish people are interpreted as precursors of the "evil Jews" of the time of the Gospels who demurred at the idea that Jesus was the result of a virgin birth and the son of God. From this perspective, all good Jews within the Hebrew bible are seen as proto-Christians, while any bad Jews are taken as precursors of Jews living after the advent of Jesus and who are thus taken to be bad. This was perhaps the most problematic aspect of the teaching from the point of view of Jews

---

53 See, for example, *CH* 1.3.98, 120. See also Skeat, ed., *Lives of Saints*, vol. 1, 472, Apollinaris, line 6.

54 E.g., *CH* 1.7.93; see also *CH* 2.13.92; 32.124.

55 E.g., *CH* 1.28.39; see also Skeat, ed., *Lives of Saints* vol. 2, 334, Edmund, line 269.

56 E.g., *CH* 1.28.100.

57 *CH* 2.8.108–11, *Dominica II in Quadragesima*.

living in communities adjacent to those of Christians. For instance, Ælfric rehearses a frequently disseminated interpretation of Cain's slaughter of Abel: that "se mægslaga cain getacnode þæra iudeiscra geleafleaste. ðe crist mid niðe acwealdon. and þæt abeles slege getacnode drihtnes ðrowunge" ([that] the murderer Cain signified the unbelief of the Jews, who killed Christ with hatred, and that Abel's killing signified God's suffering).[58]

Ælfric similarly re-interprets the narrative of the Maccabees. From the point of view of the Hebrew Bible, and of those who take it as scriptural, the Books of the Maccabees celebrate the courage and persistence of Judah Maccabee and his family members in the face of religious persecution and war. Although other versions of the narrative circulated in Anglo-Saxon England, Ælfric does not seem to have consulted any of them, but rather to have drawn on the Biblical books of 1 and 2 Maccabees.[59] The Maccabees are generally seen as "good Jews," proto-Christian figures celebrated for insisting on the right to their religious observance. Yet Ælfric frames his version of the narrative with claims that "the Jews … reject our lord" (þa iudeiscan … urne drihten forseoð).[60] Some Jews followed Jesus, but others killed him.[61] Even though some of Jesus's Jewish contemporaries accepted his divinity, the rest "live in opposition until today" (wunian wiðer-werde oþ þis).[62] The tense is important here: Ælfric does not say that Jews "rejected" Jesus, but that they "reject" him still; thus, twelfth-century Jews whose faith does not permit acceptance of a divine son of God are conflated with first-century Jews who, in Ælfric's reading of Gospel accounts, were not just complicit, but active conspirators, in the death of Jesus. The commentary on Maccabees is just one example of such insistence on the ongoing perfidy of the Jews among Ælfric's writings; he makes similar claims in several other saints' lives as well as numerous homilies.

Conclusion

As suggested by their expulsion from England in 1290, to accommodate the Jews into any category of "English" identity was impossible. And the

---

58 *CH* 2.4.107–9, *Dominia II Post Aepiphania*.
59 Halbrooks, "Ælfric, the Maccabees, and the Problem of Christian Heroism," 263–84, at 269.
60 See Ælfric's homily on the Maccabees; Lee, ed., *Ælfric's Homilies on Judith, Esther, and the Maccabees*, line 69.
61 Ibid., lines 551–3.
62 Ibid., line 526.

impossibility of such accommodation was created by a discourse about Jews that predated their arrival in England, a discourse to which Ælfric's comments in many, many sermons constitutes a significant contribution. For Ælfric in the tenth century, the figure of the absent Jew provided a way to unify Danes and Angles, Christians and recently absorbed pagans. In post-Conquest England, there was the problem of non-shared tongues: English speakers were pushed out of most positions of authority, secular and religious, by French speakers, with Latin as a possible common language. By the thirteenth century, Henry III was very much interested in Jewish conversion, though the existence of a home for converted Jews in thirteenth century London suggests that the Jews were viewed as other even if they converted to Christianity, and considered ethnically distinct even if they adopted the majority religion of the English. For readers of Ælfric's homilies two centuries after they were composed, the figuration of the actual Jew allowed Normans and Saxons to transcend the dislocations of Conquest and become one community, bound by Christianity and the otherness of the Jew.[63]

---

63 Cohen, "The Flow of Blood in Medieval Norwich," 28.

Figure 1. Portrait of Ezra. Codex Amiatinus, Florence, Biblioteca Medicea-Laurenziana, MS Amiatino I, fol. 5r. Reproduced by permission of MiBACT. Any further reproduction by any means is prohibited.

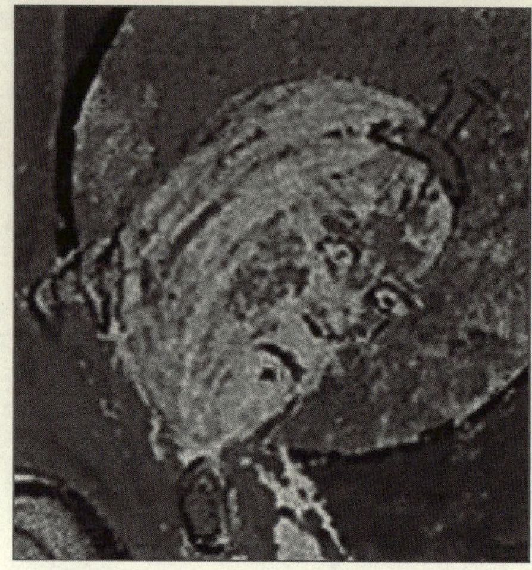

Figure 2. Detail of Ezra-portrait, showing forehead *tefillin* (?) (Codex Amiatinus, detail).

Figure 3. Portrait of Matthew. Lindisfarne Gospels, London, British Library, MS Cotton Nero D.iv, fol. 25v. © The British Library Board.

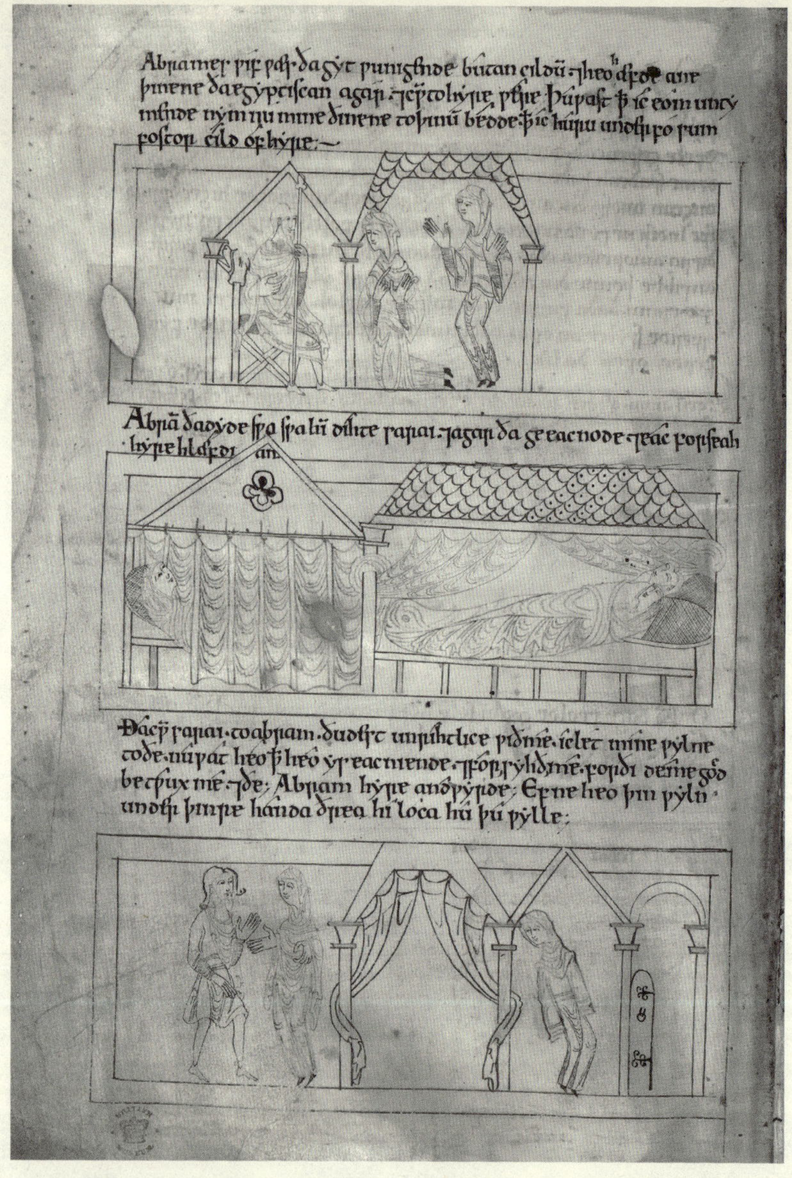

Figure 4. Sarah gives Hagar to Abraham (top), Abraham sleeps with Hagar (middle), Sarah complains about Hagar (bottom). British Library, MS Cotton Claudius B.iv, fol. 27v. © The British Library Board.

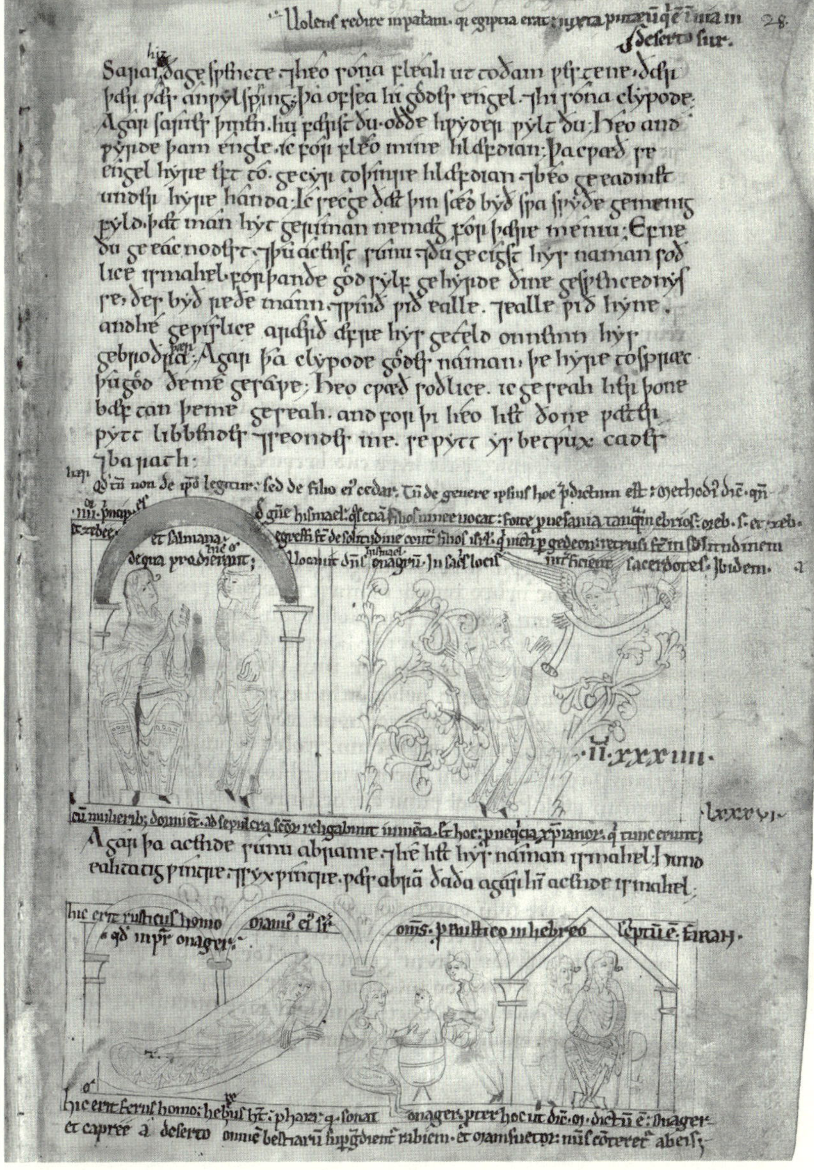

Figure 5. Sarah afflicts Hagar and Hagar flees into the desert (top), birth of Ishmael (bottom). London, British Library, MS Cotton Claudius B.iv, fol. 28r. © The British Library Board.

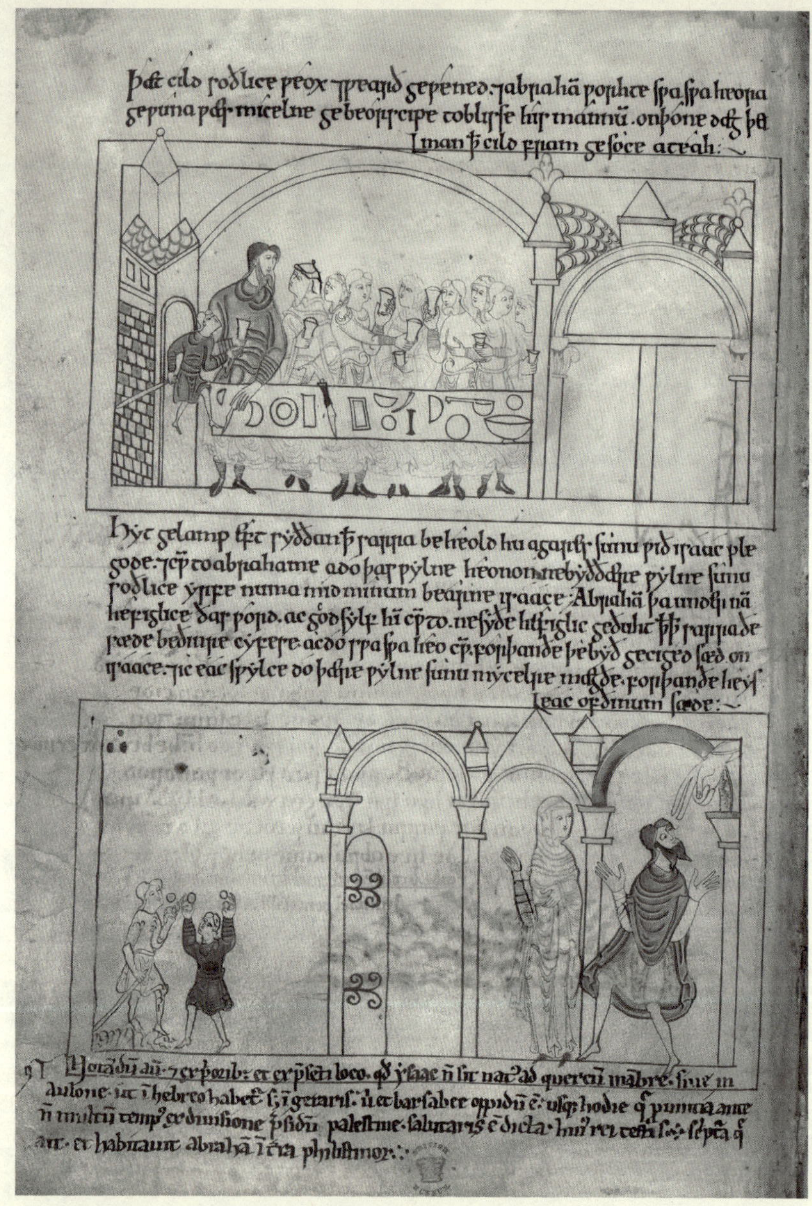

Figure 6. Weaning of Isaac (top), Ishmael playing with Isaac (bottom). London, British Library, MS Cotton Claudius B.iv, fol. 35v. © The British Library Board.

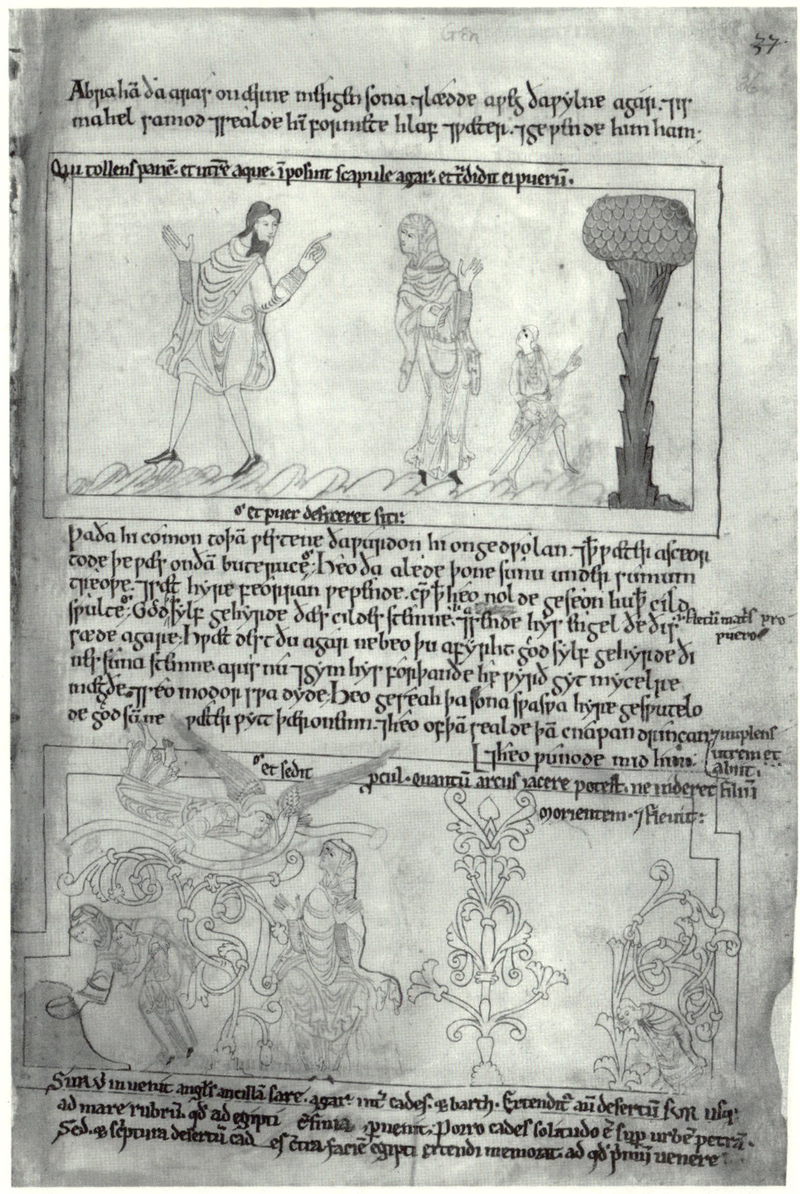

Figure 7. Hagar is exiled (top), Hagar and Ishmael in the desert (bottom). London, British Library, MS Cotton Claudius B.iv, fol. 36r. © The British Library Board.

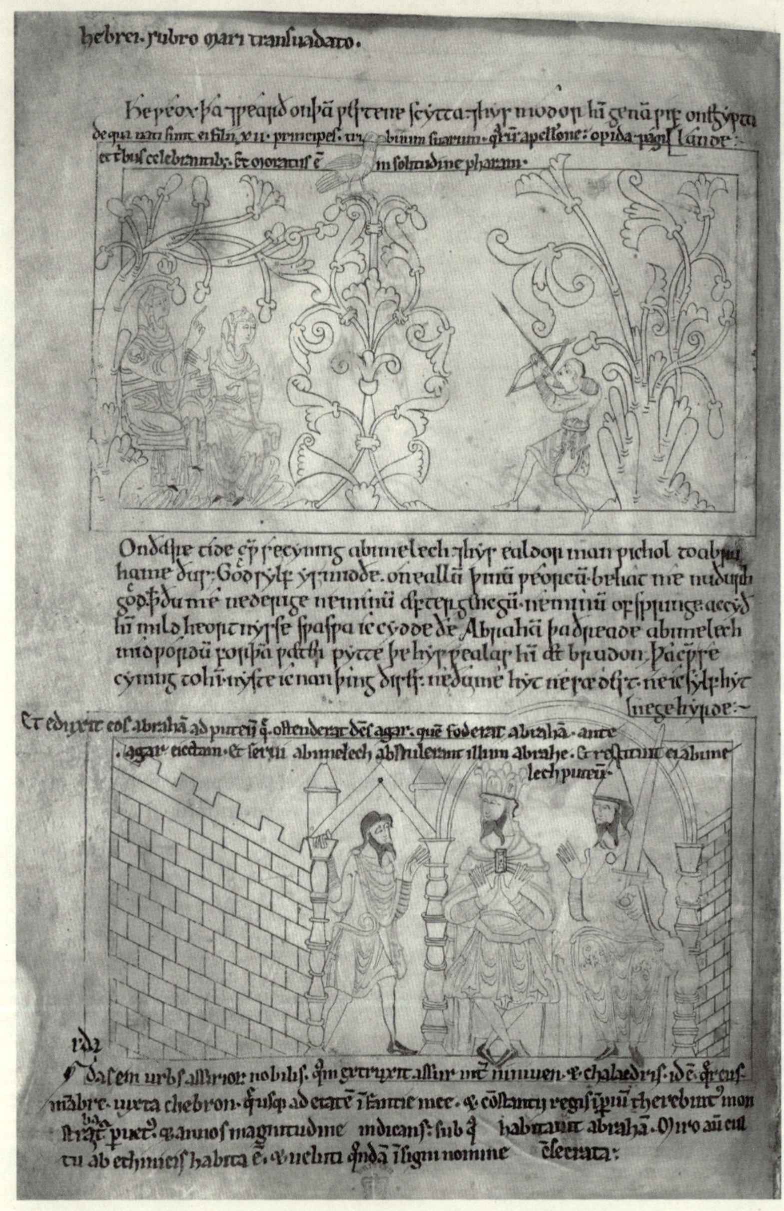

Figure 8. Ishmael the archer (top). London, British Library, MS Cotton Claudius B.iv, fol. 36v. © The British Library Board.

Figure 9. King Edgar, New Minster Charter. London, British Library, MS Cotton Vespasian A. viii, fol. 2v. © The British Library Board.

Figure 10. Latin verse, New Minster Charter. London, British Library, MS Cotton Vespasian A. viii, fol. 3r. © The British Library Board.

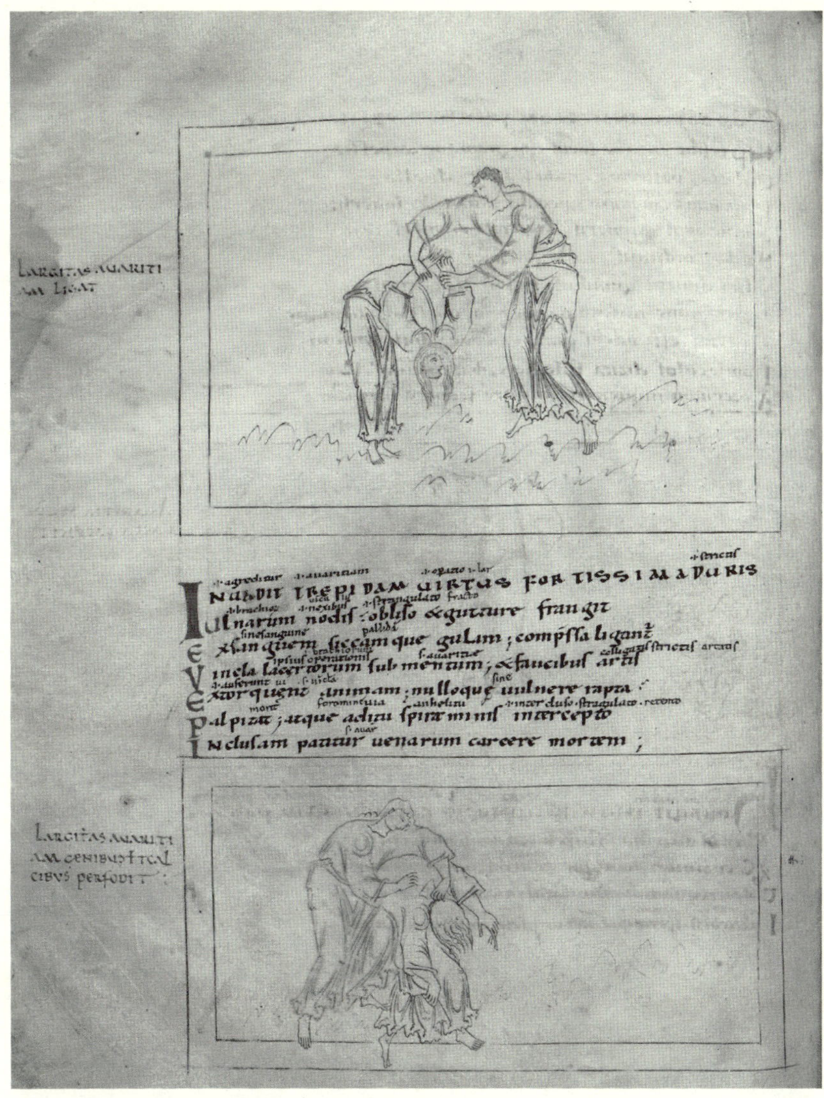

Figure 11. Personifications of Generosity and Avarice, Prudentius, *Psychomachia*. Cambridge, Corpus Christi College, Parker Library, MS 23, fol. 29v. Reproduced by permission of the Master and Fellows of Corpus Christi College, Cambridge.

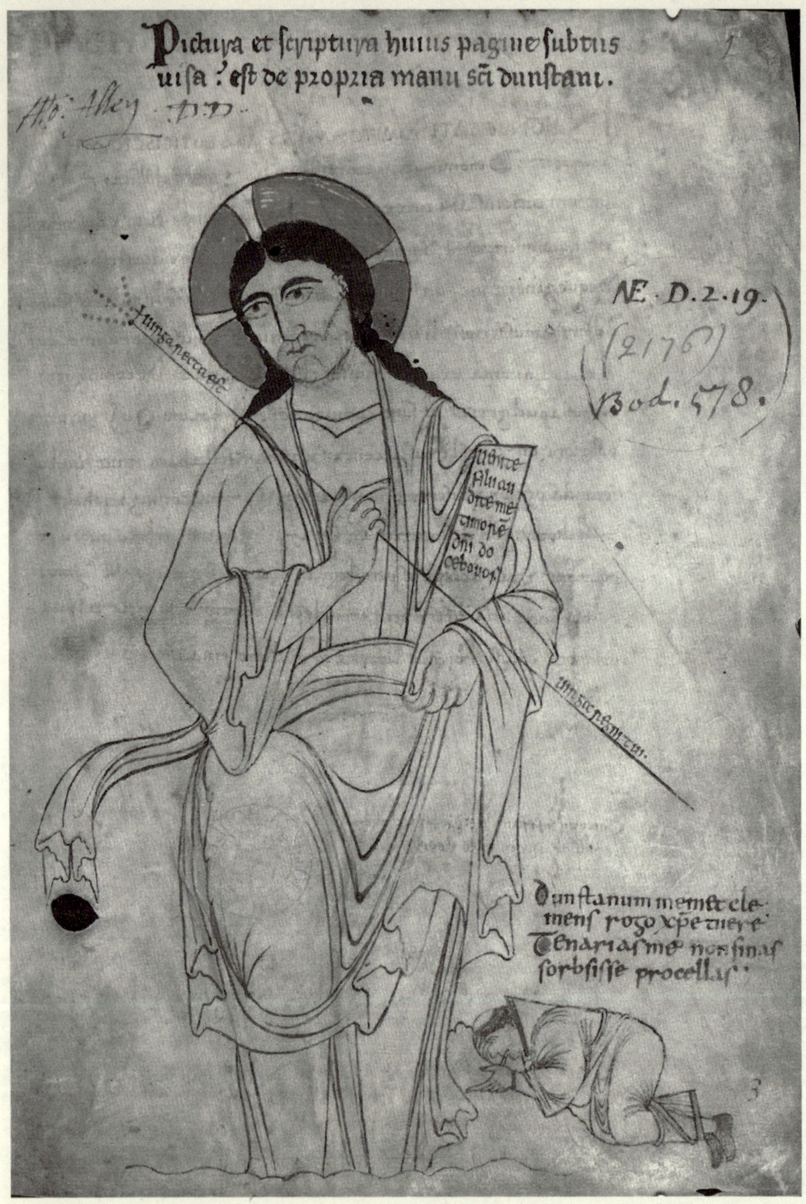

Figure 12. Dunstan Kneeling before Christ, *Saint Dunstan's Classbook*. Oxford, Bodleian Library, MS Auct. F.4.32, fol. 1r.

Figure 13. David Dancing before the Ark, Dante, *Divina Commedia*. New York, The Pierpont Morgan Library, MS M. 676, fol. 59v. Photography by Graham S. Haber, 2015.

Figure 14. David Dancing before the Ark. Sacra Parallela, Paris, Bibliothèque nationale de France, MS gr. 923, fol. 369r.

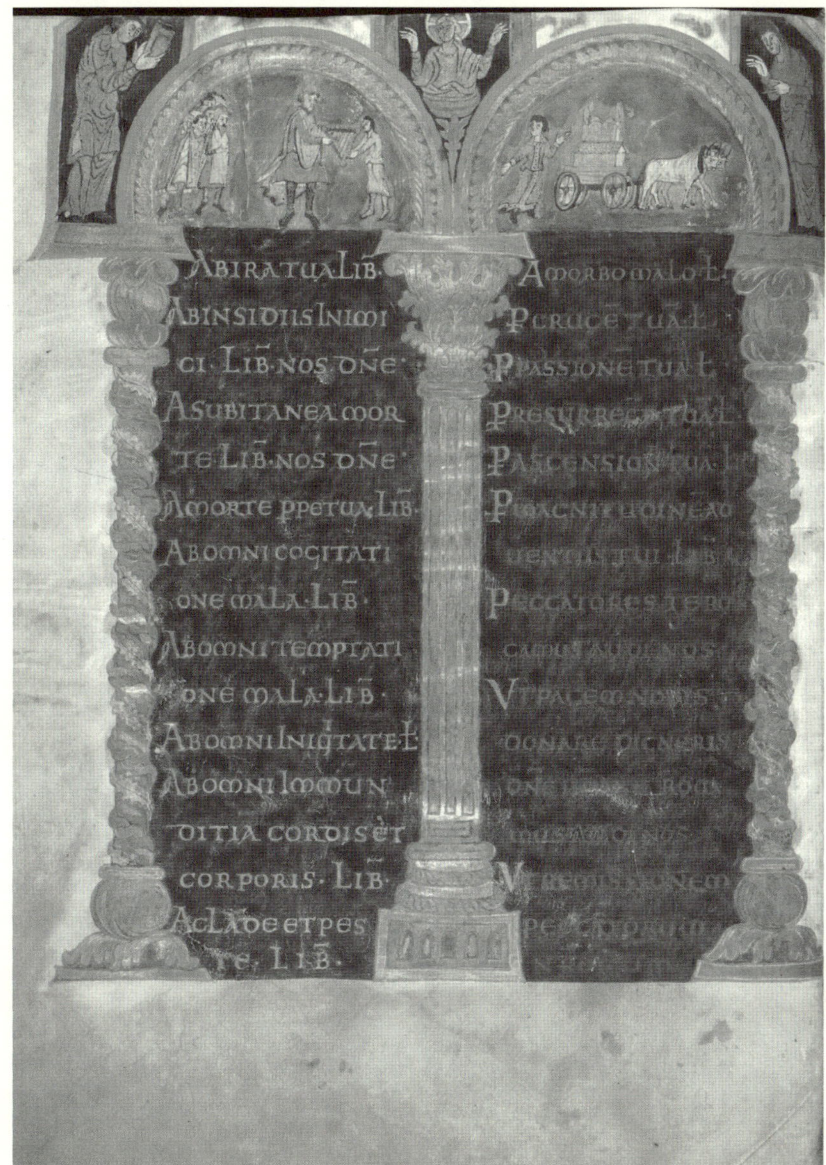

Figure 15. David Scenes; Folchart and Abbot Hartmut Dedicate Book to Christ. Folchart Psalter, St. Gall, Stiftsbibliothek, MS 23, p. 12.

Figure 16. David and Co-Psalmists, Golden Psalter (*Psalterium Aureum*). St. Gall, Stiftsbibliothek, MS 22, p. 2.

Figure 17. David and Co-Psalmists. First Bible of Charles the Bald. Paris, Bibliothèque nationale de France, MS lat. 1, fol. 215v.

Figure 18. King Aethelstan Donates Book to St Cuthbert, Bede, *Lives of St. Cuthbert*. Cambridge, Corpus Christi College, Parker Library, MS 183, fol. 1v. Reproduced by permission of the Master and Fellows of Corpus Christi College, Cambridge.

Figure 19. Ark and Cherubim, Germigny-des-Prés, Oratory of Bishop Theodulf, apse mosaic.

Figure 20. King Edgar Flanked by Archbishop Dunstan and Bishop Aethelwold, *Monastic Miscellany* containing *Regularis Concordia*. London, British Library, MS Cotton Tiberius A.iii, fol. 2v. © The British Library Board.

Figure 21. Moses Blesses the Tribes of Israel, Sees the Promised Land, Dies, and Is Mourned (Deuteronomy 33–4). London, British Library, MS Cotton Claudius B.iv, fol. 139v. © The British Library Board.

Figure 22. "there also were giants on the earth in those days" (Genesis 6). London, British Library, MS Cotton Claudius B.iv, fol. 13. © The British Library Board.

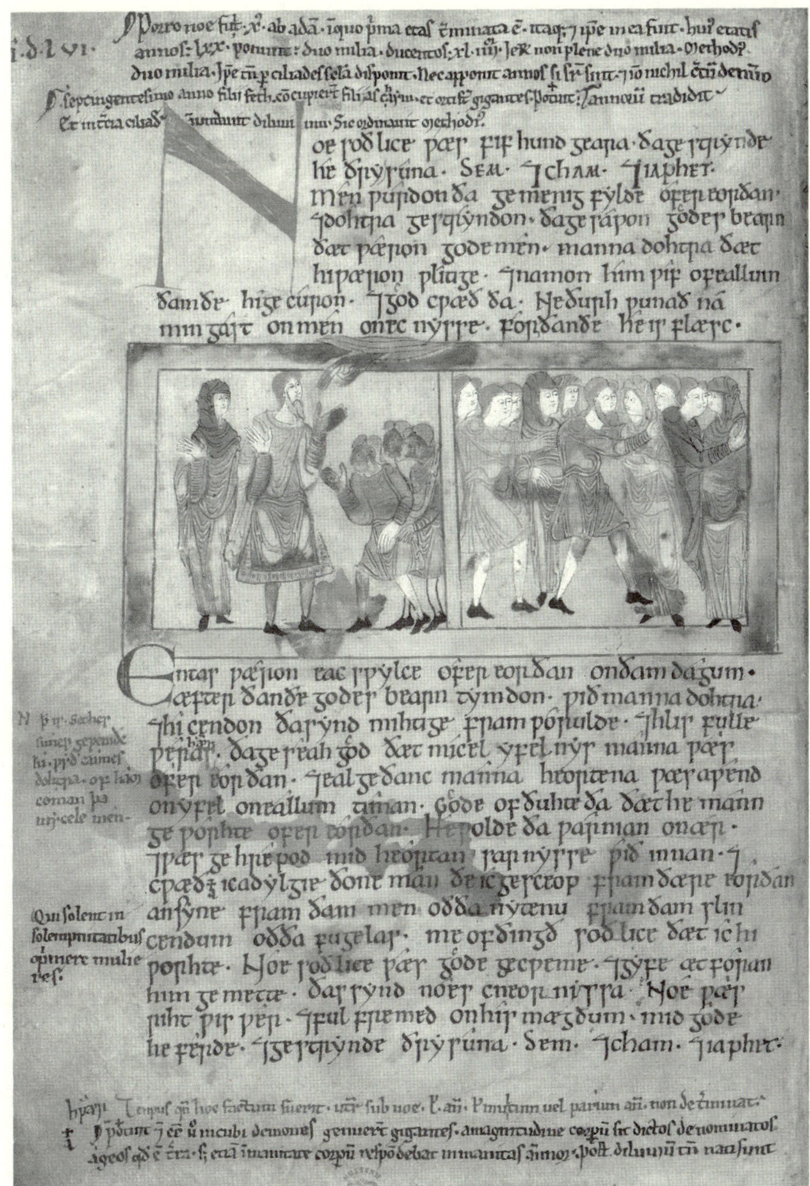

Figure 23. Noah and his Family (Genesis 5–6). London, British Library, MS Cotton Claudius B.iv, fol. 12v. © The British Library Board.

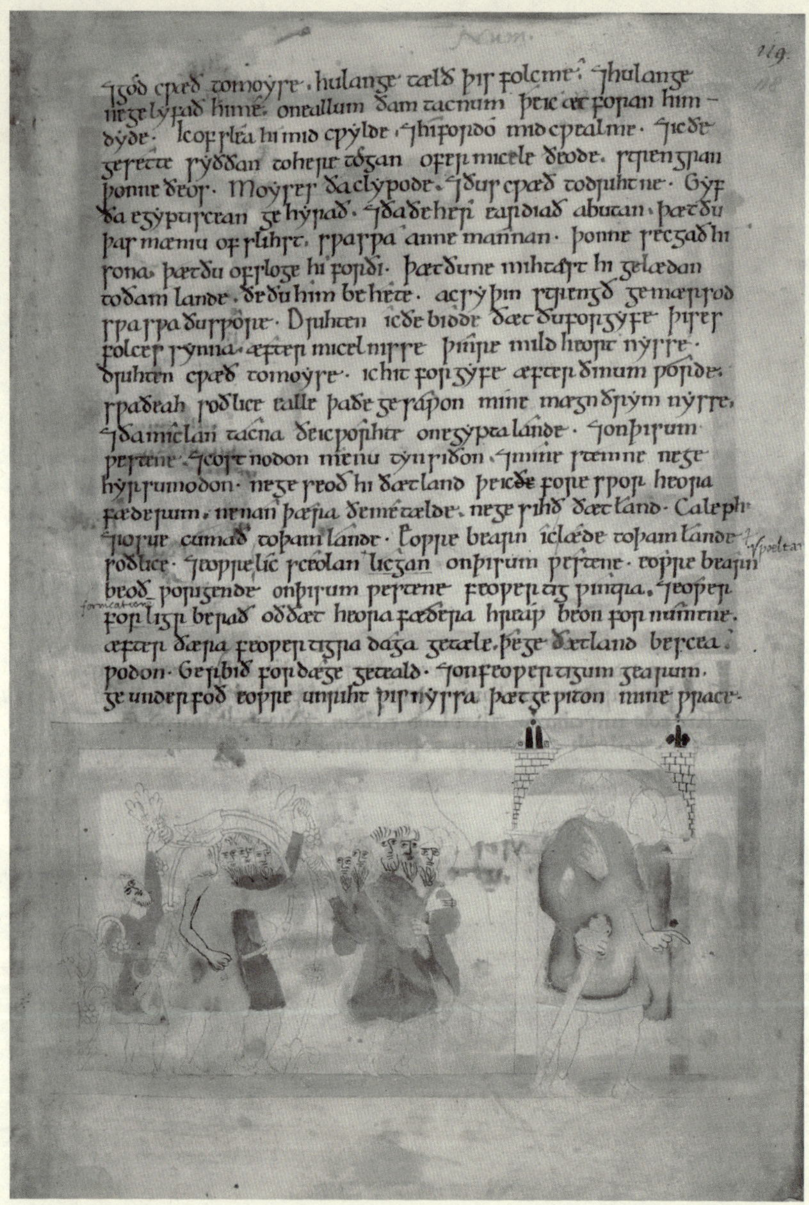

Figure 24. The Spies of Israel See the Sons of Anak (Numbers 13). London, British Library, MS Cotton Claudius B.iv, fol. 118. © The British Library Board.

Figure 25. Moses, Horned and Majestic, Receives Promise from God and the Israelites Defeat Amorrhites (Numbers 21). London, British Library, MS Cotton Claudius B.iv, fol. 124v. © The British Library Board.

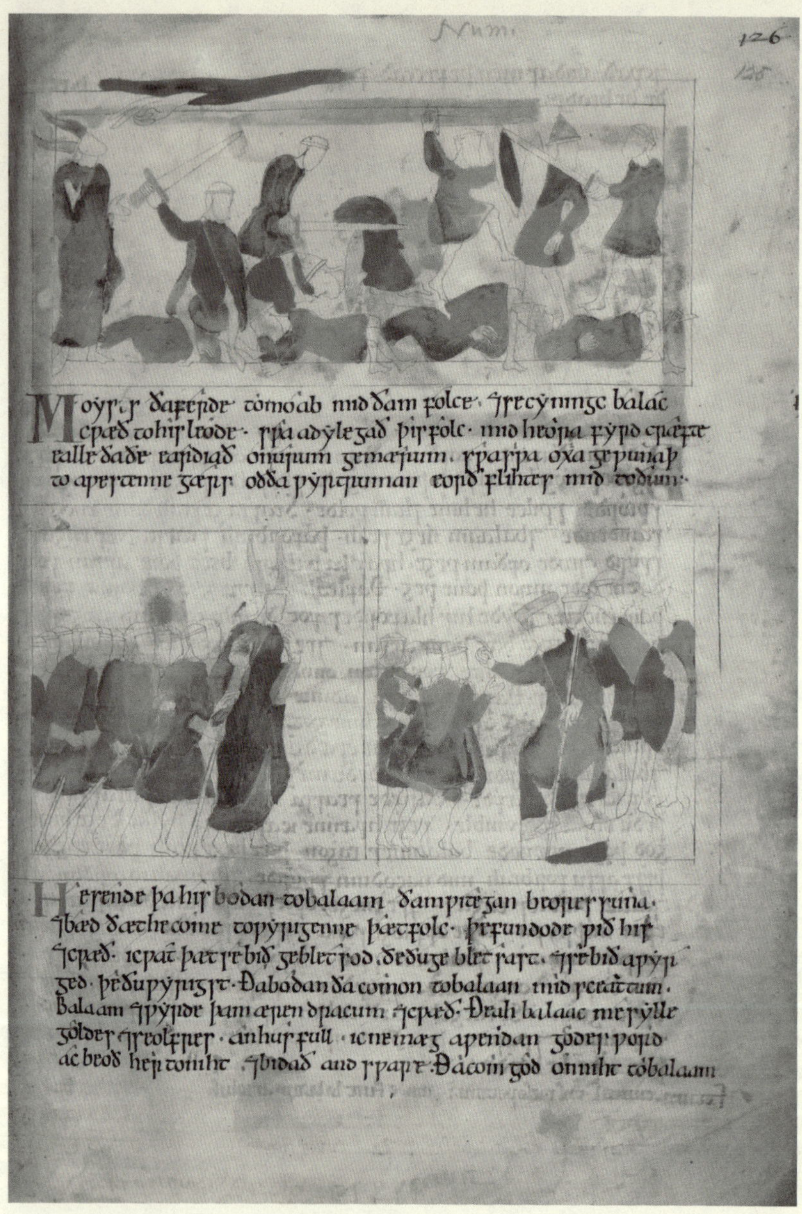

Figure 26. Moses and the Israelites Defeat Og of Bashan (Numbers 21). London, British Library, MS Cotton Claudius B.iv, fol. 125. © The British Library Board.

Figure 27. Blessing of the Tribes and the Death of Moses. Rome, Abbazia di San Paolo fuori le Mura, fol. 50v. By permission of Herbert L. Kessler.

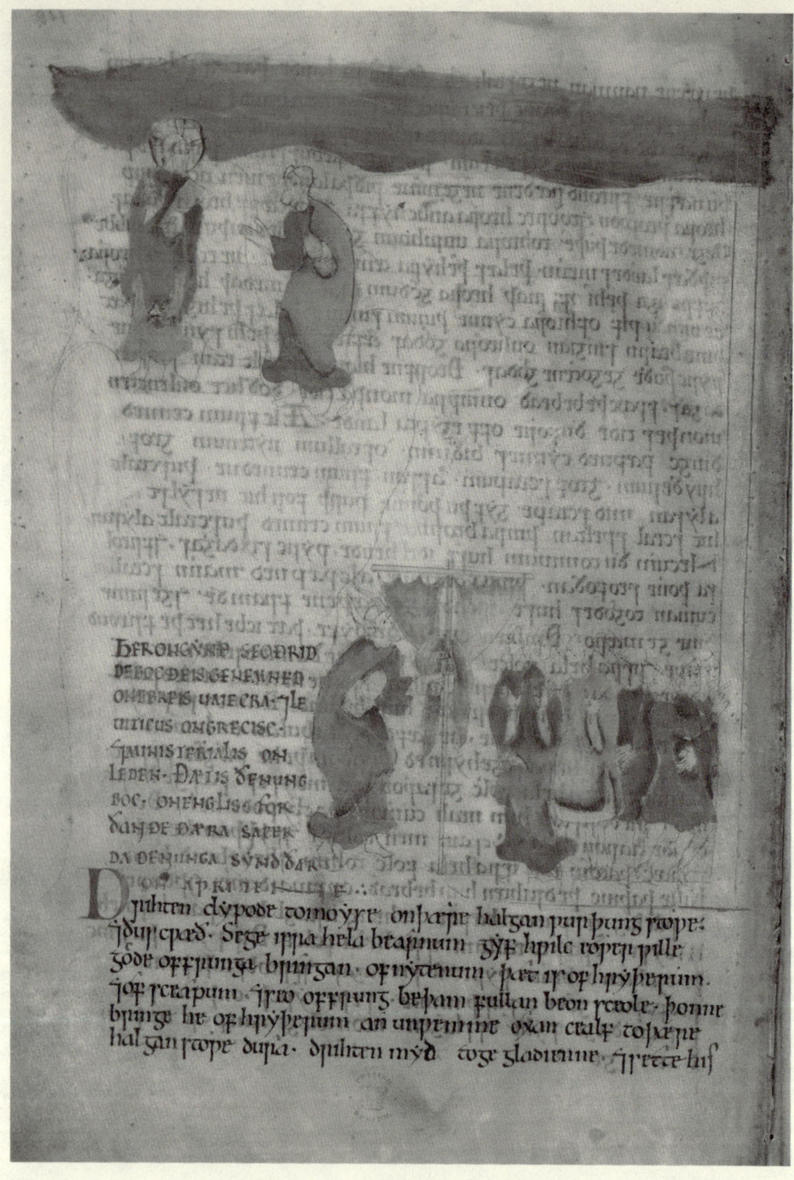

Figure 28. Moses Speaks Face to Face with God, and Returns to Israelites as a Horned Giant, with a Curtain to Separate Himself from his Followers (Exodus 34). London, British Library, MS Cotton Claudius B.iv, fol. 105v. © The British Library Board.

Bibliography

Primary Texts, Translations, Databases, Facsimiles

Acta Andreae et Matthiae apud anthropophagos. In *Die lateinischen Bearbeitungen der Acta Andreae et Matthiae apud Anthropophagos*, Beihefte zur Zeitschrift für die neutestamentliche Wissenschaft, 12. Edited by F. Blatt. Giessen: A. Töpelmann, 1930.

Acts of Andrew. *The Acts of Andrew in the Country of the Cannibals: Translations from the Greek, Latin, and Old English*. Translated by R. Boenig. New York: Garland, 1991.

Ælfric. *Ælfric's Catholic Homilies: The First Series*. Edited by P. Clemoes. London: Oxford University Press, 1997.

– *Ælfric's Catholic Homilies: The Second Series*. Edited by M. Godden. EETS, s.s., 5. London: Oxford University Press, 1979.

– *Ælfric's De temporibus anni*. Edited and translated by M. Blake. Anglo-Saxon Texts. Cambridge: D.S. Brewer, 2009.

– *Ælfric's Homilies on Judith, Esther, and the Maccabees*. Edited by S.D. Lee, 1999. http://users.ox.ac.uk/~stuart/kings/.

– *Ælfric's Life of St. Basil the Great: Background and Context*. Edited and translated by G. Corona. Woodbridge, UK: D.S. Brewer, 2006.

– *Ælfric's Lives of Saints*. Edited by W.W. Skeat. EETS, o.s., 76, 82, 94, 114. Oxford: Oxford University Press, 1881–1900. Reprinted 1966 in 2 vols.

– *Homilies of Ælfric: A Supplementary Collection*. Edited by J.C. Pope. 2 vols. London: Oxford University Press, 1967, 1968.

– *The Homilies of the Anglo-Saxon Church* 1. Edited by B. Thorpe. London: Ælfric Society, 1844.

– *The Old English Heptateuch and Ælfric's Libellus de Veteri Testamento et Novo*. Edited by R. Marsden. EETS, o.s., 330. Oxford: Oxford University Press, 2008.

– *The Old English Heptateuch, Ælfric's Treatise on the Old and New Testaments, and His Preface to Genesis*. Edited by S.J. Crawford. EETS 160. Oxford: Oxford University Press, 1922.

Agobard of Lyon. *De picturis et imaginibus*. In *Agobardi Lugdunensis opera Omnia*. Edited by L. van Acker. CCCM 52. Turnhout: Brepols, 1981.

Aided Chonchobuir. The Death-Tales of the Ulster Heroes, second reprint. Edited and translated by K. Meyer. Dublin: Dublin Institute for Advanced Studies, 1993. First published 1906 by Williams & Norgate.

Alcuin. *Liber de virtutibus et vitiis, PL* 101:613–38.

Ambrose. *De Abraham, PL* 14:417–500.

Andreas. Andreas and The Fates of the Apostles. Edited by G.P. Krapp. Boston: Ginn & Co., 1906.

Andreas. Andreas and The Fates of the Apostles. Edited by K. Brooks. Oxford: Clarendon Press, 1961.

Angelome of Luxeuil. *Enarrationes in libros Regum. PL* 115:243–550.

Anglo-Saxon Poetry. Translated by R.K. Gordon. London: Dent; New York: Dutton, 1954.

Augustine. *Contra Faustum. PL* 42:207–518.

– *De civitate Dei libri XII*. Edited by A. Kalb and B. Dombart, *Bibliotheca Scriptorum Graecorum et Romanorum Teubeneriana*. Stuttgart: Teubner, 1981.

– *De civitate Dei*. Edited by B. Dombart and A. Kalb. CCSL 47–8. Turnhout: Brepols, 1955.

– *De Genesi ad litteram libri XII*. Edited by J. Zycha, CSEL 28. Vienna: Tempsky, 1894.

– *Enarrationes in Psalmos*. Edited by. E. Dekkers et al. 3 vols. CCSL 38–40. Turnhout: Brepols, 1990.

– *Exposition of the Psalms (Ennarationes in Psalmos). The Works of Augustine: a Translation for the 21st Century, pt. 3, v. 20; Expositions of the Psalms: 121–150*. Edited by B. Ramsey. Translation and notes by M. Boulding. Hyde Park, NY: New City Press, 2004.

– *The City of God Against the Pagans*. 6 vols. Vol. 1, translated by G.E. McCracken. Vols. 2 & 7, translated by W.M. Green. Vol. 3, translated by D.S. Wiesen. Vol. 4, translated by P. Levine. Vol. 5, translated by E.M. Sanford and W. McA. Green. Vol. 6, translated by W.C. Greene. Loeb Classical Library. London: Heinemann; Cambridge: Harvard University Press, 1957–72.

Avitus. *The Poems of Alcimus Ecdicius Avitus*. Translation and introduction by G. Shea. Tempe, AZ: MRTS, 1997.

Bede. *De orthographia; De arte metrica et de schematibus et tropis; De natura rerum*. In *Opera didascalica*, vol. I. CCSL 123A. Edited by C.W. Jones et al. Turnhout: Brepols, 1975.

– *De tabernaculo, De templo, In Ezram et Neemiam.* In *Opera exegetica*, vol. IIa. Edited by D. Hurst. CCSL 119A. Turnhout: Brepols, 1969.

– *De temporum ratione.* Edited by C.W. Jones. CCSL 123B. Turnhout: Brepols, 1977.

– *Epistola ad Pleguinam.* In *Opera didascalica*, vol. III. Edited by C.W. Jones. CCSL 123C. Turnhout: Brepols, 1980.

– *Expositio actuum Apostolorum.* In *Opera Exegetica*. Edited by M.L.W. Laistner. CCSL 121. Turnhout: Brepols, 1983.

– *Homeliarum evangelii libri II.* In *Opera Homiletica*. Edited by D. Hurst, CCSL 122. Turnhout: Brepols, 1955.

– *In Tobiam.* In *Opera exegetica*, vol. IIb. Edited by D. Hurst. CCSL 119B. Turnhout: Brepols, 1983.

– *Libri quatuor in principium Genesis usque ad natiuitatem Isaac et eiectionem Ismahelis adnotationum.* In *Opera exegetica*, vol. I. Edited by C.W. Jones. CCSL 118A. Turnhout: Brepols, 1967.

– *Opera Homiletica.* Edited by D. Hurst. CCSL 122. Turnhout: Brepols, 1955.

– *Homilies on the Gospels. Book Two: Lent to the Dedication of the Church.* Translated by L.T. Martin and D. Hurst. Kalamazoo, MI: Cistercian Publications, 1991.

– *Bede: A Biblical Miscellany.* Translated by A.G. Holder and W.T. Foley. Translated Texts for Historians 28. Liverpool: Liverpool University Press, 1999.

– *Bede: On Ezra and Nehemiah.* Translated by S. DeGregorio. Translated Texts for Historians 47. Liverpool: Liverpool University Press, 2006.

– *Bede: On Genesis.* Translated by C. Kendall. Translated Texts for Historians 48. Liverpool: Liverpool University Press, 2008.

– *Bede: On the Tabernacle.* Translated by A. Holder. Translated Texts for Historians 18. Liverpool: Liverpool University Press, 1994.

– *Bede: On the Temple.* Translated by S. Connolly. Introduction by J. O'Reilly. Translated Texts for Historians 21. Liverpool: Liverpool University Press, 1995.

– *Bede: The Reckoning of Time.* Translated by F. Wallis. Translated Texts for Historians 29. Liverpool: Liverpool University Press, 1999.

– *Bede's Ecclesiastical History of the English People.* Edited by B. Colgrave and R.A.B. Mynors. Oxford: Clarendon Press, 1969.

– *The Venerable Bede Commentary on the Acts of the Apostles.* Translated by L.T. Martin. Cistercian Studies Series, 117. Collegeville, MN: Cistercian Publications, 1989.

Benedict, Abbott of Monte Cassino. *The Rule of St. Benedict. In Latin and English with Notes.* Edited by T. Fry, OSB. Collegeville, MN: The Liturgical Press, 1981.

Beowulf. Klaeber's Beowulf and The Fight at Finnsburg. 4th ed. Edited by R.D. Fulk, R.E Bjork, and J.D. Niles. Toronto and Buffalo: University of Toronto Press, 2008.

Biblia Sacra, iuxta Vulgatam versionem, 4th ed. Edited by R. Weber and R. Gryson. Stuttgart: Deutsche Bibelgesellschaft, 1994.

Blickling Book. *The Blickling Homilies*. Edited by R. Morris. EETS, o.s., 58, 63, 73. London: Oxford University Press, 1874, 1876, 1880. Reprinted 1967 in 1 vol.

Boethius (Old English). *The Old English Boethius: an Edition of the Old English Versions of Boethius's De Consolatione Philosophiae*. Edited by M. Godden and S. Irvine. Oxford: Oxford University Press, 2009.

– *The Theological Tractates. The Consolation of Philosophy*. Translated by H.F. Stewart, E.K. Rand, and S.J. Tester. Cambridge, MA: Harvard University Press, 1973.

Boniface (Wynfrith). *S. Bonifatii et Lulii epistolae*. Edited by E. Dümmler. MGH, Epistolae 3, Epistolae Karolini Aevi 1. Berlin: Weidmann, 1892.

Byrhtferth. *Byrhtferth's Enchiridion*. Edited and translated by P.S. Baker and M. Lapidge. EETS, s.s., 15. Oxford: Oxford University Press, 1995.

Caesarius of Arles. *Sancti Caesarii Arelatensis sermones*. Edited by G. Morin. CCSL 103. Turnhout: Brepols, 1953.

– *Sermons*, vol. 1. Translated by M.M. Mueller. The Fathers of the Church, 31. Washington, DC: Catholic University of America Press, 2010.

Charlemagne. *Admonitio generalis*. In *Capitularia regum Francorum I*. Edited by A. Boretius. MGH, Legum sectio II. Hannover: Hahn, 1883.

Christian Druthmar. *Expositio in Matthaeum. PL* 106:1261–1503.

Corpus Glossary. Edited by W.M. Lindsay. Cambridge: Cambridge University Press, 1921.

Coronation records. *English Coronation Records*. Translated by L.G.W. Legg. Westminster: A. Constable & Co., 1902.

Council of Aachen (816). In *Concilia Aevi Karolini I*. Edited by A. Werminghoff. MGH, Legum sectio III, Concilia II/I. Hannover: Hahn, 1906. 307–464.

Council of Laodicea (ca. 364). In *Sacrorum conciliorum nova et amplissima collectio*. Edited by G. Mansi. 31 vols. Florence; Venice: Antonius Zata, 1759–98.

Cynewulf. *Cynewulf's Elene*, revised ed. Edited by P.O.E. Gradon. Exeter: University of Exeter Press, 1977.

Cyril of Alexandria. *Glaphyra in Genesim. PG* 69:9–678.

Daniel. Daniel and Azarias. Edited by R.T. Farrell. London: Methuen, 1974.

Dictionary of Old English A–G Online. Edited by A. Cameron, A.C. Amos, and A. DiPaolo Healey. Toronto: Dictionary of Old English Project, 2007.

Epiphanius of Salamis. *The Panarion of Epiphanius of Salamis. Book I (Sects 1–46)*. Translated by F. Williams. Leiden: Brill, 1987.

Eucherius of Lyon. *Formulae spiritalis intelligentiae*. Edited by C. Mandolfo. CCSL 66. Turnhout: Brepols, 2004.

Exeter Book. *The Exeter Anthology of Old English Poetry: an Edition of Exeter Dean and Chapter Ms 3501*, revised 2nd ed. Edited by B.J. Muir. Exeter: University of Exeter Press, 2000.

Exodus, 2nd ed. Edited by P.J. Lucas. Exeter: University of Exeter Press, 1994.

Filastrius. *Diversarum hereseon liber*. Edited by F. Marx. CSEL 38. Vienna; Prague: F. Temsky, 1898.

Genesis A. Genesis A: A New Edition. Edited by A.N. Doane. Madison, WI: University of Wisconsin Press, 1978.

Geoffrey of Monmouth. *The Historia regum Britannie of Geoffrey of Monmouth*, vol.1. Edited by N. Wright. Cambridge: D.S. Brewer, 1984.

Gregory the Great. *Gregorii I papae registrum epistolarum*. Edited by L.M. Hartmann. MGH, Epistolae I. Berlin: Weidmann, 1890.

– *Grégoire le Grand: Dialogues*. 3 vols. Sources Chrétiennes 251, 260, 265. Edited and translated by A. de Vogüé and P. Antin. Paris: Cerf, 1978–80.

Haymo. *Enarratio in epistolam ad Galatas*. PL 117:669–700.

Heiric of Auxerre. *Homiliae per circulum anni* I.37. Edited by R. Quadri. CCCM 116A. Turnhout: Brepols, 1992.

Hexateuch (Old English). *The Old English Illustrated Hexateuch (London, British Library, Cotton Claudius B.iv.)*. Edited by C.R. Dodwell and P. Clemoes. EEMF 18. Copenhagen: Rosenkilde and Bagger, 1974.

Holy Bible Douay-Rheims Version. Translated by R. Challoner. London: Catholic Truth Society, 1956.

Hrabanus Maurus. *Commentariorum in Genesim*. PL 107:439–668.

– *Commentarius in Paralipomena*. PL 109:279–540.

– *De universo: the Peculiar Properties of Words and Their Mystical Significance: the Complete English Translation*. Vol. I. P. Throop. Charlotte, VT: Medieval MS, 2009.

– *Expositio in Matthaeum*. Edited by B. Löfstedt. CCCM 174A. Turnhout: Brepols, 2000.

Irenaeus. *Contra Haereses*, Lib. IV. PG 7:973–1118.

Isidore of Seville. *De fide catholica contra Iudaeos*. PL 83:449–538.

– *Isidore de Séville: Traité de la nature*. Edited and translated by J. Fontaine. Collection des Études Augustiniennes, Série Moyen Âge et Temps Modernes 39. Paris: Institut d'Études Augustiniennes, 2002.

– *Isidori Hispalensis episcopi, Etymologiarum sive originum libri XX*. 2 vols. Edited by W.M. Lindsay. Oxford: Clarendon, 1911.

– *The Etymologies of Isidore of Seville*. Translated by S.A. Barney, W.J. Lewis, J.A. Beach, and O. Berghof, with the collaboration of M. Hall. Cambridge: Cambridge University Press, 2008.

Israel Antiquities Authority. *National Treasures: Selected Artifacts from the Shelby White and Leon Levy Center for National Treasures*. http://www .antiquities.org.il.

Jerome. *Commentaria in epistola ad Galatas* 1. *PL* 26:307–438.

– *Commentarii in Hiezechielem*. Edited by F. Glorie. CCSL 75. Turnhout: Brepols, 1964.

– *Commentariorum in Matheum libri iv*. Edited by D. Hurst and M. Adriaen. CCSL 77. Turnhout: Brepols, 1969.

– *Hebraicae quaestiones in libro Geneseos*. Edited by P. De Lagarde. CCSL 72. Turnhout: Brepols, 1959.

– *Jerome: Commentary on Matthew*. Translated by T.P. Scheck. Fathers of the Church 117. Washington, DC: Catholic University of America Press, 2008.

– *Sancti Eusebii Hieronymi Stridonensis presbyteri operum, tomus tertius*. Edited by D. Vallarsi. Verona: Petrum Antonium Bernum & Jacobum Vallarsium, 1735.

Lactantius. *Lactance: Institutions divines*. Edited and translated by P. Monat. Sources Chrétiennes 377. Paris: Cerf, 1992.

Liber questionum in euangeliis. Edited by J. Rittmueller. CCSL 108F. Turnhout: Brepols, 2003.

Life of St. Cuthbert. *Two Lives of Saint Cuthbert; A Life by an Anonymous Monk of Lindisfarne and Bede's Prose Life*. Edited and translated by B. Colgrave. Cambridge: Cambridge University Press, 1940.

Missale Romanum. Editio juxta typicam Vaticanam. Malines: Dessain, 1953.

Novum glossarium mediae latinitatis ab anno DCCC usque ad annum MCC: Phacoides-Pingo. Edited by F. Dolbeau. Brussels: U.A.I., 2003.

Orosius (Old English). *The Old English Orosius*. Edited by J. Bately. EETS, s.s., 6. London: Oxford University Press, 1980.

Otfried of Weissenburg. *Glossae in Matthaeum*. Edited by C. Grifoni. CCCM 200. Turnhout: Brepols, 2003.

Peter Damian. *Sancti Petri Damiani Sermones*. Edited by G. Lucchesi. CCCM 57. Turnhout: Brepols, 1983.

Pseudo-Bede. *In Matthaei evangelium expositio*. *PL* 92:9–130.

Pseudo-Bede. *In Pentateuchum commentarii*. *PL* 91:189–392.

Pseudo-Jerome. *Quaestiones hebraicae in libros Regum et Paralipomenon*. *PL* 23:1329–1400.

Rabanus Maurus. *See* Hrabanus Maurus.

S. Benedicti Regula, 2nd ed. Edited by E.C. Butler. Paris: B. Herder, 1927.

Sedulius Scottus. *In euangelium Mathaei*. Edited by B. Löfstedt. 2 vols. Vetus Latina, aus der Geschichte der lateinischen Bibel, 14 and 19. Freiburg im Breisgau: Herder, 1989–91.

Siege of Jerusalem, The. Siege of Jerusalem. Edited by M. Livingston. TEAMS Middle English Texts Series. Kalamazoo: MIP, 2004.

Siege of Jerusalem, The. The Siege of Jerusalem in Prose. Edited by A. Kurvinen. Mémoires de la Société Néophilologique de Helsinki 34. Helsinki: Société Néophilologique, 1969.

Siege of Jerusalem, The. The Siege of Jerusalem. Edited by E. Kölbing and M. Day. EETS, o.s., 188. London: EETS, 1932.

Smaragdus. *Collectiones in epistolas et evangelia. PL* 102:15–552.

Sulpicius Severus. *Sulpice Sévère: Vie de saint Martin*. Edited and translated by J. Fontaine. 3 vols. Sources Chrétiennes 133–5. Paris: Cerf, 1967–9.

Tertullian. *Tertullien: Contre Marcion*. Edited and translated by R. Braun. 5 vols. Sources Chrétiennes 365, 368, 399, 456, 483. Paris: Cerf, 1990–2004.

– *De carne Christi* 22. *PL* 2:753–92.

The Book of Enoch, or Enoch I: A New English Edition. Edited by M. Black. Studia in Veteris Testamenti Pseudepigrapha 7. London: Brill, 1985.

Thesaurus Linguae Latinae, online version. http://www.degruyter.com/databasecontent?dbid=tll&dbsource=%2Fdb%2Ftll.

Vercelli Book, The. *The Vercelli Book*. Edited by G.P. Krapp. ASPR 2. New York: Columbia University Press, 1932.

Vindicta Salvatoris (Avenging of the Saviour). La Vengeance de Nostre-Seigneur. The Old and Middle French Prose Versions: The Cura Sanitatis Tiberii (The Mission of Volusian), the Nathanis Judaei Legatio (Vindicta Salvatoris), and the Versions Found in the Bible en français of Roger d'Argenteuil or Influenced by the Works of Flavius Josephus, Robert de Boron and Jacobus de Voragine. Edited by A. Ford. Studies and Texts 115. Toronto: PIMS, 1993.

Vita Eligii. Edited by B. Krusch. MGH, Scriptores rerum Merovingicarum, 4. Hannover: Hahn, 1902.

Secondary Texts

Aaronovitch, D. *Voodoo Histories: The Role of the Conspiracy Theory in Shaping Modern History*. New York: Penguin/Riverhead, 2010.

Abulafia, A.S. "Notions of Jewish Service in Twelfth- and Thirteenth-Century England." In *Christians and Jews in Angevin England: The York Massacre of 1190, Narratives and Context*, edited by S. Rees Jones and S. Watson. Woodbridge: Boydell & Brewer, 2013.

Adam, A. *Das Kirchenjahr mitfeiern: Seine Geschichte und seine Bedeutung nach der Liturgieerneuerung*. Freiburg: Herder, 1979. Translated by M.J. O'Connell as *The Liturgical Year: Its History and Its Meaning after the Reform of the Liturgy*. New York: Pueblo, 1981.

Akbari, S.C. *Idols in the East: European Representations of Islam and the Orient, 1100–1450*. Ithaca: Cornell University Press, 2009.

– "Placing the Jews in Late Medieval English Literature." In *Orientalism and the Jews*, edited by I.D. Kalmar and J. Penslar. Waltham, MA: Brandeis University Press, 2005. 32–50.

Allen, M.I. "Universal History 300–1000: Origins and Western Developments." In *Historiography in the Middle Ages*, edited by D. Mauskopf Deliyannis. Leiden: Brill, 2003. 17–42.

Allen, M.J.B., and D.G. Calder. *Sources and Analogues of Old English Poetry*. Cambridge: D.S. Brewer; Totowa, NJ: Rowman and Littlefield, 1976.

Anderson, E.J. "Cynewulf's *Elene* 1115b–24, the Conversion of the Jews: Figurative or Literal?" *ELN* 25.3 (1988):1–3.

Anlezark, D. "An Ideal Marriage: Abraham and Sarah in Old English Literature." *Medium Aevum* 69.2 (2000):187–210.

– "Connecting the Patriarchs: Noah and Abraham in the Old English *Exodus*." *JEGP* 104 (2005):171–88.

– "Sceaf, Japheth and the Origins of the Anglo-Saxons." *ASE* 31 (2002):13–46.

– "Understanding Numbers in London, British Library, Harley 3271." *ASE* 38 (2010):137–55.

– *Water and Fire: The Myth of the Flood in Anglo-Saxon England*. Manchester: Manchester University Press, 2006.

Anton, H.H. *Fürstenspiegel und Herrscherethos in der Karolingerzeit*. Bonn: Ludwig Röhrscheid, 1968.

Applebaum, S. "Were there Jews in Roman Briton?" *Transactions of the Jewish Historical Society of England* 17 (1951–2):189–205.

Asad, T. *Genealogies of Religion: Discipline and Reasons of Power in Christianity and Islam*. Baltimore: Johns Hopkins University Press, 1993.

Auerbach, E. "Figura." In *Scenes from the Drama of European Literature*. Minneapolis: University of Minnesota Press, 1984.

Auneau, J. "Écrits didactiques (Tobie–Judith–Baruch)." In *Les Psaumes et les autres écrits*, edited by J. Auneau. Petite Bibliothèque des Sciences Bibliques Ancien Testament, 5. Paris: Desclée, 1990. 353–87.

Bachrach, B.S. *Early Medieval Jewish Policy in Western Europe*. Minneapolis: University of Minnesota Press, 1977.

Bale, A.P. *Feeling Persecuted: Christians, Jews and Images of Violence in the Middle Ages*. London: Reaktion Books, 2010.

– "Fictions of Judaism Before 1290." In *The Jews in Medieval Britain: Historical, Literary, and Archaeological Perspectives*, edited by P. Skinner. Woodbridge, UK: Boydell and Brewer, 2003.

– *The Jew in the Medieval Book: English Antisemitisms, 1350–1500*. Cambridge: Cambridge University Press, 2006.

Barr, J. "St. Jerome and the Sounds of Hebrew." *Journal of Semitic Studies* 12 (1967):1–36.

Bartelink, G.J.M. "Phylakterion-phylacterium." In *Mélanges Christine Mohrmann: Nouveau recueil offert par ses anciens élèves*, edited by L.J. Engels. Utrecht: Spectrum, 1973. 25–60.

Bartlett, R. "Medieval and Modern Concepts of Race and Ethnicity." *JMEMS* 31 (1) (2001):39–56.

Battles, P. "'Contending Throng' Scenes and the Comitatus Ideal in Old English Poetry, with Special Attention to *The Battle of Maldon* 122a." *Studia Neophilogica* 83 (2011):41–53.

Bauer, R. *Adversus Judaeos: Juden und Judentum im Spiegel alt- und mittelenglischer Texte*. Frankfurt am Main: Peter Lang, 2003.

Bearn, G.C.F. "Wittgenstein and the Uncanny." *Soundings: An Interdisciplinary Journal* 76 (1993):29–58.

Beckwith, R.T. *Calendar and Chronology, Jewish and Christian: Biblical, Intertestamental and Patristic Studies*. Leiden: Brill, 2001.

Bedingfield, M.B. *The Dramatic Liturgy of Anglo-Saxon England*. Woodbridge: The Boydell Press, 2002.

Ben-Sasson, H.H., ed. *A History of the Jewish People*. Cambridge, MA: Harvard University Press, 1976.

Bennett, G. "Towards a Revaluation of the Legend of "Saint" William of Norwich and its Place in the Blood Libel Legend." *Folklore* 116 (August 2005): 119–39.

– "William of Norwich and the Expulsion of the Jews." *Folklore* 116 (December 2005):311–14.

Berger, K. "Abraham in der paulinischen Hauptbriefen." *Münchener theologischer Zeitschrift* 17 (1966):47–89.

Bergsma, J.S. "Qumran Self-Identity: 'Israel' or 'Judah'?" *Dead Sea Discoveries* 15 (2008):172–89.

Biale, D. *Blood and Belief: The Circulation of a Symbol between Jews and Christians*. Berkeley: University of California Press, 2007.

Biddick, K. "Paper Jews: Inscription/Ethnicity/Ethnography." *The Art Bulletin* 78.4 (1996):594–9.

– *The Typological Imaginary: Circumcision, Technology, History*. Philadelphia: University of Pennsylvania Press, 2003.

Biggs, F.M. *Sources of Anglo-Saxon Literary Culture: The Apocrypha*. Kalamazoo MI: MIP, 2007.

Biggs F.M., et al., eds. *The Sources of Anglo-Saxon Literary Culture*. Kalamazoo, MI: MIP, 2001. 264–7.

Billington, S. *Mock Kings in Medieval Society and Renaissance Drama*. Oxford: Clarendon Press, 1991.

Birchler, L. "Zur Karolingischen Architektur und Malerei in Münster-Müstair."
In *Frühmittelalterliche Kunst in den Alpenländern*. Actes du IIIe Congrès
International pour l'Étude du Haut Moyen Age, 9–14 Septembre 1951. Olten:
Urs Graf Verlag, 1954. 167–252.

Bischoff, B., and M. Lapidge, eds. and trans. *Biblical Commentaries from
the Canterbury School of Theodore and Hadrian*. CSASE 10. Cambridge:
Cambridge University Press, 1994.

Bishop, C. "*Þyrs, ent, eoten, gigans* – Anglo-Saxon Ontologies of "Giants"."
NM 107 (2006):259–70.

Bishop, N. "An Iconographical Study of the Appearance of *Synagoga* in
Carolingian Ivories." In *Jews in Medieval Christendom: Slay Them Not*, edited
by K.T. Utterback and M.L Price. Leiden: Brill, 2013.

Blair, J. *The Church in Anglo-Saxon Society*. Oxford: Oxford University Press,
2005.

Blair, P.H. *The World of Bede*. Cambridge: Cambridge University Press, 1970.

Blumenkranz, B. *Juifs et chrétiens dans le monde occidental, 430–1096*. Paris:
Mouton, 1960.

– *Les auteurs chrétiens latins du moyen âge sur les juifs et le judaisme*. Paris:
Mouton, 1963.

– "The Roman Church and the Jews." In *Essential Papers on Judaism and
Christianity in Conflict: From Late Antiquity to the Reformation*, edited by
J. Cohen. New York: New York University Press, 1991. 193–230.

Bohak, G. *Ancient Jewish Magic: A History*. Cambridge: Cambridge University
Press, 2008.

Böker, R. "Windnamen." In *Paulys Realencyclopädie der classischen Altertum-
swissenschaft. Neue Bearbeitung*, edited by G. Wissowa. 49 vols. in 58. Ser. 2,
vol. XVI. Stuttgart: Alfred Druckenmüller, 1893–1980. Cols. 2288–325.

Bolton, D.K. "The Study of the Consolation of Philosophy in Anglo-Saxon
England." *Archives d'histoire doctrinale et littéraire du Moyen Âge* 44
(1977):33–78.

Borgehammar, S. "A Monastic Conception of the Liturgical Year." In *The
Liturgy of the Medieval Church*, edited by T.J. Heffernan and E.A. Matter.
Kalamazoo, MI: MIP, 2001.

– *How the Holy Cross Was Found: From Event to Medieval Legend with an
Appendix of Texts*. Bibliotheca theologiae practicae 47. Stockholm: Almqvist
& Wiksell International, 1991.

Borst, A. *Der Turmbau von Babel: Geschichte der Meinungen über Ursprung und
Vielfast der Sprachen und Völker*. 6 vols. Stuttgart: Anton Heirsemann, 1958.

Boyarin, D. *A Radical Jew: Paul and the Politics of Identity*. Berkeley: University
of California Press, 1994.

– "The Subversion of the Jews: Moses's Veil and the Hermeneutics of
   Supersession." In *Sparks of the Logos: Essays in Rabbinic Hermeneutics*.
   Leiden: Brill, 2003. 184–210.

Boyd, W.J.P. "Aldrediana VII: Hebraica." *English Philological Studies* 10
   (1967):1–32.

Brandt, M., ed. *Das kostbare Evangeliar des heiligen Bernward*. Munich: Prestel,
   1993.

Brewer, E.C. *A Dictionary of Miracles: Imitative, Realistic, and Dogmatic*.
   Philadelphia: Lippincott, 1884.

Broderick, H.R. "The Veil of Moses as Exegetical Image in the Illustrated Old
   English Hexateuch (London, BL Cotton MS Claudius B.iv)." In *Insular
   and Anglo-Saxon Art and Thought in the Early Medieval Period*, edited by
   C. Hourihane. Princeton: Index of Christian Art, Princeton University, 2011.
   271–85.

Brown, D.P. *Anglo-Saxon England*. Totowa, NJ: Rowman and Littlefield, 1978.

Budny, M. *Insular, Anglo-Saxon, and Early Anglo-Norman Manuscript Art
   at Corpus Christi College, Cambridge: an Illustrated Catalogue*. 2 vols.
   Kalamazoo, MI: MIP, 1997.

– "'St Dunstan's Classbook' and its Frontispiece: Dunstan's Portrait and
   Autograph." In *St Dunstan: His Life, Times and Cult*, edited by N. Ramsay,
   M. Sparks, and T. Tatton-Brown. Woodbridge: The Boydell Press, 1992.
   103–42.

– "The Vivian Bible and Scribal, Editorial, and Organizational Marks." In *Making
   the Medieval Book: Techniques of Production*, edited by L.L. Brownrigg. Los
   Altos Hills: Anderson-Lovelace, 1995. 199–239.

Bulfinch, T. *Bulfinch's Mythology*. New York: Modern Library, 1979.

Cain, A. *The Letters of Jerome: Asceticism, Biblical Exegesis, and the Construction
   of Christian Authority in Late Antiquity*. Oxford: Oxford University Press,
   2009.

Cain, C. "The Apocryphal Legend of Abgar in Ælfric's *Lives of Saints*." *PQ* 89
   (2010):383–402.

Campbell, J. *The Anglo-Saxon State*. London; New York: Hambledon Press,
   2000.

– "The United Kingdom of England: The Anglo-Saxon Achievement." In
   Uniting the Kingdom? The Making of British History, edited by A. Grant and
   K.J. Stringer. London: Routledge, 1995.

Carruthers, M. *The Craft of Thought: Meditation, Rhetoric and the Making
   of Images, 400–1200*. New York: Cambridge University Press, 1998.

Carter, F.S. "Celestial Dance: A Search for Perfection." *Dance Research:
   The Journal of the Society for Dance Research* 5 (1987):3–17.

Casey, M. *An Aramaic Approach to Q: Sources for the Gospels of Matthew and Luke*. Society for New Testament Studies 202. Cambridge: Cambridge University Press, 2002.

Cassidy, F.J., and R. Ringler, eds. *Bright's Old English Grammar and Reader*. 3rd ed., 2nd corrected printing. New York: Holt, Rinehart and Winston, 1971.

Chaney, W.A. *The Cult of Kingship in Anglo-Saxon England: The Transition from Paganism to Christianity*. Berkeley, CA: University of California Press, 1970.

Chardonnens, L.S. *Anglo-Saxon Prognostics, 900–1100: Study and Texts*. Leiden: Brill, 2007.

Chazan, R. *Medieval Stereotypes and Modern Antisemitism*. Berkeley: University of California Press, 1997.

Chazelle, C.M. *The Crucified God in the Carolingian Era: Theology and Art of Christ's Passion*. New York: Cambridge University Press, 2001.

Chevalier, U. *Repertorium Hymnologicum: Catalogue des chants, hymnes, proses, séquences, tropes en usage dans l'église latine depuis les origines jusqu'à nos jours*. 6 vols. Subsidia Hagiographica 4. Louvain: Lefever, 1892–1919.

Chevin, l'abbé. *Dictionnaire latin-français des noms propres de lieux ayant une certaine notoriété principalement au point de vue ecclésiastique et monastique*. Paris: Retaux, 1897.

Cheyette, B. *Constructions of "The Jew" in English literature and Society: Racial Representations: 1875–1945*. Cambridge: Cambridge University Press, 1993.

Clemoes, P.A.M. "The Chronology of Ælfric's Works." In *The Anglo-Saxons: Studies in Some Aspects of their History and Culture presented to Bruce Dickins*. London: Bowes, 1959. 212–47.

Coatsworth, E. "The Book of Enoch and Anglo-Saxon Art." In *Apocryphal Texts and Traditions in Anglo-Saxon England*, edited by K. Powell and D. Scragg. Cambridge: D.S. Brewer, 2003. 135–50.

Cohen, A. *The Uta Codex: Art, Philosophy, and Reform in Eleventh-Century Germany*. University Park, PA: Pennsylvania State University Press, 2000.

Cohen, J. "A 1096 Complex? Constructing the First Crusade in Jewish Historical Memory, Medieval and Modern." In *Jews and Christians in Twelfth-Century Europe*, edited by Michael Signer and John Van Engen. Notre-Dame, IN: University of Notre Dame Press, 2000. 9–26.

– "Augustine's Doctrine of Jewish Witness Revisited." *Journal of Religion* 89 (2009):564–78.

– *Christ Killers: The Jews and the Passion from the Bible to the Big Screen*. Oxford: Oxford University Press, 2007.

– *Living Letters of the Law: Ideas of the Jew in Medieval Christianity*. Berkeley: University of California Press, 1999.

Cohen, J.J. *Of Giants: Sex, Monsters, and the Middle Ages.* Minneapolis: University of Minnesota Press, 1999.

– "The Flow of Blood in Medieval Norwich." *Speculum* 79, no. 1(2004):26–65.

Cohen, S.J.D. *The Beginnings of Jewishness.* Berkeley: University of California, 1999.

Cohn, N. *Warrant for Genocide: The Myth of the Jewish World-Conspiracy and the Protocols of the Elders of Zion.* New York: Harper and Row, 1967.

Cohn, Y.B. *Tangled up in Text: Tefillin and the Ancient World.* Brown Judaic Studies 351. Providence, R.I.: Brown Judaic Studies, 2008.

Collins, A.Y. *Crisis and Catharsis: The Power of the Apocalypse.* Philadelphia: Westminster Press, 1984.

Connell, M. *Eternity Today: On the Liturgical Year.* 2 vols. New York: Continuum, 2006.

Corthals, J. "The Rhetoric in *Aided Chonchobuir.*" *Ériu* 40 (1989):41–59.

Cox, C. *The Judaic Other in Dante, Chaucer, and the Gawain Poet.* Gainesville, FL: University of Florida Press, 2005.

Cramp, R. "Monkwearmouth and Jarrow: The Archeological Evidence." In *Famulus Christi: Essays in Commemoration of the Thirteenth Centenary of the Birth of the Venerable Bede*, edited by G. Bonner. London: SPCK, 1976.

Cross, J.E. "Saint-Omer 202 as the Manuscript Source for the Old English Texts." In *Two Old English Apocrypha and Their Manuscript Source: The Gospel of Nichodemus and The Avenging of the Saviour.* CSASE 19. Cambridge: Cambridge University Press, 1996. 82–104.

– ed. *Two Old English Apocrypha and Their Manuscript Source: The Gospel of Nichodemus and The Avenging of the Saviour.* CSASE 19. Cambridge: Cambridge University Press, 1996.

Cross, J.E., and J. Crick. "The Manuscript: Saint-Omer, Bibliothèque Municipale, 202." In *Two Old English Apocrypha and Their Manuscript Source: The Gospel of Nichodemus and The Avenging of the Saviour*, edited by J.E. Cross. CSASE 19. Cambridge: Cambridge University Press, 1996.

Cwi, J.S. "A Study in Carolingian Political Theology: The David Cycle at St. John, Müstair." In *Riforma religiosa e arti nell'epoca carolingia: Atti del XXIVe Congresso Internazionale di Storia dell'Arte*, edited by A. Schmid. Bologna: C.L.U.E.B, 1983. 117–27.

Czachesz, I. *Commission Narratives: A Comparative Study of the Canonical and Apocryphal Acts.* Studies on Early Christian Apocrypha 8. Leuven: Peeters, 2007.

Daniélou, J. "Abraham dans la tradition Chrétienne." In *Abraham Père des Croyants*, edited by E. Tisserant. Cahier Sionens 2. Paris: Éditions du Cerf, 1952. 68–87.

– *From Shadows to Reality: Studies in the Biblical Typology of the Fathers*. Translated by W. Hibberd. London: Burns and Oates, 1960.

– *The Bible and the Liturgy*. Notre Dame, IN: University of Notre Dame Press, 1966.

Darby, P. *Bede and the End of Time*. Burlington VT: Ashgate, 2011.

– "Bede's Eschatological Thought." PhD diss., University of Birmingham, 2009.

Davila, J.R. "Scriptural Exegesis in the *Treatise of the Vessels*, a Legendary Account of the Hiding of the Temple Treasures." In *With Letters of Light: Studies in the Dead Sea Scrolls, Early Jewish Apocalypticism, Magic, and Mysticism in Honor of Rachel Elior*, edited by D.V. Arbel and A.A. Orlov. Berlin: Walter de Gruyter, 2011. 45–61.

Davis, K. *Periodization and Sovereignty: How Ideas of Feudalism and Secularization Govern the Politics of Time*. Philadelphia: University of Pennsylvania Press, 2008.

Dean, J. "The World Grown Old and Genesis in Middle English Historical Writings." *Speculum* 57, no. 3 (1982):548–68.

Dean, J.M. *The World Grown Old in Later Medieval Literature*. Cambridge, MA: Medieval Academy of America, 1997.

DeGregorio, S. "Bede and the Old Testament." In *The Cambridge Companion to Bede*. Cambridge: Cambridge University Press, 2010.

– "Introduction: The New Bede." In *Innovation and Tradition in the Writings of the Venerable Bede*. Morgantown: West Virginia University Press, 2006.

– Review of *The Footsteps of Israel: Understanding Jews in Anglo-Saxon England*, by Andrew Scheil. *JEGP* 104, no. 4 (2005):551–3.

– ed. *The Cambridge Companion to Bede*. Cambridge: Cambridge University Press, 2010.

De Hamel, C. *The Book: A History of the Bible*. New York: Phaidon, 2005.

Dekker, K. "Pentecost and Linguistic Self-Consciousness in Anglo-Saxon England: Bede and Ælfric." *Journal English and Germanic Philology* 104 (2005):344–72.

Delany, S. *Chaucer and the Jews: Sources, Contexts, Meanings*. New York: Routledge, 2002.

Derrida, J. *Specters of Marx: the State of the Debt, the Work of Mourning, and the New International*. New York: Routledge, 1994.

Deschamps, P. *Dictionnaire de géographie ancienne et moderne à l'usage du libraire et de l'amateur de livres*. Paris: Firmin-Didot, 1870.

Deshman, R. *The Benedictional of Aethelwold*. Princeton: Princeton University Press, 1995.

– "*Benedictus Monarcha et Monachus*: Early Medieval Ruler Theology and the Anglo-Saxon Reform." In *Eye and Mind: Collected Essays in Anglo-Saxon and Early Medieval Art*, edited by A.S. Cohen. Kalamazoo, MI: MIP, 2010. 192–219.

– "Christus Rex et Magi Reges: Kingship and Christology in Ottonian and Anglo-Saxon Art." In *Eye and Mind: Collected Essays in Anglo-Saxon and Early Medieval Art*, edited by A.S. Cohen. Kalamazoo, MI: MIP, 2010. 104–36.

– "The Exalted Servant: the Ruler Theology of the Prayerbook of Charles the Bald." In *Eye and Mind: Collected Essays in Anglo-Saxon and Early Medieval Art*, edited by A.S. Cohen. Kalamazoo, MI: MIP, 2010. 137–71.

Deshusses, J. *Le sacramentaire grégorien, ses principales formes d'après les plus anciens manuscrits*. Spicilegium Friburgense, v. 16. Fribourg: Éditions universitaires, 1971.

Despres, D.L. "Adolescence and Sanctity: *The Life and Passion of William of Norwich*." *Journal of Religion* 90, no. 1 (2010):33–62.

Despres, E. "The Protean Jew in the Vernon Manuscript." In *Chaucer and the Jews: Sources, Contexts, Meanings*, edited by S. Delaney. New York: Routledge, 2002. 145–64.

Diebold, W. "The Ruler Portrait of Charles the Bald in the S. Paolo Bible." *Art Bulletin* 76 (1994):6–18.

– "Verbal, Visual, and Cultural Literacy in Medieval Art: Word and Image in the Psalter of Charles the Bald." *Word + Image* 8 (1992):89–99.

Dionisotti, A.C. "On Bede, Grammars, and Greek." *Revue Bénédictine* 92 (1982):111–41.

Discenza, N.G. *The King's English: Strategies of Translation in the Old English Boethius*. Albany: State University of New York Press, 2005.

– "The Paradox of Humility in the Alfredian Translations." *SP* 76 (2004):44–52.

Doane, N., and W.P. Stoneman. *Purloined Letters: The Twelfth-Century Reception of the Anglo-Saxon Illustrated Hexateuch (British library, Cotton Claudius B. IV)*. Tempe, AZ: MRTS, 2011.

Dobschütz, E. von. *Christusbilder: Untersuchungen zur christlichen Legende*. TU 18. Leipzig: Hinrichs, 1899.

Dobson, R.B., and H. Birkett. *The Jewish Communities of Medieval England: The Collected Essays of R.B. Dobson*. York: The Borthwick Institute, University of York, 2010.

Dodwell, C.R. "Techniques of Painting in Anglo-Saxon Manuscripts." *Artigianato e technica nella società dell'alto Medioevo occidentale (2–8 Aprile 1970), Settimane di studio del Centro italiano di studi sull'alto Medioevo 18/2*. Spoleto: Presso la sede del Centro, 1971. 643–62, 675–83.

Dunn, J.D.G., ed. *Romans 1–8*. Word Biblical Commentary, vol. 38A. Dallas, TX: Word Books, 1988.

Dutton, P., and H. Kessler. *The Poetry and Paintings of the First Bible of Charles the Bald*. Ann Arbor: University of Michigan Press, 1997.

Earl, J.W. "Christian Traditions and the Old English *Exodus*." In *The Poems of MS Junius 11: Basic Readings*, edited by R.M. Liuzza. London: Routledge, 2002. 137–72.

– "The Typological Structure of *Andreas*." In *Old English Literature in Context*, edited by J.D. Niles. Cambridge: D.S. Brewer; Totowa, NJ: Rowman & Littlefield, 1980.

Eaton, T. *Plundering the Past: Roman Stonework in Medieval Britain*. Stroud, UK: Tempus, 2010.

Edson, E. *Mapping Time and Space: How Medieval Mapmakers Viewed their World*. London: British Library, 1997.

Eerdmans, B.D. *The Covenant at Mount Sinai Viewed in Light of Antique Thought*. Leiden: Burgersdijk & Niermans, 1939.

Eggenberger, C. *Psalterium aureum Sancti Galli: mittelalterliche Psalterillustration im Kloster St. Gallen*. Sigmaringen: Jan Thorbecke Verlag, 1987.

– "Zur Illustration des St. Galler Folchard-Psalters." In *Riforma religiosa e arti nell'epoca carolingia: Atti del XXIVe Congresso Internazionale di Storia dell'Arte*, edited by A. Schmid. Bologna: C.L.U.E.B, 1983. 99–107.

Egger, K. *Lexicon nominum locorum*. Vatican City: Officina Libraria Vaticana, 1977.

Eliav, Y.Z. *God's Mountain: The Temple Mount in Time, Place and Memory*. Baltimore: Johns Hopkins University Press, 2005.

Elukin, J. "Judaism: From Heresy to Pharisee in Early Medieval Christian Literature." *Traditio* 57 (2002):49–66.

Esposito, M. "Miscellaneous Notes on Medieval Latin Literature." In *Mario Esposito: Studies in Hiberno-Latin Literature*, edited by M. Gorman. Aldershot: Variorum, 2006. 104–14 [Essay IX].

Estes, H. "Lives in Translation: Jews in the Anglo-Saxon Literary Imagination." PhD diss., New York University, 1998.

Euw, Anton von. *Die St. Galler Buchkunst vom 8. bis zum Ende des 11. Jahrhunderts*. Monasterium Sancti Galli 3. 2 vols. St Gallen: Verlag am Klosterhof, 2008.

Eve, E. *The Jewish Context of Jesus' Miracles*. London: Sheffield Academic Press, 2002.

Farmer, D.H. *The Age of Bede*. Harmondsworth: Penguin, 1983.

Fee, C. "Productive Destruction: Torture, Text and the Body in the Old English *Andreas*." *Essays in Medieval Studies* 11 (1994):51–62.

Ferhatovic, D. "Spolia-Inflected Poetics of the Old English *Andreas*." *Studies in Philology* 110 (2013):199–219.

Figgis, J.N. "The Political Aspects of S. Augustine's 'City of God.'" London: Longman, 1921.

Flach, J. *Études critiques sur l'histoire du droit romaine au moyen âge*. Paris: L. Larose et Forcel, 1890.

Fleming, D. "'The Most Exalted Language': Anglo-Saxon Perceptions of Hebrew." PhD Dissertation, University of Toronto, 2006.

Foot, S. "The Making of *Angelcynn*: English Identity before the Norman Conquest." In *Old English Literature*, edited by R.M. Liuzza. New Haven, CT: Yale University Press, 2002. 51–78.

– *Monastic Life in Anglo-Saxon England, c. 600–900*. Cambridge: Cambridge University Press, 2006.

Frantzen, A.J. "All Created Things: Material Contexts for Bede's Story of Cædmon." In *Cædmon's Hymn and Material Culture in the World of Bede: Six Essays*, edited by A.J. Frantzen and J. Hines. Morgantown: West Virginia University Press, 2007. 111–49.

Fredriksen, P. *Augustine and the Jews: a Christian Defense of Jews and Judaism*. New Haven: Yale University Press, 2010.

– "*Excaecati Occulta Justitia Dei*: Augustine on Jews and Judaism." *Journal of Early Christian Studies* 3 (1995):299–324.

Freeman, A. *Theodulf of Orléans: Charlemagne's Spokesman Against the Second Council Of Nicaea*. Aldershot: Ashgate Variorum, 2003.

Freeman, A., and P. Meyvaert. *Opus Caroli Regis contra synodum (Libri Carolini)*. MGH, Concilia 2, suppl. 1. Hannover: Hahnsche Buchhandlung, 1998.

– "The Meaning of Theodulf's Apse Mosaic at Germigny-des-Prés." *Gesta* 40 (2001):125–39.

Friedman, R.E. *Commentary on the Torah*. New York: Harper Collins, 2001.

Freud, S. "The Uncanny." In *The Standard Edition of the Complete Psychological Works of Sigmund Freud*, edited by J. Strachey. Vol. 17. London: The Hogarth Press, 2001. 217–56.

Friesen, B. "Visions and Revisions: The Sources and Analogues of *Andreas*." PhD diss., University of Toronto, 2008.

Frizzell L.E., and J.F. Henderson. "Jews and Judaism in the Medieval Latin Liturgy." In *The Liturgy of the Medieval Church*, edited by T.J. Heffernan and E.A. Matter. Kalmazoo, MI: MIP, 2001. 187–214.

Frühmorgen-Voss, H., N.Ott, and U. Bodemann, eds. *Katalog der deutschsprachigen illustrierten Handschriften des Mittelalte*rs. Munich: Kommission für Deutsche Literatur des Mittelalters der Bayerischen Akademie der Wissenschaften, 1986–.

Fulk, R.D. *A History of Old English Metre*. Philadelphia: University of Pennsylvania Press, 1992.

Gaehdem, J., and F. Mütherich. *Carolingian Painting*. New York: Chatto & Windus, 1976.

Gameson, R. *The Role of Art in the Late Anglo-Saxon Church*. Oxford: Clarendon Press, 1995.

Gatch, M. McC. *Preaching and Theology in Anglo-Saxon England*. Toronto: University of Toronto Press, 1977.

Gneuss, H. "A Preliminary List of Manuscripts Written or Owned in England up to 1100." *ASE* 9 (1981):1–60.

– *Hymnar und Hymnen im englischen Mittelalter*. Tübingen: Max Niemeyer, 1968.

Gneuss, H., and M. Lapidge. *Anglo-Saxon Manuscripts: A Bibliographical Handlist of Manuscripts and Manuscript Fragments Written or Owned in England up to 1100*. Toronto: University of Toronto Press, 2014.

Godbey, A.H. *The Lost Tribes a Myth: Suggestions towards Rewriting Hebrew History*. Durham, NC: Duke University Press, 1930.

Godden, M. *Ælfric's Homilies: Introduction, Commentary and Glossary*. EETS, s.s., 18. Oxford: Oxford University Press, 2000.

– "New Year's Day in late Anglo-Saxon England." *Notes and Queries* 237 (1992):148–50.

– "The Old English Life of St Neot and the Legends of King Alfred." *ASE 39* 2010):193–225.

Godlove, S. "Apostolic Discourse and Christian Identity in Anglo-Saxon Literature." PhD diss., University of Illinois, 2010.

– "Bodies as Borders: Cannibalism and Conversion in the Old English *Andreas*." *Studies in Philology* 106 (2009):137–60.

Golb, N. *The Jews in Medieval Normandy: A Social and Intellectual History*. Cambridge; New York: Cambridge University Press, 1998.

Goll, J., M. Exner, and S. Hirsch. *Müstair. Die mittelalterlichen Wandbilder in der Klosterkirche*. 2nd ed. Zurich: Neue Zürcher Zeitung, 2007.

Goodenough, E.R. *Jewish Symbols in the Graeco-Roman Period*. Vol. 2. New York: Pantheon Books, 1953.

Goodwin, D. *Take Hold of the Robe of a Jew: Herbert of Bosham's Christian Hebraism*. Leiden: Brill, 2006.

Gorman, M.M. "Source Marks and Chapter Division in Bede's Commentary on Luke." *Revue Bénédictine* 112 (2002):246–90.

Graesse, J.G.T. *Orbis Latinus: Lexikon lateinischer geographischer Namen des Mittelalters und der Neuzeit*, edited by H. Plechl and S.-C. Plechl. Großausgabe, 3 vols. Braunschweig: Klinckhardt & Biermann, 1972.

Gransden, A. *Legends, Traditions and History in Medieval England*. London: Hambledon Press, 1992.

Gretsch, M. *The Intellectual Foundations of the English Benedictine Reform.* Cambridge: Cambridge University Press, 1999.

Hahn, C.J. *Strange Beauty: Issues in the Making and Meaning of Reliquaries, 400–circa 1204.* University Park, PA: Pennsylvania State University Press, 2012.

Hahn, T. "The Difference the Middle Ages Makes: Color and Race before the Modern World." *JMEMS* 31, no. 1 (2001):1–37.

Halbrooks, J. "Ælfric, the Maccabees, and the Problem of Christian Heroism." *Studies in Philology* 106, no. 3 (2009):263–84.

Hall, T.N. "Medieval Traditions about the Site of Judgment." *Essays in Medieval Studies* 10 (1993):79–97.

– "The Cross as Green Tree in the *Vindicta Salvatoris* and the Green Rod of Moses in *Exodus*." *ES* 72 (1991):297–307.

– "The *Evangelium Nichodemi* and *Vindicta Salvatoris* in Anglo-Saxon England." In *Two Old English Apocrypha and Their Manuscript Source: The Gospel of Nichodemus and The Avenging of the Saviour*, edited by J.E. Cross. CSASE 19. Cambridge: Cambridge University Press, 1996. 36–81.

Harris, S.J. "Oaths in *The Battle of Maldon*." In *The Hero Recovered: Essays on Medieval Heroism in Honor of George Clark*, edited by R. Waugh and J. Weldon. Kalamazoo: MIP, 2010.

– *Race and Ethnicity in Anglo-Saxon Literature.* Studies in Medieval History and Culture 24. London and New York: Routledge, 2003.

– "The Liturgical Context of Ælfric's Homilies for Rogation." In *The Old English Homily: Precedent, Practice, and Appropriation*, edited by A.J. Kleist. Turnhout: Brepols, 2007. 143–69.

Harrison, K. "The Beginning of the Year in England, c. 500–900." *ASE* 2 (1973):51–70.

Hassel, R.C., Jr. *Renaissance Drama and the English Church Year.* Lincoln: University of Nebraska Press, 1979.

Hauer, S.R. "The Patriarchal Digression in the Old English *Exodus*, Lines 362–446." *Studies in Philology* 78 (1981):77–90.

Hausamann, T. *Die tanzende Salome in der Kunst von der christlichen Frühzeit bis um 1500: ikonographische Studien.* Zurich: Juris Druck + Verlag, 1980.

Hawkes, J. *The Sandbach Crosses: Sign and Significance in Anglo-Saxon Sculpture.* Dublin: Four Courts Press, 2002.

Heffernan, T.J., and E.A. Matter. "Introduction to the Liturgy of the Medieval Church." In *The Liturgy of the Medieval Church.* Kalamazoo, MI: MIP, 2001. 1–10.

Heimann, A. "A Twelfth-Century Manuscript from Winchcombe and its Illustrations." *Journal of the Warburg and Courtauld Institutes* 28 (1965):94–106.

Henderson, G. "Late-Antique Influences in Some English Mediaeval Illustrations of Genesis." *Journal of the Warburg and Courtauld Institutes* vol. 25, No. 3/4 (1962):172–98.

– "The Joshua Cycle in B.M. Cot. Claud. BIV." In *Studies in English Bible Illustration.* London: Pindar Press, 1985.

– "The Programme of Illustrations in Bodleian MS Junius XI." In *Studies in English Bible Illustration*, vol. 1. London: Pindar Press, 1985. 138–83.

– *Vision and Image in Early Christian England.* Cambridge: Cambridge University Press, 1999.

Heng, G. "Jews, Saracens, 'Black Men,' Tartars: England in a World of Racial Difference. In *A Companion to Medieval English Literature and Culture, c.1350–c.1500*, edited by P. Brown. Malden, MA: Blackwell, 2007. 247–68.

Herbert, J.A., ed. *Titus & Vespasian or The Destruction of Jerusalem in Rhymed Couplets.* London: Roxburghe Club, 1905.

Hermann, J.P. *Allegories of War: Language and Violence in Old English Poetry.* Ann Arbor: University of Michigan Press, 1989.

Hesbert, R.-J., ed. *Antiphonale Missarum Sextuplex.* Brussels: Vromant, 1935.

– *Corpus Antiphonalium Officii.* 6 vols. Rerum Ecclesiasticarum Documenta, Series Maior, Fontes 7–12. Rome: Herder, 1963–79.

Hessels, J.H., ed. *An Eighth-Century Latin–Anglo-Saxon Glossary*. Cambridge: Cambridge University Press, 1890.

Hieatt, C.B. "The Harrowing of Mermedonia: Typological Patterns in the Old English *Andreas*." *NM* 77 (1976):49–62.

Hill, T.D. "Hebrews, Israelites, and Wicked Jews: An Onomastic Crux in *Andreas* 161–67." *Traditio* 32 (1976): 358–61.

– "Literary History and Old English Poetry: The Case of *Christ I, II, III*." In *Sources of Anglo-Saxon Culture, Studies in Medieval Culture XX*, edited by P.E. Szarmach. Kalamazoo, MI: MIP, 1986. 3–22.

– "Sapiential Structure and Figural Narrative in the Old English *Elene*." In *Cynewulf: Basic Readings*, edited by R. Bjork. New York: Garland, 1996. 207–28.

– "The Sphragis as Apotropaic Sign: *Andreas* 1334–44." *Anglia* 101 (1983):147–51.

– "Two Notes on Patristic Allusion in *Andreas*." *Anglia* 84 (1966):156–62.

Hitler, A. *Mein Kampf*. Translated by J. Murphy. http://gutenberg.net.au/ebooks02/0200601.txt.

Hoffman, E. "Platonism in Augustine's Philosophy of History." In *Philosophy & History: Essays Presented to Ernst Cassirer*, edited by R. Klibansky and H.J. Paton. Gloucester MA: Peter Smith, 1975.

Holder, A.G. "Allegory and History in Bede's Interpretation of Sacred Architecture." *American Benedictine Review* 40 (1989):115–31.

– "Bede and the Tradition of Patristic Exegesis." *Anglican Theological Review* 72 (1990):339–411.

– "New Treasures and Old in Bede's 'De Tabernaculo' and 'De Templo.'" *Revue Benedictine* 99 (1989):237–49.

Horn, E.T. III. *The Christian Year*. Philadelphia: Muhlenberg Press, 1957.

Hourihane, C., ed. *King David in the Index of Christian Art*. Princeton: Department of Art and Archaeology, 2002.

Howe, N. "Looking for Home in Anglo-Saxon England." In *Home and Homelessness in the Medieval and Renaissance World*. Notre Dame: University of Notre Dame, 2004.

– *Migration and Mythmaking in Anglo-Saxon England*. New Haven: Yale University Press, 1989.

– "The Figural Presence of Erich Auerbach." *The Yale Review* 85 (1997):136–43.

– *Writing the Map of Anglo-Saxon England: Essays in Cultural Geography*. New Haven: Yale University Press, 2008.

Hutton, R. *The Rise and Fall of Merry England: The Ritual Year, 1400–1700*. Oxford: Oxford University Press, 1994.

– *The Stations of the Sun: A History of the Ritual Year in Britain*. Oxford: Oxford University Press, 1996.

Hvalvik, R. "Christ Proclaiming his Law to the Apostles: The Traditio Legis-Motif in Early Christian Art and Literature." In *The New Testament and Early Christian Literature in Greco-Roman Context: Studies in Honor of David E. Aune*, edited by J. Fotopoulos. Leiden: Brill, 2010. 405–35.

Hyams, P.R. "The Jews in Medieval England: 1066–1290." In *England and Germany in the High Middle Ages*, edited by A. Haverkamp and H. Vollrath. New York: Oxford University Press, 1996. 173–92.

Irving, E.B., Jr. "New Notes on the Old English *Exodus*." *Anglia* 90 (1972): 289–324.

Itzkowitz, J.B. "Jews, Indians, Phylacteries: Jerome on Matthew 23:5." *Journal of Early Christian Studies* 15 (2007):563–72.

Izydorczyk, Z. *Manuscripts of the Evangelium Nicodemi: A Census*. Subsidia Mediaevalia 21. Toronto: PIMS, 1993.

– "The Evangelium Nicodemi in the Latin Middle Ages." In *The Medieval Gospel of Nicodemus: Texts, Intertexts, and Contexts in Western Europe*. MRTS 158. Tempe: MRTS, 1997.

Jacobs, J. *The Jews of Angevin England: Documents and Records*. New York: Putnam, 1893.

Jenkins, C. "Bede as Exegete and Theologian." In *Bede, His Life, Times, and Writings: Essays in Commemoration of the Twelfth Centenary of His Death*, edited by A.H. Thompson. New York: Russell & Russell, 1966. 152–200.

Johnson, D.F. "A Program of Illumination in the Old English Illustrated Hexateuch: 'Visual Typology'?" In *The Old English Hexateuch: Aspects and Approaches*, edited by R. Barnhouse and B. Withers. Kalamazoo, MI: MIP, 2000. 169–99.

– "The Crux Usualis as Apotropaic Weapon in Anglo-Saxon England." In *The Place of the Cross in Anglo-Saxon England*, edited by C.E. Karkov, S.L. Keefer, and K.L. Jolly. Woodbridge: Boydell, 2006. 80–95.

– "The Fall of Lucifer in *Genesis A* and Two Anglo-Latin Royal Charters: "King Edgar's Privilege" and a Burton Abbey Charter." *JEGP* 97 (1998):500–21.

Jolly, K.L. *Popular Religion in Late Saxon England: Elf Charms in Context*. Chapel Hill: University of North Carolina Press, 1996.

Jones, A. "The Significance of the Royal Consecration of Edgar in 973." *The Journal of Ecclesiastical History* 33 (1983):375–90.

Jones, C.A. "The Book of the Liturgy in Anglo-Saxon England." *Speculum* 73, no. 3 (1998):659–702.

Jones, C.W. "A Legend of Saint Pachomius." *Speculum* 18 (1943):198–210.

– "Some Introductory Remarks on Bede's Commentary on Genesis." *Sacris Erudiri* 19 (1969–70):115–98.

Jones, S.R., and S. Watson, eds. *Christians and Jews in Angevin England: The York Massacre of 1190, Narratives and Context*. Woodbridge: Boydell & Brewer, 2013.

Julius, A. *Trials of the Diaspora: A History of Anti-Semitism in England*. Oxford: Oxford University Press, 2010.

Kamesar, A. *Jerome, Greek Scholarship, and the Hebrew Bible: A Study of the Quaestiones Hebraicae in Genesim*. Oxford: Oxford University Press, 1993.

Karkov, C.E. *Text and Picture in Anglo-Saxon England: Narrative Strategies in the Junius 11 Manuscript*. Cambridge: Cambridge University Press, 2001.

– *Text and Picture in Anglo-Saxon England: Narrative Strategies in the Junius 11 Manuscript*. 2nd ed. CSASE. Cambridge: Cambridge University Press, 2009.

– "The Frontispiece to the New Minster Charter and the King's Two Bodies." In *Edgar, King of the English, 959–975: New Interpretations*, edited by D. Scragg. Woodbridge: Boydell Press, 2008. 224–41.

– *The Ruler Portraits of Anglo-Saxon England*. Woodbridge: Boydell Press, 2004.

Kauffman, C.M. *A Survey of Manuscripts Illuminated in the British Isles: Romanesque Manuscripts, 1066–1190*. London: Harvey Miller, 1975.

Keck, L.E., ed. *The New Interpreter's Bible*. 12 vols. Nashville: Abingdon, 1998.

Ker, N.R. *Catalogue of Manuscripts Containing Anglo-Saxon*. London: Oxford University Press, 1957.

Kessler, H. *Seeing Medieval Art*. Peterborough, ON: Broadview Press, 2004.

– *Spiritual Seeing: Picturing God's Invisibility in Medieval Art*. Philadelphia: University of Pennsylvania Press, 2000.

– *The Illustrated Bibles from Tours*. Princeton: Princeton University Press, 1977.

Kindschi, L. "The Latin–Old English Glossaries in Plantin-Moretus MS 32 and British Museum MS Additional 32,246." PhD diss., Stanford University, 1955.

Kleinschmidt, H. *Untersuchungen über das englische Königtum im 10. Jahrhundert*. Göttingen: Musterschmidt, 1979.

Kleist, A. *Striving with Grace: Views Of Free Will in Anglo-Saxon England*. Toronto: University of Toronto Press, 2008.

Kominko, M. *The World of Kosmas: Illustrated Byzantine Codices of the Christian Topography*. Cambridge: Cambridge University Press, 2013. 109–27.

Korhammer, M. *Die Monastischen Cantica im Mittelalter und ihre altenglische interlinear Versionen*. Munich: Fink, 1976.

Kruger, S.F. *The Spectral Jew: Conversion and Embodiment in Medieval Europe*. Minneapolis: University of Minnesota Press, 2006.

Krummel, M.A. *Crafting Jewishness in Medieval England: Legally Absent, Virtually Present*. New York: Palgrave Macmillan, 2011.

Krusch, B., ed. "*Vita Eligii*." *MGH Scriptures rerum Merovingicarum* 4. Hannover: Hahn, 1902. 634–761.

Ladner, G. *The Idea of Reform: Its Impact on Christian Thought and Action in the Age of the Fathers*. Cambridge, MA: Harvard University Press, 1959.

Laistner, M.L.W. "Source-Marks in Bede Manuscripts." *The Journal of Theological Studies* 34 (1933):350–4.

Lampe, G.W.H. *The Seal of the Spirit: A Study in the Doctrine of Baptism and Confirmation in the New Testament and the Fathers*. London; New York: Longmans, Green and Co., 1951.

Lampert, L. *Gender and Jewish Difference from Paul to Shakespeare*. Philadelphia: University of Pennsylvania Press, 2004.

Langmuir, G. "Anti-Judaism as the Necessary Preparation for Antisemitism." In *Toward a Definition of Antisemitism*. Berkeley: University of California Press, 1990. 57–62.

– "Thomas of Monmouth: Detector of Ritual Murder." In *Toward a Definition of Antisemitism*. Berkeley: University of California Press, 1990.

– *Toward a Definition of Antisemitism*. Berkeley: University of California Press, 1990.

Langston, D., ed. *The Consolation of Philosophy: Authoritative Text, Contexts, Criticism*. New York: W.W. Norton, 2010.

Lapidge, M. "Aethelwold as Scholar and Teacher." In *Bishop Aethelwold: his Career and Influence*, edited by B. Yorke. Woodbridge: Boydell Press, 1988. 89–117.

– "Israel the Grammarian in Anglo-Saxon England." In *Anglo-Latin Literature 900–1066*. London: The Hambledon Press, 1993. 87–104.

– *The Anglo-Saxon Library*. Oxford; New York: Oxford University Press, 2006.

– ed. *The Cult of St Swithun*. Winchester Studies I.ii. Oxford: Clarendon Press, 2003.

– "The Life of St Oswald." In *The Battle of Maldon AD 991*, edited by D. Scragg Oxford: Blackwell, 1991.

Laqueur, W. *The Changing Face of Antisemitism*. Oxford: Oxford University Press, 2006. 95–101.

Lavezzo, K. "Gregory's Boys: the Homoerotic Production of English Whiteness." In *Sex and Sexuality in Anglo-Saxon England: Essays in Memory of Daniel Gillmore Calder*, edited by C. Pasternack and L.M.C. Weston. Tempe, AZ: MRTS, 2004. 63–90.

– *Imagining a Medieval English Nation*. Minneapolis: University of Minnesota Press, 2004.

Leclercq, Jean. *The Love of Learning and the Desire for God*. New York: Fordham University Press, 1982.

Lees, C.A. *Tradition and Belief: Religious Writing in Late Anglo-Saxon England*. Minneapolis: University of Minnesota Press, 1991. 78–105.

Leone, M. "Divine Dictation: Voice and Writing in the Giving of the Law." *International Journal for the Semiotics of the Law* 14 (2001):161–77.

Lerer, S. *Literacy and Power in Anglo-Saxon Literature*. Lincoln: University of Nebraska Press, 1991.

Lewis, S. *The Rhetoric of Power in the Bayeux Tapestry*. Cambridge: Cambridge University Press, 1999.

Liebeshcütz, H. "The Crusading Movement in Its Bearing on the Christian Attitude towards Jewry." In *Essential Papers on Judaism and Christianity in Conflict: From Late Antiquity to the Reformation*, edited by J. Cohen. New York: New York University Press, 1991.

Lilley, K. "Cities of God? Medieval Urban Forms and Their Christian Symbolism." *Transactions of the Institute of British Geographers*, New Series, Vol. 29, No. 3 (2004):296–313.

Lincicum, D. *Paul and the Early Jewish Encounter with Deuteronomy*. Tübingen: Mohr Siebeck, 2010.

Lindemann, A.S., and R.S. Levy. *Antisemitism: A History*. Oxford: Oxford University Press, 2010.

Lipsius, R.A. *Die Pilatus-Acten kritisch untersucht*. 2nd ed. Kiel: Haeseler, 1886.

Lipton, S. *Images of Intolerance: the Representation of Jews and Judaism in the Bible Moralisée*. Berkeley: University of California Press, 1999.

Liuzza, R., ed. *The Old English Version of the Gospels*. London: Oxford University Press, 1994.

Logeman, H. "Anglo-Saxonica Minora." *Anglia* 11 (1889):97–120.

Longman, T., III, and D.E. Garland, eds. *The Expositor's Bible Commentary*. Rev. ed. 13 vols. Grand Rapids: Zondervan, 2006–9.

Lowe, E.A., ed. *The Bobbio Missal: A Gallican Mass-Book*. Henry Bradshaw Society LVIII. London: Harrison and Sons, 1990.

Lynch, K.M. "The Venerable Bede's Knowledge of Greek." *Traditio* 39 (1983):432–9.

MacGillivray, H.S. *The Influence of Christianity on the Vocabulary of Old English*. Studien zur englischen Philologie 8. Halle a.S.: M. Niemeyer, 1902.

Maccoby, H. *Antisemitism and Modernity: Innovation and Continuity*. London: Routledge, 2006.

MacCormack, P. "Post-Human Teratology." In *The Ashgate Research Companion to Monsters and the Monstrous*, edited by A.S. Mittman with P. Dendle. Farnham: Ashgate, 2012. 293–309.

Maclean, G.E. "Ælfric's Version of the *Interrogationes Sigeuulfi in Genesin*." *Anglia* 6 (1883):425–73, and *Anglia* 7 (1884):1–59.

Maddicott, J.R. *Simon de Montfort*. Cambridge: Cambridge University Press: 1994.

Maguire, H. "Davidic Virtue: the Crown of Constantine Monomachos and its Images." In *The Real and Ideal Jerusalem in Jewish, Christian, and Islamic Art: Studies in Honor of Bezalel Narkiss (Jewish Art 22–23)*, edited by B. Kühnel. Jerusalem: Hebrew University, 1998. 117–23.

Marchesin, I. "Le corps musical dans les images psalmiques carolingiennes et romanes." In *Le geste et les gestes au Moyen Age*. Aix-en-Provence: CUER MA, Université de Provence, 1998. 403–27.

Markus, R.A. *Signs and Meanings: World and Text in Ancient Christianity*. Liverpool: Liverpool University Press, 1996.

Marsden, R. "Old Latin Intervention in the Old English *Heptateuch*." *ASE* 23 (1994):229–64.

– *The Text of the Old Testament in Anglo-Saxon England*. Cambridge: Cambridge University Press, 1995.

Martin, R.P., ed. *James*. Word Biblical Commentary, vol. 48. Waco, TX: Word Books, 1988.

Mayhoff, K., and L. von Jan, eds. *C. Plini Secundi Naturalis historiae libri XXXVII*. 6 vols. Bibliotheca Teubneriana. Stuttgart: Teubner, 1967–2002.

Mayr-Harting, H. *The Venerable Bede, The Rule of St. Benedict, and Social Class*. Jarrow Lecture, 1976. Jarrow: Parish of Jarrow, 1976.

McArthur, A.A. *The Evolution of the Christian Year*. London: SCM Press, 1953.

McCarthy, D. "Bede's Primary Source for the Vulgate Chronology in His Chronicles in *De Temporibus* and *De Temporum Ratione*." In *Computus and Its Cultural Context in the Latin West, AD 300–1200. Proceedings of the 1st International Conference on the Science of Computus in Ireland and Europe, Galway, 14–16 July, 2006*, edited by I. Warntjes and D. Ó Cróinín. Turnhout: Brepols, 2010. 159–89.

McClintock, A. "The Angel of Progress: Pitfalls of the Term 'Post-Colonialism'." *Social Text* 31/32 (1992):84–98.

McClure, J. "Bede's Old Testament Kings." In *Ideal and Reality in Frankish and Anglo-Saxon Society: Studies Presented to J. M. Wallace-Hadrill*, edited by P. Wormald. Oxford: Blackwell, 1983. 76–98.

McCone, K. *Pagan Past and Christian Present in Early Irish Literature*. Maynooth: An Sagart, 1991.

McCulloh, J.M. "Jewish Ritual Murder: William of Norwich, Thomas of Monmouth, and the Early Dissemination of the Myth." *Speculum* 72, no. 3 (1997):698–740.

McKitterick, R. *The Frankish Church and the Carolingian Reforms, 789–895*. London: Royal Historical Society, 1977.

Meaney, A. *Anglo-Saxon Amulets and Curing Stones*. BAR British Series, 96. Oxford: B.A.R., 1981.

Mellinkoff, R. "Cain's Monstrous Progeny in *Beowulf*: Part II, Post-Diluvian Survival." *ASE* 9 (1981):183–97.

– "More about Horned Moses." *Jewish Art* 12/13 (1986–7):184–98.

– *Outcasts*, 2 vols. Berkeley: University of California Press, 1993.

– "Sarah and Hagar: Laughter and Tears." In *Illuminating the Book: Makers and Interpreters: Essays in Honour of Janet Backhouse*, edited by M. Brown and S. McKendrick. London: British Library Publishing, 1998.

– *The Horned Moses in Medieval Art and Thought*. Berkeley: University of California Press, 1970.

– "The Round, Cap-shaped Hats Depicted on Jews in BM Cotton Claudius B. Iv." *ASE* 2 (1973):155–65.

– "The Round-Topped Tablets of the Law: Sacred Symbol and Emblem of Evil." *Journal of Jewish Art* 1 (1974):28–43.

Menache, S. "Faith, Myth, and Politics: The Stereotype of the Jews and Their Expulsion from England and France." *The Jewish Quarterly Review* 75, no. 4 (1985):351–74.

Merras, M. *The Origins of the Celebration of the Christian Feast of Epiphany: An Ideological, Cultural and Historical Study*. Joensuu, Finland: Joensuu University Press, 1995.

Meyer, A.R. *Medieval Allegory and the Building of the New Jerusalem.*
Woodbridge, UK: D.S. Brewer, 2003.

Meyer, M. "Did the Daughters of Israel Come Out Dancing and Singing to
Meet David? A Biblical Image in Christian-Imperial Attire." *Byzantion* 73
(2003):467–87.

Meyvaert, P. "Bede, Cassiodorus, and the Codex Amiatinus." *Speculum* 71, no. 4
(1996):827–83.

– "The Date of Bede's *In Ezram* and His Image of Ezra in the Codex Amiatinus."
Speculum 80 (2005):1087–1133.

Michelson, H. *The Jew in Early Medieval Literature.* Amsterdam: H.J. Paris,
1926.

Millar, B. *The Siege of Jerusalem in its Physical, Literary and Historical Contexts.*
Dublin: Four Courts Press, 2000.

Mittman, A.S., and S.M. Kim. "Locating the Devil 'Her' in MS Junius 11." *Gesta*
54:1 (2015):3–25.

Monroe, L.A.S. *Josiah's Reform and the Dynamics of Defilement: Israelite Rites
of Violence and the Making of a Biblical Text.* Oxford: Oxford University
Press, 2011.

Moore, R.I. *The Formation of a Persecuting Society: Authority and Deviance in
Western Europe, 950–1250.* Malden, MA: Blackwell Publishing, 2007.

Morrison, K.F. 1988. *"I Am You": The Hermeneutics of Empathy in Western
Literature, Theology, and Art.* Princeton: Princeton University Press, 1988.
8–11.

Mundill, R. *England's Jewish Solution: Experiment and Expulsion, 1262–1290.*
Cambridge: Cambridge University Press, 1998.

– *The King's Jews: Money, Massacre and Exodus in Medieval England.* London:
Continuum, 2010.

Nardone, R.M. *The Story of the Christian Year.* NY: Paulist Press, 1991.

Nelson, J. "Coronation Rituals and Related Materials." In *Understanding
Medieval Primary Sources: Using Historical Sources to Discover Medieval
Europe*, edited by J. Rosenthal. Abingdon and New York: Routledge, 2012.

– *Politics and Ritual in Early Medieval Europe.* London: Hambledon Press, 1986.

– *Rulers and Ruling Families in Early Medieval Europe: Alfred, Charles the
Bald, and Others.* Aldershot: Ashgate Variorum, 1999.

– "The Political Ideas of Alfred of Wessex." In *Kings and Kingship in Medieval
Europe*, edited by A. Duggan. London: University of London, 1993. 125–58.

Nelson, R.D. "Josiah in the Book of Joshua." *Journal of Biblical Literature* 100
(1981):531–40.

Neuman de Vegvar, C. "*In Hoc Signo*: The Cross on Secular Objects and the
Process of Conversion." In *Cross and Culture in Anglo-Saxon England:*

Studies in Honor of George Hardin Brown, edited by K.L. Jolly, C.E. Karkov, and S.L. Keefer. Morgantown: West Virginia University Press, 2008. 79–117.

Neusner, J. *Jeremiah in Talmud and Midrash: A Source Book*. New York: University Press of America, 2006.

Neville, J. *Representations of the Natural World in Old English Poetry*. Cambridge: Cambridge UP, 1999.

Nibley, Hugh. "Christian Envy of the Temple." *Jewish Quarterly Review* 50 (1959):97–123, 229–40.

Niles, J.D. "Pagan Survivals and Popular Belief." In *The Cambridge Companion to Old English Literature*, edited by M. Godden and M. Lapidge. Cambridge: Cambridge UP, 1986. 126–41.

Nirenberg, D. *Anti-Judaism: The Western Tradition*. New York: W.W. Norton & Company, 2013.

– *Communities of Violence: Persecution of Minorities in the Middle Ages*. Princeton, NJ: Princeton University Press, 1996.

– "Figures of Thought and Figures of Flesh: 'Jews' and 'Judaism' in Late Medieval Spanish Poetry and Politics." Speculum 81 (2006):398–426.

– "The Rhineland Massacres of Jews in the First Crusade: Memories Medieval and Modern." In *Medieval Concepts of the Past: Ritual, Memory, Historiography*, edited by P.J. Geary. Cambridge: Cambridge University Press, 2002. 279–310.

Nolland, J., ed. *Luke 1–9:20*. Word Biblical Commentary, vol. 35A. Dallas, TX: Word Books, 1989.

O'Neill, P. "The Old English Introductions to the Prose Psalms of the Paris Psalter: Sources, Structure, and Composition." *Studies in Philology* 78, no. 5 (1981):20–38.

O'Reilly, J. "Islands and Idols at the ends of the earth: Exegesis and Conversion in Bede's *Historia Ecclesiastica*." *Histoire et littérature de l'Europe du Nord-Ouest* 34 (2005):119–45.

Ohly, F. *Sage und Legende in der Kaiserchronik: Untersuchungen über Quellen und Aufbau der Dichtung*. 2nd ed. Darmstadt: Wissenschaftliche Buchgesellschaft, 1968.

Orchard, A. *Pride and Prodigies: Studies in the Beowulf-Manuscript*. Cambridge: D.S. Brewer, 1995.

Orchard, N., ed. *The Sacramentary of Ratoldus* (Paris, Bibiothèque Nationale de France, lat. 12052), Henry Bradshaw Society 116. London: The Boydell Press, 2005.

Owen-Crocker, G. *Dress in Anglo-Saxon England*. Manchester: Manchester University Press, 1986.

Parkes, M.B. *Pause and Effect: An Introduction to the History of Punctuation in the West*. Aldershot: Scolar, 1992.

Payne, A.F. *King Alfred & Boethius. An Analysis of the Old English Version of the Consolation of Philosophy*. Madison: University of Wisconsin Press, 1968.

Pelteret, D.A.E. *Slavery in Early Medieval England: from the Reign of Alfred until the Twelfth Century*. Woodbridge: Boydell Press, 1995.

Pitra, J.B., ed. *Spicilegium solesmense sanctorum Patrum*, vol. 1. Paris: Firmin Didot, 1852.

Pratt, D. "Kings and Books in Anglo-Saxon England." *ASE* 43 (2014):297–377.

– *The Political Thought of King Alfred the Great*. Cambridge: Cambridge University Press, 2007.

– "The Voice of the King in 'King Edgar's Establishment of Monasteries'." *ASE* 41 (2012):145–204.

Propp, W. "The Skin of Moses' Face – Transfigured or Disfigured?" *The Catholic Biblical Quarterly* 49 (1987):375–86.

Puhle, M., and C.-P. Hasse, eds. *Heiliges Römisches Reich Deutscher Nation 962 bis 1806: Von Otto dem Grossen bis zum Ausgang des Mittelalters*. 2 vols. Dresden: Sandstein, 2006.

Pulsiano, P. "Old English *Nomina ventorum*." *SN* 66 (1994):15–26.

Quinn, E.G., et al., eds. *Dictionary of the Irish language*. Dublin: Royal Irish Academy, 1911–76.

Rabin, A. Review of *The Footsteps of Israel: Understanding Jews in Anglo-Saxon England*, by Andrew Scheil. *Modern Philology* 103, no. 2 (2005):227–30.

Ray, R. "Bede, Rhetoric, and the Creation of Christian Latin Culture." The Jarrow Lecture, 1997.

– "Cicero and Bede." *ASE* 16 (1987):1–15.

– "What Do We Know about Bede's Commentaries?" *Recherches de théologie ancienne et médiévale* 49 (1982):5–20.

– "Who Did Bede Think He Was?" In *Innovation and Tradition in the Writings of the Venerable Bede*, edited by S. DeGregorio, Morgantown: West Virginia University Press, 2006. 11–35.

Reimer, A.M. *Miracle and Magic: A Study in the Acts of the Apostles and the Life of Apollonius of Tyana*. London; New York: Sheffield Academic Press, 2002.

Remley, P.G. *Old English Biblical Verse*. Cambridge: Cambridge University Press, 1996.

Revel-Neher, E. "'By Means Of Colors': A Judeo-Christian Dialogue in Byzantine Iconography." In *Jews in Byzantium: Dialectics of Minority and Majority Cultures*, E.R. Bonfil et al. Leiden: Brill, 2011. 501–34.

– "Du Codex Amiatinus et ses rapports avec les plans du tabernacle dans l'art juif et dans l'art byzantine." *Journal of Jewish Art* 9 (1982):6–17.

– *The Image of the Jew in Byzantine Art*. Translated by D. Maizel. Oxford: Pergamon Press, 1992.

Robbins, J. *Prodigal Son, Elder Brother: Interpretation and Alterity in Augustine, Petrarch, Kafka, Levinas.* Chicago: University of Chicago Press, 1991.

Rohmann, G. "The Invention of Dancing Mania: Frankish Christianity, Platonic Cosmology and Bodily Expressions in Sacred Space." *The Medieval History Journal* 12 (2009):13–45.

Rokéaḥ, Z.E. *Medieval English Jews and Royal Officials: Entries of Jewish Interest in the English Memoranda Rolls.* Jerusalem: The Hebrew University Magnes Press, 2000.

Roll, S.K. *Toward the Origin of Christmas.* Liturgia Condenda 5. Kampen: Kok Pharos, 1995.

Rollason, D. "St Cuthbert and Wessex: the Evidence of Cambridge, Corpus Christi College MS 183." In *St. Cuthbert, His Cult and His Community to AD 1200*, edited by G. Bonner, D.W. Rollason, and C. Stancliffe. Woodbridge: Boydell, 1989. 413–24.

Roth, C. *A History of the Jews in England.* Oxford: Clarendon Press, 1964.

– "Jewish Antecedents of Christian Art." *Journal of the Warburg and Courtauld Institutes* 16 (1953):24–44.

– *The Intellectual Activities of Medieval English Jewry.* London: Oxford University Press, 1948.

Royle, N. *The Uncanny.* Manchester: Manchester University Press, 2003.

Rubin, M. *Gentile Tales: The Narrative Assault on Late Medieval Jews.* New Haven: Yale University Press, 1999.

Rumble, A. *Property and Piety in Early Medieval Winchester: Documents Relating to the Topography of the Anglo-Saxon and Norman City and its Minsters.* Winchester Studies 4: The Anglo-Saxon Minsters of Winchester, pt. 3. Oxford: Clarendon Press, 2002.

Scarfe Beckett, K. *Anglo-Saxon Perceptions of the Islamic World.* CSASE 33. Cambridge: Cambridge University Press, 2003.

Schade, H. "Zum Bild des tanzenden David im frühen Mittelalter." *Stimmen der Zeit* 172 (1962/3):1–16.

Scheibe, C. "Alcuin und die *Admonitio Generalis.*" *Deutsches Archiv für Erforschung des Mittelalters* 14 (1958):221–9.

Scheil, A.P. "Space and Place." In *A Handbook of Anglo-Saxon Studies*, edited by J. Stodnick and R.R. Trilling. Malden, MA: Wiley-Blackwell, 2012. 197–213.

– *The Footsteps of Israel: Understanding Jews in Anglo-Saxon England.* Ann Arbor, MI: University of Michigan Press, 2004.

Schlauch, M. "The Allegory of Church and Synagogue." *Speculum* 14, no. 4 (1939):448–64.

Schmidt, R. "*Aetates mundi*: die Weltalter als Gliederungsprinzip der Geschichte." *Zeitschrift fur Kirchengeschichte* 67 (1955–6):288–317.

Schramm, P.E. *Kaiser, Könige und Päpste. Gesammelte Aufsätze zur Geschichte des Mittelalters*, 4 vols. Stuttgart: Anton Hiersemann, 1968.

Schreckenberg, H. *Die Flavius-Josephus-Tradition in Antike und Mittelalter.* Leiden: Brill, 1972.

Scragg, D.G. *Edgar, King of the English, 959–975: New Interpretations.* Woodbridge: Boydell Press, 2008.

Seiferth, W.S. *Synagogue and Church in the Middle Ages: Two Symbols in Art and Literature.* New York: Ungar Press, 1970.

Shapiro, J. *Shakespeare and the Jews.* New York: Columbia University Press, 1996.

Shaw, B. "Translation and Transformation in *Andreas*." In *Prosody and Poetics in the Early Middle Ages: Essays in Honour of C. B. Hieatt*, edited by M.J. Toswell. Toronto: University of Toronto Press, 1995. 164–79.

Siker, J.S. *Disinheriting the Jews: Abraham in Early Christian Controversy.* Louisville, KY: Westminster, 1991.

Simon, M. *Verus Israel: A Study of the Relations between Christians and Jews in the Roman Empire (135–425).* Translated by H. McKeating. Oxford: Oxford University Press, 1986.

Skemer, D.C. *Binding Words: Textual Amulets in the Middle Ages.* Philadelphia: Pennsylvania State University Press, 2006.

– "Written Amulets and the Medieval Book." *Scrittura e civiltà* 23 (1999):253–305.

Skinner, P. *Jews in Medieval Britain: Historical, Literary and Archaeological Perspectives.* Woodbridge: Boydell & Brewer, 2003.

Smetana, C. "Ælfric and the Early Medieval Homiliary." *Traditio* 15 (1959):163–204.

– "Ælfric and the Homiliary of Haymo of Halberstadt." *Traditio* 17 (1961): 457–69.

Smith, J. "Rulers and Relics c.750–c.950: Treasure on Earth, Treasure in Heaven." *Past and Present* 206, suppl. 5 (2010):S73–S96.

Smith, S. "The Bride Stripped Bare: a Rare Type of the Disrobing of Christ." *Gesta* 34 (1995):126–46.

Smith, S.T. "The Edgar Poems and the Poetics of Failure in the *Anglo-Saxon Chronicle*." *ASE* 39 (2010):105–37.

Southern, R.W. "Bede." In *Medieval Humanism and Other Studies.* Oxford: Basil Blackwell, 1984. 1–8.

Stacey, R.C. "Anti-Semitism and the Medieval English State." In *The Medieval State: Essays Presented to James Campbell*, edited by. J.M. Madicott and D.M. Palliser. London: The Hambledon Press, 2000.

– "Jewish Lending and the Medieval English Economy." In *A Commercializing Economy: England 1086 to c. 1300*, edited by R.H. Britnell and B.M.S. Campbell. Manchester: Manchester University Press, 1995. 78–101.

– "Parliamentary Negotiation and the Expulsion of the Jews from England." In *Thirteenth-Century England*, VI, edited by R.H. Britnell, R. Frame, and M. Prestwich. Woodbridge: Boydell Press, 1997. 77–101.

Stanley, E. "Dance, Dancers and Dancing in Anglo-Saxon England." *Dance Research: The Journal of the Society for Dance Research* 9 (1991):18–31.

Stanton, R. *The Culture of Translation in Anglo-Saxon England*. Cambridge: D.S. Brewer, 2002.

Steger, H. *David Rex et Propheta. König David als vorbildliche Verkörperung des Herrschers und Dichters im Mittelalter, nach Bilddarstellungen des achten bis zwölften Jahrhunderts*. Nuremberg: Verlag Hans Carl, 1961.

Stemberger, G. "Der Dekalog im frühen Judentum." In *Judaica Minora 1: Biblische Traditionen im rabbinischen Judentum*. Texts and Studies in Ancient Judaism, 133. Tübingen: Mohr Siebeck, 2010. 149–50.

Stephens, W. *Giants in Those Days: Folklore, Ancient History, and Nationalism*. Lincoln: University of Nebraska Press, 1989.

Stephenson, R. "Scapegoating the Secular Clergy: The Hermeneutic Style as a Form of Monastic Self-Definition." *ASE* 38 (2010):101–37.

Stinson, C. "'Northernmost Israel': England, the Old Testament, and the Hebraic 'Veritas' as Seen by Bede and Roger Bacon." In *Hebrew and the Bible in America: The First Two Centuries*, edited by S. Goldman. Hanover: University Press of New England, 1993. 14–42.

Stookey, L.H. *Calendar: Christ's Time for the Church*. Nashville: Abingdon Press, 1996.

Stow, K.R. "Jews and the Catholic Church." In *Dictionary of the Middle Ages*, edited by J.R. Strayer. 13 vols. New York: Scribner's, 1986.

Strickland, D.H. *Saracens, Demons & Jews: Making Monsters in Medieval Art*. Princeton, NJ: Princeton University Press, 2003.

Suckale-Redlefsen, G. *Die Bilderzyklen zum Davidleben von den Anfängen bis zum Ende des 11. Jahrhunderts*. PhD diss., Munich, 1972.

Suggs, M.J., K. Doob Sakenfeld, and J.R. Mueller, eds. *Oxford Study Bible: Revised English Bible with the Apocrypha*. New York: Oxford University Press, 1992.

Sutcliffe, E.F. "St. Jerome's Pronunciation of Hebrew." *Biblica* 29 (1948):112–25.

– "The Name 'Vulgate'." *Biblica* 29 (1948):345–52.

– "The Venerable Bede's Knowledge of Hebrew." *Biblica* 16 (1935):300–6.

Swarzenski, H. *Monuments of Romanesque Art: The Art of Church Treasuries on North-West Europe*. Chicago: University of Chicago Press, 1954.

Szittya, P. "The Living Stone and the Patriarchs: Typological Imagery in *Andreas*, ll. 706–810." *JEGP* 72 (1973):167–74.

Temple, E. *Anglo-Saxon Manuscripts, 900–1066*. London: Harvey Miller, 1976.

Teviotdale, E.C. "Latin Verse Inscriptions in Anglo-Saxon Art." *Gesta* 35 (1996):99–110.

Thormann, J. "The Jewish Other in Old English Narrative Poetry." *Partial Answers: Journal of Literature and the History of Ideas* 2, no. 1 (2004):1–19.

Tigay, J.H. "On the Term Phylacteries (Matt 23:5)." *The Harvard Theological Review* 72, nos. 1–2 (1979):45–53.

Tischendorf, C. von, ed. *Evangelia apocrypha adhibitis plurimis codicibus Graecis et Latinis maximam partem nunc primum consultis atque ineditorum copia insignibus*. 2nd ed. Leipzig: Mendelssohn, 1876.

Toch, M. "The Jews in Europe 500–1050." In *The New Cambridge Medieval History: Volume I, c. 500–c. 700*, edited by P. Fouracre. Cambridge: Cambridge University Press, 2005. 547–70.

Tomasch, S. "Postcolonial Chaucer and the Virtual Jew." In *The Postcolonial Middle Ages*, edited by J.J. Cohen. New York, NY: Palgrave, 2000. 243–60.

Tompkins, J.P. "The Reader in History." In *Reader-Response Criticism: From Formalism to Post-Structuralism*. Baltimore: Johns Hopkins University Press, 1980. 201–32.

Trachtenberg, J. *Jewish Magic and Superstition: A Study in Folk Religion*. Philadelphia: Jewish Publication Society of America, 2004.

– *The Devil and the Jews: The Medieval Conception of the Jew and Its Relation to Modern Antisemitism*. New Haven: Yale University Press, 1943.

Trahern, J.B. "Joshua and Tobias in the Old English *Andreas*." *SP* 42 (1970):330–2.

Tristram, H.C.L. *Sex aetates mundi: Die Weltzeitalter bei den Iren und den Angelsachsen*. Heidelburg: Carl Winter, 1985.

Turner, S., S. Semple, and A. Turner, eds. *Wearmouth and Jarrow: Northumbrian Monasteries in an Historic Landscape*. Hertfordshire: University of Hertfordshire Press, 2013.

Turville-Petre, T. *England the Nation: Language, Literature, and National Identity, 1290–1340*. Oxford: Clarendon Press, 1996.

Ussani, V., ed. *Hegesippi qui dicitur Historiae libri V*. CSEL 66. Vienna: Hölder, Pivhler, Tempsky, 1932.

Van Court, E.N. "*The Siege of Jerusalem* and Recuperative Readings." In *Pulp Fictions of Medieval England: Essays in Popular Romance*, edited by N. McDonald. Manchester: Manchester University Press, 2004.

Vermes, G., trans. *The Complete Dead Sea Scrolls in English*. New York: Penguin, 1997.

Vigouroux, F., ed. *Dictionnaire de la Bible*. 5 vols. in 10. Paris: Letouzey et Ané, 1912–22.

Waite, G. "Old English *lybesn* and *æ-becn*: A Gloss in Oxford, Corpus Christi College MS 279B." *Notes and Queries*, n.s., 60 (2012):14–19.

Wallace-Hadrill, J.M. *Early Germanic Kingship in England and on the Continent. The Ford Lectures Delivered in the University of Oxford in Hilary Term 1970*. Oxford: Clarendon Press, 1971.

Wallis, F. "Bede and Science." In *The Cambridge Companion to Bede*, edited by S. DeGregorio. Cambridge: Cambridge University Press, 2010. 113–26.

– "Cædmon's Created World and the Monastic Encyclopedia." In *Cædmon's Hymn and Material Culture in the World of Bede: Six Essays*, edited by A.J. Frantzen and J. Hines. Morgantown: West Virginia University Press, 2007. 80–110.

Walsh, M.M. "The Baptismal Flood in the Old English *Andreas*: Liturgical and Typological Depths." *Traditio* 33 (1977):137–58.

Wasserstein, D.J. "The First Jew in England: 'The Game of the Evangel' and a Hiberno-Latin Contribution to Anglo-Jewish History," in *Ogma: Essays in Celtic Studies in Honour of Próinséas Ní Chatháin*, edited by M. Richter and J-M. Picard. Dublin: Four Courts Press, 2002. 283–8.

Weinfeld, M. "Jeremiah and the Spiritual Metamorphosis of Israel." *Zeitschrift für die Alttestamentliche Wissenschaft* 88, no. 1(1976):17–56.

Weitzmann, K. *Miniatures of the Sacra Parallela*. Princeton: Princeton University Press, 1979.

Weitzmann, K., and H. Kessler. *The Frescoes of the Dura Synagogue and Christian Art*. Washington, DC: Dumbarton Oaks, 1990.

Wenham, G.J., ed. *Genesis 1–15. Word Biblical Commentary*, vol. 1. Dallas, TX: Word Books, 1994.

Whatley, G. "The Figure of Constantine the Great in Cynewulf's *Elene*." *Traditio* 37 (1981):161–202.

White, C.L. *Ælfric: A New Study of his Life and Writings*. Hamden, CT: Archon Books, 1974. First published 1898 by Lamson, Wolffe & Co.

Whitehead, C. *Castles of the Mind: A Study of Medieval Architectural Allegory*. Cardiff: University of Wales Press, 2003.

Whitelock, D., ed. *English Historical Documents I, c. 500–1042*, 2nd ed. London: Eyre Methuen, 1979.

Wirth, K.-A., ed. *Pictor in Carmine: ein Handbuch der Typologie aus der Zeit um 1200: nach MS 300 des Corpus Christi College in Cambridge*. Berlin: Gebr. Mann, 2006.

Withers, B. "Interaction of Word and Image in Anglo-Saxon Art II: Scroll and Codex in the Frontispiece of the Regularis Concordia." *Old English Newsletter* 31 (1997):36–40.

– *The Illustrated Old English Hexateuch, Cotton Claudius B.iv: The Frontier of Seeing and Reading in Anglo-Saxon England*. Toronto and Buffalo: The British Library and University of Toronto Press, 2007.

Wittekind, S. *Kommentar mit Bildern: zur Ausstattung mittelalterlicher Psalmenkommentare und Verwendung der Davidgeschichte in Texten und Bildern am Beispiel des Psalmenkommentars des Petrus Lombardus (Bamberg, Staatsbibliothek, Msc. Bibl. 59)*. Frankfurt: Peter Lang, 1994.

Wormald, P. "Bede, The *Bretwaldas* and the Origins of the *Gens Anglorum*." In *Ideal and Reality in Frankish and Anglo-Saxon Society: Studies Presented to J.M. Hadrill*, edited by P. Wormald with D. Bullough and R. Collins. Oxford: Blackwell, 1983. 99–129.

– "*Engla Lond*: The Making of an Allegiance." *Journal of Historical Sociology* 7 (1994):1–24.

– *English Drawings of the Tenth and Eleventh Centuries*. London, Faber and Faber, 1952.

– "The Making of England." *History Today* (February 1995):26–32.

– *The Making of English Law: King Alfred to the Twelfth Century*. Oxford: Blackwell Publishers, 1999.

Wright, C.D. "Insulae Gentium: Biblical Influence on Old English Poetic Vocabulary." In *Magister Regis: Studies in Honor of R.E. Kaske*, edited by A. Groos, et al. New York: Fordham University Press, 1986. 9–21.

– "Matthew's Hebrew Gospel in *Andreas* and Old English Prose." *Notes and Queries*, n.s., 30 (1983):101–4.

Wright, S.K. *The Vengeance of Our Lord: Medieval Dramatizations of the Destruction of Jerusalem*. Studies and Texts 89. Toronto: PIMS, 1989.

Wright, T. *Anglo-Saxon and Old English Vocabularies*, edited by R.P. Wülcker. 2nd ed. 2 vols. London: Trübner, 1884.

Wütrich, L. *Wandgemälde von Müstair bis Holder. Katalog der Schweizerischen Landesmuseums Zurich*. Zurich: Verlag Berichthaus, 1980.

Wutz, F. *Onomastica Sacra: Untersuchungen zum Liber interpretationis nominum Hebraicarum des hl. Hieronymus*. 2 vols. TU 41. Leipzig: Hinrichs, 1914–15.

Yeager, S.M. "Racial Imagination and the Theater of War: Captivity and Execution in *Richard, Coeur de Lion*." In *A Companion to British Literature*, vol. 1, edited by R. DeMaria, Jr, H. Chang, and S. Zacher. Chichester: Wiley-Blackwell, 2014. 81–96.

– "The Crusade of the Soul in *The Siege of Jerusalem*." In *Jerusalem in Medieval Narrative*. Cambridge Studies in Medieval Literature 72. Cambridge: Cambridge University Press, 2008. 78–107.

Yuval, I.J. *Two Nations in Your Womb: Perceptions of Jews and Christians in Late Antiquity and the Middle Ages.* Translated by B. Harshav and J. Chipman. Berkeley: University of California Press, 2006.

Zacher, S. "Circumscribing the Text: Views on Circumcision in Old English Literature." In *Old English Literature and the Old Testament*, edited by M. Fox and M. Sharma. Toronto: University of Toronto Press, 2012. 89–118.

– "Multilingualism at the Court of King Æthelstan: Latin Praise Poetry and *The Battle of Brunanburh*." In *Conceptualizing Multilingualism in England, 800–1250*, edited by E.M. Tyler. Turnhout: Brepols, 2012. 77–104.

– *Rewriting the Old Testament in Anglo-Saxon Verse: Becoming the Chosen People.* New Directions in Religion and Literature. London; New York, NY: Bloomsbury Academic, 2013.

– "The Chosen People: Spiritual Identities." In *The Oxford Handbook of Medieval English Literature*, edited by E. Treharne and G. Walker. Oxford: Oxford UP, 2010.

Zettel, P.H. "Ælfric's Hagiographic Sources and the Latin Legendary Preserved in B.L.MS.Cotton Nero i + CCCC MS.9 and other Manuscripts." DPhil diss., Oxford, 1979.

Zimmermann, J. "Histrio fit David. König Davids Tanz vor der Bundeslade in der Ikonographie und Literatur des Mittelalters." In *König David. Biblische Schlüsselfigur und europäische Leitgestalt*, edited by W. Dietrich. Freiburg: Universitätsverlag, 2003. 531–61.

Index

163, 172, 175, 177, 185–8, 192–3,
271, 274, 279
Paul, Pauline doctrine, 7, 19, 20, 27,
33, 34, 83, 102, 143, 155, 179–80;
Pauline universalism, 12; Pauline
hermeneutics (letter versus spirit),
8, 19, 20, 80, 83, 84, 86–7, 94, 132,
135–6, 137, 151, 155, 158, 180, 277.
See also Bible: New Testament
Paulinus of Nola, 15
Peter, Apostle, 33, 86, 175, 220, 222
Peter Comestor, 252
Peter Damian, 53–4n34
Pharisees, 169–80, 185–8
Philo of Alexandria, 136, 155
Pontius Pilate (NT), 41–3, 46, 50, 57–60
post-colonial theory, 8
Promised Land, 34, 90, 133, 136n12,
139–41, 146–51, 153–5, 207, 251,
256–7, 260, figure 21. *See also*
Jerusalem
Prudentius, Aurelius Clemens, 222,
233–4, figure 11
Pseudo-Bede, 172
Pseudo-Jerome, 179nn51–2

race, 16, 18, 36n29, 41, 52, 57, 138,
245, 248, 266–7
Red-Sea crossing, 147, 152
Regularis Concordia, 235–6, figure 20
Richard I, King, 24, 265, 268, 273
Rome, 12n36, 22, 43–8, 50, 91, 104
Ruin, The, 252

Saducees, 173
Salvian, 15, 30
Saracens, 49–50, 200–1, 217–18
Sarah, 23, 49, 136, 197–218, figure 4,
figure 5
Sedulius, Caelius, 233, 234n54

Sedulius Scottus, 35n24, 172
Septuagint, 64–9, 72–7, 181n58, 184
seraphim, 175
Sermon on the Mount, 185
Siege of Jerusalem, 17–18, 40n1, 41n5,
48n20, 51nn27–8
Slaughter of the Innocents, 118, 120–1
Smaragdus of St Mihiel, 172, 227
Solomon, King, 52, 54, 81–2, 85, 102,
183, 229n37, 230. *See also* Temple
of Solomon
St Augustine's Abbey, Canterbury,
237, 257n83
Stephen, Protomartyr, 119–23, 140–1,
158
stone, 58–9, 75, 80–6, 89–103, 109,
125, 135, 175–8, 180–5; as faithful
Christians, 95–8, 102; as faithful
Jews, 95–8; as senseless, stubborn Jews, 83, 95–8, 102, 106–7;
Christ as the cornerstone, 19, 36,
85, 91, 95, 123–4n49; living stones,
81, 86–7, 91, 95–6, 106, 176n40,
180n56; Roman walls, 99; sepulcher of Christ, 51, 58–9, 82–3, 89,
162; "sepulchral Jew," 19, 82–6, 88,
90–3, 102, 106–7. *See also* buildings;
materialism, materiality; Temple of
Solomon
Sulpicius Severus, 48n19
supersession, 9, 11, 19–20, 80, 82,
84, 86–7, 90–4, 107, 110, 112n13,
114, 140, 193, 277. *See also* Jewish
stereotypes; Jews; Paul
synagogue, 4, 144, 217, 225, 266

tabernacle, 37–8, 79–107, 226n21, 232;
mystical and spiritual interpretation, 91–2. *See also* Bede: Works: *De
Tabernaculo*; buildings

Toronto Anglo-Saxon Series

General Editor
ANDY ORCHARD

Editorial Board
ROBERTA FRANK
THOMAS N. HALL
ANTONETTE DIPAOLO HEALEY
MICHAEL LAPIDGE
KATHERINE O'BRIEN O'KEEFFE